Europe's Reformations, 1450–1650

T. H. Deeds

Critical Issues in History

Series Editor: Donald T. Critchlow

Europe's Reformations, 1450–1650

James D. Tracy

ROWMAN & LITTLEFIELD PUBLISHERS, INC.
Lanham • Boulder • New York • Oxford

ROWMAN & LITTLEFIELD PUBLISHERS, INC.

Published in the United States of America
by Rowman & Littlefield Publishers, Inc.
4720 Boston Way, Lanham, Maryland 20706
http://www.rowmanlittlefield.com

12 Hid's Copse Road
Cumnor Hill, Oxford OX2 9JJ, England

British Library Cataloguing in Publication Information Available

Library of Congress Cataloging-in-Publication Data

Tracy, James D.
  Europe's reformations, 1450–1650 / James D. Tracy.
       p.   cm. — (Critical issues in history)
    Includes bibliographical references and index.
    ISBN 0-8476-8834-8 (alk. paper). — ISBN 0-8476-8835-6 (pbk.: alk. paper)
    1. Reformation.   2. Europe—Church history—15th century.
  3. Europe—Church history—Modern period, 1500–   I. Title.
  II. Series.
  BR290.T73 1999
  274'06—dc21   99–34167
                                                                          CIP
Printed in the United States of America

♾ ™The paper used in this publication meets the minimum requirements of
American National Standard for Information Sciences—Permanence of Paper for
Printed Library Materials, ANSI/NISO Z39.48–1992.

For Sue

Contents

Figures

Note Regarding
Endnotes, References,
and Abbreviations

Endnotes are used for giving background information that may not be familiar to all readers. References to fuller discussion of matters treated here are found in the bibliography. There are also general works of reference that should be mentioned. The *Oxford Encyclopedia of the Reformation*, edited by Hans J. Hillerbrand (4 vols., Oxford University Press, 1995), has capsule summaries for important figures, ideas, and events, up to about 1600. Because this book covers events up to 1650, not all topics mentioned here are treated in the *Encyclopedia*, but readers may turn to the *Encyclopedia* with confidence for topics occurring before 1600. Readers interested in the flavor of debate among scholars may turn to the forty essays (many on themes relevant to this book) contained in the *Handbook of European History during the Late Middle Ages, Renaissance, and Reformation, 1400–1600*, edited by Heiko A. Oberman, Thomas A. Brady, Jr., and James D. Tracy (2 vols., Leiden, 1994; paperback edition Grand Rapids, Mich., 1995), abbreviated in the bibliography as *Handbook*. To get a sense of scholarship as it takes shape, the most helpful scholarly journals are *Archiv für Reformationsgeschichte / Archive for Reformation History* (articles in English and German), abbreviated here as *ARG*, and the *Sixteenth Century Journal*.

Series Editor's Foreword

The Reformation, the religious revolution of the sixteenth century, shattered western Christendom by dividing it into two camps, Roman Catholic and Protestant. In the process, Europe itself would be reconfigured geographically, political power realigned, and new social forces realized. Moreover, this religious revolution inalterably changed perspectives of individual conscience, moral judgment, and the relationship between church and state. And, as James Tracy astutely observes, communities on the local level underwent dramatic changes, as religious loyalties now cut across all others, dividing "villager from villager, parishioner from parishioner, guild brother from guild brother." Yet, in the end, the Reformation revitalized the Catholic Church, created new opportunities of practice for Protestants, and allowed greater freedom to others not to practice any religion at all. Thus, as Tracy concludes, "the Reformation created a new world in Europe, one recognizably similar to our pluralistic world."

The consequences of this religious reformation continued long after Martin Luther, an Augustinian friar and university professor at Wittenberg, drafted his *Ninety-five Theses* on the indulgence system in 1517. Luther's break with the church led to the political separation of Germany into Protestant and Catholic camps, a peasant's revolt in June 1524, and the eventual legalization of Lutheranism with the Peace of Augsburg. Meanwhile, Reformation activities spread to Geneva with arrival of John Calvin in 1536; found political expression in France with the formation of a Protestant party; swept through the Netherlands, Denmark, and Sweden; and even penetrated areas in Poland.

The speed with which these heretical fires spread through these areas suggests how brittle the Catholic Church had become over many countries. From the early twelfth century onward, criticism of the church found expression in some of its most devoted adherents. By the sixteenth century, friction between clergy and their flocks seemed to be increasing rather than decreasing.

Yet the Reformation unleashed more than adamant calls for reform in the church; it raised a fundamental question that went beyond institutional reform: Is the Bible to be interpreted by the individual for his own soul's sake or by the church for the individual's soul's sake? This simple question opened the floodgates for revolutionary changes in the individual's relationship to the community, the state, its rulers, and to God. The Catholic Church responded to this religious, cultural, and political crisis by calling for internal reform and a Counter-Reformation against Protestantism.

Tracy captures the complexity and drama of one of the most remarkable and important episodes in world history. Sensitive to the positions of both reformers and the established church, acute in his observations about the ramifications of social and cultural changes in these years, and vivid in his capturing of the complexity of the period, Tracy provides his readers with a first-rate account of Europe's Reformations.

Donald T. Critchlow
Series Editor

Acknowledgments

This book is a weaving together of the ideas of many scholars, whose complicated arguments I have ventured to compress into paragraphs or even sentences. I owe special thanks to my friend and colleague David Kieft and to my father-in-law, Robert Soman, for judicious, nonspecialist readings of the manuscript. This book will be a success if it conveys something of the sustained intellectual pleasure I have had from over thirty years of professional association with the colleagues whose works are cited in the bibliography.

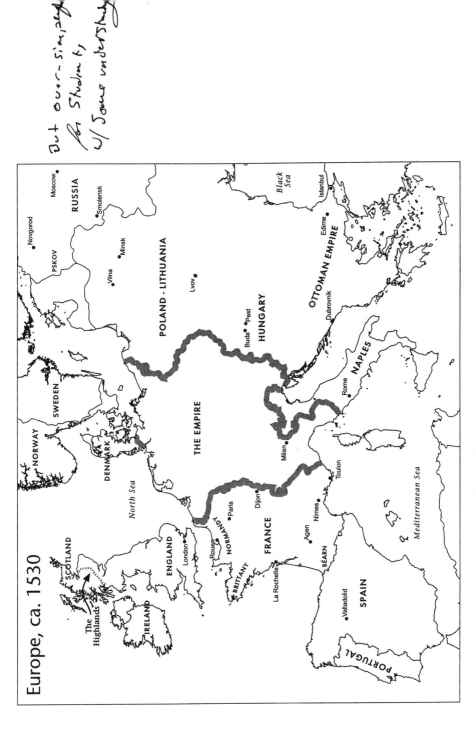

Europe, ca. 1530

Details of the area labeled "The Empire" are presented on p. xx.

Basic +
good for
Students w/
No Knowledge

But over-simplify
for Students
w/ Some understanding

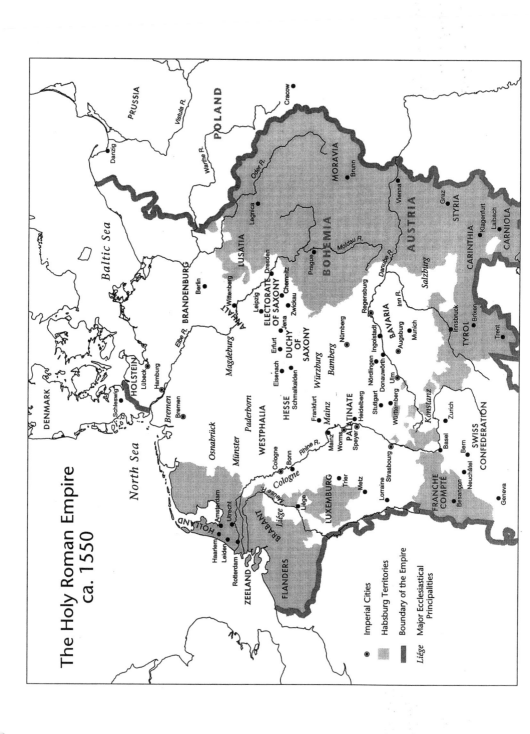

The Holy Roman Empire
ca. 1550

Imperial Cities
Habsburg Territories
Boundary of the Empire
Liège Major Ecclesiastical
Principalities

I | INTRODUCTION

In 1517, Latin Christendom[1] was a larger society made up of a nearly endless multitude of corporate bodies,[2] each ready and willing to defend its lawful turf against all comers. The one thing most people had in common in this rather contentious world was their belief in the Holy Catholic Church. But in that year Martin Luther unwittingly began what was to become the Protestant Reformation when he proposed a public debate on certain aspects of church practice regarding the forgiving of sins. By the time of Luther's death (1546), there were many churches, not just one, and "Lutherans" were battling the followers of Geneva's John Calvin (d. 1564), among others, for the loyalty of new converts. Most of the new religious bodies were backed by governments that had armies as well as printing presses to defend their beliefs. Thus religious loyalties now cut across all the others, dividing brother from sister, villager from villager, parishioner from parishioner, guild brother from guild brother. Many Europeans drew spiritual consolation and a more confident view of life from the new religious communities, including the Catholic Church, which found new vigor in facing the Protestant challenge. Others found in the spaces created by open conflict among the contending forms of Christianity greater freedom not to practice any religion at all. Religious rivalry also became a potent additive to the normal stew of political conflict that bred incessant warfare among Europe's many states. Thus the Reformation created a new world in Europe, one recognizably similar in some ways to the pluralistic world that we ourselves inhabit. This book tells the story of what Europe was like before the Reformation, how the Reformation itself developed, and how Europe was changed by it. In this introductory section, Chapter 1 explains the premises of my own approach to the Reformation. Chapter 2 briefly discusses some of the Reformation's more distinctive features in the overall context of European history.

1

1 | Premises

This book has two premises, each of which will be discussed in turn. The first is that we can best understand the historical significance of the Protestant movement by viewing it not as unprecedented, but as the high point in a series of "reformations" that convulsed the Latin or western half of Christendom from the eleventh to the eighteenth centuries. The second and more general premise is that religious belief is a motive force in history, but only one among many, so that the outcome of a religious movement can never be explained solely on the basis of religion.

When Martin Luther sent off copies of the *Ninety-five Theses* to church authorities (31 October 1517), "reformation" was a familiar word. In southern France in the tenth century, the monastery of Cluny spearheaded a *reformatio* of the Benedictine order based on a return to its original discipline and austerity of life. Pope Gregory VII (d. 1085) launched an effort to reform the church as a whole by attacking the regnant political system of the Holy Roman Empire.[1] Since bishops were chosen from families loyal to the emperor, emperors found it convenient to have these spiritual rulers exercise secular power in their territories as well. In a ceremony known as investiture or "clothing" with the symbols of office, "prince-bishops" received both their spiritual and their temporal authority from the emperor.

This was the arrangement Pope Gregory now denounced as corrupt, demanding that it cease immediately. The emperor, not surprisingly, took a different view. After nearly fifty years, a struggle that convulsed much of Europe ended in compromise: Bishops would still be "invested" by the emperor or his representative as temporal rulers, but they would henceforth be "invested" with spiritual authority by the pope or by other bishops. In retrospect, this acceptance on both sides of a clear distinction between spiritual and secular authority can be seen as a necessary precondition for the much later (and distinctively European) idea of a separation between church and state. At the time, however, neither party was satisfied by the compromise, and tension between the claims of pope and emperor continued. Beginning around 1150, the focal point of conflict shifted to efforts by the emperors to gain control over the populous towns of northern Italy, close to the Papal States, a band of territory stretching from Rome north to the Adriatic Sea. This struggle ended only when Emperor Frederick II, bitterly opposed by several successive popes, died without a legitimate heir (1250).

Meanwhile, a many-sided movement largely under lay leadership sought to reform the church by urging that men of God must imitate the poverty of Christ and his apostles, rather than living in the lavish style favored by popes and prince-bishops. In southeastern France during the twelfth century, a merchant named Peter Waldo, with his followers, sought permission to travel from town to town preaching the gospel, as the apostles had done. But when local bishops were unyielding (canon law provided that only ordained clergymen could preach),[2] they rejected church authority and formed by their preaching a growing underground movement, until royal officials joined with the church in a campaign of suppression. In remote Alpine valleys seldom seen by the king's men, Waldensians survived to welcome the Protestant Reformation of the sixteenth century.

Other branches of the broad apostolic poverty movement remained within the church. Francis of Assisi in Italy (d. 1226) and Dominic de Guzman in Spain (d. 1221) cast off all trappings of wealth and begged in the streets for their food. Their followers, Franciscans and Dominicans, came to be known as begging brothers, or mendicant friars. They made it their mission to preach to the inhabitants of Europe's now burgeoning cities. But as people flocked to the new mendicant churches, resentment grew among the secular or parish clergy,[3] who defended their spiritual turf with lawsuits and even fisticuffs. Moreover, as the new mendicant orders accumulated property through the donations of pious folk, the Franciscans especially quarreled bitterly among themselves about how strictly the rule of poverty must be observed. To some, it seemed true reform was farther away than ever.

The problems of the papacy in the late Middle Ages brought new demands for reform. When popes resided at Avignon in southern France (1304–1378), the papacy seemed to be under the thumb of the French king. Then came the papal schism from 1378 to 1414, when two factions of cardinals (backed by rival rulers) maintained two lines of claimants to the papal throne, one in Rome, the other at Avignon. To deal with this dilemma, some professors of theology and canon law rejected the idea that the pope alone wielded final authority, arguing that an ecumenical council could depose a wayward pope.[4] Conciliarism, as this doctrine was called, seemed to triumph when the Holy Roman Emperor summoned the bishops of Latin Christendom to the German city of Constance. The Council of Constance (1414–1417) ended the schism, elected a new pope, and proclaimed the right of future councils to govern the church. But hopes for lasting change were again thwarted. The next council bogged down in squabbles between bishops from territories whose rulers were at war. The pope once again became sole head of the church, but by default, since many theologians and canon lawyers north of the Alps still advocated a conciliar doctrine of church authority.

Meanwhile, the Council of Constance had touched off a war by its treatment of a Czech preacher and theology professor named Jan Hus. Hus taught (among other things) that lay people were unjustly deprived of their right to receive in the sacrament of the eucharist, or communion, not just the host (the bread) consecrated by the priest at mass but also the wine, now consumed only by the priest.[5] Hus's appeal to the spiritual dignity of lay people was extremely popular in Prague, notably among fellow Czechs, who chafed under Prague's German-speaking minority's control of the city and the university.[6] Charged with heresy on various points by German professors at the university, Hus accepted a safe-conduct from the council, meaning he could return safely after having been heard. But having determined that some of his opinions were indeed heretical, and that he violated the terms of his safe-conduct by preaching to the populace in Constance, the council had Hus burned at the stake. The reaction in Czech-speaking lands shows the explosive power of two sentiments that will also be visible in the Reformation: (1) lay resentment of clerical privilege and (2) national pride. Czech-speaking priests and nobles led a rebellion against Bohemia's king, forming a new polity backed by a strong citizen army.[7] Over time, the Hussites, or Utraquists, in Bohemia split into competing parties.[8] One reconciled with the papacy, retaining the right for lay people to receive the consecrated wine. But a more radical faction survived, like the Alpine Waldensians, to greet the new dawn proclaimed by Protestant Reformers.

Martin Luther's instant and enormous popularity easily matches the enthusiasm for Hus in Bohemia a century earlier. Luther was not a martyr, unlike Hus, but the printing press made him virtually an overnight sensation all across the German-speaking lands of central and eastern Europe (see Chapter 4).[9] But if the failure of reform efforts in earlier centuries

Figure 1.1. St. Francis of Assisi renounces his father's wealth. Francis's father, a cloth merchant, holds the clothes his son has renounced. Giotto di Bondone (1266–1336), "St. Francis renounces his worldly goods." Church of San Francesco, Assisi. (*Art Resource, New York, NY.*)

Figure 1.2. The Burning of Jan Hus. The Czech preacher and theologian Jan Hus, burned at the stake in 1414 by order of the Council of Constance (right) and the Holy Roman Emperor (left): Diebold Schilling, "Berner Chronik." (*Bugerbibliothek Bern, Ms. h .h. I 1, p. 367.*)

proved to many that Luther's Reformation was necessary, it proved to others that the Catholic Church must once and for all reform itself. Charles V, Holy Roman Emperor from 1519 to 1556, would have preferred to see Luther burned as a heretic, like Hus. But Charles had little control over the German heartland of his empire, where authority rested with local rulers such as Luther's prince and protector, the elector of Saxony. Beginning in the 1520s, a growing number among the empire's many cities and territories declared exclusively for the Reformation, forcing stubborn Catholics to choose between conformity or exile and placing in doubt the very survival of Catholicism in Germany. After many false starts, the pope; Charles V; and the emperor's great rival, the king of France, set aside their quarrels long enough to permit convening a desperately needed ecumenical council. Meeting at intervals over a period of years, the Council of Trent (1545–1563) clarified Catholic doctrine on points challenged by the Reformers and laid the groundwork for creating a better-educated and better-disciplined parish clergy to compete with the new Protestant pastorate.

Meanwhile, a different kind of Catholic reform was already underway in Spain and Italy, through the emergence of new religious orders, in particular the Society of Jesus, or Jesuits, founded by a Basque nobleman, Ignatius of Loyola (d. 1556), and the Capuchins, begun as a reform movement among the Franciscan friars. As Jesuits and Capuchins labored to regain for Catholicism territories that had largely been lost to Protestantism, their zeal imparted a new sense of hope to dispirited Catholics in Germany. When preaching alone failed to achieve the objective, Jesuits counseled ardent Catholic rulers on a judicious use of princely power to make stubborn Protestants choose between conformity and exile.

Was the Catholic resurgence that began around 1550 an attempt to roll back the advance of Protestantism, or an outgrowth of new forms of Catholic spirituality? Clearly, it was both a "Counter-Reformation" and a "Catholic Reformation" at the same time. Current scholarship, leaving this older debate aside, focuses on the many similarities between Tridentine[10] Catholicism and the new state churches of Protestant lands—Lutheran in much of Germany and Scandinavia, Reformed[11] in Switzerland and several other areas, Anglican in England.

In each of these cases, leaders of the favored confession worked closely with government officials toward three objectives. First, there must be a well-educated clergy, solidly grounded in correct or orthodox doctrine. Second, all inhabitants of the territory must learn at least the rudiments of true doctrine, through sound preaching, the establishment of primary schools, and Sunday catechism classes for the young. Last, there must be a betterment of popular behavior and belief, particularly an improvement of the sexual mores that all reformers now saw as intolerably lax, and an all-out assault on resort by the people to a whole spectrum of practices seen as superstitious or diabolical, ranging from magical incantations to outright witchcraft.[12]

Inducing ordinary folk to change the ways their ancestors had lived and thought for centuries was no easy task. Scholars debate whether the desired transformation was accomplished or not (see Part IV). But it is clear that, despite the obvious differences in doctrine, the rival churches breathed a shared atmosphere and struggled to move forward along a similar path. This time, the reformation of Christian society was going to be made to stick.

The call for reformation was not stilled by the relative success of the new churches. For one thing, small sects[13] that lacked all the trappings of wealth and authority roundly condemned churches that had made their compromises with state power in order to become established.[14] For another, each of the established churches harbored zealous believers not satisfied by changes they saw as half-hearted. Under Queen Elizabeth I (d. 1603), England's Puritans called for removal of "popish" elements still to be seen in Anglican worship. In the Lutheran churches of Germany in the seventeenth century, a long struggle to define the true, orthodox, meaning of Luther's teaching was followed by a Pietist movement that aimed to get away from dry doctrinal formulas, back to the personal experience of God's forgiveness described in Luther's writings. Rather than forming a new church, Pietists met in small groups to pray and read scripture, like devout dissidents elsewhere, such as the Jansenists[15] of Counter-Reformation France and the Collegiants[16] of the officially Calvinist Dutch Republic. In the following century Lutheran Pietism grew stronger, while Jansenism survived as an underground movement, despite persecution by the French king. In England, John Wesley's preaching launched a spiritual revival that led to a separate Methodist Church, echoed by the Great Awakening in far-off America.

These reform movements form a continuum, but in this book we need only include enough of that continuum to provide a proper framing for the events of the sixteenth century. Each part of the book will begin with a chapter on "late medieval background" (fourteenth and fifteenth centuries), followed by chapters on the main lines of development down to about the middle of the seventeenth century. My treatment of the sixteenth century will include the Catholic Reformation while emphasizing Protestantism.

Until about forty years ago, most scholars understood the Protestant Reformation as the proclamation of a leading idea that took concrete form in social, political, and economic institutions. In German universities, scholars influenced by an idealist philosophy of history pored over the doctrines of the principal Reformers, especially Martin Luther and John Calvin.[17] One scholar argued that doctrinal syntheses had been forged at various times during the history of Latin Christendom, each one pointing

toward a form of government and society that represented its logical outcome. Thus, the scholastic theology of medieval university professors,[18]
epitomized in the natural law[19] doctrine of St. Thomas Aquinas (d. 1274),
legitimized the rights of subjects and pointed to a monarchy in which the
king's power was limited by a parliament. But Luther's sharp distinction
between the realms of faith and power undercut any religious justification
for active resistance to rulers, and thus pointed to the absolute or unlimited monarchy some seventeenth-century rulers claimed to exercise. By
contrast, Calvin's rejection of episcopacy in favor of a quasi-republican
form of church government, together with his followers' defiance of
Catholic monarchs in France and elsewhere, pointed toward the eventual
emergence of democracy.[20]

In North America, the Reformation was until fairly recently a topic of interest mainly for students in Protestant theological seminaries and denominational colleges. Courses on Reformation history did not become
common on state university campuses until the 1960s.[21] In the common
Protestant view, Martin Luther, by his courageous protest, had freed ordinary believers from the domination of a corrupt and greedy clergy. Centuries of superstition, imposed on a gullible people by the Catholic
Church, had melted away when Luther proclaimed that scripture was the
sole source of authority and that lay men and women were free to read the
Bible and interpret it for themselves. Thus, the Reformation was the dawn
of an era when, for the first time, individuals were encouraged to think for
themselves.

Meanwhile, in Catholic seminaries and denominational colleges, scholars idealized not the Reformation, but the high Middle Ages, especially the
thirteenth century, when universities flourished and virtuous rulers and
urban guilds worked to lay the foundations of a just social order.[22] From
this perspective, when Luther made his personal religious experience the
measure of Christian faith, he loosed upon the world a destructive individualism, a wanton tearing down of beliefs and institutions laboriously
built up over the centuries—as in the case of Protestant iconoclasts (image
breakers) who smashed to pieces the religious art cherished by their ancestors. Interestingly, the competing denominational interpretations both
emphasized the emergence in the Reformation of a modern form of individualism, for good or for ill.[23]

The historical-materialist interpretation of the Reformation, first put
forward by Karl Marx (d. 1883) and Friedrich Engels (d. 1895), was in
more recent times cultivated in the German Democratic Republic
(1945–1989).[24] The Communist state required scholars to work within the
parameters of official ideology, but East German historians found ways
of making the argument interesting. In this view, the Reformation was an

"early bourgeois revolution," that is, an attempt by the burghers of Germany's many towns to overthrow the power of an aristocracy of feudal nobles, rooted in their control of agricultural land and peasant labor.[25] The movement was premature, since the burghers were not yet strong enough to seize control of state power, but it was a revolution nonetheless, because Luther's attack on the authority of the church undermined the religious respect for the status quo that propped up the power structure of feudal society.

In this great struggle, loyalties followed class interests. The most prestigious urban families—the so-called patricians—favored the old religion.[26] Up-and-coming merchants, not yet part of the ruling elite, rallied to Luther's cause. Lower down the economic scale, members of the craft guilds endorsed the more thoroughgoing rejection of Catholic belief and practice preached by Huldrych Zwingli in Zurich and later by John Calvin in Geneva. Unskilled laborers,[27] often recent migrants from the countryside, showed themselves the true revolutionaries by embracing the most radical of theological options, that of Anabaptist preachers who were often of humble origin themselves.[28]

During the latter half of the twentieth century, proponents of these three very different lines of interpretation—idealist, denominational, and materialist—have criticized but also borrowed from one another's work, resulting in a great melting pot of opinions that makes for a much richer understanding of the Reformation. The ecumenical movement among Christians has enabled scholars working in the context of a faith community to set aside hostile stereotypes.[29] Meanwhile, the growing interest among historians at large in the lives and beliefs of ordinary men and women has generated new questions about how the teachings of the Reformers—or of the pre-Reformation Catholic Church—were understood and practiced in daily life. Finally, and especially in the Germany that was until recently two distinct countries, scholars from East and West initiated multiple contacts that softened earlier dichotomies. Those starting from a materialist perspective began to recognize religious ideas as having a motive force of their own not strictly derived from class interests. Those starting from a theological perspective began to recognize that the religious choices of sixteenth-century men and women were not completely individualistic, because religion—and religious change—also had a social dimension.

From this dazzling variety of possible ingredients for an interpretative stew, each historian will cook up his or her own recipe. I confess an attraction to a principle first stated by the German philosopher Georg W. F. Hegel:[30] the great movements of history involve a convergence of ideal principles and selfish interests, woven together in such a way that those involved often cannot tell one from the other.[31] In general, Hegel's principle means that while ideas have a definite impact on history, it is never the impact expected by their proponents. As applied to the Reformation, it means that men and women will not willingly die a martyr's death for material interests, but neither will they in great numbers willingly disrupt the normal inertia of their daily lives solely for the sake of religious principles. This seems to me a reasonable premise for the present book: one of my aims is to give ideal and material motives the respect that each deserves.

2 | The Reformation in European Perspective

It is precisely by looking at the Protestant movement in the wider chronological framework suggested in the previous chapter that one can best discern its distinctive features. I believe there are six: (1) *sola scriptura*, the Protestant insistence on the sole authority of scripture; (2) *sola fide*, the doctrine of salvation or justification "by faith alone";[1] (3) the doctrine of the priesthood of all believers; (4) the reform of worship and religious practice, focusing attention on the sermon rather than on ritual action; (5) the holy community, meaning that for a genuine reformation the town or village as a whole must conform itself to God's law; and (6) the confessional state, meaning that rulers use their powers to promote the true Christian confession. Each of these points involves a message preached by the Reformers, reactions to that message from various levels of society, and outcomes that neither the Reformers nor their Catholic opponents could have predicted.

1. Sola scriptura. At medieval universities, theologians-in-training lectured on the writings of earlier scholars before being allowed to lecture on the Bible. Theologians who organized their findings into massive *Summae* (Summaries), like St. Thomas, sifted the Bible for answers to all their questions. To be sure, they consulted other authorities as well—Church Fathers like St. Augustine (d. 430) and pagan philosophers like Aristotle—but the Bible came first. Theologians offered their own interpretations of scripture, but only the church pronounced with authority, through the decrees of ecumenical councils or the papal pronouncements held by some theologians to be infallible.[2] Luther, though trained as a scholastic theologian, challenged this tradition on two fundamental points. First, scripture to him was not a repository of answers to all questions. Rather, it was a single message of overpowering clarity, an answer to the one question that mattered most: How can sinful human beings be saved from the everlasting fires of hell? Second, he rejected the church's claim to control interpretation. By 1519, he was convinced that one could not rely on ecumenical councils or the Fathers, not even St. Augustine, from whom he himself had learned a great deal.[3] "Scripture alone" (*sola scriptura*) had saving truth— all else was mere "human opinion."

Luther's conviction that the Bible was only now being understood, after centuries of darkness, parallels the views of humanists like Erasmus of Rotterdam (d. 1536).[4] Italian humanists of the fifteenth century learned Greek from refugee Byzantine scholars, thus gaining direct access to works previ-

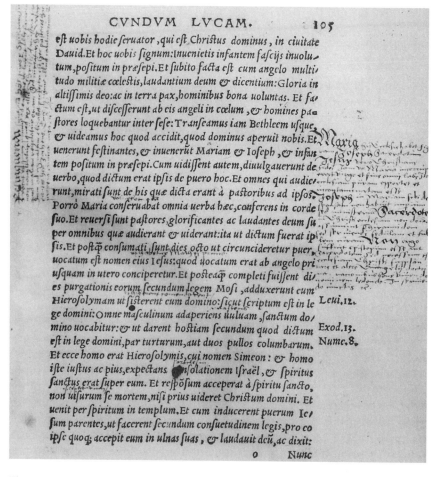

Figure 2.1. Studying the scriptures. An unknown sixteenth-century reader makes marginal notes on Luke 2 in his copy of a separately published edition of Erasmus's new Latin translation of the New Testament; Erasmus, Novum Testamentum ad Graecam Veritatem Recognitum (Basel: Froben, 1521). (*Special Collections, University of Minnesota Library.*)

ously known only in translation.[5] One Venetian humanist now argued that the scholastics had not even understood Aristotle, their great hero, because of reliance on faulty Latin texts. Scripture was open to the same kind of study. Pope Nicholas V commissioned Lorenzo Valla (d. 1457) to compare Vatican Library manuscripts of the Greek New Testament with the Vulgate translation, used for centuries in the Latin liturgy. Inspired by Valla's work, Erasmus published the first Greek New Testament in 1516, with copious notes on how the precious original differed from the Vulgate. Though not a humanist by training, Luther learned New Testament Greek and, going Erasmus one better, the Hebrew of the Old Testament as well. Erasmus saw the original New Testament text as a "fountain" of pure truth from which Christians could now drink in the plain meaning of the gospel, obscured for so many centuries by the errors of copyists and translators. This was Luther's belief too, even though he and Erasmus did not read the Gospels the same way (see chapter 5).

Most people in Europe were peasants, and few peasants could read in their own language, much less Latin or Greek. Yet Luther's contrast between "scripture alone" and "mere human opinion" had an astonishing resonance in many a humble household. The printing press provides part of the answer to this puzzle—short pamphlets featured cartoons setting forth "scripture alone" in terms that anyone could understand.[6] But there was also a great hunger for preaching in late medieval Germany, which led to the building of so-called hall-churches, free of the interior pillars that made it hard to see the pulpit. This hunger for preaching was a hunger for God's Word.[7] Events of the 1520s make it clear that people who could not read harbored deep-seated beliefs about the meaning of scripture. To them, God's Word must have answers not just to the question of salvation, but also to social and economic injustices pressing in on their daily lives. Luther was to find, to his dismay, that German peasants who rallied to the cause of God's Word understood "scripture alone" quite differently than he did.

2. *Sola fide.* Justification "by faith alone." The common opinion among medieval theologians was that sinners are "justified" when they freely accept the grace or favor that God extends to them and do the "good works" that God's commandments require. For Luther, this belief in the competence of human free will obscured the one truth on which the very salvation of humankind depended. From his own struggle to live as a pious monk, and from his study of St. Paul's Epistles, he was convinced that man is saved not by any work or act of will, but solely by grace. God's law commands unselfish love, but no human being can overcome his inborn selfishness. The true purpose of the commandments is to convince the sinner of his utter impotence, opening the door to an unqualified faith or trust that a gracious God will freely grant a forgiveness he does not deserve. Thus "Christian liberty" means that the sinner who experiences the joy of

faith is freed from the dread of God's punishment that necessarily shadows all who vainly imagine they must achieve His forgiveness by their own good actions. It is by this faith alone that one can be saved.

In the cloister, fellow monks saw Luther as a "scrupulous" brother—a touch too anxious about averting God's wrath. The very notion of "scrupulosity" does not appear in monastic literature until after about 1300, suggesting a heightened sense of sin among men and women who, like Luther, had vowed their lives to God. Meanwhile, theologians placed

Figure 2.2. Luther outbowls his foes. The reason Luther (in his garb as an Augustinian friar) bowls so well—to the dismay of pope and cardinals to the right—is that his bowling ball is labeled "Holy Scripture": Otto Clemen, Flugschriften aus der ersten Jahren der Reformation (4 vols., Leipzig: R. Haupt, 1907–1911), vol. 3. (*University of Minnesota Library.*)

AETHERNA IPSE SVAE MENTIS SIMVLACHRA LVTHERVS
EXPRIMIT·AT VVLTVS CERA LVCAE OCCIDVOS

·M·D·X·X·

Figure 2.3. Luther as an Augustinian friar. Lucas Cranach the Elder (1472–1553), "Martin Luther as a Monk," 1520. (*Metropolitan Museum of Art, New York, NY.*)

more and more stress on what man must do to attain his own salvation, and preachers constantly warned their congregations of the pains of hell, urging layfolk to imitate the devotion of monks and nuns in doing good works and avoiding sin. Manifestations of popular anxiety to ward off the wrath of God, like the flagellant movement, suggest that such sermons were not falling on deaf ears.[8] Indeed, it seems the medieval centuries were marked by a process of "guiltification"—raising in believers a conscious-ness of their own sinfulness—which for some had reached a breaking

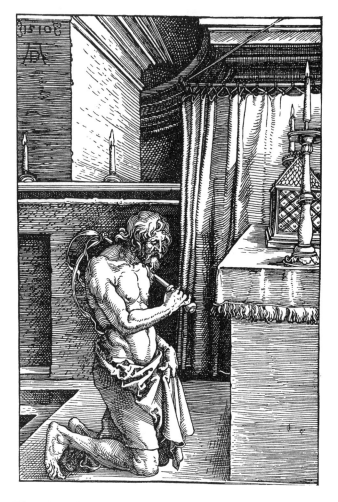

Figure 2.4. The spirit of penance. Scourging oneself in penance for one's sins was encouraged among members of religious orders and pious lay people: Albrecht Dürer (1471–1528), "The Penitent." (*British Museum, London.*)

point by Luther's time. A number of his followers left personal accounts of the deliverance from the burden of anxiety they too found in the Christian liberty of which he spoke.

But followers of John Calvin, who also condemned justification by works, believed that God's grace served a purpose beyond the spiritual consolation of the individual: it guided believers in truly good works to glorify His name. Adherents of the Catholic Reformation sought to live out a doctrine of good works that was essentially medieval, yet purged of excesses and adapted to new circumstances. Thus if Luther's "scrupulosity" disclosed a larger crisis in the religious sensibility of Latin Christendom, his solution was but one of several to be considered here.

3. *The priesthood of all believers.* Priests and members of religious orders enjoyed freedom from taxation and other special privileges, seen by the clergy as proof of their God-given preeminence in Christian society. In the clerical conception of the church lay people had but a passive role. But as towns and villages gained a measure of political autonomy, lay boards (the English term for them was "churchwardens") took over management of the church building and other parish property. As urban craftsmen formed guilds to govern their own trades, men and women formed religious confraternities whose aims were usually devotional and sometimes social, like founding a hospital. As literacy among the laity slowly increased, especially in urbanized regions like northern Italy and the Low Countries, dealers in manuscript books had a brisk trade in pious treatises in the languages of the people.

The clergy of the late Middle Ages were not particularly corrupt—by and large, priests fulfilled their duties in celebrating mass and administering the sacraments. But as lay people grew more active in the life of the church, they held the clergy to a higher standard. For many, it was no longer acceptable if parish priests, despite the church's rule on celibacy, had women who were wives in everything but name, or if the Franciscan friars claimed for their taverns exemption from the beer tax that other innkeepers had to pay. Anticlericalism—resentment of the wealth and privileges of the clergy—was widely diffused among lay people in the late Middle Ages, though more in some parts of Europe than others. Bohemia's Hussite revolution was one expression of this resentment; the Reformation was another.

Here, too, Luther touched off feelings more explosive than he realized. He appealed to the laity's sense of spiritual worth in his idea of the "priesthood of all believers"—every Christian man and woman has a priestly dignity in the sight of God; ministers of God's Word are only delegated to exercise an authority vested in all. But Luther wanted monasteries to be dissolved in an orderly fashion by town governments, not sacked by angry mobs, as sometimes happened. He wanted new preachers of the Word, trained in the biblical languages, to wield an authority not unlike what most of them had been used to as former Catholic priests. But Anabaptist preachers drew crowds when they proclaimed that the Bible was fully accessible to humble folk in the vernacular, never mind book-learning or priestly authority. Owing to his distinctive doctrine of church governance,

Figure 2.5. Anabaptist meeting. Persecuted by town and territorial governments alike, Anabaptists were sometimes captured in the midst of worship: "Nocturnal Anabaptist Gathering Taken by Surprise." (*Wick Collection, Zentralbibliothek Zurich.*)

John Calvin made a further concession to the dignity of the laity by including lay elders in church decisions. Yet it was in Calvinist towns that one heard complaints that the new ministers were displaying all the arrogance of the old priests.

In the end, Lutheran and Calvinist pastors did consolidate their authority, but only with the backing of town and territorial governments (see points 5 and 6). Meanwhile, in Catholic lands, the first goal of reformers (again with state support) was to form a parish clergy that could regain, among lay people, the respect that had been lost. Thus, if the Reformation's initial effect in the 1520s was to shatter the prestige of the clergy, the next century or so was occupied with competing strategies for rebuilding it.

4. *The reform of worship.* Protestantism was founded on a new understanding of God's Word, proclaimed from the pulpit by preachers learned in Greek and Hebrew. For the literate minority, this religion of the Word built on existing pious practices, for the private reading of scripture now encouraged was not all that different from the private reading of books of hours that had long been common among devout lay people, especially women.[9] Worship services in the language of the people, not the Latin that few of the laity understood, bridged the gap between those who could read and those who could not, as did the vernacular hymns, rare in Catholic worship, that helped rally people to the new faith.

Yet the traditional religious culture of the illiterate, especially in the countryside, had a life and power of its own. Worshipers usually did not receive communion more than once or twice a year, and in country parishes, where priests had little education, there was not always a Sunday sermon. The most solemn moment of Sunday mass came when the priest held aloft the consecrated host for the veneration of all. Also important were the processions in which the whole parish participated: around the boundaries of the parish, to invoke God's blessing on the crops; on the feast day of the parish's patron saint, usually the chief festival of the village year; and in the torch-lit funeral corteges, held at dusk to convey the faithful departed to the next life at the very hour that daylight gave way to darkness. People also took comfort in the familiar sacred furnishings of the church interior, statues and stained glass windows, many of them endowed by prominent families or, in towns, by the guilds. Statues in particular were a focal point for personal devotion. Moreover, statues and relics of the saints could work miracles, as attested by stories circulating in almost every vicinity.[10] Thus, for the majority of Europe's Christians, religion meant participating in the solemn public rituals by which one gained access to heavenly protection.

Figure 2.6. Books of Hours. Late medieval patrons often had themselves represented (as here) praying from a book of hours: Jan van Eyck (1390–1441), "The Madonna of Chancellor Rolin." (*Musée du Louvre, Paris.*)

In Luther's German liturgy, the sermon became the highlight of the service, and country people were confronted, often for the first time, with learned orations from men trained in university theology faculties. With the aid of Luther's *Short Catechism*, youngsters were to master the main points of doctrine, either in newly established village schools or in Sunday afternoon catechism classes. But the order of the worship service and for a time even the priestly vestments were kept as before. Luther saw religious images as encouragements to piety, and in many churches that became Lutheran all statues and paintings remained in place.

Figure 2.7. Elevation of the Host. For worshipers on most occasions in this era, the most solemn moment of the mass: Richard Muther, Die deutsche Bücherillustration der Gothik und Frührenaissance (Munich: G. Hirth, 1922), p. 240. (*University of Minnesota Library.*)

Zwingli and Calvin made no such concessions to tradition. In their view popular belief was nothing but a rank growth of idolatry and superstition to be torn up by its roots: no more saints, no religious images of any kind, no funeral processions, no more festivals that blended Christian themes with worldly celebration, like the parish saint's day or Christmas, with its popular carols. Even more than in Lutheran territories, the sermon was the main event of the service. In the Great Church of Zurich, where Zwingli had preached, the altar was removed, the communion table that replaced it was kept to one side, and at the front of the church was built a large pulpit supported by braces anchored in the wall. Nowhere is the new religion of the Word more graphically expressed. Thus, the Reformation also involved something like a cultural war between university-trained preachers grimly resolved to raise their ignorant flocks to a higher level of religious consciousness, and a mute, largely illiterate peasantry whose capacity for resisting unwanted innovations is only now beginning to be appreciated.

Figure 2.8. Preaching from a wooden pulpit in Zurich. Though it represents a scene from the mid-fifteenth century, this drawing gives an idea of how Zurich's Reformers had makeshift pulpits built in front of the high altar, to focus attention on God's Word: from Christoph Silberisen, Schweizer Chronik, as reproduced in Walter Muschg, E. A. Gessler, Die Schweizer Bilderchroniken des 15en/16en Jahrhunderts (Zurich: Atlantis, 1941), no. 198. (*University of Minnesota Library.*)

5. The holy community. Between approximately 1050 and 1400, towns all over western and central Europe organized themselves as "communities." This meant having a body of officials whose decisions were binding on all. There would be a mayor or mayors, aldermen (to use the English term) who served as a court for certain kinds of cases, as well as a legislative council, and a sheriff. Often surrounded by high protective walls built by the burghers themselves, town communities were proud of their distinctiveness in a society dominated by agriculture and by the estates of noble families. After about 1300 villages too began organizing as communities, in part to protect their interests against towns that sought to control trade in agricultural products. Sheriffs were usually appointed by the territorial ruler, but mayors and aldermen served by election in villages as well as towns, and despite oligarchical election procedures, those chosen were keenly aware of having to answer to fellow citizens.[11]

Thus, while mayors and aldermen sitting jointly spoke as "the community" in making decisions in behalf of all, "the community" also meant everybody—especially the so-called common man, the small farmer, or, in towns, the members of craft guilds. This dual meaning of "community" reflects the gulf that separated the great majority, strug-

Figure 2.9. The free imperial city of Nuremberg. Early sixteenth-century artists often exaggerated the distinction between town and countryside by showing cities (as here) free of suburban development beyond the walls: "Nuremberg in the Reichswald," 1516. (*Germanisches Museum, Nuremberg.*)

gling to earn their bread day by day, from the wealthy stratum that monopolized the more important local offices. In many parts of Europe, some time between roughly 1200 and 1400, merchant and artisan guilds demanded and got a share of power, giving the common man a voice in public affairs. But whether local governments were broad or narrow in their social composition, they all had the same problem: making the community in name a community in fact, in which people focused on interests that united them against the outside world, rather than on the economic and family rivalries that pitted burgher against burgher, villager against villager.

Since the idea of community had a moral connotation, it was to be expected that local governments took an interest in religion and morality.

From about 1300, towns began imposing civil penalties for offenses like adultery, blaspheming the name of God, drunken brawling, or engaging in prostitution outside the special districts now created. Many issues relating to worship were beyond the reach of magistrates, since the right to appoint the pastor of a town's parish church was often held by a monastery or noble family outside the walls. But towns exercised what influence they could to procure the appointment of native sons. They also sought to foster public devotion by taking over the management of local religious institutions—convents, hospitals, schools—and by enacting laws that prohibited taverns from opening their doors on Sunday mornings, when mass was being celebrated. In the minds of sixteenth-century men and women, the community was a corporate body not just according to human law, but also in the sight of God.

This sense of standing as a community under God's judgment helps explain the appeal of Reformation doctrine. For if the true doctrine was now being preached for the first time, one could hope for the formation, at last, of a true community, holy and pleasing in the eyes of the Lord. This yearning for a more godly manner of life seems to have been felt most keenly by folk who toiled in their artisan shops or tilled modest parcels in the countryside. These men and women saw themselves as persons of honor, not like the wandering rabble whose only thought was of their next meal, nor like the rich and powerful, who allowed themselves to be tempted by the idea that God's rules were more lenient for important people.

Yet urban ruling families were now demanding to be addressed as "lords" of the city, like noble lords ruling their country properties. Fearful for their own position, they also tended to be very cautious about approving any radical change in a town's form of worship. From the standpoint of the common man, if the self-styled better sort of people were not minded to follow the call of God's Word, then perhaps it was time for a change in the way the community governed itself. In not a few towns, the triumph of the Reformation was coterminous with efforts to achieve broader participation of the citizenry in local government. More generally, across Europe, in Lutheran, Catholic, and Reformed areas, hard-working people from the lower-to-middling sector of the population gave strong support for raising the standards of behavior in public, compelling sons and daughters to be more obedient of parental wishes (especially in the important matter of marriages where property was involved), and rooting out altogether the diabolical evil of witchcraft.

6. *The confessional state.* The legislation of Emperor Constantine (d. 337) and his successors gave the Catholic Church a privileged place in the late Roman world. There was now only one path to salvation and one true doctrine to guide people along the way. Over time, Christians professing what

the church identified as false doctrine came to be liable for prosecution by secular judges for the civil crime of heresy. What may be called the principle of intolerance—that no one person may be allowed to endanger the spiritual well-being of the community—was forged in this early period and would remain the common belief of Christian Europe down through the seventeenth century. Those who confessed true doctrine formed a single great family in the sight of God, the *corpus Christianum* (Christian body) or Christendom. It was not entirely clear, however, who was the earthly head of this Christian body—Was it the pope in Rome or the Holy Roman Emperor in Germany?[12]

In fact, struggles between temporal and spiritual authority were not limited to the conflicts between papacy and empire noted in Chapter 1. Each major ruler made demands that were not acceptable to Rome, especially regarding control over appointments to key ecclesiastical posts in his realm—the bishoprics and the important monasteries[13]—as well as the right to tax the income from the landed endowments by which they were supported. During the centuries when the papacy was weakened first by its years of exile in Avignon and then by the schism of 1378–1414, strong monarchs in France, England, and Castile (in Spain) gained effective control over ecclesiastical appointments as well as the taxation of church wealth. Popes were allowed to levy their own taxes on the income of bishops and abbots in these lands, but within limits, and only if they sanctioned the king's right to do likewise.

In Germany, by contrast, the relatively strong monarchy of earlier centuries, weakened in part by conflicts with the papacy, gave way after 1250 to an ineffective central government. Emperors of the late Middle Ages were not strong enough to interpose themselves between the papacy and the German church. Moreover, since Germany's prince-bishops were in the unique position of being able to pass the burdens of papal taxation on to the subjects whom they ruled as temporal princes, the flow of revenues to Rome became a political issue here as nowhere else. Germany, so went a common refrain, was "the pope's cow." Of all the reasons why the obscure monk who challenged papal authority became a hero in Germany almost overnight, this national resentment of papal control of the German church was probably the most important. This was the sentiment to which humanists among Luther's supporters appealed by dubbing the Saxon professor the "liberator" of Germany.[14]

It might seem that the teachings of the Reformers were hostile to prevailing notions about the unity of church and state in one Christian body. Luther's early writings condemned coercion of any kind in matters of faith, whether by the pope or by the secular ruler. John Calvin held that the church must have a government of its own, lest princes or town councils be tempted to meddle in affairs that did not properly concern them. In practice, however, the Reformers could not accept the possibility that pastors might teach the new doctrines or not, as they saw fit, and neither rulers nor their subjects could accept a permanent religious division among Christians living in the same city or territory.

Only one doctrine could be the true form of Christianity, and in the common belief, the ruler who tolerated falsehood risked calling down upon his land the wrath of God. Thus it was state power, at the town or territorial level, that cleared the churches of clergy who refused to accept the new teachings and state power again that forced ordinary men and women to choose between accepting what was now deemed the correct confession of faith or finding a new place of residence. Having control over the religious life of his territory was of course an asset to the prince. Well-educated preachers were good at reminding people of their solemn duty of obedience to the prince and useful for keeping the baptism and marriage registers that made it easier to assess the taxable wealth of the prince's subjects. Still, we should be wary of imputing overly calculating motives to princes and their councillors. They too were caught up in a spirit of enthusiasm for the great enterprise of making a more godly world.

This dependence of reform movements on state power had a further implication. Preachers of all eras stressed that a prince's highest duty was to govern his subjects well, but in fact the "honor and reputation" of a prince came from his success in making war.[15] Thus as confessional states based on hostile creeds emerged in states that were neighbors but not good neighbors, garden-variety territorial rivalries came to be infused with a new religious intensity. In the Swiss Confederation, the autonomous cantons had quarrels among themselves, partly due to the fact that each canton had the same standing, regardless of its population.[16] Hence, when the more populous cantons eagerly embraced the Reformation, the others enthusiastically proclaimed their loyalty to Catholicism. Conflict between the two confessional parties led to the first of the Reformation era's religious wars in 1531, only fourteen years after Luther had circulated his *Ninety-five Theses*.

Friction between Emperor Charles V and Germany's Protestant princes, papered over in numerous compromises, broke out into war in 1547, again from 1552 to 1555. Soon thereafter France fell into a series of civil wars pitting one religious faction against another, lasting from 1562 to 1598. Religious issues were also important in the long rebellion of the Low Countries provinces against their sovereign, the king of Spain (1572–1648), in the Thirty Years' War in Germany (1618–1648), and in the civil war in England between adherents of the crown and of Parliament (1641–1660). This conjunction between war and religion is an important part of our story. In many cases, a territory's ultimate religious identity depended not on what the people seem to have wanted, or what the preachers preached, but on who won the last battle.

The six points highlighted here have to do not just with questions of religious belief, but also with power politics and conflicts of various kinds within European society. The Reformations of the sixteenth century represent a confluence of distinct developments, each having its own trajectory. This multilayered process cannot be captured by a chronological narrative. Hence the three topical sections of the book that follow aim to show how different strands of the story came together, rather as in a novel or a film that recounts the same events more than once, each time from the perspective of a different character. The doctrinal issues presented in Part II, "Doctrine," include *sola scriptura* (point 1) and *sola fide* (point 2). Part III, "Politics," considers, as in point 6 (the confessional state), how princely governments and their rivalries shaped the outcome of the various Reformations. Part IV, "Society and Community," treats the antagonisms within society (between different lay groups and between laity and clergy, as in point 3) as a problem that each of the Reformations sought to overcome through reforming worship and building a true Christian community (as in points 4 and 5). Each part will begin with a chapter on pertinent late medieval background, followed by chapters on the Reformations in the German and Swiss lands and then in other parts of Europe.

II DOCTRINE TO LIVE BY

Doctrine has always been the way Christians explain who they are. In early centuries, the Latin word *doctrina* meant a "teaching" that formed the hearts of believers as well as instructing their minds in the "right" or orthodox understanding of God's dealings with humankind. This is not to say that religion begins with doctrine—according to an ancient Christian maxim, formal statements of faith represent an articulation of what people mean when they worship in a certain way.[1] But doctrine was the test of agreement: if certain Christians professed false doctrine, there must be something wrong also with how they lived and worshiped. For sixteenth-century Christians the question was, which is the orthodox doctrine—the teaching that had been accepted for so many centuries or the new doctrine that was (so its proponents claimed) the good, old doctrine of the ancient church, and thus not really new at all? Historical scholarship shows that doctrine itself was not the only issue—the political and social tensions that divided sixteenth-century Christians are also reflected in their newfound differences on matters of belief. But one must begin by taking seriously the understanding that contemporaries had of their own experience. As far as is possible, the discussion in Chapters 3–7 will focus on matters of doctrine, reserving discussion of the pertinent political and social issues to Parts III and IV.

3 | Doctrine

Late Medieval Background

People in fourteenth- and fifteenth-century Europe were religious, but not in the way readers may think. Surrounded by the technological sophistication of the late twentieth century, we find it hard to grasp the raw insecurity of life in earlier ages. Plagues that carried off whole families appeared seemingly from nowhere, as did the flooding and adverse weather conditions that made for a poor harvest and the famine that almost inevitably followed. The fact that the causes of human disease and plant blight were so poorly understood added to the psychological insecurity of an era when such things were commonly ascribed to evil spells cast by one's enemies or to machinations of the perfidious Jews.[1] Ordinary folk were also at risk in time of war. Commanders deemed it risky to accept battle with the enemy's army and safer to punish his towns, or at least his villages, since the towns were often surrounded by stout walls. Humble folk could take some satisfaction in the fact—as expressed by the "wheel of fortune" image popular in the fifteenth century—that not even the powerful were secure. Great nobles could be ruined by intrigues at court, rich merchants by sudden price changes in far-off lands.

Medieval Europeans did not suffer these afflictions passively. Their strategies for making life more predictable included new farming methods that increased yield, extensive dikes and drainage canals to contain waters, regular correspondence among merchants about commodity prices, and stockpiles of grain by city governments to hold prices down during a scarcity. Over time these multiple improvements fed into a technological revolution that, by the eighteenth century, put Europe well in advance of other areas of the globe. Yet no one cherished the illusion that man by his puny efforts could bend the power of nature, or the will of God.

In pre-Christian times, the peoples of Europe, like peoples everywhere, practiced various rituals to invoke the blessing of the gods and ward off

Figure 3.1. Dame Fortune and the Wheel of Fortune. Dame Fortune and her wheel, from a manuscript translation (1503) of Francesco Petrarca's *De Remediis Utriusque Fortunae* ("On the Remedies for Good and Bad Fortune"). (*Bibliothèque nationale de France, Paris.*)

Figure 3.2. San Bernardino of Siena preaching in the Piazzo del Campo. Sano d. Pietro (1406–1481), from the Duomo in Siena. (*Art Resource, New York, NY.*)

the power of evil spirits. Traces of this ancient paganism persisted long after the peoples of Europe were Christianized.[2] For example, Bernardino of Siena (d. 1444), a famous Franciscan preacher later canonized as a saint,[3] found in one midsize Italian city the custom of attempting to cure eye afflictions with water from "the spring of Apollo," named after one of the ancient gods. When he demanded that the source of such open paganism be stopped up, he was told to take his preaching elsewhere. He came back some years later and had his followers destroy the superstructures, proposing that the spring itself be incorporated into a church to be dedicated to the Virgin Mary, under the title of Our Lady of the Favors. Since they would still have their healing waters, now under Christian auspices, the townsfolk agreed.

This one incident may stand for thousands over a span of centuries, as Europeans came to accept a monotheistic religion. Christianity focused on eternal salvation but was never a religion of the spirit alone, for the God of biblical faith is Lord of the universe, and His power extends to storms and plagues and battles. Ordinary people believed in the promise of life eternal, but they attached at least as much importance to the promise of God's protection in their daily lives, including protection against the evil spirits that in a Christian view of the world were now seen as devils, minions of Satan. Like Bernardino, preachers had to frame their message so as to appeal to listeners who had priorities of their own. This chapter traces the interaction between Christian teaching, promulgated by learned men of the fourteenth and fifteenth centuries, and the religious inclinations of ordinary folk.

Each bishop was responsible for guarding against the teaching of false doctrine, or heresy, in his diocese.[4] Theology—the formal study of scripture and the Fathers—was cultivated at first by the bishops themselves, later by monastic scholars. With the rise of universities, this function of reflecting on doctrine was claimed by professors at the new faculties of theology, masters of arts and doctors of theology.[5] Theologians like Thomas Aquinas (d. 1274) and John Duns Scotus (d. 1308), whose training in the arts centered on Aristotle's philosophy, sought to reconcile biblical faith with the findings of human reason. They maintained that certain truths of faith (like the existence of God) could be demonstrated by human reason and that others were at least compatible with truths discoverable by reason, even though Aristotle, the greatest of philosophers, had held certain opinions contrary to faith.[6]

Aquinas and Scotus founded "schools" of thought that continued, but the philosophy and theology of the next two centuries took a different turn, known to contemporaries as "the modern way" and to historians as nominalism.[7] Aquinas and Scotus believed that the human mind can grasp in a general way the principles by which God has ordered the world. Take, for example, the Ten Commandments God gave to Moses on Mount Sinai or the summary of the commandments cited by Jesus in the Gospel: to love God above all things and to love one's neighbor as oneself.[8] We may infer, Aquinas and Scotus argued, that these are the precepts that God in his wisdom knows will best enable us to fulfill our true nature as human beings. But any such claim to discern the mind of God, especially when combined with the astrological determinism that was also a legacy from pagan antiquity,[9] seemed to many theologians an attempt to confine the awesome power of God within limits invented by human reason. The tendency of the "modern way" was to scale back reason's claims and make room for the sovereign freedom of God's impenetrable will. Concerning the commandments, "modernists" held that we know only that these are the precepts God commands, nothing more; any speculation as to why He may have given us these commands and not others is unwarranted by reason and dangerous to the faith.

The "modern" emphasis on the sovereignty of God's will developed in two strikingly distinct ways. The more common trend was to exalt the freedom of the human will. Just as God was free to accept a person's "merits" or good works as the basis for salvation, man was able, by strenuous effort, to achieve a degree of conformity with the commandments that God would find acceptable. Gabriel Biel (d. 1495), the leading German theologian of his day, put the matter succinctly: "do what is in you" and God's grace will supply whatever may be lacking for salvation.

But other "modernists," especially among the order of Augustinian Friars, came to very different conclusions on the basis of their study of the writings of St. Augustine. That Church Father spent his later years in controversy with followers of a British monk named Pelagius, who believed (as Augustine thought) that man could attain salvation by his own efforts, without any need for God's grace.[10] Augustine believed that owing to the "original sin" of Adam and Eve in the Garden of Eden, man's whole nature is steeped in selfishness, alienated from God, and of its own power utterly incapable of fulfilling God's law.[11] Only God's freely given grace frees man from the shackles of sinfulness.[12] But God grants his grace only to those whom He chooses, for reasons that no man may know. Moreover, it is false to say (as Augustine himself had said in earlier writings) that man is free to accept or reject the grace of God, for God's choice brooks no resistance. Taking up a term used in the Epistles of St. Paul,[13] Augustine maintained that those chosen for salvation are "predestined" from all eternity, according to God's inscrutable will.

Thus the two branches of the "modern way" reached diametrically opposed conclusions about how human beings can be saved from damnation. In the person of Martin Luther, the clash between these two theological tendencies would become a clash within the mind and heart of a single man. As an Augustinian friar, he was familiar with the recent revival of Augustine's thought. But as a theology student at the University of Wittenberg he was taught by a professor who had been Gabriel Biel's pupil.

Luther was unusual among professors of theology in that he also had an appointment as a preacher. Preaching to the laity was not a high-status activity among the clergy, and university professors or canons of cathedral chapters who preached regularly were considered an oddity.[14] The famous preachers of the late Middle Ages were almost all members of the orders of mendicant friars that took preaching as their special mission, the Franciscans (like Bernardino of Siena), the Dominicans, and also Luther's Augustinian Friars. Friars had chairs of theology reserved for their orders in university faculties, but they also had churches of their own in the towns and made circuits of pulpits in outlying parishes. In urban parish churches, staffed by the secular clergy, the pastor himself (even if resident) usually did not preach.[15] In the larger German towns of the fifteenth century, this task was increasingly taken over by holders of endowed preacherships, established by pious donations. The better-known urban preachers, friars or secular priests, frequently had university degrees in theology. But in small towns and especially in the countryside, there was often no one to preach but the pastor or (especially in rural areas) his vicar.[16] Most vicars had never seen the inside of a university, and if they preached at all (some did not) they might read aloud to their congregations from manuals of listener-friendly sermons prepared by someone higher up in the chain of learning and prestige.

Preachers knew from experience that among common people the accepted way of proving a point was by telling a story. Hence, sermons were full of stories—incidents from scripture or from the lives of the saints, accounts of local miracles, or tales of how God raised up the lowly and cast down the proud. Sermons were meant to point out a moral; introducing a theological argument was more difficult. This leads to a second observation: preachers concentrated on morals and had relatively little to say about doctrine. To be sure, church leaders expected even simple believers to be able to recite two basic prayers, the Our Father and the Hail Mary, as well as the Apostles' Creed. There is precious little information about whether people knew their prayers, but knowledge of doctrine at this rudimentary level was in fact diffused in many ways, perhaps most effectively through popular devotions like the angelus and the rosary, common from the fifteenth century.[17] Pulpit rhetoric tended to focus on how people ought to live. To be a good Catholic was to love God, obey the commandments of God and the church,[18] and to live at peace with one's neighbors.

No doubt many people lived more or less in this way. But Satan and his minions were abroad in the world setting snares for unwary souls—neither the preachers nor their listeners had the slightest doubt on this point. Vice was not just a moral failing, it was evidence of the power of the devil in the human heart, and preachers saw it as their sacred duty not to mince words in denouncing sin. Accordingly, their sermons depict a world obsessed by sexual license, boundless greed, and lust for the blood of one's enemies. The seeming contrast between the norms of Christian life and how people actually lived (as described in sermons) becomes even sharper if one considers the importance of monastic ideals.

Lay Christians had long imitated the example of monks and nuns in one way or another. For example, the "Tables of the Holy Spirit"[19] that first appeared in city parishes in France during the twelfth century provided food for the urban poor, just as monasteries provided for the rural poor. But now that many of the leading urban preachers were themselves members of religious orders—mendicant friars—sermons often held up the simplicity and austerity of monastic life to be emulated by individual lay people. In increasing numbers, ordinary men and women joined "third orders" for the laity,[20] participated in the canonical hours,[21] or left instructions in their wills that they be buried in the habit of a religious order. But the appeal to monas-

Figure 3.3. The Seven Corporal Works of Mercy. The doctrine of good works meant in particular the seven corporal works of mercy (from lower left, clockwise, feeding the hungry, giving drink to the thirsty, visiting the imprisoned, burying the dead, giving shelter to the homeless, visiting the sick, and clothing the naked): Pieter Bruegel the Elder (ca. 1525–1569), "Charitas" (Charity) in René van Bastelaer, Les Estampes de Peter Bruegel l'Ancien (Brussels: G. Van Oest, 1908), no. 134. (*Special Collections, University of Minnesota Library.*)

tic ideals also implied a higher moral standard for the laity, consistent with the monastic practice of carefully examining one's conscience for sins against God and one's neighbor. By this measure a layman must find himself guilty of adultery if he merely desired another man's wife or guilty of the grave sin of hatred if he but fervently wished ill to his enemies.

This raising of moral consciousness or "guiltification" leads to a final observation. There was, after all, a theology implicit in late medieval preaching, one that resembled the "free will" school of the modern way. It was not that all preachers had studied the works of theologians like Gabriel Biel, though some had. Rather, preachers had to get through to the hardened sinners they saw before them, and many found no better way of doing so than by hammering home the fear of God. At the same time, lest they leave listeners wallowing in despair, preachers also emphasized the concrete steps sinners could take—indeed must—to save themselves from the wrath of God. Paradoxically, the same centuries that witnessed a revival among some theologians of Augustine's doctrine of predestination were marked by a tradition of preaching that stressed, more than ever, human free will and the good works by which men aided in their salvation.

How listeners reacted to sermons is not easy to reconstruct. Some people ignored the church altogether, as many as 10 to 15 percent in one area that has been studied; they simply never went to Sunday mass. But there is also evidence of a higher level of religious engagement on the part of devout laity. Treatises on how to achieve a sense of personal union with God through prayer were written not just for lay people but by lay people, like those written by England's Richard Rolle (d. 1349) and Margery Kempe (d. 1440). The fourteenth and fifteenth centuries saw few new religious orders but a number of lay brotherhoods and sisterhoods that emulated monastic life without binding vows. The Beguines, communities of unmarried women and widows, lived in enclosed courtyards carved out of crowded urban centers, each woman contributing to the common chest through a craft like spinning, and each free to leave and marry as she wished. The Brothers of the Common Life sometimes operated schools aimed at recruiting boys for the priesthood. Although the most famous document of their spiritual outlook, *The Imitation of Christ* (1476), was written by a priest-member, most Brothers were laymen who, like the Beguines, could leave and marry if they wished.

Most people fell somewhere between the two extremes—the irreligious and the devout. For those who had enough property to make a bequest, wills offer a window on religious attitudes. Many bequests went for pious purposes, sometimes more than half the total, and two types of such gifts are of special interest here: the endowing of masses for the release of one's soul from purgatory and donations to charitable foundations. Formalizing the suggestions of earlier Christian writers, theologians of the eleventh century proposed that many souls at the point of death, perhaps most, will not be found worthy either of admission to God's presence in heaven or of condemnation to an eternity of punishment in hell; there must therefore be an intermediate state, a place of purgation where souls are cleansed of the dross of sin and so prepared for admission to paradise. The doctrine of purgatory was quickly accepted by the church, and wealthy clergy and members of the aristocracy began leaving sums in their wills to endow masses to be said for their souls as a way of speeding their release from purgatory. Belief in purgatory was immortalized in the middle section of the greatest of medieval poems, the *Divine Comedy* of Dante Alighieri (1265–1321).[22]

In Dante's lifetime, the practice of endowing soul masses was democratized, as men and women even of modest means began designating proportional sums in their wills for this purpose. Indeed, the custom came to be so widespread that a whole class of "chantry-priests" were able to make a living, barely, by saying masses for various testators and collecting the small fees provided by their wills.[23] Late medieval wills also reflect the emphasis of preachers on good works, particularly works of charity. Merchant testators often earmarked bequests to the poor to atone for the sin of usury.[24] Wealthy persons also left funds to build hospitals for the sick or enclosed courtyards with small dwellings to house the poor or the aged. The largest foundation of this kind, endowed in 1519 by the great merchant-banker of Augsburg, Jakob Fugger, still exists, operating according to rules established by the benefactor.[25] Many other testators made smaller bequests to one or more of their city's charitable foundations.

For people who did not have money enough to leave a will, the evidence available points in the same general direction. Ordinary believers of the late Middle Ages set great store by indulgences, promises by the church that all who met certain conditions could have stated periods of punishment in purgatory remitted, either for themselves or for their deceased kinfolk.[26] Churches where an indulgence was to be obtained on a particular day might have to open their doors at four or five in the morning to accommodate the crowd.

Especially in the cities, people also joined in great numbers the religious fellowships known as confraternities. These came in many kinds, for men, for women, for both sexes, some headed by priests, most by lay people. Each had a common devotion, gathering on a certain day in a certain church for particular prayers, but many also had charitable aims: giving alms to the poor, raising funds for dowries for poor but honorable girls,[27] or operating a hospital. Some confraternities even took on the vital but life-threatening task of burying the victims in times of plague. All of these practices varied

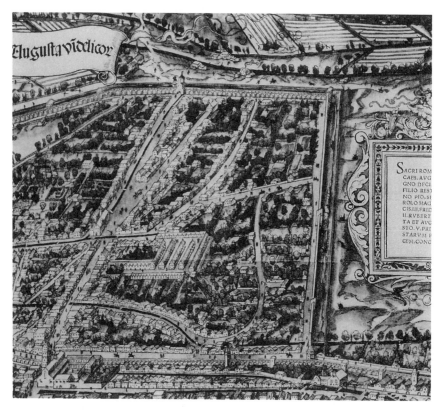

Figure 3.4. The Fuggerei in Augsburg. The row-houses on this section of a late sixteenth-century map of Augsburg mark Jacob Fugger's city for the poor, built in 1519: from G. Braun and F. Hogenberg, Civitates Orbis Terrarum, as abridged in Adrien Romain, Parvum Theatrum Urbium Praecipuarum Totius Orbis Terrarum (Frankfurt, 1595). (*James Ford Bell Library, University of Minnesota.*)

considerably with time and place. For example, the endowing of soul masses waned in fifteenth-century Italy but waxed in sixteenth-century Spain. It also became more common for confraternities to concern themselves with preparation for a good death[28] or praying for the souls in purgatory. Charitable bequests increased in some parts of Europe but decreased in others. In Germany, indulgences were distinctly less popular if the monies donated were sent across the Alps to papal Rome rather than going to local churches. But the overall pattern of religious activity among the laity does seem to reflect the constant stress of preachers on the fires of hell and on the good works man must do to attain his own salvation.

Lay people also had concerns that were uniquely their own. The custom of processing along the boundaries of the parish, to invoke God's blessing and cast out any devils that might be infesting the area, long established in the countryside, was adopted by urban parishes as well. There might even be a fight if groups from two different parishes met along the boundary, each suspecting the other of driving its demons into their parish. According to a belief condemned by some clergy as superstitious but actively promoted by others, anyone who gazed upon the consecrated host would not die that day. Hence, in some areas the priest at daily mass took to elevating the host not just once, as the rubrics prescribed,[29] but twice, for the benefit of those who came late. Parish boards began commissioning craftsmen to create elaborate golden "monstrances" with glass windows, so that the host might be carried aloft in procession and seen by all. During the fifteenth century, the church authorized a new feast, that of "Corpus Christi" (the Body of Christ), a day on which people from all of a town's parishes followed the monstrance in solemn procession, invoking God's blessing on the whole city. The confraternities, always founded for purposes of prayer and charitable works, seem to have functioned for their members as a surrogate extended family, creating bonds that were social as well as spiritual. Rules were often vague about prayers to be said at meetings but detailed and precise about support for the families of deceased members and prayers for their souls.

Thus, if the clergy were getting through to the laity, lay people were using practices sanctioned by the church for their own purposes. This does not mean that lay people did not grumble about the power and privileges of the clergy—in fact such resentment seems to have been growing (see Part IV). But to grasp the religious life of the late Middle Ages, one must recognize that Christians high and low, theology professors and illiterate peasants, shared to a significant degree a common understanding of doctrine. Theologians of the "free will" modernist school wrote learned treatises on what each person must do to be saved; preachers expounded a similar message in plain language; and lay people recited their prayers, gave to the poor, endowed masses for their souls, and joined confraternities, all in the earnest hope of doing what was needed for God's blessing in this life and the next.

At a more speculative level, one can argue that participants in this good-works Catholicism of the late Middle Ages had something else in common, a pattern of thought that encouraged repetitious behavior. Scholastic philosophers and theologians continued to multiply their subtle distinctions in a language that was increasingly technical. Preachers introduced more and more subcategories into their catalogues of the various types of sin that good Christians must be careful to avoid. Ordinary be-

lievers could not have enough of a good thing, whether it be the endowing of thousands of soul masses by some, an endless collection of indulgences by others, or the proliferation of confraternities, thirty or more in
not a few urban parishes. This pattern of activity may also be compared to
the "flamboyant" Gothic architecture of the same period, with its arches
within arches and traceries within traceries. Scholars who make such comparisons have suggested—plausibly, I think—that this repetitious behavior, this topping-up of good works with yet more good works, betrays a
certain underlying anxiety, a fear that by doing as much as possible one
still might not be doing enough.

Meanwhile, the authority that university professors of theology claimed
in matters of doctrine was coming under challenge from the devotees of a
new kind of learning. In Italy there were still traces of ancient Roman educational practices, based not on logic but on oratory, the art of speaking
and writing eloquently.[30] Small schools run by teachers of oratory offered
an alternative to the university liberal arts curriculum based on Aristotle's
logic. Around 1300, Italian teachers of oratory began modeling their instruction on what is now called classical Latin, dating from the era of authors like Cicero (d. 43 B.C.) and Livy (d. 17 A.D.). They also contended that
poetry, history, and moral philosophy—what Cicero had called "the studies of humanity"—were the best preparation for an orator. Accordingly, as
teachers of these subjects gained a foothold in universities, students nicknamed them "humanists." Mastering the classical style required knowing
the history of the Latin language and if possible Greek as well, a language
well known to classical Latin authors. Some humanists proved the value
of their craft by acting as textual detectives, showing, for example, that a
particular document, for reasons of style, could not possibly be assigned
to the author or period to which it was ascribed.

Thus was born philology, the scientific study of texts. Armed with the
new philological method of inquiry, humanists like Lorenzo Valla (d.
1457) challenged the monopoly over the interpretation of texts claimed by
university professors. Working as an independent scholar, Valla showed
that law professors misunderstood the texts of ancient Roman law[31] because they tried to take them apart according to the rules of scholastic
logic, instead of setting them into their proper historical context. Working
for the king of Naples, he demonstrated beyond reasonable doubt that a
text used by the popes to buttress their territorial claims against Naples
was a crude forgery.[32] Working for a humanist pope, and making use of
Latin and Greek manuscripts housed in the Vatican Library, he showed
that the Vulgate Latin New Testament was riddled with mistranslations,
some of which distorted the meaning of the Greek original.

In Italy, where most universities were of recent origin, debates between humanist scholars like Valla and university professors steeped in scholastic logic were conducted with civility. But a real battle was joined when, by about 1500, humanist scholarly methods began to penetrate northern universities, where the privileges of the professorate were deeply entrenched. Erasmus of Rotterdam (1469–1536) was the standard-bearer of humanist scholarship in this more combative era. The illegitimate son of a priest, Erasmus (by his telling) entered a monastery for lack of a better way of continuing the life of study he had chosen. There he chafed under constraints real or imagined, above all the superstitious fear that Christians might be contaminated by contact with pagan Latin poets of the classical era, like his beloved Horace (d. 8 B.C.). Given the chance to serve as Latin secretary to a local bishop, Erasmus "escaped" from his monastery and never went back. After years of scrounging support from semiliterate patrons, he gained the attention of the learned world through his collection of *Adages,* or pithy sayings from Greek and Latin authors , especially in the second edition of 1508.

His real passion was for "ancient theology," that is, the vision of Christian life propounded by the Fathers of the Church, and closely based on scripture. The Fathers were themselves trained in the art of oratory, not logic, and Erasmus admired their way of weaving scripture into their works and writing so as to reach the heart, making readers better Christians. (By contrast, he and other humanists charged that scholastics were mainly interested in displaying their own argumentative skills[33]). He set himself to master Greek, even though no teacher was available, and thus gained access to the Greek Fathers, especially Origen (d. 255), a sophisticated thinker and biblical scholar. When he found a manuscript of Valla's unpublished treatise on the New Testament (1505), Erasmus also found his calling. It took eleven years to prepare the first-ever printed edition of the Greek New Testament that appeared in 1516, to be followed by four subsequent editions. Each was accompanied by copious notes discussing the Greek and Latin manuscripts he had examined and, where manuscripts or quotations of the New Testament by the Fathers offered different readings, explaining why he had chosen one rather than another. As a New Testament philologist, Erasmus was a scholar of unparalleled brilliance, improvising as he went along interpretative techniques that would not be recognized as standard procedure until 150 years after his death.[34]

Scholarship was never an end in itself for Erasmus, only a means to a badly needed reform of Christian doctrine. If people lived as they did— slaughtering one another in senseless wars—it was because they had been taught that religion was only a matter of ritual practices, like not eating meat on Fridays or confessing one's sins to a priest once a year.[35] This false "religion of ceremonies" rested on a misreading of the Gospels. For example, when John the Baptist prepares the way for Jesus' coming by urging listeners to "do penance," the term used in the Latin Vulgate was referred by medieval interpreters to the penance one was assigned by the priest in the sacrament of confession.[36] Erasmus pointed out, correctly, that the original Greek word means "have a change of heart," and thus does not refer to any ecclesiastical ritual.

Erasmus did not believe such distortions were accidental. He claimed that members of religious orders, especially the mendicant friars,[37] "twisted" scripture deliberately in order to promote religious practices that feathered their own nests, like the custom of having oneself buried in a Franciscan habit. The grip that these "mendicant tyrants" had on the minds of the common people could be broken only by the power contained in the native meaning of scripture. Theologians must set aside Aristotle's logic and study scripture in the original languages. Preachers must set aside their talk of ceremonies and teach people about the love that Christians are to bear one another. And lay people must find their own ways of prayer, based on reading scripture, and forget about imitating the monks. Despite vociferous objections from scholastic theologians, who found it unseemly that mere "grammarians" like Erasmus meddled in sacred theology, this message found an audience among laymen and wealthy clerics who could read Erasmus's Latin and conscientious young men preparing for the priesthood. University lectureships in Greek and Hebrew were endowed at Louvain (1517) and Paris (1519), for study of the Old Testament as well as the New. Graduates trained in the new theology were beginning to occupy endowed preacherships in important churches. By about 1520, Erasmus's program for a reform of doctrine was taking shape as an alternative to the prevailing vision of Christian life. By this time, however, it was not the only alternative.

4 | Doctrine

Martin Luther, to 1521

Few individuals have shaped history as Martin Luther did. The way he overcame his personal religious anguish became the model for a new understanding of Christian life. His keen mind and passionate spirit, breaking through the conventions of academic theological discourse, won over men who had sat down to read the works of this notorious heretic in order to refute him.[1] His courageous challenge of papal authority gave him immense prestige among those who joined in the inchoate "evangelical" movement,[2] so that his word sufficed to guide many into one channel rather than another, forming in the end a new church. But Luther's greatest importance to history lies in the fact that his protest against Rome touched off a many-sided explosion that no man could control. This chapter will consider Luther's early life and thought down to 1521. Chapter 5 will take up the extraordinary and often conflicting proliferation of responses to Luther's message during the years 1520–1526.

Luther speaks in his writings of a breakthrough moment, when he felt himself delivered from the dread of God's punishment by a new insight into the meaning of scripture. Assuming that Luther had this experience before his life of public controversy began (1517), some scholars have combed surviving notes of the early lectures he gave at Wittenberg, looking for evidence of his new understanding of scripture. Others point to the fact that Luther's fullest description of his "tower experience" dates it from the time of his second course of lectures on the Psalms (1518–1519).[3] Perhaps the most sensible view is that Luther's theology cannot be reduced to a single point; rather, it is made up of several strands, some of which appear in the early lectures, others not before 1518. Thus the climax of his

47

inner struggle came in the midst of furious battle with his enemies. At least in this case, religious doctrine takes shape not in a quiet compartment unto itself, but right in the middle of that tangled nexus of conflicts we call history.

Luther was born in 1483, the son of a Saxon miner. Hans Luther, Martin's father, rose from laborer to partner in one of the small operations typical of Saxony's mining boom in this era. It was a measure of the family's rising status that Martin was the first Luther to receive a bachelor of arts degree, from the University of Erfurt. He followed the traditional scholastic curriculum, dominated at Erfurt by the "modern way," though he also had friends among Erfurt's upstart humanist scholars. Martin was a strong student, and he doubtless made Hans Luther proud when he enrolled in the law faculty in 1505. But en route back to Erfurt from a visit home, passing through a frightening summer storm, he impulsively vowed to St. Ann, the patron saint of miners, that he would become a monk if she delivered him from peril. His father had misgivings and friends were surprised, but Luther persisted. He entered the Erfurt cloister of the reformed Augustinian Friars, a congregation distinguished for its learning.[4] Johann Staupitz (d. 1525), father-superior of Germany's reformed Augustinians, was called by the elector of Saxony to help found a new university in Wittenberg (1502). Staupitz was the first holder of the theology chair reserved for his order; Luther would be the second.

The traditional monastic routine emphasized self-scrutiny. Friars regularly confessed their sins to a father confessor, and there was a weekly "chapter of faults" at which each recounted his failings publicly. But Brother Martin was unusually scrupulous. He later recalled that when he sang in choir the Psalm verse "In Thy righteousness deliver me" he recoiled inwardly, measuring his own sinful heart against the righteousness of God.[5] He could not confess his sins often enough or long enough: "Once I confessed for six hours." Even when his confessor absolved him from the guilt of his sins he was not content, for the formula of absolution required the penitent to be sorry for his sins: How could one be sure of being truly sorry, that is, sorry for having offended God, not because one feared the pains of hell?[6] Work was a standard remedy for monks unduly preoccupied by their sins. Luther apparently began the study of theology at Erfurt, shortly after his ordination as a priest (1507). The next year Staupitz bade him transfer to Wittenberg to earn his doctorate. When Brother Martin proffered a list of fifteen reasons why he was unworthy to be a theologian, Staupitz commanded him under his monastic vow of obedience to go.[7]

At first, Wittenberg intensified Luther's anxiety.[8] Since one of his theology professors had been a student of the late Gabriel Biel, the monk who could never be sure of being properly sorry for his sins was confronted with the calm assurance of a late-great theologian that one need only "do what is in you" in order to be saved. Staupitz, a noted student of St. Augustine, came to the rescue by admonishing his protégé not to give heed to "recent" theologians, that is, the scholastics. True wisdom was to be gleaned from the Church Fathers, above all St. Augustine. Luther's lectures on St. Paul's Epistle to the Romans (1515–1516) show how carefully he studied Augustine, especially his writings against Pelagius. The prevailing scholastic view was that man with the help of divine grace could perform actions that were inherently righteous in the sight of God. But Luther, following Augustine, taught his students that man is too corrupted by sin ever to do anything truly righteous in the sight of God. Rather, God in his mercy imputes[9] righteousness to those who freely confess that they are steeped in sin, utterly incapable of living up to the commandments. Augustine maintained that those who are saved by God are predestined for salvation from all eternity, and this too Luther accepted. But knowing the duplicity of his own heart, he could not believe that God had chosen such a sinner as himself for eternal glory. Hence he adopted from other sources the view that the true Christian is one who resigns himself to the prospect of damnation in hell and still praises the justice of God. In fact, he could not resign himself to an eternal punishment, and the awful spells in which he was numbed by a dread of God's justice only grew worse. Somehow, Augustine was not the full answer.

Luther had been named superior of the reformed Augustinian Friars in Wittenberg in 1512. In this capacity he developed what would later be important contacts at the court of Elector Frederick the Wise (d. 1525). As preacher at the elector's castle church (since 1514), he was also gaining a sense of how difficult it was for ordinary folk to accept the hard truths of Christian life as taught by St. Augustine and St. Paul. Within the theology faculty, however, he built an Augustinian "school," as may be seen from the "theses" or propositions that were posted and then publicly defended by doctoral candidates he had trained. He also began winning over faculty colleagues, such as Andreas Bodenstein von Karlstadt (d. 1541), who abandoned his allegiance to the "way" of Aquinas once Luther persuaded him to read Augustine.

This busy but quiet life was disrupted by a small incident that became the hinge of something huge. In Rome, Pope Leo X (ruled 1513–1521) was rebuilding the great basilica of St. Peter. He proclaimed indulgences for all who contributed to the project and recited certain prayers. This was a familiar practice, for popes claimed to have disposal over a spiritual "treasury" consisting of the merits of all the saints through the ages, so that by his fiat these merits could be applied to the remission of punishment in purgatory. Frederick the Wise, mindful of widespread complaints that

Chapter 4

Figure 4.1. Sale of indulgences. Anonymous caricature of the sale of indulgences (by Dominican Friar Johann Tetzel) to which Luther's *Ninety-five Theses* responded: the last couplet of the text reads, "As soon as the gulden in the basin rings, another soul to heaven springs." (*Stiftung Luther-Gedenkstätten in Sachsen-Anhalt, Wittenberg.*)

Germany was "the pope's cow,"[10] had barred the pulpits of his land to the preaching of any indulgence that involved sending contributions to Rome. But the indulgence was preached in a neighboring territory by a Dominican friar who had circulars printed with a catchy jingle: "As soon as the coin in the coffer clings, another soul from purgatory springs."

To Luther, the popularity of this indulgence among his parishioners showed how easily people were misled by quick and easy paths to salvation. Some even thought the certificates of indulgence they obtained involved a remission of their sins, not just of time in purgatory.[11] So, on 31 October 1517, he made public his *Ninety-five Theses*, written in academic Latin, challenging the whole practice of indulgences.[12] Among other things, he asserted that the true treasure of the church is the gospel, not the merits of the saints, and that the pope had no power to release souls from purgatory. Moving on to related subjects, he also maintained that whoever receives absolution from a priest in the sacrament of confession must have firm faith that his sins are forgiven.

Quite unexpectedly, the *Ninety-five Theses* were circulated all over Germany, even translated into the vernacular, and Luther became an overnight celebrity. German humanists who resented what they saw as papal domination of their country seized on the fact that a German monk was challenging Rome.[13] Printers sensed there would be a market for anything of Dr. Luther's they could get their hands on, and they were not mistaken. In Rome and elsewhere, Dominican theologians came to the aid of their indulgence-preaching confrere by heaping abuse on the "heretic" of Wittenberg. Luther responded in kind, and then some—invective was one of his real talents. He also published an *Assertion of the Ninety-five Theses,* defending everything he had said, point by point.

Meanwhile, Luther continued his work as a professor of theology. In his second course of lectures on the Psalms (1518–1519) he wrestled once more with the question of how sinful man might escape God's judgment, and this time he found some new answers. First, to those whom God has chosen for salvation, He imputes a righteousness that is "passive," not active, given by God, not accomplished by man. The sinner does nothing for his own salvation, not even (as Luther had said in earlier lectures) accusing himself of sin before God. Sorrow for sin, faith in God—in short, everything that conduces to salvation—is from God alone. Second, to have faith means the sinner has firm confidence that God has forgiven him his own sins. For Luther there is a vital distinction between believing in one's mind that Christ by his life and death has redeemed humankind from sin and believing in one's heart that Christ is one's own redeemer, sinner though one knows oneself to be. The latter, not the former, is what St. Paul means when he says (Rom., 1:17) "the just shall live by faith."

This doctrine of "salvation by faith" was henceforth for Luther the "key of scripture," opening up the mystery of how sinful man might be saved. Though he would still be plagued all his life by doubt and anxiety, Luther never forgot the deliverance he felt when this key of scripture was given to him, possibly in the early months of 1518. He could now see the torment of earlier years as a necessary preparation: had he not been driven to despair of his ability to do anything worthy in the sight of God, he could never have experienced the joy of Christ's wondrous and gratuitous mercy.

This new understanding of Christian faith was soon tested in a confrontation with Pope Leo X's emissary to Germany, Cardinal Tommaso de Vio (d. 1534), known from the town of his birth as Cajetan. Initially, the papal court did not take seriously the ruckus caused by an obscure professor at a fledgling German university. But Rome did have important business in Germany. For centuries, the papacy had sought to rally Latin Christendom against the military might of Islamdom, first in an ultimately futile campaign for possession of the Holy Land during the era of the Crusades (1096–1293),[14] then in a struggle to stem the steady advance of the Ottoman Turkish Empire. Since the Ottoman sultan had recently (1517) subdued a rival Muslim empire based in Egypt,[15] there was every likelihood of further Turkish attacks against Christian Europe. Hence, in the summer of 1518, Pope Leo sent Cajetan, a seasoned diplomat, to address the princes and the envoys of Germany's cities assembled for a diet in Augsburg.[16] Cajetan carried proposals to mobilize a Christian army with German support, but he could not overcome deep skepticism of papal motives in Germany, where people could remember previous occasions when money was collected but no crusade was ever launched.

Cajetan was also instructed to lay down the law to the troublesome professor from Wittenberg, summoned to Augsburg for the meeting (12–14 October 1518). Cajetan, who was also a respected theologian, had evidently decided that all questions raised in the *Ninety-five Theses* could be treated as still open to dispute, except for two points. Speaking as a defender of papal authority, he demanded that Luther recant his assertion that popes had no power to declare that souls were released from the pains of purgatory. Luther replied that he could not do so, unless taught from scripture that his opinion was false. Speaking for the theological tradition (including Augustine), which held that no man could ever be certain of his standing before God, Cajetan demanded that Luther recant his assertion that anyone absolved by a priest must believe he is free of sin. This too Luther refused; to him, Cajetan was contradicting the plain meaning of St. Paul's words, "the just shall live by faith." He appealed from the pope's emissary to the pope himself, or to a council of the church. Word spread that he had defied Cajetan. Luther returned to Wittenberg, meeting admiring crowds en route.

Johann Eck (d. 1543), a theology professor at the university of Ingolstadt and a celebrated debater, thought he could bring Luther to heel. He challenged Karlstadt (Luther's Wittenberg colleague) to a debate, confident that Luther too would take up the gauntlet. The debate was held in Leipzig, under the auspices of the duke of Saxony,[17] whose lands had been ravaged within living memory by Hussite armies from nearby Bohemia. In debate with Luther (4–13 July 1519), Eck played to his audience, pointing to similarities between Luther's writings and those of Jan Hus, the Bohemian heretic condemned and burned by the Council of Constance (1414).[18] Since he evidently discounted the authority of Constance, did Luther still wish to appeal to a council of the church, as he had done in Augsburg? This attack placed Luther at a crossroads. He would have much company among theologians if he merely questioned papal authority, but none at all if he rejected the common belief that ecumenical councils cannot err in matters of faith. Having asked for a few days' time to examine Hus's writings, Luther returned with an unequivocal answer: Hus had been unjustly condemned, Constance had erred, and councils of the church were not infallible. By implication, the only source of religious authority was scripture itself—*sola scriptura.*

Events now moved rapidly toward schism in Latin Christendom. In Wittenberg, studying the papal decrees constantly cited against him, Luther found little he could respect. In letters to close friends, he wondered if the papacy had fallen under the grip of Satan. The New Testament Book of Revelation prophesies a day when many of the faithful will be deceived by Christ's great adversary, described in one text as the seven-headed beast, in another as the Whore of Babylon.[19] Reform-minded visionaries of the medieval era predicted that the Antichrist would some day occupy the emperor's throne or even the seat of St. Peter in Rome.[20] In private, Luther now believed the day had come: papal Rome was the Whore of Babylon.

In public, he set forth his understanding of the gospel in three influential treatises published in 1520. *The Freedom of a Christian* explains his doctrine of salvation by faith, starting from the sharp distinction in the Epistles of St. Paul between the false righteousness of works and the true righteousness of faith. Only those who despair in the righteousness of their own deeds can grasp what faith in Christ means and how it makes Christians free from the anxiety that oppresses all who place any trust whatsoever in their own righteousness. In effect, Luther's own spiritual journey had become the model of Christian life. *An Address to the Christian Nobility of the German Nation* called on the secular leaders of German society to take a hand in reforming the church, since no help was to be expected from the pope or his bishops.

The Babylonian Captivity of the Church tears down the church's authority point by point. The pope claims to be the final interpreter of scripture, but scripture's message—the promise of forgiveness in Christ—is clear and needs no interpreter. The church claims to govern the lives of Christians by canon law, but coercive authority belongs only to the secular rulers to whom God has given it, not to those designated to preach the Word. The church teaches that God's grace must be mediated by an ordained priesthood, but this claim too is false. For Luther there are indeed unique rituals or sacraments of the church through which believers have access to divine grace. But for him the efficacy of the sacraments depends solely on Christ's promises in the gospel, not on a power-to-make-holy received by priests in ordination.[21]

Furthermore, for Luther there were not seven sacraments,[22] as in Catholic doctrine, but only two, baptism and the Lord's Supper—and the latter was distorted by false teaching. With his disciples at the Last Supper, Jesus had said of the bread He blessed, "This is my body," and of the wine, "This is my blood . . . Do this in memory of me."[23] Luther believed, as Catholics did, that these words meant the body and blood of Christ were truly present in the consecrated bread and wine. But he rejected the Catholic doctrine of transubstantiation, according to which the substance (an Aristotelian term) of the bread and wine is transformed into that of the body and blood of Christ. The words of Jesus must speak for themselves, unencumbered by human efforts to explain God's ways.

Meanwhile, the papal court moved toward a formal condemnation. Johann Eck volunteered his help in combing Luther's writings for propositions worthy of censure as heretical (he claimed to have found 4,000). *Exsurge, Domine* ("Rise up, O Lord"), a papal bull demanding that Luther recant forty-one specific assertions, was issued on 15 June 1520.[24] Luther greeted the news with derision. When a copy of the bull finally reached Wittenberg some months later, he celebrated with a bonfire (10 December) fed by the papal bull and a copy of the canon law. A further bull (3 January 1521) excommunicating Luther for refusing to recant was anticlimac-

Figures 4.2 and 4.3. The papacy as Antichrist. While Christ Himself refuses the crown offered by the man to the right of St. Peter, a greedy pope "fishes" money from secular rulers: engravings by Lucas Cranach the Elder (1472–1553). Passional Christi und Antichristi (Wittenberg, 1521), as reproduced in Harmann Grisar, S.J., and Franz Heege, S.J., Luthers Kampfbilder (4 vols., Freiburg: Herder, 1921–1923). (*Michigan State University Library.*)

tic.[25] Luther shed his hesitation to speak publicly about the papacy: the see of Peter had become a cesspool of iniquity, the Antichrist.

The voice of Emperor Charles V was yet to be heard. At the death of Maximilian I of Habsburg (ruled 1493–1519), two great princes had vied for the succession, King Francis I of France (ruled 1515–1547) and Maximilian's grandson Charles of Habsburg (b. 1500), hereditary ruler of the Low Countries and king of Castile and Aragon.[26] Charles won the contest by offering larger bribes to the electoral princes (including the elector of Saxony) by whose vote the emperor was chosen.[27] Patriotic German humanists rejoiced: as archdukes of Austria, the Habsburgs were hereditary German princes. Many hoped the new Habsburg emperor would defend the empire against papal domination as well as French aggression. But Charles himself had no sympathy for Luther's rebellion against the papacy. Raised in the belief that he as emperor would be the divinely appointed leader of the Christian world,[28] he resolutely opposed any division within Christendom, especially at a moment when Islamdom, led by the Ottoman sultan, seemed more dangerous than ever.

One of Charles's first acts as emperor was to request that the princes and urban deputies assembled for the Diet of Worms condemn Luther. Since the diet would not act without hearing what the Saxon monk had to say, Luther was summoned to Worms. He told the emperor (17–18 April 1521) he could not in conscience recant his opinions unless taught from scripture. Many at Worms were deeply impressed. The pope's representative at Worms exaggerated only slightly when he reported that "nine-tenths of the people here cry 'hurrah for Luther', the other tenth cry 'death to the pope'." But once Luther had departed, under safe-conduct, Charles induced a majority of the diet to issue the Edict of Worms, placing Luther outside the protection of the law (whoever harmed him would not be punished) and prohibiting the dissemination of his teachings.

The emperor now returned to his Spanish kingdoms, threatened by impending war with France, leaving behind as his deputy for imperial affairs his younger brother, Archduke Ferdinand of Austria (1503–1564). As for Luther, he was fortunate in that his prince, Elector Frederick the Wise, did not believe he had received a fair hearing. Under Frederick's protection, and living in disguise as a nobleman at the Wartburg, one of the elector's castles, Luther disappeared from view for the better part of a year (April 1521–March 1522). When he emerged from seclusion, it would be a different world.

5 | Doctrine

The German and Swiss Reformation, 1520–1526

At the Wartburg, Luther completed a translation of the New Testament from Greek into German, published in 1522, and began learning Hebrew for the Old Testament. (His epoch-making translation of the full Bible would be published in 1526.[1]) In Wittenberg during these months, his designated spokesman was Philip Melanchthon (1497–1560), a brilliant young professor of Greek who had switched to theology at Luther's suggestion. But Karlstadt took the lead by pushing ahead with reform on several fronts—he introduced a new German-language liturgy and persuaded the city council to remove images from the churches. To make it clear there was no longer any real distinction between clergy and laity, Karlstadt took a wife,[2] breaking with the church's rule of clerical celibacy, and also began dressing as a layman.

Meanwhile, three men had taken refuge in Wittenberg after being expelled from nearby Zwickau for professing religious ideas the city council deemed too radical, including the abolition of infant baptism (see below). The so-called Zwickau prophets claimed direct inspiration from God. Melanchthon and others hesitated—Could these men be right? The city dissolved in furious controversy among ardent, image-smashing supporters of Karlstadt, angry defenders of the now-abolished Latin mass, and followers of the three prophets. Alarmed, Luther came out of hiding and laid down the law from his accustomed pulpit (March 1522): The "prophets" must leave town; the Latin mass must be restored until such time as people could be weaned away from it (Luther introduced his own German liturgy four years later). The university faculty prohibited Karlstadt from publishing anything. Dr. Luther could still control the flow of events in Wittenberg. The rest of Germany and Switzerland was a different matter.

In far-off Zurich, Huldrych Zwingli (1484–1531) launched the most important alternative to Luther's understanding of the evangelical message. As a student at the Universities of Vienna and Basel, Zwingli became a part of the humanist movement, as is evident from his study of Erasmus. He displayed a typically humanist patriotism while serving as a pastor in the town of Glarus, writing poems in praise of the noble Swiss nation. He was also chaplain to the men of his town who, as was their custom, marched across the Alps (1512, 1515) to fight under the papal banner as mercenary soldiers in Italy's wars. For his services, Zwingli received an annual papal pension. He used the extra income to purchase works in "ancient theology," including Erasmus's Greek New Testament of 1516 and a grammar for learning ancient Greek.

Erasmus's critique of contemporary warfare, together with bitter memories of his second Italian campaign,[3] emboldened Zwingli to speak out against the current vogue for mercenary contracts with the king of France,

Figure 5.1. View of Zurich, ca. 1500. The Grossmünster, the church where Zwingli would become People's Preacher in 1519, may be seen clearly in Franz Leu, the Elder, "View of Zürich," ca. 1500. (*Schweizerisches Landesmuseum, Zürich.*)

whose agents were signing up Swiss cantons one after another. The town council of Glarus, eager for French pensions, dismissed Zwingli from his pastorate, forcing him to take a parish in a smaller town.[4] But Zwingli's stance won admirers in the important city of Zurich, a holdout against the French alliance, where he became endowed preacher of the "great church" in January 1519. It was the custom to preach each Sunday on the scripture texts assigned for the mass of that day. But Zwingli, mindful of the differences among New Testament authors to which humanist scholars had called attention, broke with precedent by announcing a series of sermons on the Gospel of Matthew, from beginning to end.

He also attacked the cult of the saints, indulgences, and other long-established practices. He preached justification by faith, a doctrine he claimed to have learned directly from scripture rather than from Luther. Zwingli's emphasis was in any case slightly different, because of his belief that God's grace made it possible for the righteous to live according to the commandments.[5] How Christians lived was for him a touchstone of doctrinal truth. For example, he now believed it was wrong for Christians to fight as mercenaries in any war, not just for the French. It was a victory for Zwingli (January 1522) when the city council banned all inhabitants of the canton from signing up as mercenaries, despite opposition from the countryside, where men supplemented their income by soldiering. Knowing he had the support of the council, Zwingli arranged a disputation (January 1523) in which he defended *sola scriptura* against Catholic opponents, and attacked clerical celibacy, monasticism, and belief in purgatory.

The council declared Zwingli the winner on the main issue, *sola scriptura*, but it took two years to overcome resistance to the abolition of Catholic worship throughout the city and the canton. Guided by Zwingli, the council sanctioned a new German liturgy (April 1525) and mandated removal from the churches of all images—crucifixes,[6] statues, paintings, and stained glass windows. Zwingli believed the Christian people, like the Hebrews of Old Testament times, had a covenant with God and were thus bound to honor His commandments to the Jews of old,[7] including the prohibition of graven images. Prior to 1525 there had already been outbreaks of spontaneous iconoclasm, as people convinced of a new faith laid violent hands on the "idols" by which they had so long been deceived. Like all educated men of the era, Zwingli abhorred riots, and he counted on the city council to ensure that the remaining "idols" would be removed from the churches in an orderly fashion. Orderly on not, Luther viewed this whole development with misgiving. He believed images encouraged piety and should be kept. He also found that those who were zealous to cleanse the churches of images (like Karlstadt in Wittenberg a few years earlier) seemed to think

Figure 5.2. Swiss mercenaries crossing the Alps. One of Zwingli's accomplishments was to stop (in the canton of Zurich) the practice by which Swiss men earned their bread fighting in foreign wars: from Diebold Schilling, Amtlicher Luzerner Chronik, as reproduced in Walter Muschg, E. A. Gessler, Die Schweizer Bilderchoniken des 15en/16en Jahrhunderts (Zurich: Atlantis, 1941), no. 135. (*University of Minnesota Library.*)

they were performing a righteous deed in the sight of God—thus reintroducing the old idea of justification by works.

Differences between Wittenberg and Zurich became acute when Zwingli espoused a new understanding of the Lord's Supper. In 1524 a visitor from the Low Countries showed him a treatise arguing that the words

Figure 5.3. Image of a patron saint. Albrecht Dürer (1471–1528), "St. Sebald," from Valentin Scherer, *Dürer. Des Meisters Gemälde und Kupferstiche* (Berlin/Leipzig: Deutsche Verlagsinstitut, 1926); the church model Sebald holds is recognizable as the Seballdskirche (St. Sebald's church) in the artist's native Nuremberg. (*University of Minnesota Library.*)

of Jesus at the Last Supper had been grossly distorted by the church. "This is my body" should be taken figuratively, not literally, as had been believed for so many centuries. In 1525 Zwingli presented this view in a treatise of his own. The true body of Christ, he maintained, was not a piece of bread, but the assembly of the faithful gathered to commemorate the Last Supper. Luther reacted much as his Catholic adversaries did: this was blasphemy, plain and simple. How could anyone who so capriciously dismissed the plain meaning of scripture be counted as a Christian? And how could sinners trust in the promises of Christ if His very words in the

Gospel were not to be believed? The pamphlet war between Wittenberg and Zurich that now began lasted into the following century.

One thing Luther and Zwingli had in common was that German and Swiss-German humanists were of incalculable importance in spreading their doctrines.[8] These men, mostly a bit younger, had been moving into influential positions as endowed preachers, secretaries to town councils, and councillors to princes. They cheered the two Reformers on as they attacked the established scholastic theology in the name of a new or rather "ancient theology" based on scripture and the Fathers. As patriotic students of the German past, they also blamed the papacy for waging war against the great emperors of the medieval centuries, indeed, treating them shamefully—and thus weakening the empire.[9] During Emperor Maximilian I's occasional conflicts with the papacy,[10] humanists in imperial service promoted the common view that Germany was being exploited by papal greed.

Figure 5.4. The Difference between the True Religion of Christ and the False Religion of Antichrist. God the Father rains blessing on Dr. Luther and his hearers, fire and damnation on the fat friar and avaricious pope to the right: Pankratz Kempf, broadside, before 1554: from Walter L. Strauss, The German Single-Leaf Woodcut, 1550–1600 (3 vols., New York: Abaris, 1975), II, pp. 508–509. (*University of Minnesota Libraries.*)

Northern humanists also connected papal Rome with a special kind of Italian snobbery. Italian humanists, styling themselves heirs to the glories of ancient Rome, heaped scorn on "barbarian" lands north of the Alps that had no history worth remembering. Young scholars eager for study in Italy, the font of humanist learning, often found that "barbarians" speaking correct classical Latin with a northern accent were treated with the curiosity one might bestow on a talking ape. Hence, German and Swiss-German humanists combed old manuscripts for evidence of forgotten heroes whose great deeds would give the lie to Italian arrogance. One whose name came to light was Arminius, a war chieftain who kept Rome out of northern Germany by annihilating three legions that crossed the Rhine in 9 A.D.[11] When Luther came on the scene, humanists acclaimed him as the new Arminius, the man destined to free the German nation from Roman tyranny in its modern and clerical guise.

Many believed, in the words of a humanist friar who heard Luther preach at Augsburg (October 1518), that Luther was saying what Erasmus said, only more boldly.[12] Zwingli's career illustrates the possibility of a seamless progression from "ancient theology" to Reformation doctrine. Yet there was no necessary connection between the humanist agenda—sound biblical

Figure 5.5. Iconoclasm in the Netherlands, 1566. Engraving of "Iconoclasm in the Netherlands," 1566, from Michael Eytzinger, *Novus de Leone Belgico eiusque Topographiae et Historiae Descriptione* (Cologne, 1588). (*British Library, London.*)

scholarship as the basis for a reform of Christian life—and the doctrine of salvation by faith. This became clear in Erasmus's debate with Luther.

After publication of the first edition of his Greek New Testament (1516), Erasmus settled at the University of Louvain, near Brussels, where the endowment by a wealthy friend of chairs in Latin, Greek, and Hebrew laid an institutional foundation for the new theology. But the growing controversy over Luther made Louvain more and more difficult, as conservative theologians, already suspicious of the mere "grammarian" they had admitted to their faculty, now blamed Erasmus's novel approach to scripture for all of Luther's heresies. Moreover, Emperor Charles V expected that the most famous scholar of his Low Countries provinces must surely take up his pen against Luther, sooner or later.[13] Erasmus himself had feared from the start that Luther's vehement "spirit" portended schism in Christendom, a prospect he deeply abhorred. Yet he also admired Luther as an expositor of the Gospel, and he saw "mendicant tyrants" reigning supreme in the church if Luther, their great foe, were laid low. Thus, he could neither support Luther nor attack him. Late in 1521 he moved to Basel, where his publisher was, lest he be confronted with a request from Charles V to write against Luther.

In Basel, part of the Swiss Confederation, evangelical zealots assailed Erasmus as a hypocrite for continuing to profess loyalty to the pope, after he himself had so sharply attacked superstitious practices of the church. On the other hand, it also became clear he would lose credibility among those in the church who defended him—including officials at the papal court—if he remained silent. He therefore decided to write against Luther, but chose an issue he felt would not give support to the errors of the "mendicant tyrants." Erasmus's *Consideration of Free Choice* (September 1524) assumed the stance of one willing to weigh the evidence pro and con: Did man have free will in matters pertaining to salvation?

Erasmus thought scholastically trained theologians (Luther included) had a tendency to dogmatize, to see their own opinions as binding on all Christians. He preferred to be "skeptical" of dogmatic assertions, save for doctrines supported either by the clear teaching of scripture or by the "consensus" of the church over the centuries—and he asserted that Luther's complete denial of free will was not defended by any respected theologian.[14] But as a concession to Luther's insistence on *sola scripura*, Erasmus limited his discussion to evidence from scripture. There were, he admitted, passages in the Epistles that seem to support Luther's interpretation of St. Paul's teaching on predestination.[15] But as theologians taught, the

Figure 5.6. The older Erasmus. Hans Holbein the Younger (1497–1543), "Erasmus of Rotterdam." (*Robert Lehman Collection, 1975. Metropolitan Museum of Art, New York, NY.*)

fact that God foreknows every choice human beings make does not mean that God causes us to make one choice rather than another. On the other hand, Erasmus argues, the many scriptural passages that summon believers to walk in the way of the Lord leave no doubt that man must have some freedom to respond to God's grace.

Luther's *Bondage of the Will*, published a year later, attacked Erasmus as an "atheist" for his skepticism about dogmatic assertions. Where Paul speaks plainly about divine predestination and human impotence, Luther argued, Erasmus stops up his ears, unwilling to hear a truth that human vanity cannot bear. Scripture is indeed full of commandments, not because man will ever be capable of achieving perfect love or the other virtues commanded by God, but because sinners must be taught to despair in their own powers before they can learn to place their trust in Christ. Luther ridiculed the idea that God's foreknowledge does not exclude human freedom. It is, he insisted, God's foreknowledge that causes human beings to make one choice rather than another: "This bombshell knocks free will flat." This debate, perhaps the most important of the Reformation era, showed that Luther and Erasmus were not after all pursuing the same goals, as so many who admired both men had thought. On the whole, younger humanists continued in Luther's wake (or Zwingli's). Men of Erasmus's generation now placed their hopes, as he did, in a reform of the church from within.

Much as Erasmus, Zwingli, and Luther differed from one another, they all believed ordinary folk should be guided in matters of faith by learned men like themselves. No one appreciated the fact that the advent of the printing press allowed men and women of little formal education to join in public discussion of any and all questions. From 1521 to 1525, even as the number of books published in Latin for scholars and churchmen declined in the German-speaking lands, there was an explosion of books published in German for those who could read only in their native tongue. Printers in Strasbourg, an important book market, turned out nearly ninety books in German per year during these years, as opposed to the twenty or so books per year published during the previous decade. This was largely because Luther and other reformers made a conscious decision to appeal to the lay public by writing in the vernacular or having Latin works translated. In Strasbourg, over half the German-language books in the peak years dealt with the Reformation controversy, and Catholic writers attacking Luther were significantly outgunned by their adversaries. Works by Luther accounted for 49 percent of religious books in the vernacular, evangelical preachers in Strasbourg for another 11 percent. Yet 22 percent of the vernacular books on religion were penned by lay authors, mostly in support of Luther's cause, but from their own perspective. Women too dared to make use of the possibilities the printing press offered. Katherine Zell, wife of a former priest and Protestant preacher, published as a pamphlet a letter of consolation she had written for the women of a small Habsburg town, whose husbands had chosen exile rather than submission to the Catholicism prescribed by their Catholic ruler.[16]

Luther's rebellion against Rome provided powerful justification for long-standing lay grievances against the clergy that are treated in great detail in lay pamphlets.[17] On the major doctrinal issues, some lay writers grasped exactly what Luther meant by the freedom of a Christian, for they too found in his doctrine of salvation by faith a deliverance from the dread of God's punishment.[18] As a group, however, they attached greater importance to his doctrine of *sola scriptura,* the issue most often discussed in books and pamphlets by lay authors. Lay men and women took great comfort in the idea that God's Word was just as accessible to them, through vernacular translations of scripture, as it was to clerics who flaunted their Latin learning. They also tended to find Zwingli's interpretation of salvation by faith more congenial than Luther's. Man is saved by grace rather than by his own works, but the gift of grace is given that Christians might live righteously. Luther's insistence that even the sinner who has been saved does nothing at all for his own salvation was not easy to grasp, certainly not for hard-working men and women reared in the good-works Catholicism of the late Middle Ages.

The Anabaptist current of the broad evangelical movement provided the greatest scope for a distinctively lay theology. Rejection of infant baptism can be seen as a final stage in the tearing down of the Catholic sacramental system and with it the authority of the priesthood that administered the sacraments. Luther had rejected five of the traditional seven sacraments, retaining only baptism and the Lord's Supper. Zwingli demystified the Lord's Supper by proposing that the bread and wine remained bread and wine, nothing more. Once baptism came to be understood as a profession of faith by adults, not a ritual by which even infants may receive forgiveness of sin,[19] nothing was left of the Catholic idea that God has entrusted to the priesthood certain signs or actions that are efficacious in the communication of His grace.

The attack on infant baptism originated among Saxon evangelicals who felt Luther himself was moving too slowly, including Karlstadt and Thomas

Müntzer, a preacher whose radical ideas got him expelled from Zwickau shortly before the three "prophets" (his disciples), who then went to Wittenberg. The theory of adult baptism was first put into practice among a circle of Zurich evangelicals who felt Zwingli was moving too slowly.[20] Meeting privately for prayer and scripture reading, they laid great stress on literal interpretation of the New Testament as a guide for Christian life. For example, true Christians must refuse to take oaths, whether in a law court or elsewhere, because Jesus instructed his disciples not to swear.[21] The first adult baptism took place among this group, in a village outside Zurich (January 1525). Their leader was Konrad Grebel (1498–1526), scion of a leading Zurich family. This clean break with over a thousand years of religious tradition sparked intense religious excitement as the men of Grebel's circle fanned out, preaching their version of the gospel. Huge crowds gathered in the open air, witnessing what many saw as a spiritual rebirth in the Holy Spirit, with men and women, lifted out of their ordinary selves, speaking in tongues, as is recorded in the Acts of the Apostles.[22]

Those who agreed on rejecting infant baptism often disagreed on many other points. Münzter believed the righteous were entitled to take up arms against their oppressors, but for Grebel and his followers, true Christians must eschew violence, following Jesus' command in the gospel: "Resist not evil."[23] Further differences may reflect the fact that subsequent Anabaptist leaders (unlike the university-trained Grebel) often had the assurance of the self-taught, having learned theology from their own study of scripture in the vernacular. For example, Melchior Hoffman (1495–1543), a furrier by trade, believed the Holy Spirit had given him the power to discern a hidden or spiritual meaning that was superior to the literal meaning of scripture. Anabaptists debated among themselves whether they should practice community of goods, as described in the Acts of the Apostles,[24] but Jacob Hutter (1500–1536), a hatter, made community of goods the test of a true following of Jesus.

None of these differences mattered to civil authorities, Catholic or evangelical, for they saw all Anabaptists as dangerous radicals bent on undermining public order. Without infant baptism, what was the shared foundation for a Christian society? Without the taking of oaths, and the belief that perjurers would answer to God, who could be trusted to keep his word? Thus the spread of Anabaptism evoked ferocious persecution, of which Grebel himself would have been an early victim had he not escaped from a Zurich prison, only to die of the plague.

In south and central Germany Anabaptism never claimed more than a miniscule fraction of the population. But the religious ideas of the "common man" found a broader expression in the Peasants' War that broke out

Figure 5.7. Feeding the hungry in Alkmaar, province of Holland, 1504. Feeding the hungry, one of seven panels on "The Corporal Works of Mercy" by the anonymous Master of Alkmaar (province of Holland), ca. 1504. Note that Christ himself stands among the people (cf. Matt. 25:35). *(Rijksmuseum—Stichting, Amsterdam.)*

across much of southern and central Germany from 1524 to 1526, by far the
greatest peasant rebellion of medieval or early modern European history.
The circumstances that drove so many peasants to fury against their noble
and monastery landlords will be discussed in Part IV. Some radical evangelical preachers, notably Thomas Müntzer, preached rebellion from their
pulpits; others aided in drafting the states of grievances used by peasant
assemblies to justify their actions. But the ideas seem to have come mainly
from the peasants themselves. The connection with Reformation doctrine
lies in the fact that in a traditional society ordinary folk can accept as legitimate a social order in which they are badly treated, so long as they see
it as part of a world willed by God, rather like the unforgiving order of nature. A great rebellion thus needs a rationale, a reason for believing God
has not in fact willed the world to be so. This the peasants of Germany
found in the teaching of the Reformers, especially Zwingli. Unlike Luther,
Zwingli saw scripture as a "law" in the sense that it provided true Christians with a guide to righteous living.[25]

The *Twelve Articles* (1525) published by leaders of the peasant movement
takes this view one step farther. The law of scripture—godly law—is a
guide not just for personal conduct, but also for social relations within a
Christian society. Was it godly to discriminate among men and women redeemed in the blood of Christ so that some were held as serfs by others
who claimed to be their lords and masters?[26] Surely not. For many peasants, the "freedom of a Christian" meant that no Christian man or woman
must be kept in bondage. Luther, initially sympathetic to peasant grievances, reacted sharply to what he saw as a perversion of the gospel. In two
pamphlets he urged princes to cut down in good conscience all who
showed their contempt for divine law by rebelling against the authorities
God had set over them. In fact, princes and noble lords needed no encouragement. Despite victories here and there under peasant commanders
trained as mercenary soldiers, rebel armies were crushed one after another.

In the long perspective of religious history, the ferment of the years
1520–1526 was uncommonly creative. Most forms of Protestant Christianity now active in the world can trace their roots to this brief period. But for
many who lived through the turmoil in Germany and Switzerland, it
seemed as if the world were coming apart at the seams. What was left of
all that people had been taught to revere? The pope was unmasked as the
Antichrist, the consecrated host as a mere piece of bread, and miracle-
working statues as "idols" to be smashed to bits. Scripture, learned men

now said, was guide enough for Christian folk. But these same learned men—Luther, Zwingli, Erasmus—were at one another's throats, figuratively at least, about what scripture had to say. The "common man" had rendered his interpretation of scripture with powder and shot. Was there to be a time of naked repression, as princes drowned in blood the remnants of peasant resistance? Or was the social order again to be shaken to its foundations by another great uprising? Where amid all the chaos was the gospel? Or was the gospel itself somehow responsible for the chaos? These questions, shaped by the events of several years, demanded a response. Hammering out answers would take several decades.

6 | Doctrine

The German and Swiss Reformation, 1526–1555

The Holy Roman Empire was not a unitary state, but rather a loose federation of territories ruled by princes and of free cities.[1] The diet was the only forum in which the major imperial princes meet regularly with representatives of the major free cities. Because of the many prince-bishops, the Catholic party had a majority in the diet and was determined to maintain the Edict of Worms (1521), which prohibited the dissemination of Luther's doctrines, even if it could not now be enforced. But evangelical princes and magistrates were under pressure from townsfolk to dismantle altogether what remained of the old religion. In these circumstances, it seemed unlikely the diet could play in Germany's religious conflict the peacemaking role it had so often played in the political conflicts of earlier centuries.

The turmoil of the Peasants' War changed everything. Many Catholic princes were now persuaded that a religious order imposed by heretical governments was better than the chaos that seemed to loom on the horizon. The Habsburg dynasty, the anchor of Catholicism in Germany, also had reasons for compromise. Archduke Ferdinand wanted evangelical princes to help defend Austria against a possible Ottoman invasion, but their cooperation had a price. His brother the emperor was at this time less willing to countenance negotiation with heretics, but all his resources were engaged in conflicts outside of Germany.[2] Hence, both sides were able to agree to the Recess (closing statement) of the Diet of Speyer (1526): until an ecumenical council of the church should be convened to settle disputed issues, princes and imperial cities were free to regulate religious matters according to the dictates of conscience. In effect, the Edict of Worms was suspended.

This compromise allowed the diet to become a forum for further discussion of religious differences. Meanwhile, local governments proceeded with the implementation of evangelical reform, even as radical preachers proposed visions of reform that no government could accept. This chapter, organized chronologically, follows each of three different tracks: deliberations at the diet; the reforms implemented by evangelical governments; and the continuing spread of radical religious ideas, despite everything the diet and the territorial governments could do to stop it.

The Recess of Speyer provided legal cover for governments eager to build a new religious order. The landgrave of Hesse, Philip the Magnanimous (1504–1567), was the first to seize the opportunity. Philip had a church ordinance drawn up for presentation to the parliament or estates of his territory.[3] Like similar ordinances soon to be adopted elsewhere, it prescribed worship in the vernacular language, preaching based on the doctrine of salvation by faith, reception by the laity of the wine as well as the bread in the Lord's Supper, a married clergy, and catechism classes to instruct the young. These were the founding principles of a new, distinctly evangelical church. The Hessian ordinance was accepted by the estates (October 1526) but was never implemented because it was in effect vetoed in Wittenberg. Luther had no fixed ideas on how an evangelical church should be governed, but he objected to the provision that each congregation in Hesse would be free to choose its own preacher. Events in Electoral Saxony had convinced him that congregational autonomy was not a good idea.

Luther's protector, Elector Frederick (d. 1525), was traditional in his beliefs and respected the authority of the Catholic hierarchy in Saxony. But for many of his subjects that authority had now ceased to exist. Thus the Saxon clergy had little or no supervision. Radicals like Karlstadt and Müntzer were free to gain acceptance from local congregations and preach whatever doctrines they wished—rejection of infant baptism or even rebellion against the prince. But Frederick's nephew and successor, Elector John (ruled 1525–1532), was an ardent evangelical. Luther now had direct access to the ruler; indeed, because of long friendship with Georg Spalatin, a humanist councillor, he now had virtually an alter ego at the prince's side. The elector expressed to Luther his concern about the lack of discipline for rural pastors. Luther in turn wanted assurances that Saxon nobles would not be allowed to grab for themselves all the properties of the monasteries that were now to be dissolved—something had to be kept back to support the ministers of the Word.

One first had to take stock of things. For this purpose Wittenberg theologians reinvented the practice of visitation, whereby a bishop toured the parishes of his diocese at regular intervals. In canon law, visiting bishops had the right to dismiss unworthy pastors. But there were (as yet) no bishops in Germany who supported the new doctrines.[4] Hence, Luther proposed that the prince be seen as a "stopgap bishop," so that visitors acting in his name had power to deal with pastors found to be wild-eyed radicals or stubborn "papists." Preliminary visitation of a few areas in 1526 was followed by systematic visitation of the whole territory between 1527 and 1529, with Luther himself acting for a time as a visitor.

The problems the visitors uncovered were sobering. It was now clear that the present clergy would have to be replaced as soon as possible by a new body of clergy trained in evangelical theology at a university theology faculty and paid at a level that would compensate educated men for spending their days among peasants. This goal would take decades to achieve. But Saxony served as a model for evangelical princes and town councils by making a beginning.

In the canton of Zurich, a much smaller territory, supervision of the clergy was relatively easy. Rural pastors, many with little education, were kept in line by a council requirement that they read their Sunday sermons from sermon books prepared by clergy in the city. Urban pastors had to participate in weekly "prophecies," or discussions of scripture, organized and led by Zwingli himself. To educate a new evangelical pastorate, Zwingli persuaded the city council to set aside for creation of a theological school the income from tithes that peasants were still required to pay.[5]

The problem Zwingli could not control stemmed from the fact that Zurich was but one among thirteen Swiss cantons. The two other cantons based on sizable cities, Bern and Basel, embraced the Reformation soon after Zurich, as did two smaller cantons. But seven others remained fiercely loyal to Catholicism, including the founding members of the Swiss Confederation (1291), the so-called forest cantons high in the Alps.[6] Since each canton had one vote in the Confederation Diet, the Catholic party confidently arranged a disputation (1526) in which their spokesman, Johann Eck, was adjudged the winner over an evangelical preacher from Basel.[7]

What sparked real bitterness on both sides was the treatment of lands that had been conquered by the confederation, each ruled as a subject territory, each year by a different canton. Under evangelical rule, evangelical preachers were installed even if parishioners did not want them. Under Catholic rule, the new preachers were forced out even if people wanted them, and in a few cases they were tried and executed for the crime of heresy. This changing of religious truth with every change of administration was not sustainable, especially not in a country with Switzerland's military traditions. Evangelical cantons formed a Christian Civic Union (1529); Catholic cantons responded with a Christian Union.

Zurich was ready to go to war in 1529, until Bern arranged a peace acceptable to the Catholic cantons. When tensions mounted again, Bern proposed economic warfare. The evangelical cantons controlled the Swiss lowlands, between Germany and the Alps. Their Catholic adversaries, concentrated in the Alpine valleys, depended on imports of grain from the German side, since access was more difficult via the steeper slopes of the Italian Alps.[8] In May 1531, Bern, Zurich, and their allies blocked roads leading into the mountains, hoping to compel Alpine "idolaters" to submit. Seeing no end to the blockade, the men of the forest cantons mobilized for a sudden strike on Zurich. There was no time to summon aid from Zurich's allies. At Kappel, near Zurich (11 October 1531), a large Catholic force overwhelmed the men of Zurich. Huldrych Zwingli, a chaplain once more, lay among the dead.

This defeat had consequences. All of Switzerland now agreed to a treaty prescribing that no canton would interfere in another's religious affairs. In Zurich, mourning hundreds of its young men, many put the blame on the fact that Zurich's relations with other cantons had been guided by the religious zeal of Zwingli and his party. Zwingli believed the "Christian magistrates" of his city would govern the church wisely. They appointed the preachers (like himself) and approved the order of worship. Only the interpretation of scripture was, in his view, reserved to the competence of the clergy. But one reason Zwingli had such confidence in the magistrates

Figure 6.1. The Battle of Kappel (1531). The larger army of the Catholic cantons is at the right, Zurich's force at the left: from the Chronicle of Johannes Stumpf (1548). (*Zentralbibliothek Zurich.*)

was that he himself, in the words of a Catholic critic, "acted like a burgomaster." For example, he seems to have participated in meetings of an informal inner circle of magistrates known as the secret council. This was to change. In 1532 the council decreed that neither the preachers nor the secret council would be allowed to interfere in Zurich's external affairs.

Heinrich Bullinger (1504–1575), the humanist scholar who succeeded Zwingli as leader of Zurich's clergy, understood that a line had been drawn. It was the preacher's duty to tell magistrates how the teaching of scripture might bear on contemporary issues, but magistrates were not obliged to listen. Bullinger could accept this arrangement because he believed, as had Zwingli, that the magistrates had a God-given mandate to govern the religious life of Christian society, except as regards the interpretation of scripture. This explicit acceptance of state control of the church was a hallmark of the Zwinglian branch of the evangelical movement.

Meanwhile, confessional alliances were also forming in Germany, where many feared a much wider religious war. Catholic princes, including the powerful dukes of Bavaria, sometimes consulted together, but with little practical result. Common action to stem the advance of heresy would have required cooperation with Habsburg Austria, against which Bavaria (Austria's neighbor) had unsettled grievances. In 1528 one of Philip of Hesse's councillors made public what he claimed was a secret pact among Catholic princes to attack their evangelical confreres.[9] Alarmed, Philip of Hesse and Elector John of Saxony mobilized their armies, standing down only when it was clear no attack was forthcoming.[10]

Amid growing suspicion on both sides, the Catholic party in the diet pushed through at the 1529 Diet of Speyer a Recess nullifying the 1526 Recess and reinstating the Edict of Worms, with added clauses prohibiting the dissemination of other new doctrines besides Luther's. Six evangelical princes, together with the representatives of fourteen free cities, signed a protest against this action: they could not submit to the will of the majority in a matter of conscience. This was a milestone, the first time leaders of the evangelical movement were sufficiently conscious of their common interests to act as a body. The Protestant Reformation takes its name from the "protestants" of Speyer.

Full unity among evangelicals was impeded by discord between Wittenberg and Zurich. Elector John of Saxony insisted that parties to any political alliance must accept the articles of belief recently drawn up by Wittenberg theologians. Philip of Hesse, hoping for a broader theological consensus to allow inclusion of Swiss and south German cities that sup-

HEINRYCHVS... BVLLINGERVS
GVNDECIMAM NVNC LABVNTVR SYDERA LVSTRI,
HÆC ÆTAS, FORMAM PICTA TABELLA REFERT
NIL EGO VEL FORMAM VEL VITÆ TEMPORA SPECTO
SED CHRISTVM, VITÆ QVI MIHI FORMA MEÆ EST.

Figure 6.2. Heinrich Bullinger (1504–1575). An anonymous portrait of Zwingli's successor in Zurich (1531–1575). (*Zentralbibliothek Zurich.*)

ported Zwingli, invited Luther and Zwingli to meet in his city of Marburg (October 1529), along with many other evangelical theologians. The climactic moment of the Marburg Colloquy came when Luther met privately with Zwingli and one other Swiss preacher. Taking a piece of chalk, Luther wrote the Latin for "This is my body" on the table, insisting on the literal meaning of Jesus's words at the Last Supper. Zwingli offered a modification of his purely symbolic interpretation, but to no avail. Wittenberg and Zurich would henceforth go their separate ways, politically as well as doctrinally.

Charles V now announced his intention to come to Germany (his first visit since 1521) for the diet to be held in Augsburg in the summer of 1530. Protestants had feared the emperor would insist on the terms decreed by the recent Diet of Speyer. Instead, he called for consultations concerning the resolution of Germany's religious conflict. Charles wanted religious unity in Germany, not necessarily by force. One of his Spanish advisors, Alfonso de Valdes, was promoting an idea first proposed by Erasmus, namely, that the doctrinal disputes might be settled if reasonable men from both sides could be brought together under the auspices of a great prince.[11] Erasmus had suggested that concessions would have to be made to legitimate complaints against clerical privilege, for example, by allowing lay people to receive the wine as well as the bread in the Lord's Supper and allowing priests to marry.

Erasmus rightly guessed that Philip Melanchthon might be willing to enter into such a discussion on behalf of the evangelical party.[12] Melanchthon had taken the lead in framing a statement of Lutheran belief for presentation at the diet (June 1530). Without diluting Luther's teachings, Melanchthon's Augsburg Confession answered the emperor's goodwill gesture by stressing points of agreement with Catholics, notably in the belief that Christ's body and blood are truly present in the eucharist. At Augsburg, many Catholic observers were impressed by the confession's moderate tone. Melanchthon in turn was impressed by the flexibility he found in private conversations with Valdes and with Cardinal Lorenzo Campeggi, the representative of Pope Clement VII (ruled 1523–1534). They discussed, for example, a plan whereby Lutherans would recognize the papacy as wielding an authority that had evolved historically, but not (as in Catholic belief) as wielding an authority originally granted by Christ to St. Peter.[13]

But no agreement was forthcoming. The Catholic majority in the diet resumed its agenda from the previous year. Enforcement of the imperial legislation prohibiting the spread of evangelical doctrine was now entrusted to the Imperial High Court, made up of judges appointed exclusively by Catholic princes.[14] Fearing the worst, Elector John of Saxony and Phillip of Hesse met (December 1530) in the small town of Schmalkalden to conclude a defensive alliance with several other Protestant princes. Luther at first objected to the idea of an agreement directed against the emperor; in his view, scripture did not permit Christians to rebel against the rulers God had set over them.[15] Others persuaded him, however, that princes of the empire were not mere individual believers, but rulers in their own right, whose duty it was to prevent the emperor from behaving in tyrannical fashion. Thus was born the Schmalkaldic League, led by Saxony and Hesse and limited to signatories of the 1530 Augsburg Confession. Other territories joined as they converted to the Reformation, so did Strasbourg and other evangelical cities in south Germany that were Zwinglian in theology but accepted Luther's doctrine of the Lord's Supper as the price to be paid for the protection afforded by the league.[16]

Catholic princes were sobered by this development; they were not willing to go to war to stop the spread of heresy. Also, some of those involved in the discussions at Augsburg took away the impression that agreement might yet be possible. Hence, the next diet (Regensburg, 1532) issued a Recess suspending religious proceedings before the Imperial High Court and declaring that if no ecumenical council were convened in the interval, the following diet, slated for 1534, would attempt to craft a religious compromise on its own authority.

This was alarming news in Rome. Pope Clement VII refused to convene the ecumenical council that many were calling for—he feared a council, invoking fifteenth-century conciliar doctrine, might challenge the authority of the papacy.[17] But he was even more opposed to seeing an imperial diet usurp the role of a council by claiming to decide matters of doctrine. The pope urged Charles and Ferdinand not to convene the diet slated for 1534. As it happened, Charles was again distracted by affairs outside Germany.[18] There would not be another diet until he returned in 1540.

In the interim, both the Lutheran and the Zwinglian versions of the evangelical movement continued winning new adherents. So too did doctrines that may be called "radical" in two senses of the term.[19] First, most proponents of these doctrines consciously rejected an assumption Luther and Zwingli had taken over from the Catholic past, namely, that all baptized Christians, saints and sinners alike, were members of the church as well as subjects of their territorial government. In this view, church and state, the dual aspects of a single Christian commonwealth, were obliged to support each other in multiple ways. By contrast, radical preachers held that the church embraced only those dedicated to the following of Christ; the brutal power of the state was established by God not for true Christians, but only to curb the evil ways of sinners.[20]

Second, radical preachers also rejected one or more of the elements of orthodox Christian belief that Luther and Zwingli retained, such as the doctrine of the Trinity, the need for a visible church, or infant baptism. Luther and Zwingli (like their Catholic foes) expected Christian rulers to suppress all who preached against such fundamental doctrines. But radical reformers saw in the hostility of the state a proof of their claim to be the true Christians who in this wicked world must need be persecuted.

The doctrine of the Trinity—that Father, Son, and Holy Spirit are three distinct Persons in one God—had been professed by all Christians since the great theological controversies of the fourth century.[21] But Michael Servetus, a Spanish physician, published his *On the Errors of the Trinity* in Basel in 1531. Drawing on sources from an impressive array of religious and intellectual traditions, Servetus argued that the New Testament named the one and only God using different terms, including "Father," "Son," and "Holy Spirit," just as the Old Testament had different names for the one and only Lord. The doctrine of the Trinity was thus a great falsehood, demeaning to the unity of God. Catholics and Protestants were equally shocked. But theologians who wrote books refuting Servetus unintentionally disseminated his doctrines by summarizing them, and when Servetus himself was burned at the stake in Geneva (1553),[22] martyrdom gave his teaching added prestige, especially among Italian religious refugees living in Switzerland. These men[23] became apostles for the Anti-Trinitarian or (as it was later called) Unitarian gospel in other parts of Europe.

Kaspar von Schwenkfeld (1489–1561), a noble courtier in the duchy of Legnica (part of Bohemia), led the way in questioning the need for a visible church. Having experienced what he believed was a revelation from God convincing him of the truth of Luther's teaching, Schwenkfeld became the leader of an influential Lutheran party at the ducal court. Distressed by the quarrel over the Lord's Supper, he experienced a second divine visitation that persuaded him that Zwingli's symbolic interpretation was correct.[24] From 1526 Schwenkfeld refused to partake in a ritual that caused so much hatred among Christians and urged his followers to do likewise. Schwenkfeld also objected to the fact that churches, like states, employed coercion in matters of belief—true Christians know that belief comes from the Holy Spirit, not from force. Hence, Schwenkfeld became an early advocate of religious toleration.[25] Local Lutherans joined with Archduke Ferdinand of Austria, now king of Bohemia, to expel Schwenkfeld from his homeland (1529). He spent the rest of his years in south Germany, traveling and living among friends he had won over to his spiritual interpretation of the gospel.[26]

Figure 6.3. Caspar Schwenkfeld (1489–1561). Engraved portrait, "Caspar Schwenkfeld von Ossing in his 56th Year, 1566." (*British Museum, London.*)

The radical religious movement that had the greatest numerical appeal was a form of Anabaptism tracing its origins to a lay preacher from the Baltic coast, Melchior Hoffman (1495–1543). Having espoused first Lutheran and then Zwinglian ideas, Hoffman was expelled from several northern territories for claiming the God-given ability to discern a "spiritual" or hidden meaning of scripture that was superior to the literal meaning. Arriving in Strasbourg (1529), he accepted the Anabaptist view of baptism and also fell in with a circle whose members believed they were prophets inspired by God. Hoffman now began preaching a spiritual interpretation of scripture that confirmed the prophecies of his new comrades. The Final Days foretold in the Book of Revelation were drawing near: very soon, Christ would come again to establish on earth his kingdom, the Heavenly Jerusalem.[27] Expelled from Strasbourg, Hoffman took his message to Emden in East Friesland, where he was able to baptize over 300 adults before being expelled yet again. As Hoffman returned to Strasbourg, some of his converts crossed from East Friesland into the Habsburg

Netherlands, where their message found fertile ground. Owing to war, grain was scarce in the Netherlands, and prices were at historical highs.[28] Hungry folk flocked to hear the "Melchiorite" message of imminent deliverance, especially in the populous province of Holland. Meanwhile, seeing his Strasbourg followers arrested in droves, Hoffman suspended the practice of adult baptism. By now, however, Melchior was no longer in control of the Melchiorite movement.

Jan Matthijs, a Holland Melchiorite, resumed adult baptism in 1533. In contrast to Hoffman's belief that true Christians must suffer persecution meekly, as Christ himself did, Matthijs announced that the time had come for God's elect to take up the sword against their oppressors. With Jan Bockelszoon, another Hollander, Matthijs traveled to nearby Münster in Westphalia,[29] which had recently ejected its prince-bishop and adopted the Lutheran Reformation. He quickly won over the city's chief evangelical preacher and his followers. Back in the Netherlands, the faithful received an urgent message: God's Kingdom was to be erected in Münster; true Christians must sell their possessions and be in Münster before the Last Days were to begin (March 1534). Thousands streamed toward Münster from the Low Countries,[30] just as unbelievers—Catholics and Lutherans—were being forced out. Lutheran princes in Westphalia joined Münster's prince-bishop in besieging the city. When Jan Matthijs fell in battle (April 1534), Jan Bockelszoon succeeded him and had himself proclaimed king of the Heavenly Jerusalem. Pointing to examples of polygamy among Old Testament patriarchs, King Jan decreed that God's elect were no longer bound by monogamy—he set the example by taking sixteen wives. When Münster fell to its besiegers, Bockelszoon and his chief supporters were punished with exemplary cruelty (June 1535).

The debacle at Münster marked a turning point for the Anabaptist movement. A persecution that was already fierce became ferocious. Even in the few places where Anabaptists had been tolerated, civil authorities now suspected that seemingly peaceful folk secretly harbored violent Münsterite fantasies.[31] In Moravia, part of the kingdom of Bohemia, followers of Jacob Hutter (1500–1536) had established themselves as a peasant community practicing the common ownership of goods. Their landlords—Hussite noblemen and an open-minded prince-abbess—had no problems with these hardworking tenants. After Münster, however, Archduke Ferdinand, the king of Bohemia, saw to it that the "Hutterites" were expelled. They were not able to return to Moravia for several years.[32]

Among Anabaptists in the Low Countries, reactions to Münster led to a stronger form of organization. When the city fell, some Münsterites took up an outlaw existence, robbing churches to support themselves.

Figure 6.4. The Trek to the Anabaptist Kingdom of Münster, 1534. Engraving of "Anabaptists Selling Their Jewels for the Trek to Münster," from Lambertus Hortensius, *Het Boek . . . van den Oproer der Weder-Doper.* (*Mennonite Historical Musem, Goshen College, Goshen, Indiana.*)

Menno Simons (1496–1561), a priest in Friesland, came to the fore among Anabaptists who denounced the excesses of Matthijs and Bockelszoon, traceable to false doctrine. Scripture must be interpreted literally, Menno insisted, not according to the imaginings of self-styled prophets. Discipline was another problem: loose living among those who claimed to be the true followers of Christ was a terrible scandal. Menno and his supporters introduced the ban, a form of excommunication in which public sinners were to be shunned by all believers. Com-

Figure 6.5. Menno Simons (1496–1561). Engraved portrait of Menno Simons, bound with Christoffel van Sichem, Beschryvinge ende Afbeelindinge der Voornemste Hooft Ketteren (Amsterdam, 1608). (*Special Collections, Bridwell Library, Southern Methodist University.*)

munities formed along these lines proved to have the strength to withstand continuing persecution.[33]

What Menno Simons achieved for Anabaptism, John Calvin (1509–1564) was to achieve for a major segment of the broader evangelical movement. Calvin's father was a lay official in the service of the bishop of Noyon (northern France). When John took his bachelor's degree at the University of Paris he enrolled in the theology faculty, preparing for a career in the priesthood, as his family wished. But Calvin senior quarreled with the bishop, and John switched to the faculty of law at Orleans. This faculty was known for its humanist approach to legal scholarship,[34] and the taste he acquired for pagan and Christian antiquity made Calvin shift direction once more. Returning to Paris to study ancient languages, he fell in with a group of humanist students and professors who were also eager for religious reform. When a leader of this circle gave a public address endorsing the doctrine of salvation by faith (November 1533), the inquisitor of the diocese of Paris demanded action by royal officials.[35] For the speaker and his associates, including Calvin, France was no longer safe.

As a refugee in Basel, Calvin embarked on a period of study resulting in his *Institutes of the Christian Religion* (1536), the single most important doctrinal work of the Protestant Reformation, especially in its final and most complete edition (1555). The *Institutes* adopted many of the teachings first put forward by Zwingli. God's commandments serve a "pedagogical" purpose for sinners who must be taught to despair in their own ability to fulfill the commandments, but for those to whom God grants saving faith the commandments serve also as a guide to holiness. Indeed, the grace of forgiveness is given so that God may be glorified in the lives of his saints.[36]

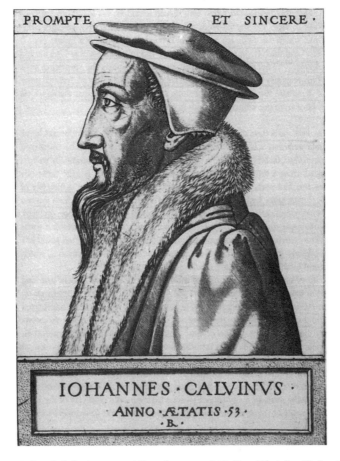

Figure 6.6. John Calvin (1509–1564) at the age of 53. René Boivin, "John Calvin at the Age of 53," 1562. (*Bibliothèque Publique et Universitaire de Genève, Geneva.*)

Like Zwingli, Calvin believed that religious images of any kind were an abomination in the sight of God: churches must be cleansed of all "idols," whether sculpted, painted, or molded in stained glass. Finally, Calvin too rejected Luther's belief that the body and blood of Christ are truly present in the Lord's Supper, though he did not endorse Zwingli's view that the bread and wine were mere symbols. Instead, he contended, one receives in the sacrament the "virtue" or power of Christ's flesh, even though the Lord's body itself is not in any way present. Because of these areas of agreement, Calvin and Zwingli are often grouped together as the founders of a "Reformed" Protestantism that was the major alternative to the Lutheran Reformation in continental Europe. But there were also differences, as became evident when Calvin accepted a post as preacher in Geneva (1536).

Geneva's choice for the Reformation was connected with its struggle for independence from its two Catholic overlords, the duke of Savoy and the prince-bishop of Geneva. Geneva was able to defy both princes because it had found a backer in neighboring Bern, largest and most powerful of the Swiss cantons. Bern sought to cement the alliance by having Geneva adopt a French-language version of its evangelical worship service. The eagerness of Geneva's city council to comply placed Calvin at a crossroads, comparable to that faced by Luther at the Leipzig debate. Had he obeyed Geneva's Christian magistrates, no one in the Zwinglian tradition of reform would have had any words of blame. But the fact that a civil government proposed to decide questions of worship offended his sense of what scripture taught about the church. Rather than accept the new order of worship, Calvin, together with his colleague Guillaume Farel,[37] chose exile in Strasbourg (1538).

Calvin's convictions about the autonomy of the church were greatly strengthened in Strasbourg (1538–1541), where he served as pastor for a congregation of Protestant refugees from France. Martin Bucer, Strasbourg's leading evangelical preacher, had a tale of woe to tell. Like other Swiss and south German reformers, Bucer expected the proclamation of the true gospel to bring a change in the way people lived. In fact, Strasbourgers went about their sinful ways much as before: The Reformation was incomplete, and Bucer thought he knew why. The problem was that Strasbourg's magistrates governed the church, just as in Bullinger's Zurich. If preachers demanded stronger action against religious radicals (like Melchior Hoffman), the magistrates cited the need to avoid coercion in matters of belief. If preachers wanted some prominent person excommunicated from the church as a public sinner, the magistrates preferred not to add one more feud to the many they already had to contend with. When Bucer published a treatise proposing that the church rather than the civil government take over the supervision of morals—"we must decide once and for all if we mean to be Christians"—the magistrates pointedly ignored it. Casting about for some way to free the church from control by the magistrates, Bucer toyed with the idea of a limited recognition of the religious authority of Strasbourg's prince-bishop, which had ceased to exist in the city with the triumph of the Reformation in 1529.

Calvin had a better idea. His study of the New Testament convinced him that the primitive church had a clearly articulated governing structure, which needed only to be re-created. In the Acts of the Apostles, Christian communities are headed by (ἐπισκοποί = overseers) or by (*presbuteroi* = elders). In subsequent centuries, bishops (a word derived from the first of these Greek terms) had come to be recognized as sole rulers of their religious communities, with full authority over those called elders or, somewhat later, priests. Calvin believed that this historical development falsified the collegial relationship between "overseers" and "presbyters" in the New Testament. Each local church should be governed by a minister of the Word (the overseer) together with a board of lay elders, joined in what Calvin called (using a canon law term) a consistory. A church government so constituted, based on the teaching of scripture, could reclaim the authority that civil magistrates had wrongfully usurped. When he was again given the opportunity to lead Geneva's church (see below), Calvin would know how to proceed.

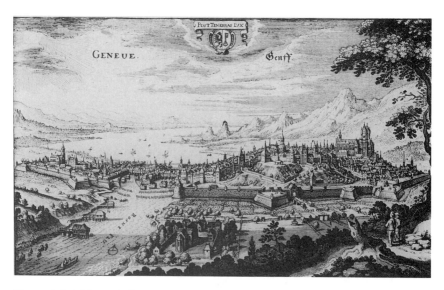

Figure 6.7. A View of Geneva in the Seventeenth Century. From Matthaeus Merian, Martin Zeiller, Topographia Germaniae (17 vols. facsimile reprint of second edition [Frankfurt, 1655], Kassel: Bärenreiter, 1959–1967), vol. 4, Topographiae Heluetiae, following p. 68. (*University of Minnesota Library*.)

In 1540 Charles V summoned a diet in order to resume negotiations between the religious parties. During his absence from Germany several princes had sponsored "colloquies" between the two sides. In the process, important theologians had developed genuine interest in reaching agreement, notably Martin Bucer, Strasbourg's leading preacher, and Johann Gropper, a Catholic scholar from Cologne who promoted the study of Augustine as a possible common ground. When the Diet of Hagenau convened (June 1540), Protestant estates[38] insisted on starting from the 1530 Augsburg Confession. Many Catholic princes urged the emperor to reject this demand. But in Charles's council the "soft hand" faction that favored negotiation had won out over the "hard hand" faction that favored war in order to end Germany's politically dangerous religious division.[39] Thus Charles accepted the Augsburg Confession as the basis for discussion at the forthcoming Diet of Worms (November 1540–January 1541). Meanwhile, a committee of Protestant theologians, including Bucer and Calvin as well as Melanchthon, agreed on the text of a revised Augsburg Confession that was more acceptable to south German evangelicals.[40]

Some progress was made at Worms.[41] But Charles's advisers wanted to move things along more quickly. Prior to the next diet, to be held in Regensburg, Gropper and Bucer were secretly commissioned to draft articles of agreement on each of the main points of doctrine. The Regensburg Colloquy (April–July 1541) featured three theologians on each side, including the Protestant Bucer and the Catholic Gropper. When the conferees met, Charles's spokesman placed before them as the new basis for their discussion the "book" by Bucer and Gropper, without telling the others whence it had come. Between meetings the Catholic conferees consulted with Cardinal Gasparo Contarini, whom Pope Paul III (ruled 1534–1549) had sent as his representative. The choice of Contarini boded well for compromise, since this respected theologian and diplomat was also known to be unusually sympathetic to Luther's theology.[42]

The six conferees found themselves in accord on one issue after another. When several days of hard bargaining led to an agreement on salvation by faith, Regensburg's church bells rang out in celebration of this apparent victory for religious peace. But subsequent discussion stalled over language describing the authority of the church and reached a dead end on the Lord's Supper. Catholic conferees reluctantly dropped the term "transubstantiation," as Protestants demanded, but Contarini reinserted it in the text. Charles summoned Contarini to ask why it was so important to insist on a single word. In reply, Contarini called to mind the great controversy of the fourth century, when a single word that many Christians rejected was deemed necessary by others to assert the full divinity of

Figure 6.8. Philip Melanchthon. Albrecht Dürer, "Philip Melanchthon," 1526, from Valentin Scherer, Albrecht Dürer. Des Meisters Gemaelde und Kupferstiche (Berlin/Leipzig: Insel, 1926), p. 172. (*University of Minnesota Library.*)

Christ.[43] The emperor needed peace in Germany, but politics was not the final reality.

No one realized it at the time, but with the failure of the Regensburg Colloquy, the moment for theological compromise had come and gone. Following the article to which the six conferees agreed in 1541, there would not be another joint Lutheran-Catholic statement on salvation by faith until the last quarter of the twentieth century.[44] As the chance for reconciliation faded, so too did the reputations of those who had promoted the idea of compromise. In 1535, a year before his death, the aging Erasmus had declined a cardinal's hat offered by Pope Paul III. Twenty-four years later, in 1559, all of Erasmus's works were placed on the *Index of Forbidden Books* promulgated by Pope Paul IV (ruled 1555–1559).[45] Melanchthon too came under attack (see below). On either side of the confessional divide, thinkers (often humanists) seeking to reach out to men of goodwill in the other camp faced increasing suspicion among their coreligionists.

Conversely, those who all along took a dim view of theological compromise gained in credibility. German Catholics were strengthened in the belief that only an ecumenical council could provide a remedy for the church's ills. The obstacle to a council now lay not in Rome, as previously, but in Paris.[46] Charles needed, for the sake of unity in Germany, the reform of abuses in the church that only a council could mandate. Precisely for this reason, the king of France made it clear that no French bishops would be permitted to attend a council—and without their participation, a council would be seen as a mere imperial enterprise, not a truly ecumenical assembly. This problem Charles dealt with by force of arms. In the treaty concluded following a two-year war begun by France (1542–1544), the king of France undertook not to obstruct a future council.

Pope Paul III then summoned the bishops of the Latin Christian world to a council in Trent, an imperial city on the Italian side of the Alps. The doctrinal decisions of the first session of the Council of Trent (1545–1547) will be discussed in Chapter 7. The point to be made here is that those who argued for adopting language that Protestants might conceivably accept were in the minority.[47] On key issues, the council's majority preferred language that sharply distinguished between the false teachings of the Reformers and what was henceforth to be orthodox Catholic doctrine. For the bishops and their theologian-advisers, the moment for compromise had passed. Now it was time to mobilize the minds and hearts of the faithful for a protracted struggle on behalf of Catholic truth.

Within Charles's council, the failure at Regensburg meant that the Schmalkaldic League would probably have to be dealt with as the "hard hand" councillors had envisioned. German affairs had to wait their turn on the emperor's agenda—war with France engaged his full attention from 1542 to 1544. But in the treaty ending this war Charles also compelled the king of France to abandon his alliances with Germany's Protestant princes; one could not make war against the Schmalkaldic League without assurances that France would not interfere. When Charles returned to the empire in 1545, he spoke of resuming the theological discussions broken off at Regensburg. This time, however, his soothing words were meant to calm the fears of the leaders of the league, Philip of Hesse and Elector John's son John Frederick of Saxony (ruled 1532–1547), and to conceal his preparations for war—including a secret treaty with John Frederick's Lutheran cousin, Duke Moritz of Saxony.

Following Charles's defeat of Hesse and Electoral Saxony in the First Schmalkaldic War (1547), he imposed on the parts of Protestant Germany that had submitted to him an "Interim" religious settlement promulgated at the Diet of Augsburg (May 1548).[48] There were some concessions to evangelical sensibilities: Preachers would be free to profess the key doctrine of salvation by faith, clergy would still be allowed to marry, and lay people would still receive the wine as well as the bread in the Lord's Supper. In all other respects, the Interim mandated full restoration of Catholic worship, including the Latin mass and the seven sacraments. These provisions evoked sullen acquiescence in Lutheran territories that had submitted to the emperor and redoubled the determination to resist among those that had not. As fighting sputtered on, it began to seem that Charles's victory was not irreversible. A new coalition between France and a revived league (Second Schmalkaldic War, 1552–1555) shattered Charles's hopes for restoring religious unity to Germany.[49]

The ensuing Peace of Augsburg (1555) guaranteed freedom of religious choice in the empire, but only for ruling princes and the governments of free cities. "Where there is one lord," the treaty declared, "let there be one religion."[50] Subjects who disagreed with the religious policy of their rulers were promised the right to sell their property and move elsewhere, nothing more. Moreover, the choices were limited to Roman Catholicism and the religion of the Augsburg Confession. These two faiths were recognized in imperial law, but "sects" like Anabaptism, Zwinglianism, or Calvinism (see below) had no rights whatever.

The Augsburg Interim caused deep division among Germany's Lutherans. Prior to Luther's death (1546), there had been occasional complaints that Philip Melanchthon was sympathetic to the doctrine of free will or to John Calvin's interpretation of the Lord's Supper. Melanchthon had in fact evolved his own views on both of these points, but his close personal collaboration with Luther kept such disputes in the background so long as Luther lived. The Interim put a spotlight on Melanchthon. His and Luther's University of Wittenberg was part of Electoral Saxony, hitherto ruled by Charles's defeated enemy, John Frederick. But Duke Moritz now claimed Electoral Saxony as his reward for assisting in the emperor's victory—John Frederick was left with the lesser title of duke and a smaller territory. Moritz did not seek to impose the unpopular Augsburg Interim on his new lands. Instead, he had his Catholic councillors[51] and the Wittenberg theologians, including Melanchthon, work out (1549) a version of the Interim more consistent with evangelical theology. Melanchthon thus gave his name to a partial restoration of Catholic ceremonies. He did so because he believed that outer forms of worship were "indifferent things"[52] that could be accepted if essential doctrine was not compromised.

This policy was bitterly attacked by Matthias Flacius Illyricus (1520–1575), a professor of Hebrew at Wittenberg. Flacius argued that "indifferent things" imposed by a secular government became violations of Christian freedom. He fled Wittenberg for Magdeburg, a city that had renounced the rule of its prince-archbishop some time previously and was now the center of Lutheran resistance to Charles V and his Interim. With Magdeburg's preachers, Flacius and others who now claimed to represent the "Genuine Lutheran"[53] party took it on themselves to expose the errors of the all-too-compromising Melanchthon and his 'Philippist' disciples. If Melanchthon held (following Luther) that Christians must obey their rulers as far as possible, Magdeburgers argued it was the Christian duty of their city council and other "lesser magistrates" to resist the tyranny of the emperor. Genuine Lutherans also attacked Wittenberg theologians for not issuing a blanket condemnation of John Calvin's teaching on the Lord's Supper.[54] Many of these controversies were eventually settled in a credal statement adopted by a majority of Lutheran territories, the Formula of Concord (1580).[55] In the intervening years, however, just as Germany's Lutheran territories gained full recognition in imperial law (1555), their theologians were at daggers drawn. Further expansion of Lutheranism was curtailed by this discord, if not halted altogether.

Just in these years the Calvinist movement, based in Geneva, was reaching the height of its influence. Geneva's city council had asked Calvin to return in 1541.[56] He quickly gained the council's approval for a confession of the evangelical faith and for a church ordinance embodying his distinctive ideas on ecclesiastical polity, or church government. Geneva's church was to be ruled by a minister of the Word (appointed by the council) acting with lay elders elected by citizens, along with deacons to serve the needs of the poor. Minister and elders together formed the consistory, to which the supervision of morals was entrusted. Questions of doctrine were to be settled not by the consistory, but at periodic synods including ministers and elders from each of the towns in a given territory. As the church was being organized along these lines, city officials went door to door with copies of the new confession of faith. Persons above the age of fifteen were given a choice between swearing to these articles of belief or leaving the city. Calvin's Geneva was not to be a haven for the godless.

There was, however, a sticking point. Like other Swiss and south German Reformers, including Zwingli, Calvin believed that the test of true doctrine was how church members lived. To have public sinners numbered among those receiving the Lord's Supper was a great scandal, to be warded off by the excommunication of errant believers. Calvin's self-governing church polity, unlike a city council, could be expected to uphold God's law regardless of the person of the offender. But not everyone in Geneva accepted this view of church authority, and the 1541 church ordinance was vague about whether the city council could or could not overrule consistory decisions on excommunication. Calvin had many supporters among prominent families, but other Genevans, having cast off the tyranny of the papal clergy, had no taste for a new kind of clerical power and made no secret of their feelings. One man, for example, was cited before the consistory for naming his dog "Calvin." For many years the outcome was uncertain, as city council elections yielded majorities for or against Calvin's vision of the place of the church in Geneva. The breakthrough came when Calvin's foes, having lost badly in the elections of 1555, attempted a coup d'etat with help from Bern. They were defeated in a street battle.

The new council solidified the church's position by undertaking not to interfere in decisions regarding excommunication and by changing citizenship rules to allow religious refugees to gain voting rights more quickly.[57] Geneva now became a magnet for men and women who suffered or feared persecution for their Protestant beliefs in France, Italy, the Low Countries, and parts of Germany. The Word of God was proclaimed in many areas, but only Geneva had a church polity capable of making God's Word efficacious in the life of the commonwealth. Gauging how people actually behaved is notoriously difficult for historians,[58] but it seems the refugees were right in thinking that godly discipline was becoming a visible reality in Geneva: Children learned their catechism, men were less likely to indulge in casual swearing, and magistrates were less likely to line their own pockets.

When the council established an academy (1559) for the training of pastors, many of the first graduates were refugees who made the dangerous trip back whence they had come, eager to plant in their home countries the seeds of godly commonwealths like Geneva. Calvin's study, and later that of his successor, Theodore Beza (1516–1605),[59] became a command post for communications from the new mission territories. Thus, just in the years when papal Rome was regaining its lost authority in the Catholic Church, Calvin's Geneva was becoming a Protestant Rome.

In addition to the aura of godly discipline that drew refugees from far and wide, Calvinism was also distinctive in certain aspects of its theology. In the early editions of his *Institutes* Calvin did not highlight predestination, but he insisted there was no such thing as chance. Everything that happened in the world happened by God's will: If one blade of grass greened while another did not, if one nursing mother had milk for her infant but another did not, it was because God had willed it so. During the course of controversies with Protestant as well as Catholic opponents, this emphasis on God's will crystallized in a specific formulation of the doctrine of predestination. In 1550 Calvin debated before the city council of Geneva an ex-friar[60] who maintained that while God does indeed predestine for salvation all who are saved, He offers his grace to all men; those who are damned are damned through their own fault, not because God decrees it so. Calvin responded that it made no sense to say that God decrees the salvation of those who are saved but not the damnation of those who are damned. God offers his grace only to those whom He chooses, and if man has no free will to participate in his own salvation, neither has he the free will to turn aside from God's decree. God displays his infinite mercy by saving those sinners He chooses to save and his infinite justice by condemning to hell those sinners He chooses to condemn. Neither Bullinger in Zurich nor Luther's heirs in Wittenberg accepted Calvin's unusual doctrine of "double predestination."[61] But for Calvin and his followers this awesome understanding of God's power was a great source of spiritual comfort. The person who trusted that he or she was predestined for salvation by such a God had, in an ultimate sense, nothing to fear.

By comparison with Lutheranism in particular, Calvinism was also much more emphatic in its rejection of Catholic tradition, root and branch. Luther's conception of the Lord's Supper was close enough to the Catholic view to permit discussion at Regensburg, even if there was no agreement. Calvin believed that the Catholic mass "swarmed with idolatry" from top to bottom. Luther's acceptance of religious images permitted Lutherans and Catholics in some north German villages and small towns to use the same church, even if they were careful to use it at different times. Calvin, like Zwingli, insisted that the churches be cleansed of "idols" of every sort, as may be seen from the whitewashed walls and clear-glass windows of churches where Calvinism triumphed. Nowhere is it recorded for the sixteenth century that Calvinists and Catholics used the same house of worship. In the absence of firm disciplinary structures, Lutherans often found it prudent to attend Sunday mass in countries with a vigilant Catholic government. Calvinists who did the same had to face the consistory; in effect, they had to choose between the fires of persecution and the fires of hell. Meanwhile, the Counter-Reformation church was forming a generation of Catholics who took an equally uncomplimentary view of Protestantism and of Calvinism in particular. The next chapter portrays the two movements that battled most fiercely for the allegiance of Christian Europeans during the century between 1550 and 1650: militant Calvinism and militant Catholicism.

7 | Doctrine

The European Reformations

CATHOLICISM

Both as a movement for internal reform and as a campaign against Protestantism, the Catholic Reformation (or Counter-Reformation) was blended from locally differing proportions of four basic elements: the spiritual energy of new religious orders; a slow restoration of the moral authority of the priesthood, starting with legislation by the Council of Trent; popular loyalty to the old religion; and rulers who legitimized their authority by criminalizing Protestant dissent and backing Catholic reform. These four strands of the story overlap chronologically, but it will be simpler to treat them one by one.

Ignatius of Loyola (1491–1556), a Basque[1] nobleman, had his leg broken by a cannonball in his first military engagement (1521). For want of the chivalric tales[2] he was familiar with, during a long convalescence he read and reread a traditional compilation of saints' lives.[3] By the time he was able to walk again, Ignatius found himself daydreaming not about achieving great feats of valor, but about preaching to infidels in the Holy Land. This conversion of the imagination was the door to a new life. Ignatius sold his property and gave the money to the poor, went on pilgrimage to Jerusalem, and returned to a wandering life in his native Spain, seeking spiritual counsel from holy men and holy women.

The Spiritual Exercises, a record of Ignatius's own spiritual quest, eventually became a manual of initiation and daily prayer for his followers. The technique of prayer Ignatius adopted was known as meditation. Starting from an incident in Jesus' life as recorded in the Gospels, one was to fix the scene as vividly as possible in one's imagination and dwell on Jesus' words

Figure 7.1. St. Ignatius Loyola. Jacopino del Conte, Posthumous Portrait of Ignatius of Loyola, 1556. (*Curia Generalizia of the Society of Jesus, Rome.*)

and actions. In later years, Ignatius guided each new member of his company through the full thirty-day sequence of meditations outlined in the *Exercises*. The objective was to build as it were a mental armory against temptation, so that at crucial moments scenes from the life of Christ would come to mind as if unbidden.[4] It is not known if Ignatius had even heard of Martin Luther when he first wrote the *Exercises*. But those who learned from the *Exercises* to use the powers of the mind in shaping their thoughts to the service of Christ would have little patience for Luther's assertion that the human will is incapable of any action pleasing to God.

Needing a university education to make himself heard in the world, Ignatius as a mature man took his place among teenagers at the arts faculty in Paris. Bachelor's degree in hand, he and a small group of followers planned to sail from Venice to the Holy Land. Prevented from embarking because of war, the company instead offered their services to the pope in Rome. In 1540 Pope Paul III recognized the Society of Jesus as a religious order. As the first elected father-general (1540–1556), Ignatius charted the new society's future. Jesuit overseas missions[5] began in 1542, when, heeding a request from the king of Portugal, Ignatius sent Francis Xavier, one of his Paris companions, as a missionary to Portugal's new possessions in India. In 1548 Ignatius prescribed a humanist curriculum for the first Jesuit secondary school, at Messina in Sicily. Jesuit schools quickly became the preferred means, even in some Protestant territories, for young men of prominent families to acquire the polish of a classical education. Ignatius also provided a form of governance unprecedented among religious orders. Local superiors were appointed by the father-general, not elected by their confreres; general meetings of the order convened not annually, as was customary, but only as the father-general and his advisers deemed necessary. Ignatius envisioned his men as troops to be sent quickly wherever the church needed help. Increasingly, they were to be enlisted in the battle against Protestantism.

If the tight, top-down structure of the Jesuit order resembled the ambitions of monarchs in the early modern era,[6] the Oratories of Divine Love made up a loose-knit federation more typically medieval in structure. What these cells of piety had in common was the example of Caterina Fieschi Adorna (1447–1510), later venerated as St. Catherine of Genoa. A daughter of Genoa's premier families, Catherine chose to live as a celibate lay woman, devoting herself to prayer and to the poor of her native city. She attracted disciples, often wealthy bankers like her kinfolk, and it was they who founded the first Oratory (Genoa, 1497), which in turn founded Italy's first hospital for the incurably ill. Oratories soon appeared in other Italian cities, similar to traditional confraternities in their stated goals but animated by a new fervor.

The Roman Oratory was a training ground for men who carried a zeal for reform into higher echelons of the church. Four of its members (including one who later became pope[7]) founded a new order for priests, the Theatines (1524), aimed at fostering common prayer and devotion to the unfortunate, especially the incurably ill. A fifth, Gasparo Contarini (d. 1542), was the pope's representative at the Regensburg Colloquy.[8] In 1525, a Franciscan friar in a small central-Italian town, Matteo da Bascio, resolved to devote himself to prayer and preaching, based on a literal observance of the rule of St. Francis. The pointed hood (*capuccio*) he chose to wear gave its name to the Capuchins, recognized by the pope in 1528 as a separate branch of the Franciscan movement. The Capuchins were to be, with the Jesuits, the great preachers and literary protagonists of the Counter-Reformation. In 1535 Angela Merici and twenty-eight young women of her native Brescia founded the Company of St. Ursula. They took vows of virginity, as nuns did, but each was to live with her family, dress in lay garb, and devote herself to the Christian education of girls. Church authorities, ever suspicious of religious women not living in convents,[9] eventually forced the Ursulines to adopt a cloistered life, but they continued their work of operating schools for girls. The Ursulines' devotion to the traditional works of mercy exemplifies a Catholic Reformation understanding of "good works" that was very different from Luther's.[10]

The Council of Trent convened in three sessions (1545–1547, 1551–1552, and 1561–1563), interrupted twice by war and once by the reign of an autocratic pope who refused to reconvene it.[11] At its first session the council took up doctrinal issues raised by the Reformers, none of which had ever previously been the subject of any dogmatic pronouncement by the church

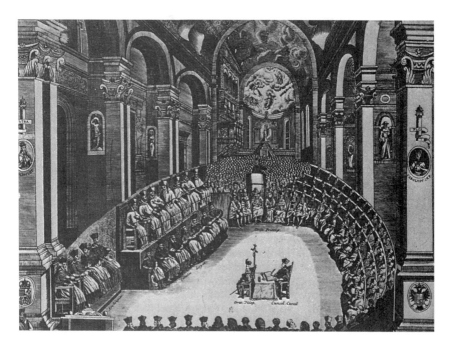

Figure 7.2. The Council of Trent. Sixteenth-century engraving of the Council of Trent. (*British Museum, London.*)

as a whole. First on the agenda was justification (salvation). Girolamo Seripando (d. 1563), father-general of the Augustinian Friars,[12] proposed wording similar to what Protestant and Catholic conferees had accepted at Regensburg (1541). Diego Lainez (d. 1565), one of Ignatius Loyola's early companions, proposed instead a vigorous statement of traditional Catholic beliefs concerning free will.[13] Though it shows traces of Seripando's language, the council's decree on justification flatly asserts what Luther and Calvin had flatly denied: the human will is free to accept or reject God's grace. The next question concerned scripture and tradition. Catholic theologians were agreed that the traditions of the church were authoritative, but what did this mean in relation to scripture? The minority view, which some Protestants might have accepted, was that "tradition" was the way in which the church had always understood scripture. The view that prevailed was that unwritten traditions in the keeping of the church are a distinct source of divine revelation, having an authority equal to that of scripture. These doctrinal definitions ensured that it would henceforth be clear (up to a point) which opinions were Catholic and which were not.[14]

Reform of the clergy came to the table at the council's third session (1561–1563). Bishops were supposed to be shepherds of the faithful, but they were commonly appointed at the behest of the ruler, for political reasons,[15] and many seldom actually saw the dioceses of which they were titular heads.[16] The council was unable to reach agreement on the precise nature of a bishop's obligation to reside in his diocese,[17] and it did not even attempt to set aside the various agreements, formal and informal, by which popes had recognized local rulers as having a voice in the selection of bishops. What it did was strengthen the authority of bishops vis-à-vis the regular as well as the secular clergy. Bishops were given more say in the appointment of pastors by noble "patrons" of parish churches,[18] as well as the right to "visit" monasteries and other religious establishments that had previously gained exemption from episcopal control.[19]

The priesthood needed reform as much as the episcopate. Canon law provided that only men of a certain age be ordained, following an examination of their theological competence by the ordaining bishop. Both provisions were widely ignored, the first in favor of younger sons of prominent families being groomed for important positions, the second in favor of men of humble background who hoped only to scrape out a meager existence.[20] The council forcefully reasserted the law: only men of twenty-five or older were to be ordained, and only with a university-level education including training in theology. To make this possible, the council mandated that each bishop find the resources (this was not easy) to endow a "seminary" for the training of diocesan priests.[21]

Most in need of reform was the papacy itself, as late medieval reform treatises often pointed out. The Roman Curia was both a collection of networks based on nepotism and a vast bureaucracy whose members had a natural interest in perpetuating the functions that kept them gainfully employed. One of their more lucrative functions was the granting of dispensations that exempted recipients from given provisions of canon law, such as the rule prohibiting "pluralism," that is, the holding of ecclesiastical positions in two or more locations at once. The Council of Trent issued new regulations that, over time, had some effect in curbing clerical double-dipping, but it played little role in reorganizing the Curia (this was to be done somewhat later by the popes themselves).[22]

The council's real significance for the papacy lay in the fact that this great engine of Catholic reform was called into being by the popes, who also guided the council's deliberations through emissaries who always presided at formal sessions. Bolstered by Rome's new standing, papal *nuncios* fanned out to advance the Catholic cause.[23] Armed with the *Index of Forbidden Books* promulgated by Pope Paul IV in 1559, permitting ready identification of allegedly dangerous authors, they pressed bishops and secular rulers to join in the repression of heretical books and other expressions of false doctrine. The church had its own procedures for trying persons accused of heresy, but the effective suppression of dissent required active cooperation from the secular courts (see below). Papal emissaries also pushed for the appointment of zealous clergymen to important positions in the local church. They urged princes to accept the Tridentine decrees for their territories, countering as best they could the influence of those whose interests would be adversely affected by their implementation—noble patrons of parish churches and monasteries that objected to having some of their property taken to endow the new seminaries. By these means, the papacy assumed leadership of the movement for Catholic reform and of the battle against Protestantism, gaining by about 1600 a moral prestige in the Catholic world such as it had not enjoyed for centuries.

"Innovation" was not a friendly word for sixteenth-century Europe's rural majority. Novelties came not from the peasants themselves (at least not in ways they were conscious of), but from the landlord's counting-house or from lawyers at the prince's court, who, like city-bred preachers, appealed to books illiterate folk could not read. The old ways were the ways country dwellers could control (who else knew the local customs?) or could at least bear because of their familiarity. By and large, the old ways meant the old religion, with its familiar rites and gestures. The alliance between the grievances of Germany's peasants and Reformation doctrine had proven to be temporary, and in France Reformation doctrine had very little appeal to the peasantry, save in a few areas. To be sure, where peasants had a generation or two to get used to Lutheranism, they strongly resisted efforts by princes to make them change their minds again.[24] But in the outward forms by which illiterate people measured religious propriety, Lutheranism was not so different from Catholicism, save for the use of the vernacular. In territories where Lutheranism was imposed from above, like Norway and Finland,[25] the fact that a largely Catholic peasantry offered little active resistance seems related to efforts by authorities to change as little as possible in the outward ceremonies of religion.

Reformed Protestantism had a different trajectory. Zwinglian as well as Calvinist doctrine required that worship be thoroughly "cleansed" of all the artifacts and all the gestures of the Catholic cult, and this was often accomplished by violent outbursts of iconoclasm, with or without the encouragement of Reformed preachers.[26] To provocations of this kind, Catholic people in Switzerland and France (not the Low Countries) responded with violence of their own.[27] Sympathizers of the Reformation were chased out of Switzerland's forest cantons well before the conflict between Catholic and Protestant cantons had crystallized into open warfare. Since Switzerland's cantons enjoyed an unusual degree of local autonomy, not being subject to any kind of control by a princely court, it is perhaps not surprising if individual cantons made their collective decisions about the Reformation, for or against, quickly and with force. France was a different story.

Beginning in the 1520s and 1530s, France was crisscrossed by itinerant Catholic preachers, prophesying that men and women now living would yet see the Last Day, the hour of God's final victory over Satan and all the forces of evil. Apocalyptic[28] rhetoric of this sort was a common theme of medieval preaching, concentrated in certain periods and regions in a way that can sometimes but not always be linked to social and economic crises. French preachers of these decades seem to have been influenced in part by widespread astrological prognostications to the effect that a rare alignment of the planets portended some momentous change on earth.[29] Whatever its source, this wave of doomsday preaching prepared people on both sides of France's eventual religious divide to believe that combating the devilish evils they saw before them ("heresy" for some, "idolatry" for others) was of transcendent significance.

The centralizing claims of France's monarchy made the struggle that was to come more intense than it might otherwise have been.[30] For the king and his officials, all aspects of French life, including religion, properly came under the scrutiny of royal judges. The antiheresy legislation of Kings Francis I (ruled 1515–1547) and Henry II (ruled 1547–1559), even if occasionally relaxed,[31] created a mechanism of judicial repression that was ineffective in stamping out dissent, but odious to friends and kinfolk of its victims.[32] The anger that built up, fueled by the fiery rhetoric of Reformed preachers, found a ready target in the visible symbols of "idolatrous" Catholic worship.

French Catholics, egged on by their preachers, responded by targeting the "heretics" themselves. By 1560 France was gripped in a deepening spiral of reciprocal violence. For example, in Paris, passersby, hearing the distinctive tones of Protestant plainsong from a merchant's house, quickly became a Catholic mob that stormed the house and murdered its occupants. At Christmas Eve mass in a Paris church, two young Huguenots (as French Protestants were called)[33] rushed up to the altar at the moment of the elevation, stabbed the priest, and trampled on the host; they were killed immediately by the congregation. When quarrels among the great families of

Figure 7.3. A Catholic view of Protestant violence in France. "Horrible Crimes Perpetrated by the Huguenots," from Richard Verstegen, Teatrum Crudelitatum. (*Thomas Fisher Rare Book Library, University of Toronto.*)

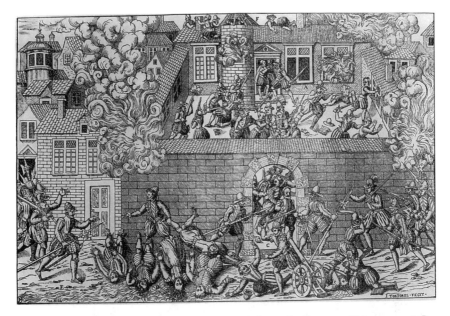

Figure 7.4. A Protestant view of Catholic violence in France. "Massacre at Ca-hors, 19 November 1561," from Alfred Franklin, *Les Grandes Scènes Historiques due XVIe Siècle, Reproduction Fac-Simile du Recueil de J. Tortorel et J. Perrissin* [1586] (Paris: Fisachbacher, 1881). (*University of California at San Diego Library.*)

the realm were added to this volatile mixture, France fell into a long cycle of civil and religious wars (1562–1598).[34]

The fanatical zeal with which Catholics in France defended their faith was a striking example of a more diffuse phenomenon. So long as Protestant preaching had not had a generation or more to take root, Catholic authorities could count on a certain residual loyalty to traditional beliefs. But it was a loyalty that ordinary men and women gave on their own terms. The religious temper of ardently Catholic Paris made it difficult for France's monarchs to make the concessions to the Huguenot party that peace in the realm required. Reform-minded Catholic pastors were to find their flocks unwilling to accept modification of traditional observances. As far as country people were concerned, innovation was still innovation, even if propounded in the name of the old religion.

As in France during the first half of the sixteenth century, Catholic rulers in other countries typically responded to the Reformation by attempting

Figure 7.5. The Spanish Inquisition. In the terminology of the Inquisition, the burning of heretics was an "act of faith" (auto da fe): Pedro Bereguette (1450–1504), "St. Dominic Presiding at an Auto-da-Fe." (*Art Resource, New York, NY.*)

to suppress it. The religious justification for this policy was that since princes were seen as ruling "by the grace of God,"[35] they had a responsibility to see that God was worshiped properly. The legal justification was that medieval law codes often defined heresy as "treason against God," meaning that it was a crime punishable by death, as was treason against the ruler. At least since the thirteenth century, rulers had cooperated with the church in putting convicted heretics to death. Each diocese had an official known as the inquisitor, in whose court accused heretics could be tried and convicted, but not sentenced to death. Convicted heretics were handed over to "the secular arm," which alone had the power of capital punishment.

Queen Isabella of Castile (ruled 1476–1504) pioneered a closer princely involvement in the suppression of heresy when she established the Spanish Inquisition (1478), a court made up of churchmen appointed by the crown. Especially in its early decades, the Inquisition conducted a savage persecution of "Judaizers"—that is, descendants of Spanish Jews who had converted to Christianity but still practiced the Jewish rites of their ancestors.[36] In some provinces of the Low Countries, Charles V relied on a territorial inquisition based on the Spanish model; in others, he relied on provincial courts that were more willing to prosecute people for crimes of belief than were the town courts. The dukes of Bavaria followed the latter course, issuing laws that criminalized behavior recognizable as "Lutheran"[37] and were enforceable in the secular courts. In France, too, the crown was content to leave the enforcement of heresy laws in the hands of the chief law courts, known as *parlements*.[38]

This church-state collaboration in Catholic Europe claimed an estimated 3,000 Protestant martyrs in the years between 1520 and 1600.[39] Where dissenters were few in numbers and poorly organized, like Lutherans in the Netherlands in the 1520s, or Protestants of any kind in Spain,[40] the application of brute force was effective. Where they were strong in numbers and well organized, like Calvinists in France or in the populous province of Flanders, persecution made martyrs, and the blood of martyrs was, as in early Christian times, the seed of new conversions. Repression was not working.

Another strategy was to improve the training and discipline of the Catholic clergy. Charles V carefully checked the religious and educational qualifications of those he proposed for high positions in the church, but this was in Castile, which had an unusual tradition of royal involvement with church reform, tracing back to Queen Isabella.[41] In other Catholic lands, bishops continued to be appointed first and foremost for their family connections. Change came only with a generation of Jesuit-educated princes willing to override opposition to reform of the clergy. Archduke

Charles of Inner Austria[42] (ruled 1564–1590) and Archduke Albert of the Spanish Netherlands (ruled 1595–1621) accepted the Council of Trent's decrees as a basis for regulating the often contentious issue of lay patronage of ecclesiastical appointments. In Bavaria Duke William V (ruled 1579–1598) functioned as the effective ruler of the church. In France, where the civil wars had ended with a formal grant of toleration for the kingdom's Huguenot minority (1598),[43] the Parlement of Paris refused to recognize the Tridentine decrees as part of French law. But the crown began exercising more care in the appointment of bishops, while members of parlement joined the crown in promoting the new religious orders. By the early seventeenth century, many areas had zealous bishops who were indefatigable in "visiting" their dioceses. The ranks of the parish clergy were being filled a new kind of priest, making new demands on populations that were often loyal to Catholicism, if seldom enthusiastic for reform.

CALVINISM

Certain features of the Calvinist movement in Geneva reflected the character of Geneva itself. As a self-governing commune, whose citizens formed one body, Geneva had no tolerance for religious dissension; citizens were given a choice between acceptance of the new Calvinist confession or exile.[44] Though dependent on Bern's aid against enemies like the duke of Savoy, Geneva was a self-standing republic, with no need for any kind of church authority at a higher level than that of the city. Hence, it was the large and complex canton of Bern, not Geneva, that developed Reformed synods, with pastors and lay elders elected by local churches deliberating on matters of doctrine. With the collaboration of men who had come to Geneva as exiles and returned as missionaries to their native lands, Calvin guided the building of similarly structured Reformed churches in places as far away as Hungary. But the Calvinism of larger and more complex territories also assumed characteristics suitable to each local context. The varieties of Calvinism may be illustrated by looking at churches in France, the Low Countries, Scotland, and, in Germany, the Rhineland Palatinate.

In France, reform of the church was promoted by a circle of preachers and scholars around Jacques Lefèvre d'Étaples (1460–1536), a scholastic professor of Aristotle's logic who ended his learned career as a humanist biblical scholar. One of the preachers was Guillaume Farel (1489–1565), later to be Calvin's collaborator in Geneva. Enthused for Luther's works,

Farel went to Basel, where he made contact with Zwingli and his ideas. Bern installed him as the first Protestant preacher in the French-speaking city of Neuchâtel (1530), a Bernese dependency, which then began printing Protestant works for distribution in France, including vernacular Bibles. Farel's intemperate zeal was evident in the broadsides denouncing "the horrible, gross and insupportable popish mass" (1534), printed in Neuchâtel and posted all over France, including on the door of the royal bedchamber.

During the 1540s Geneva replaced Neuchâtel as the command post for diffusion of Protestant works into France, and Calvin's personal influence began to be felt in many of the places where Reformed movements coalesced. In the city of Nîmes, to the south, a strong Protestant movement formed around the staff of the humanist secondary school, whose rector (from 1542) had met Calvin in Strasbourg. In the Rhone valley city of Lyon, France's mercantile capital, local Protestants became numerous enough to appoint a regular pastor (1546), one of Calvin's correspondents. Near the southwestern port city of La Rochelle, a Benedictine abbot of noble birth, another correspondent, converted all his monks to the new faith in 1553.

From about 1555, Calvinism expanded rapidly. Nobles accepted the new faith in large numbers, often at the behest of their female kindred.[45] A spectacular example at the highest level of French society was Jeanne d'Albret (d. 1572), Queen of Navarre, who made a public announcement of her conversion in 1560.[46] Her husband, Antoine de Bourbon, was less steadfast in his loyalty to the new creed than she was, but he had the great advantage of being first in rank among the princes of the royal blood, who were closest to the throne after King Henry II and his sons.[47]

At the local level, the visible presence of armed noblemen allowed Huguenots to worship in public, often in the open air, without fear of disturbance by the king's officers. Meanwhile, in a number of cities in the south and southwest, merchants, magistrates, and even some royal officials joined hands with the artisans who were often the earliest recruits to the Protestant cause. Many congregations could now support more than one preacher; presbyters were elected and consistories met, after the Genevan model, to discipline the wayward. Strong in numbers as well as social prestige, Huguenot communities demanded (but did not get) churches for their own use. Their preachers joined with nearby colleagues to form "colloquies," or regular meetings of regional clergy, to ensure uniformity of doctrine and to provide pastors for new congregations.

The capstone of this organizational edifice was achieved in 1559, when deputies elected by the colloquies met secretly in Paris for a national synod, which adopted, with slight modifications, a confession of faith drawn up by Calvin. Not all French Protestants accepted Calvin's views on church governance. A treatise published in 1562 argued that decisions regarding the appointment of preachers should be made by each congregation, not by a "colloquy" or synod. But these ideas, though not forgotten,[48] were condemned by two national synods of the French church. By 1561, leaders of the Huguenots counted some 2,000 congregations that were "organized" in the Genevan manner, with pastor, elders, and consistory. This suggests that some 10 percent of France's roughly twenty million people were Protestant.

Many in France clamored that true Christians would be justified in striking out against their tyrannical oppressors. But despite the continuing persecution, Calvin insisted, time and again, that the gospel must never be compromised by any use of force. The 1559 edition of his *Institutes* urged "magistrates" to prevent rulers of their realms from acting as tyrants—Calvin may have been thinking of France's princes of the blood and of Antoine de Bourbon in particular. This became more than a theoretical question when King Henry II, a lover of jousting,[49] was killed by an errant lance (1559), leaving the throne to a weak boy whose council of regency was dominated by Duke Francis of Guise, a determined foe of the Reformation. Huguenot nobles led by the prince of Condé, Bourbon's younger brother, plotted to seize the person of the king and install Bourbon as head of a new council of regency.[50] When the plot was uncovered (1560) suspicious eyes turned toward Geneva. Calvin kept aloof, but it seems his second-in-command and eventual successor, Theodore Beza (1516–1605), signaled approval of the attempted coup. Calvin's attempt to limit the right of resistance to potentates of the realm, though intellectually defensible, was not readily comprehensible to zealous Huguenots who had seen coreligionists burned at the stake by order of the king's courts.

Whether Calvin wished it so or not, French Calvinism was becoming a revolutionary movement. When a party of Protestant worshipers was massacred by the duke of Guise (1562), Condé called Huguenot nobles to arms, and Huguenot factions seized control of twenty cities, including Nîmes, Lyon, and La Rochelle. This first of France's religious wars began auspiciously for the Huguenot rebels, but by the time the last war was concluded (1598) they gladly accepted a recognition of their rights limited to the few parts of the kingdom they still controlled. Calvin's caution about mixing violence and religion had been vindicated. The Protestant movement in France never again reached its numerical strength of 1561, just before the religious wars began.

Charles V's attempt to create in the Low Countries a special state tribunal modeled on the Spanish Inquisition evoked a firestorm of opposition, as provincial parliaments demanded respect for their customary legal privileges, never mind the claim that such privileges were suspended in cases of "treason against God."[51] Nonetheless, the new territorial inquisition was able to snuff out a nascent Lutheran movement by targeting the highly visible preachers and scholars who were its natural leaders.[52] In Lutheranism's stead more radical forms of dissent emerged, especially among men and women of humbler background who were almost invisible to the authorities. Anabaptists and "Sacramentarians"[53] were put to death, but there was no wholesale rounding up of suspects until the Melchiorite scare of the 1530s,[54] when town governments—usually loath to prosecute citizens for crimes of belief—took a real interest in enforcing heresy laws. By about 1540, magistrates in some towns began to realize that new-style Mennonite congregations posed no danger to public order. During the 1540s there were relatively few martyrs.

Just at this time, however, Calvinism appeared in the French-speaking provinces closest to France and started making its way to Netherlandish-speaking provinces farther north, like Flanders and Brabant. With Geneva-style consistories monitoring their behavior, Calvinists found it difficult to compromise with idolatry by attending Sunday mass now and then to avoid drawing attention. Together with local Anabaptists, they were targets for the territorial inquisition in Flanders, led by Peter Titelmans, a zealous Louvain theologian.[55] The courage of the martyrs won sympathy, especially among skilled workers in the centers of Flanders's "new textile" industry.[56] Even apart from the spread of Protestant ideas, townsfolk in the Low Countries had a peculiar dislike[57] for seeing men hung or burned at the stake merely because of their beliefs.[58] In Holland, a crowd gathered in Rotterdam for the execution of five Anabaptists rioted, freeing the prisoners and chasing the magistrates into the relative safety of town hall (1558). In the new textile towns of Flanders, starting in 1562, Calvinists were broken out of jail by sizable parties of men.

Facing these disorders was Margaret of Parma, regent[59] in the Low Countries for King Philip II of Spain, who had succeeded his father Charles V in 1556. Philip made things more difficult for Margaret when he decreed (with papal cooperation) the creation of new bishoprics for his Low Countries lands (1561). There would now be fifteen bishoprics instead of three, the better to supervise reform of the clergy as well as the campaign against heresy. But noble families feared diminution of their control over high positions in the church, powerful abbots were loath to release monastic properties to endow the new bishoprics, and magistrates flatly refused to allow heresy-hunting bishops within their town gates. The great nobles who sat in Margaret's council of state gave voice to widespread dissatisfaction in the country. Led by William of Nassau, the Prince of Orange (1533–1584),[60] the council demanded and got (1564) the dismissal of Philip's key adviser,

Figure 7.6. King Philip II of Spain. Ruled 1556–1598. Pompeo Leoni (ca. 1533–1608), Bust of Philip II. (*Kunsthistorisches Museum, Vienna.*)

whom they blamed for the new bishoprics plan.[61] Sensing that further change was possible, the council sent two of their number to Spain to ask the king to suspend the heresy laws. Philip's reply (1565) came as a rude shock: heretics were to have no mercy whatever.

Margaret's government now seemed to lose its grip. Four hundred noblemen presented a petition for relaxation of the heresy laws. Thousands of people flocked to rural settings for the illegal "hedge sermons" of Calvinist preachers. In August 1566 zealous Calvinists returned from exile in England to organize a systematic tearing-down of "idols" in Flanders's new textile district. Led by preachers who sometimes paid image-breakers by the hour, the wave of iconoclasm spread through much of the country. Did this smashing of the symbols of the old religion represent the will of the people? And would the guildsmen who made up the town militias stand to arms to prevent it? No one knew. In most towns, magistrates did little to ward off the destruction they knew was coming.

But public order was not so fragile as it seemed. Nobles and magistrates sent Margaret their expressions of support, and when the dust had settled it seemed the number of convinced Calvinists was fairly small. Margaret sought to calm the waters by allowing towns to set aside one of their churches for "the new religion," an arrangement that seemed in some areas to work. Meanwhile, however, Philip II had already made his decision, based on the panic-stricken reports he initially received from Brussels. A trusted commander, the duke of Alba, marched north from Italy at the head of ten thousand Spanish troops (1567).[62] Once in Brussels, Alba disregarded notions of due process deeply ingrained among Netherlanders, ordering all key decisions made by a three-man group, known to Spaniards as the council of troubles, and to Netherlanders as the council of blood.[63] This council issued death sentences at a rate that dwarfs all persecutions of the Reformation period, but the number of actual victims was much smaller.[64] Hearing that Alba was coming, leaders of the Calvinist movement had fled into exile, some to England, others to the city of Emden in East Friesland, a neighbor of the Netherlands province of Friesland. While in exile, Netherlands Calvinists adopted rules for church governance, based on French models: each town congregation would have a consistory, including lay elders; pastors of nearby congregations would form a *classis*[65] for supervision of doctrine and preaching; and for the resolution of important matters, each *classis* would elect delegates to a synod.

William of Orange carried on an armed struggle, but without the resources to match Alba's ten thousand men. His forces defeated wherever they took the field, Orange retired to Germany (1568). The only remaining center of active resistance was in England's channel ports, where Calvinist exiles, following an old Netherlands pattern, expressed their rebellion by taking to the sea as pirates. The Sea Beggars disrupted the maritime commerce of the Netherlands but could not prevent Alba from reducing the country to obedience.[66] In Alba's judgment the only thing lacking was a source of revenue that would allow his troops to remain in the Netherlands without being a drain on Spain's treasury. He thought he had the consent he needed from the provincial parliaments, but he did not understand their slow deliberative procedures. When his officials went out in the early months of 1572 to collect the tenth-penny tax, a new levy based on Spanish precedents, they met a wall of hostility—it seems no money at all was actually collected. This form of "Spanish tyranny" the people of the Low Countries would not stomach.[67]

The Sea Beggars seized an opportunity. Drawing their fleet up before the small port of Brill (April 1572), they promised protection from the Spaniards

Figure 7.7. The capture of Brill by the Sea Beggars, April 1572. Disembarking from their ships, the rebel army draws up in formation and marches toward the main gate of Brill ("Briele"). (*The British Library, London.*)

and respect for the religion of the inhabitants. Once in control they cleansed the churches of "idols" and installed Calvinist preachers—but they did keep the Spaniards out. As other cities in the seafaring provinces of Holland and Zeeland submitted to the Beggars, townsfolk seem to have accepted an implicit bargain: no Spaniards, but no public Catholic worship either. The exiles now returned, often to become magistrates of their native towns, and William of Orange guided the revolt from a headquarters in Holland. He too had become a Calvinist, recognizing that committed Calvinists were the natural leaders of the war against Spain. But Orange also made it clear that all Christians ought to be free to worship in public as they chose: to him, the revolt against Spain was about defending the traditional "liberties" or privileges of the Netherlands provinces, not about religion. Calvinist leaders were adamant about not permitting any public expression of Catholic idolatry. But their worshipers made up only a small fraction of the population, and forcing everyone to conform to Calvinism would alienate those who opposed the king of Spain but not his religion. Moreover, Mennonites, now freed from fear of the king's heresy laws, competed with Calvinists for the allegiance of evangelical Christians. With their strict community discipline,

Mennonites would rightly scoff at the moral pretensions of a Protestant church that claimed to incorporate the whole community, the indifferent as well as the devout.

Hence, Netherlands Calvinists renounced the idea of inclusiveness. Theirs was to be what they called "the public church" of rebel territory. No other form of Christian worship was permitted in public; Catholic worship was banned in private as well.[68] But no citizen would be constrained to join the public church—in fact, admission to formal membership was carefully controlled, in the interests of good discipline.[69] The underlying question—whether the war against Spain was being fought for freedom from tyranny or for true religion—would be sorted out during the long decades of revolt (1572–1648).

Scotland's history was shaped by conflicts with its larger and more powerful neighbor to the south. In the late medieval wars between England and France,[70] France and the royal house of Stuart formed what Scots called "the auld alliance." But in the sixteenth century a disastrous defeat at the hands of the English, together with a combination of English bribes and border raids, led some of Scotland's great nobles to rethink the French connection.[71] King James V kept Scotland in France's orbit, choosing as his bride Mary of Guise, daughter of one of France's premier families.[72] But James perished in a counterraid against England (1542), leaving his throne to an infant daughter, Mary Stuart.[73] Pro-English and pro-French factions now vied for control of the kingdom.

This conflict had a religious coloration, since King Henry VIII and his Parliament had severed England's ties with Rome in 1536.[74] Scots Protestants, concentrated in the coastal towns, counted on England for support, while pro-English Scots saw Protestantism as a way of ending French influence. George Wishart, Scotland's leading Protestant preacher, had a Zwinglian theology acquired on his travels to Germany and Switzerland and connections with pro-English lesser nobles. David Beaton, archbishop of St. Andrews and a pillar of the pro-French party, worked at bringing reform to a poorly educated and ill-disciplined Catholic clergy. In 1546 Beaton had Wishart tried and executed for heresy. A band of pro-English nobles then murdered the archbishop and occupied his castle. John Knox (1513–1572), a former priest and member of Wishart's circle, gained attention with a fiery sermon to the conspirators in St. Andrews castle, denouncing the papacy as the Antichrist. Royal forces captured the castle, and Knox got two years in the galleys,[75] but his career as a reformer had barely begun. He preached in England until Mary Tudor's accession to the English throne brought a restoration of Catholicism (1553–1558)[76] and

Figure 7.8. John Knox (1514–1572). Portrait of John Knox engraved by Hondius. (*British Museum, London.*)

thereafter to a congregation of English and Scots refugees in Calvin's Geneva.

Mary of Guise assumed control of the regency council for her daughter in 1554. Mary Stuart had been betrothed as a young girl to Francis, eldest son of France's King Henry II, and their marriage, celebrated in 1558, seemed to bind Scotland to France. But Scots were growing resentful of the visible signs of French control, like French garrisons in key castles, and the accession to England's throne of the Protestant Elizabeth I, also in 1558, opened new possibilities. Returning from the continent, Knox fanned an incipient rebellion by preaching a fiery sermon (May 1559) urging alliance with England against France and the papacy.[77] Unlike Calvin, who limited the right of rebellion to those holding positions of responsibility, Knox believed private individuals had the right to strike down a tyrant ruler. In fact, Scotland's rebellion was firmly guided by the lesser nobility and bolstered by troops sent from England. When Mary of Guise died (June 1560), France withdrew its troops. The Scots parliament, with an unusual number of lesser nobles in attendance, abolished papal authority, forbade the mass, and adopted a Calvinist confession of faith. Even though it seems the majority of Scotland's population was Catholic for some years thereafter, parliament's decision was not to be reversed.

Mary Stuart, now a widow, returned to her kingdom in 1561.[78] She insisted on Catholic worship in her own chapel but had no power to restore Catholicism in her realm, and she also had other interests. Following a series of plots animated by her claims to the English throne, Mary fled to England (1568), where, after one more plot, she was executed by order of Elizabeth (1587).[79] The question that remained was how the new Scots church was to be governed. Initially, decisions on church appointments were made by a council of leading Protestant nobles. This authority was soon transferred to a general assembly in which clergy also voted, though they were outnumbered by lay representatives of the towns and the nobility. A Geneva model, favored by some, would have decisions made by assemblies in which clergy had the dominant voice. But there were also bishops who accepted the Reformation and continued governing their churches, despite the change in theology; some leading Scots, looking to conformity with England, argued for an episcopal form of church government.[80] The debate among these options would continue until Scotland again rose in rebellion in the 1630s, this time against an English king and his bishops.[81]

The Wittelsbach ruler of the Rhineland Palatinate was one of the seven electoral princes of the Holy Roman Empire.[82] Elector Louis V (d. 1544), a close ally of Charles V, kept aloof from the Reformation that was steadily gaining ground in his corner of south Germany. Louis's brother and successor, Elector Frederick II (d. 1556), set his course by the political weathervane: he introduced a Lutheran church order in 1546; rescinded it in 1548, after Charles V's victory in the First Schmalkaldic War; and restored it again in 1553, when the tide had turned against the emperor. Frederick's nephew Ottheinrich (ruled 1556–1559) gave Protestantism a firm footing by recruiting leading Protestant scholars for the university of Heidelberg and reorganizing his privy council along confessional lines. He also created a church council to govern religious affairs.[83] The only question was which kind of Protestantism the Palatinate was embracing.

Elector Frederick III (ruled 1559–1576), from a junior branch of the Wittelsbach family, had been converted to Lutheranism by his wife. Offended by a bitter dispute over the Lord's Supper between Lutheran and Calvinist theology professors brought in by Ottheinrich, he dismissed both of the chief antagonists. Convinced by his study of the issue that the Calvinist interpretation was correct, he took the bold step of announcing his intention to introduce Calvinism in his lands. Calvinism had no legitimate standing in the empire according to the 1555 Peace of Augsburg, a fact made clear at a 1561 meeting that was intended to demonstrate unity among Germany's Protestant princes but showed instead the deep division between the Lutheran majority and a small Calvinist party led by Frederick III. But persistence by a capable ruler of such an important territory brought tacit recognition of Calvinism in the empire. The *Heidelberg Catechism* (1563), drafted by two theology professors Frederick had appointed, was to be widely used and admired in other Calvinist churches.

The next step was to ensure good discipline, to prevent God's church from being sullied by the presence of ungodly members. The church council's proposal (1564) to leave discipline in the hands of civil officials touched off an important family dispute between the two main branches of Reformed Protestantism. Geneva and Zurich had reached agreement on the Lord's Supper in 1549, and since then theologians of both camps formed a common front against Lutheran and Catholic attacks by minimizing their remaining differences. But Calvin stood for control of church affairs by the church itself, while Zwingli's heirs believed discipline was the prerogative of godly magistrates. Thomas Erastus (1524–1583), a medical professor at Heidelberg, prepared a statement of the Zwinglian view, arguing that the jurisdiction civil authorities exercised over offenses against God (like blasphemy) properly extended to excommunicating public sinners from the church. Theodore Beza, Calvin's successor in Geneva, asserted that only officers of the church, not civil magistrates, were called upon to make judgments based on divine law.[84] The Palatinate's 1570 church ordinance threaded a path between both views: boards of lay elders were created, as the Calvinists wished, but only civil officials had the authority to excommunicate sinners or even scold them in public.

Frederick III knew that his eldest son and heir, a devout Lutheran, would change course once more. In fact, Elector Louis VI (ruled 1576–1583) brought in Lutheran professors for the university, Lutheran pastors for the churches, and Lutheran jurists for his administrative councils. But Frederick III in his later years gained immense prestige in the Calvinist world by sending troops to the aid of embattled coreligionists in France and the Netherlands, commanded by his younger sons, John Casimir and Christopher. As regent of the Palatinate (1583–1592) for his nephew, the son of Louis VI, John Casimir was able to bring back the Calvinist professors and administrators his older brother had sent packing. This time the Calvinist imprint took hold. By the time of Elector Frederick V (ruled 1610–1623), Louis VI's grandson, a thoroughly Calvinist Palatinate was ready for a leadership role in a grand alliance of European Protestant powers.[85]

These four Calvinist movements differed from one another as well as from their Genevan model. French Calvinists created the first national church organization, Dutch Calvinists embraced for various reasons a more selective idea of church membership, and Scottish Calvinists departed even more than their French and Dutch confreres did from Calvin's caution about mixing the gospel with political rebellion. The experience of the Palatinate shows that Calvinism, a revolutionary movement in the three other countries, could also accommodate itself to princely rule. What these four churches had in common was an allegiance to Calvin's teaching (with bits of Zwinglian influence) and to the Reformed tradition's thoroughgoing repudiation of the religious past.

Just as Catholicism in its Counter-Reformation form found nothing of any value in Protestantism, Protestantism in its Calvinist form found nothing of any value in Catholicism. The warfare between adherents of these competing doctrines that broke out along many fronts may thus seem to have been inevitable. In fact it was not. Street fighting (as in France) between groups that despise each other's beliefs makes a riot, not a war. The next three chapters will show that the religious wars fought by Europeans of this era must also be understood from the perspective of what contemporaries called reason of state.

III | POLITICS

Not all rulers in sixteenth-century Europe were princes. The Republic of Venice, a major trading and naval power, was governed by its large hereditary aristocracy, all of whose adult males had the right to attend meetings of the Senate. Florence, a major banking and cloth-manufacturing center, was a republic until one of its great families, the Medici, succeeded in transforming themselves into hereditary princes. When Switzerland defeated the armies of the Holy Roman Empire (1499, see below), the Swiss cantons too were republics, recognizing no princely authority. Throughout Europe, large and midsize cities thought of themselves as republics, for they governed their internal affairs without much interference from the princes whose military protection they depended on, and whose taxes they paid.

Whether princely or republican, all European regimes of this era had three things in common. First, like governments in other parts of the world, they saw themselves as ruling in the name of God.[1] This meant it was their duty to take measures to ensure that the Lord on high did not withdraw His protection from their land. Late medieval Catholic governments promoted shrines and patron saints especially associated with the territory or its ruling dynasty and closely watched how the clergy conducted its business, to make sure divine worship was performed properly according to church law. Further, since God entrusted the temporal affairs of the realm to its government, rulers had the right to make the temporal wealth of the church serve the common good of the territory. For example, if it seemed money were being drained off to Rome for no good purpose, a ruler like Saxony's Elector Frederick the Wise presumed authority to ban the preaching of papal indulgences within his borders.[2]

Princes preserved the loyalty of great families in part by promising them honorable positions in the church for their younger sons and daughters.[3]

121

Territorial treasuries also had some benefit from revenues that could be extracted from ecclesiastical foundations, despite their claims to immunity from taxation. Since state interests of this kind collided with the papacy's claims to control both the taxation of church wealth and appointments to high positions, governments had to ward off unwanted interference from Rome.[4] Late medieval rulers did this by having friends in the Roman Curia. By about 1450, the college of cardinals[5] had become a kind of central station for Europe's multiple lines of political conflict, as great princes obtained red hats for their own bishops, while lesser ones formed connections among the college's numerous Italian cardinals. Protestant rulers of the Reformation era would solve these problems more simply, by seizing control of church property and claiming the right of appointment for themselves.

Second, the control that every regime had over its own territory represented a fragile truce among potential foes. Town governments had great difficulty containing long-simmering feuds among their great families, and there was also social conflict between the body of great families, who saw themselves as naturally suited to govern, and commoners who did not see their interests being served through rule by the self-styled better sort of people.[6] Kings depended on their nobles to command their armies and staff certain administrative posts, but nobles knew their ancestors had been virtual princes in their family lands and could easily be mobilized to rebellion against the crown, with the backing of their kinsmen who occupied high positions in the church. Towns built and maintained their own defensive walls and had citizen militias to defend the walls against the ruler himself if he infringed on their privileges. These powerful groups— the nobles, the high church officials, and the towns—each had a voice in the representative assemblies or parliaments that were common throughout Latin Christendom.[7] Fortunate was the prince who mobilized the three estates (as they were called) behind his policies, especially for the approval of new taxes.[8] Unfortunate was the prince against whom the three estates raised a common standard of revolt. In the Reformation era these internal conflicts were overlaid with new religious differences, making new enemies or leading traditional foes to fight one another with real appetite.

Third, every regime had external enemies, usually not very far away. To a monarch nothing was more important than his own honor or esteem; a ruler whose neighbors believed they could injure him with impunity afforded his subjects little protection. Hence, a young prince who did not go to war in the early years of his reign was thought peculiar and might even begin losing the respect of powerful subjects. The prince's councillors, many trained in the law, had no trouble pointing to nearby territories of which their master's ancestors had been wrongfully deprived. Towns of any size had well-defined economic interests putting them at odds with their neighbors; it was not uncommon even for towns subject to the same prince to fight their own miniwars for control of markets or access to the sea—hence, the wisdom of the ancient Roman maxim, "divide and conquer." To weaken an enemy territory, one offered bribes and suitable promises to powerful men who hated the current regime. Cross-border conflicts were always entangled with internal rivalries in each of the warring states. The complicating factor of sixteenth- and early seventeenth-century warfare was that invading armies of a given religious persuasion also counted on the support of beleaguered coreligionists within the borders of an enemy territory where a rival creed held sway.

This section of the book illustrates the Reformation era entanglement of politics and religion, each influencing the other. Chapter 8, "The Wars of Italy, 1494–1559," reviews the primary nexus of conflicts bequeathed by late medieval rulers to their sixteenth-century successors. This inherited pattern of warfare explains why Charles V, the ardently Catholic emperor, could only devote part of his time and resources to settling accounts with Protestant Germany's Schmalkaldic League. Chapter 9, "Wars of Religion, 1562–1648," focuses on a series of wars fought by the fervently Catholic Habsburgs of later generations. Here one sees the impact of religion on politics, because the Habsburgs' Protestant foes, backed at crucial moments by anti-Habsburg Catholic powers, were able to prevent Europe from coming under the hegemony of a single dynasty. Chapter 10, "The European Reformations," examines the impact of politics on religion through government-sponsored reformations in Scandinavia, the Dutch Republic, and Habsburg Austria. The complex story of England's many rulers and many Reformations requires separate discussion (Chapter 11).

8 | Politics

The Wars of Italy, 1494–1559

To understand the network of conflicts that Charles V inherited from his late medieval forebears, it will be helpful to start by glancing at six major players: the Italian states, the Ottoman Empire, Spain, France, the Holy Roman Empire, and the Low Countries.

Italy was Europe's teacher in many respects,[1] but it was not unified as a nation until 1870. There were not nearly as many separate states in 1450 as in 1250, since larger territories had gobbled up smaller ones until there were only five major powers: the Duchy of Milan; the Republic of Venice; Florence; the Kingdom of Naples, which from 1453 also included Sicily;[2] and the Papal States. These five signed a treaty (1454) implicitly recognizing a balance of power: further aggrandizement by any one would be resisted by the others. But during the forty years of relative peace that ensued, wealthy Italy invited the envious gaze of the "barbarian" kingdoms.[3] From 1494, Italy became the preferred battleground for contests between Europe's great powers.

The portion of Italy's Lombard plain[4] covered by the duchy of Milan was thickly dotted with flourishing cities and famous for its highly developed agriculture, tracing back to monasteries that drained marshes and enterprising noble landowners who pioneered in introducing new crops. Milan's political evolution was typical for cities in north and central Italy. Burghers formed a self-governing commune during the eleventh century, but the communal government was never strong enough to suppress violent feuding among the great families.[5] By the end of the thirteenth century, burghers accepted rule by a single dominant family as a means of restoring order. The family of city-lords[6] that controlled Milan from 1313 to 1451[7] conquered or annexed other cities far and wide, until their ambition was checked by Venice (see below). The new Sforza dynasty

(1454–1498) was more modest in its aims. After 1494, rich and compact Milan would be the favored target of foreign invaders.

By tradition, Venice limited her ambitions to the sea. She rose to commercial dominance in the eastern Mediterranean first by supplying the Byzantine empire with badly needed naval power, then by fighting off a century-long challenge from Genoa, Italy's other great maritime power.[8] But Milan's expansion toward the Adriatic during the fifteenth century caused Venetians to realize that the republic's small strip of mainland territory did not provide adequate protection.[9] With their characteristic energy, Venetian statesmen built up the needed infrastructure for land warfare, hired the best mercenary generals, and conquered a large swath of northeastern Italy. Unlike the restive subject towns of other Italian states,

Figure 8.1. The Christ of late Renaissance art. Titian (ca. 1488–1576), "The Temptation of Christ" (Cf. Matt. 4:4). (*William Hood Dunwoody Fund, Minneapolis Institute of Art.*)

like Milan,[10] Venice's mainland cities were ruled with moderation and fortified by the latest military technology. Venice was without doubt Italy's
best-governed state and most formidable power, on land as at sea. This
made her dangerous to foreign invaders but untrustworthy to all other
Italian states.

Florence, proud of its communal traditions, resisted longer than other
cities the transition to rule by a single family. In the century following the
beginning of Medici rule in 1434, citizen revolts re-created the communal
republic from 1494 to 1512 and again from 1527 to 1530. The Medici finally
secured their authority through alliance with Habsburg Spain, now Italy's
dominant power (see below).

In Naples, the kingdom's fractious nobility was strong enough over the
centuries to limit the influence of quasi-autonomous cities along the coast
and to prevent the crown from undertaking any unwanted administrative
streamlining, while dominating the rural economy in ways that left peasant cultivators few incentives for improvement. Naples was the largest
and most populous of Italy's great states, but in time of war no one could
predict whether its nobles would rally to the king or to his enemy. The
strong governance of Charles V's viceroy, Pedro Alvarez de Toledo
(1532–1553), brought the nobility to accept Spanish rule, but did not significantly curtail their control of the countryside and the inland towns.

The Papal States were unified more in name than in fact.[11] Anarchy
reigned following the Avignon papacy and the papal schism (1304–1414),[12]
forcing popes to devote their energies to squalid wars against bandit chieftains. Finally, Pope Julius II (ruled 1503–1513) donned armor himself and
led his troops to some important victories. This violated canon law—no
priest was to shed blood in battle, much less Christian blood[13]—but by
handing his conquests over to papal officials, not to his own relatives, Julius
enabled his successors to have their hands free for other matters.[14]

The Ottoman Empire. The first Ottoman sultans were chieftains of a Turkish band influenced by the Islamic warrior ideal of battling infidels on the
frontier. Starting from a base in central Asia Minor, the Ottomans were
making conquests in Europe's Balkan Peninsula by the fourteenth century.
Their capture of Constantinople and the remnants of the Byzantine Empire
(1453) created a unified domain stretching from eastern Asia Minor deep
into the Balkans. Land taxes supported a formidable military machine:
Janissaries (footsoldiers), who were taken as boys from Christian villages
and raised to be Islamic warriors,[15] and the mounted Turkish archers
whose rapid wheeling tactics were never effectively countered by Christian armies. Ottoman rule also provided the justice that stable government
requires; many Christian peasants in the Balkans found the taxes demanded by their new Turkish masters more predictable and hence more
tolerable than the arbitrary exactions of their erstwhile Christian lords.

The early years of the sixteenth century witnessed a series of triumphs that made Ottoman arms seem invincible. The Asia Minor frontier was secured when the armies of Iran's new Safavid dynasty were crushed in 1514. Egypt's Mamluk Sultanate collapsed in a single battle (1517), giving the Ottomans control of the North African coast as far west as what is now Tunisia. Great Christian citadels on the island of Rhodes and in Belgrade, capital of what remained of the Orthodox Christian kingdom of Serbia, fell in the same year (1522). In 1526 Hungary's army was destroyed and its rash young king killed in battle against a vastly larger Ottoman force at Mohàcs, south of Budapest. Sultan Suleyman the Lawgiver (ruled 1520–1566) was young, vigorous, and intelligent. What would be his next conquests? This was Christian Europe's nightmare.

Spain's two separate kingdoms, Castile and Aragon, were united but not amalgamated by the marriage of Isabella of Castile and Ferdinand of Aragon (1476). Each kingdom, hitherto torn by its own civil war, welcomed the peace this marriage brought. Hence, the parliaments, or *cortes*, in both realms willingly endorsed most of the new measures proposed by Spain's "Catholic Kings," as Ferdinand and Isabella styled themselves.[16] Isabella (d. 1504) tackled Castile's internal affairs with uncommon energy.[17] She reformed the religious orders by backing the efforts of her confessor to make Castilian houses join the observant branch of their respective congregations.[18] She reformed judicial and financial administration by excluding the great nobles from posts they traditionally occupied and replacing them with university-trained lawyers from burgher or lesser noble families. With the consent of Castile's *cortes*, she also required each village to provide a proportional number of able-bodied men for repressing banditry.

Ferdinand (d. 1516) found a military use for Isabella's recruitment system: Granada, last of the Islamic principalities that had once encompassed most of the Iberian Peninsula, was conquered in 1492. Ferdinand next turned his ambitions to Naples, ruled by a cousin who represented the illegitimate branch of his family. Meanwhile, his military advisers designed, and devised training exercises for, new infantry units that combined the latest in weaponry[19] with tactical methods recommended in Roman military manuals. Spain's fighting men would prove their mettle in Italy, first in Ferdinand's time, then under his grandson, Charles V.

France became a different kind of kingdom in the course of its eventual victory in the Hundred Years' War (1337–1453), a struggle with England that dominated European politics of the era.[20] As with other monarchs in Europe, earlier French kings needed the approval of their estates or representative assemblies to introduce and maintain new forms of taxation. But during the last stages of the war, the Estates General[21] made grants of taxation without attaching the usual three-year time limit. It may be that the assembled deputies simply wanted their king to end the dreary years of war by whatever means necessary, but no reason for this novelty is given in the documents. The provincial estates still had to be consulted on some issues,[22] but France's king henceforth had what no other European prince had—the freedom to levy taxes and even raise the rates at will. King Charles VII (ruled 1422–1461) used the opportunity to create so-called companies of ordinance, a permanent or standing army, the first in Europe since the collapse of the Roman empire;[23] in peacetime units were garrisoned in the towns.

Charles VII's son Louis XI (ruled 1461–1483) displayed a new and exalted understanding of royal authority. He was not merely the overlord of

Figure 8.2. Sketch of a Janissary. Sketch of a Janissary by the Venetian artist Giovanni Bellini, who visited Istanbul during the reign of Sultan Mehmed II (1451–1481). (*British Museum, London.*)

his vassals,[24] France's great nobles, he also was their sovereign, a Roman law term denoting the source of all lawful authority.[25] Instead of socializing with his nobles, as was customary, Louis preferred the company of honest burghers, loyal to the crown. The great vassals rose in rebellion under the leadership of Duke Charles the Bold of Burgundy (ruled 1467–1477), a prince of the royal blood whose family now controlled most of the Low Countries (see below). But Louis XI used the companies of ordinance to quell the revolt. When the same Charles of Burgundy aimed at building a powerful kingdom along France's eastern border, Louis used royal tax revenues to pay the Swiss pikemen who brought Burgundy's dreams to a dismal end.

Louis XI's son Charles VIII (ruled 1483–1498) inherited the throne as a boy, and as he grew to manhood the court was abuzz with plans for France's greater glory. Seasoned commanders pointed to nearby provinces that might be incorporated within the kingdom without much risk, but the young and inexperienced king had grander ideas: the royal family had recently inherited a claim to the Kingdom of Naples, a thousand miles beyond France's borders. In 1494 Charles VIII marched across the Alps at the head of 30,000 men, including the companies of France's standing army and a large contingent of Swiss and German mercenaries.

Foremost among the rulers of the *Holy Roman Empire*'s approximately 3,000 separate jurisdictions were the imperial princes, especially the seven princes who had the right to elect the emperor. Four of the electors were lay princes,[26] and three were from the ranks of the prince-bishops.[27] Far more numerous were smaller territories, mostly in south Germany, that had purchased from the emperor grants of immunity freeing them from the authority of one of the princes and submitting them instead to a merely nominal control by the emperor himself. There were eighty free imperial cities, including many once ruled by their prince-bishops; over a thousand free imperial knights reigning over postage-stamp territories; and a few communities of free imperial peasants.

The emperor could not overcome this multiplicity of jurisdictions, because his effective authority was limited to the lands in which he was also the hereditary prince. Emperor Frederick III (ruled 1440–1493)[28] rarely set foot outside his Habsburg family's Austrian duchies. To make up for the lack of imperial leadership, late medieval towns and princes had formed regional federations among themselves, but only two of these survived into the sixteenth century: the Hanseatic League, a powerful association of merchant cities in north Germany,[29] and the Swabian League, a union of princes and free cities in southwestern Germany.

The imperial diet, dating from the fourteenth century, provided the only forum for a national discussion of Germany's problems. Imperial princes attended in person or sent representatives, as did the magistrates of south Germany's more important free imperial cities.[30] One issue the diets discussed was the lack of public order.[31] Since there was no national judicial frame-work for settling quarrels, princes, knights, and towns regularly resorted to arms instead.[32] Merchants crossing the borders of Germany's many territories with their goods were liable to encounter robber barons exacting what they called tolls[33] or bandits who made off with the merchandise altogether.

From about 1450, there was talk of addressing this problem through a diet-sponsored "reformation" of imperial government. The plan involved a court to which Germany's princes and towns would be obliged to take their differences, a small standing army to enforce the court's verdicts, and an empire-wide tax (the first ever) to pay the troops. Frederick III was not enthusiastic about seeing the diet increase its authority in this way. But in his first year as emperor Frederick's son and successor, Maximilian I (1493–1519), struck a bargain with leaders of the diet: He approved the imperial reform plan, and the diet in return granted him money for a military expedition across the Alps to punish Venice for encroaching on Habsburg land. As it turned out, Maximilian failed to capture the city in Venetian territory he besieged, and imperial reform did not fare much better. The diet duly created an Imperial High Court and approved a Common Penny tax, but the Swiss Confederation refused to pay; the troops sent by the diet to make the Swiss change their minds met an ignominious defeat (1499). This did not bode well for compliance with the tax nor for the prestige of the new court. For Germans of Luther's generation, imperial reform was one more "reformation" that fell short of its promises.

For much of the Middle Ages, the *Low Countries*[34] was a purely geographical expression, denoting the low-lying lands formed by the North Sea deltas of the Rhine, Meuse, and Scheldt Rivers. Some of the principalities to be found here were mainly French-speaking, but the most important were three Netherlandish-speaking territories with large urban populations: the county of Flanders, including the great cities of Ghent and Bruges; the duchy of Brabant, with Antwerp and Brussels; and the county of Holland, with numerous small cities, such as Amsterdam, that only became important in later centuries. Set in an area where major trade routes converged,[35] the Low Countries harbored northern Europe's greatest wool-manufacturing centers (Ghent and Bruges) and its main banking and mercantile hub (Bruges in the fourteenth century, Antwerp in the fifteenth). Peasant cultivators in this market-oriented region developed new farming techniques that increased grain yields dramatically.[36] It remained for the dukes of Burgundy to create a unifying political framework for these enterprising provinces.

Duke Philip the Bold (d. 1404), the first of his line, ruled the French province of Burgundy as the younger brother of King Charles V (d. 1380). By marrying the daughter and sole heiress of the count of Flanders, he put himself in position to arrange further marriages that ultimately brought most of the Low Countries provinces, including Brabant and Holland, under Burgundian rule. His son and grandson played key roles in the long war between England and France, first as allies of England, then in the final stages as an ally of their royal cousin, the king of France.[37] The Burgundian rulers kept a lavish court in Brussels, engaging the talents of some extraordinary regional artists[38] and using their tax revenues to fund magnificent pageants that glorified the chivalric values of the European aristocracy. Young Low Countries noblemen connected with the court were reared in a culture that prized above all things the honor that was gained by having vengeance against one's enemies and also by making war in distant lands against the foes of Christendom.[39]

The grandest of Burgundian dreams were those of Duke Charles the Bold (ruled 1467–1477), last of his family in the direct male line. Charles overrode the deep-rooted political separatism of his lands and squeezed their wealth in order to finance plans for a new kingdom in the western borderlands of the Holy Roman Empire, between his Low Countries provinces and Switzerland.[40] Twice defeated by the Swiss, he perished in a foolish assault on the fortified city of Nancy in Lorraine (1477). Louis XI took the opportunity to repossess the duchy of Burgundy, a rich prize.

Mary of Burgundy, Charles the Bold's daughter and heiress, chose as her husband and protector Maximilian of Habsburg, the future Emperor Maximilian I. When Mary died in a fall from her horse a few years later

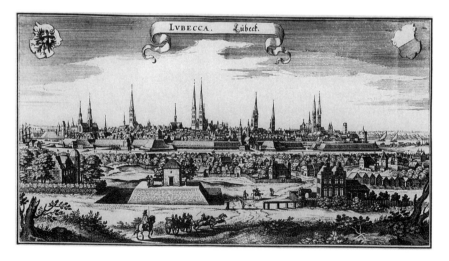

Figure 8.3. The free imperial city of Lübeck. From Matthaeus Merian, Martin Zeiller, Topographia Germaniae (17 vols. facsimile reprint of second edition {Frankfurt, 1655], Kassel: Bärenreiter, 1959–1967), vol. XIV, following p. 154. (*University of Minnesota Library.*)

(1482), Maximilian had to weather some very difficult years in dealing with provinces that rejected the centralizing machinery put in place by Charles the Bold[41] and resented being ruled by a foreigner. The Habsburg dynasty survived here only because Maximilian's son and grandson were accepted as "natural" princes.[42] Archduke Philip died relatively young (1506), but his wife Juana of Castile (daughter of Ferdinand and Isabella) had given birth to a son in Ghent in 1500. This boy, christened Charles, would in manhood bring together the imperial title of his paternal grandfather, Maximilian of Habsburg; the Spanish lands of his maternal grandparents, Ferdinand and Isabella; and the Burgundian dreams of his great-grandfather and namesake, Charles the Bold.

During the campaigning season of 1494 France's Charles VIII led a magnificent army through Italy toward Naples. A force of 30,000 men had not been seen in the peninsula for centuries, and France's innovative military engineers had in their train siege cannon that cracked open strongly walled fortresses one after another. As Florence's Medici ruler[43] went out to meet in person the king whose passage he dared not oppose, his pro-French subjects rebelled, creating the Second Florentine Republic (1494–1512).[44] In Naples the king's[45] armies melted away, allowing Charles to be crowned as king. But even France's treasury did not permit an army on the march to be paid and fed for months at a time, and Charles had not reckoned on the malarial fevers of the southern kingdom's marshy lands. As his men sickened or deserted, Charles ordered a withdrawal, but it was too late to preserve his prestige. States that had hailed his southward march sniped at his northward retreat, and the troops he left behind could not hold Naples for France. Some at the French court were sobered by this great waste of treasure and blood. But dreams of glory do not die so easily.

Upon the death of the childless Charles VIII, the throne passed to his cousin, the duke of Orléans, who became king as Louis XII (ruled 1498–1515). Louis immediately focused on the duchy of Milan, to which his branch of the French royal family nurtured a claim tracing back more than a century.[46] French armies repeated their initial victories of four years earlier, so quickly that Louis entered upon a further campaign, to make good his predecessor's claim to Naples. Ferdinand of Aragon had made Louis an offer he could not refuse: the two monarchs would jointly conquer Naples and divide it between them. But Ferdinand gave his remodeled army orders to attack not the armies of Naples, whose loyalty to their own king was doubtful in any case, but the unsuspecting French. Their success left Spain in control of the kingdom of Naples, while France held Milan.

What historians have dubbed the Wars of Italy (1494–1559) were just beginning. Like the great-power conflicts of more recent times, including the Cold War, the Italian wars drew states great and small into a vortex of rivalry. Pope Julius II, hoping to end Venetian occupation of what had been a part of the Papal States, made an alliance with France (1508–1509). Emperor Maximilian I, having an eye on certain other lands held by Venice, joined the anti-Venetian coalition, setting aside for the moment his long-standing grievances against France.[47] Hard-pressed, Venice was forced to disgorge some of her recent conquests in separate treaties with the coalition partners. Julius then recruited Venice and Spain for a campaign against the French in Milan, promoted in Italy as a war to drive out the "barbarians" and in the rest of Europe as a Holy League to free the pope from French domination (1511–1512). England's young Henry VIII (ruled 1509–1547), eager for a good war, agreed with Ferdinand of Aragon on a joint invasion of southern France. But Ferdinand had other plans. While French troops in the region were kept busy watching the English encampment, Spanish forces occupied the Spanish portion of the hitherto independent kingdom of Navarre.[48] In Italy, French forces won signal victories in Lombardy but were driven from Milan following defeat by Swiss troops fighting under the papal banner (1513). Meanwhile, Spanish troops had restored Medici rule in Florence (1512)[49] and now controlled the vital port of Genoa as well. Though Milan itself was not in Spanish hands,[50] Spain was becoming the dominant power in the north of Italy as well as the south.

A new French king meant a new cycle of war. Francis I (ruled 1515–1547) regained Milan through a brilliant victory at Marignano (1515), in which many of the Swiss units, won over by French gold, changed sides at the last minute.[51] But in Brussels Archduke Charles, soon to be France's great enemy, was just now reaching manhood. Following the death of his maternal grandfather Ferdinand (1516), Charles entrusted the regency of the Low Countries to his aunt, Margaret of Austria (d. 1530), and sailed to Spain, where he was recognized by the separate parliaments of each realm as king of Castile and king of Aragon (1517). But the Holy Roman Empire was not a hereditary monarchy. Upon the death of Charles's paternal grandfather, Emperor Maximilian I (1519), Francis I of France announced his candidacy for the imperial throne. Charles, backed by loans from south Germany's great banking families,[52] had to outbid Francis in buying the votes of the seven electoral princes. In Castile and Aragon there were rumbles of trouble over the free-spending ways of the office-hungry courtiers whom Charles had brought with him from the Low Countries. Leaving his subordinates behind to deal with major revolts in both Spanish kingdoms,[53] Charles sailed to the Low Countries and made his way to the German city of Aachen, near Cologne, for his solemn recognition as Emperor

Charles V.[54] Since Charles had decided to reside in Spain, the richest of his realms, he delegated control of Habsburg Austria to his younger brother Ferdinand (ruled 1521–1564), who was also to represent him in the affairs of the empire. This was the origin of the later division between the Spanish and the Austrian branches of the house of Habsburg.

Having secured his multiple inheritances, Charles was ready for his contest with Francis I. The Habsburg-Valois[55] rivalry was more than a series of battles over territory. French diplomats saw France itself as beset on three sides by Habsburg might—the Low Countries in the north, the empire in the east,[56] and the Pyrenees mountain frontier with Spain in the south. By maintaining a foothold in Italy, France could break out of this encirclement and also serve the larger interests of Christian Europe by preventing its domination by a single power. From Charles's point of view, the interest of Christian Europe lay in having stronger defenses against Ottoman Turkish expansion; he himself was the natural leader in this great cause, but he was prevented from giving it his full attention because the perfidious French refused to accept Charles's control of lands of which he was the lawful overlord.

Charles was as eager as other young rulers to prove himself in combat, but he could only reach the Italian theater of war by crossing seas controlled by his enemies. North African corsairs patrolled the western Mediterranean and raided coastal settlements in Charles's kingdoms of Naples and Aragon. The chief Christian naval power in the area was Genoa, which had cast off Spanish rule and was now allied with the French. Hence, Charles remained in Spain, depending on the German mercenaries whose passage across the Alps was arranged by his brother Ferdinand. The seasoned Spanish commanders and pro-Habsburg Italian princes who led Charles's forces in Italy served him well. On 24 February 1525, the emperor's birthday, a multinational Habsburg army overwhelmed the French at Pavia, near Milan; 8,000 French were killed, and King Francis I, taken prisoner, was sent off to captivity in Spain. In long and courteous discussions with his royal captive, Charles extracted the fruits of victory. In the Treaty of Madrid (1526) Francis I promised to restore to Charles the duchy of Burgundy, the country of his ancestors.

In fact, no French king could give away Burgundy and keep his throne—especially after Burgundy's estates refused to accept the treaty that would have severed their province from France.[57] Moreover, Francis's repudiation of a treaty he claimed he had signed under duress met with a sympathetic reaction in many quarters. In Italy, even if Charles refrained from asserting his own claim to Milan,[58] Spanish regulars garrisoned key citadels of the duchy, within easy reach of a number of other states. On the wider European stage, after the defeat and death of Hungary's king at Mohàcs

(1526), Ferdinand of Habsburg, the king's brother-in-law, moved in to claim the kingdom of Bohemia and what was left of the kingdom of Hungary.[59] Hence, Charles and his family now seemed dangerously close to a hegemony[60] that made other powers nervous. Little realizing that France was already conducting secret discussions with the Ottomans for military collaboration against the Habsburgs, Pope Clement VII signed a secret treaty of alliance with Francis I (1526).

In 1527, Genoa's fleet ferried a large French army to Naples; by pre-arrangement (as Habsburg diplomats rightly suspected), Naples's defense forces had been drawn off elsewhere by the attacks of North African corsairs. Quick French victories in Naples threatened to overturn Habsburg power in Italy altogether. But one of Charles's Neapolitan commanders

Figure 8.4. King Francis I of France (reigned 1515–1547). Jean Clouet (1485/ 90–1540/41), "Francis I." (*Musée du Louvre, Paris.*)

saved the day by reporting that Andrea Doria, Genoa's leading admiral, was unhappy with his treatment by the French. Suitable overtures brought a change of allegiance. Doria's fleet ferried Spanish troops to Naples, where they began pushing out the French. Doria himself, the era's greatest naval strategist, became one of Charles's key advisers.

Meanwhile, some 10,000 German mercenaries, again sent by Ferdinand, were marching across the Alps. But since Charles's credit was overextended, money to pay the troops was not forthcoming,[61] and, as mercenaries often did if not paid, they jumped the traces. They became not so much an army as an angry, ill-disciplined rabble storming through Italy. Since many of the Germans were Protestants (if not the Spaniards, who had joined them from garrisons in Lombardy), they had no trouble choosing one among the emperor's enemies on whom to wreak their fury: papal Rome. The best that Charles's viceroy of Naples could do was to help Pope Clement VII himself escape from his fortified castle of Sant'Angelo. Rome itself was less fortunate: thousands of civilians were slaughtered, untold women were raped, and many of the city's churches were plundered and desecrated. At first, Charles's advisers and pamphlet-writers[62] tried to claim credit for this vindication of the emperor's position as head of the Christian world at the expense of a perfidious pope.[63] Only as the horror of the Sack of Rome (May 1527) became more widely known did they switch to arguing that the emperor himself was not responsible for what had happened.

With the protection afforded by Doria's fleet, Charles was able to bring an army to Italy himself, intending to push across the Alps into France. But France now agreed to a treaty (1529) accepting the status quo in Italy.[64] Since another of Charles's goals was reconciliation with Pope Clement VII, a member of the Medici family,[65] he used his army to besiege Florence, which had again rebelled against the Medici and created a republic (1527–1530). Even before Florence was conquered, he arranged to have himself crowned by the pope as Holy Roman Emperor.[66] The ceremony, preceded by talks between pope and emperor, took place in Bologna (November 1529–April 1530), because Charles was en route to Germany. Pope and emperor agreed that the rage visited on Rome by German mercenaries a few years before was but a token of the evils that might be expected if heresy continued to spread unchecked. Clement demanded that Charles combat heresy by any means necessary, including the force of arms. Charles demanded that Clement combat heresy by convoking a council to reform the Catholic Church, but he suspected (rightly) that Clement was too fearful for his own authority to risk a council. Might Charles have to arrange a religious settlement in Germany on his own authority, as some of his advisers suggested? Or could he trust that France would keep the recently concluded peace treaty, permitting him, if need be, to deal with his heretical subjects by sterner means? In this uncertain frame of mind, Charles crossed the Alps, en route to the Diet of Augsburg.

In Germany Charles faced a host of problems. Most worrisome was the security of the empire's southeastern frontier. At Vienna (1529), a massive siege army led by Sultan Suleyman himself had been held off only because a relief garrison force approved by the imperial diet (Protestants as well as Catholics) arrived in the nick of time. To this Turkish provocation there had to be a Christian and imperial response, the sooner the better. Meanwhile, Ferdinand had been complaining that he had no respect among Germany's princes. His solution—to which Charles assented—was to have the electoral princes elect him as King of the Romans, a title sometimes borne by the emperor's designated successor.[67] Not surprisingly, it was the leading Protestant princes—Philip of Hesse and Elector John of Saxony—who objected most loudly to this presumption of a Habsburg family claim to the imperial office. Thus Charles needed Protestant cooperation both to have his brother elevated to a new dignity and to build an army to send against the Ottomans. In these circumstances, the fact that Hesse and Saxony were forming what they claimed was a purely defensive alliance (the Schmalkaldic League), though worrisome, was of lesser concern.[68]

Ferdinand was recognized as King of the Romans, even by Saxony and Hesse, and in 1532 a large imperial force took the field to march against the Turks. Charles's participation in this campaign was minimal, and he turned his face homeward as soon as the withdrawal of an opposing Turkish army made it decent for him to do so. The emperor wanted Ferdinand to negotiate a truce with the Ottomans, rather than incurring the risk of war.[69] Charles had great difficulty deploying his resources as far away as Vienna, but he was not shirking his duty as Christendom's defender; rather, as he wrote to Ferdinand, he would do his crusading at sea.

In response to a Habsburg naval assault on Ottoman territory,[70] Sultan Suleyman commissioned Khair-ad-din Barbarossa, a former corsair, as admiral of the Ottoman fleet. In 1534, Barbarossa, with seventy galleys, unchallenged by Doria's twenty, raided at will along the coasts of Sicily and Naples, then seized Tunis in North Africa as a base for further operations. With Doria as his strategist, Charles devoted the better part of a year to supervising preparations for a massive onslaught on Barbarossa's new headquarters. Meanwhile, a Schmalkaldic League army paid for by France conquered the southwest-German duchy of Württemberg, hitherto a Habsburg-administered territory;[71] this was troublesome, but France—the root of the problem—could be dealt with later. The huge armada that sailed against Tunis (1535) won a great victory, perhaps the greatest of Charles's military career. Prints and tapestries showing the crusading emperor taking counsel with his commanders before Tunis were produced in the Low Countries for wide distribution. This was how Charles wanted to be remembered.

It was now time to deal with France. Charles sailed for Italy with a large army and pushed across the Alps into Provence (1536). But this campaign accomplished nothing, and for the next two years fighting on various fronts alternated with negotiations, until another peace with France was concluded (1538). But even as he finally turned his attention to Germany (1539), the emperor was still preoccupied by Muslim corsairs—especially Barbarossa, whose fleet was now based at Algiers. If the theological negotiations recommended by his "soft hand" advisers could solve Charles's problems in Germany,[72] he would be able to deploy his resources for a second great maritime crusade, this time against Algiers. Hence, while Charles kept an ear closely tuned to the doctrinal discussions at the Diet of Regensburg (1541), he was also dictating long missives to Spain full of instructions on topics like providing biscuit for soldiers on board the galleys. In the end, this dual-track strategy was another of Charles's failures. The conferees at Regensburg did not agree, and since Charles insisted on staying almost to the end, his travels were one of many circumstances that contributed to postponing the armada's departure to a dangerously late date (17 October). A few days after his men had disembarked near Algiers, galleys were smashed and supplies sunk by a fierce and premature winter storm. The campaign was over before it had begun.

Following upon this great blow to his prestige, the next year (1542) was an evil time for Charles. Barbarossa's galleys, openly welcomed for the first time in France's Mediterranean harbors, imperiled the sea link between Spain and Italy. Mary of Hungary, regent of the Low Countries,[73] had reliable information that two armies were preparing to invade, one from France, another from a formerly Habsburg Rhineland territory that the duke of Cleves had occupied with French help.[74] Preoccupied by dangers along the Pyrenees front, Charles could only tell his sister to withstand the shock of invasion as best she could.[75] Meanwhile, the Schmalkaldic League occupied Brunswick, a duchy whose staunchly Catholic ruler was threatening to punish towns that claimed to be independent of his jurisdiction and had introduced the Reformation.[76] The league now discussed extending membership to the same duke of Cleves who had now occupied part of the Low Countries with French help. This encroachment by the league on his hereditary lands Charles could not tolerate. When he assembled an army in the Low Countries in 1543, the duke of Cleves was his first target.

Charles quickly overran Cleves, forcing the duke to disgorge the Low Countries province he had conquered and renounce his hopes of joining the Schmalkaldic League.[77] From his base in the Rhineland, the emperor marched into France the next spring. A French army followed him along the opposite bank of the Marne River but did not offer battle; instead France proposed negotiations that resulted in a treaty.[78] France made no cession of territory, and observers wondered why an emperor with an army pointed at Paris had not insisted on more. Money was part of the answer, since Charles had barely enough to pay his mercenary soldiers their "going home" fee. But there were also secret clauses[79] reflecting a new focus by Charles on German affairs. This was the treaty in which Francis I promised to break off his contacts with the Schmalkaldic League and to allow French bishops to attend an ecumenical council convened by the pope.[80]

In Germany, there was friction between the Schmalkaldic League's two leaders, Philip of Hesse and John Frederick of Saxony, because of Philip's bigamous marriage to a young noblewoman attendant on his lawful wife, John Frederick's second cousin.[81] Charles's diplomats prepared for war by massaging the interests of other princes. The league counted on tacit support from the Catholic Duke William of Bavaria, known for his long-standing quarrel with the house of Austria. But William was won over by a promise of marriage between his son Albert and Ferdinand's daughter Anna. Duke Moritz of Saxony was a Lutheran, but Charles knew that he coveted the electoral title of his cousin, John Frederick. Secret agreements served the emperor well. When it was clear that war was coming, but before Charles had gathered his forces, the league passed up an opportunity to strike at a still-vulnerable emperor for fear of offending the duke of Bavaria,[82] little realizing he was already in Charles's camp. Once hostilities were joined Charles did not have to invade Electoral Saxony—the job was done for him by Duke Moritz, who waited until after his cousin had marched south for what he thought was their common struggle against the emperor.[83] It remained for Charles and his chief commander, the duke of Alba,[84] to pursue and defeat John Frederick's retreating forces near the Saxon town of Mühlberg (April 1547). John Frederick was captured; Philip of Hesse soon surrendered.

Charles was better at winning a victory than at exploiting it wisely. He was right to think that most of the league's member cities and territories would sue for terms once the two leaders were in his custody, but some (like Magdeburg) stubbornly continued to resist. Familiar Catholic ceremonies were duly reintroduced, as prescribed by the Augsburg Interim of 1548, but evoked real hostility. The force of such specifically Protestant religious convictions was difficult for Charles to comprehend. Moreover, he overestimated the strength of his position. First, he declared that his son Philip would follow Ferdinand as emperor, not Ferdinand's own son Maximilian, so that the two branches of the Habsburg family would have the imperial title by turns. This deeply offended Ferdinand and Maximilian and also the imperial princes, for whom the popular Maximilian was a fellow German and Philip (who spoke only Spanish) a foreigner. Next, Charles alienated Moritz by deciding that some of his promises to Saxony's new elector did not have to be kept. Some Lutheran princes were trying to revive the Schmalkaldic League as a defensive alliance. Moritz, secretly joining their counsels, proposed a more ambitious plan: with French help, the Augsburg Interim could be overturned. France's Henry II (ruled 1547–1559) was interested but sought recognition of his occupation of three imperial cities in the border province of Lorraine—Metz, Toul, and Verdun;[85] when the league's negotiators agreed, a treaty was signed (January 1552).

Charles V, suddenly facing armies converging against him from two directions, fled across the Alps to southern Austria. Ferdinand, now willing to act without his brother's approval, agreed to suspend the Augsburg Interim in return for Moritz's help in an attack he launched against Ottoman strongholds in Hungary. Straining all the resources of a now fragile Castilian treasury,[86] Charles gathered funds to assemble a sizable army in southern Germany by the late summer of 1552. How was this precious force to be employed? Charles could have attacked his Schmalkaldic foes in an attempt to revive the Interim. Alternatively, he might have concentrated on Margrave Albrecht Alcibiades of Bayreuth, a rogue Protestant prince who had been terrorizing his neighbors without much regard to confessional differences. Instead, the emperor added Albrecht Alcibiades and his men to his own forces and marched against the imperial city of Metz, now held by the French. This choice revealed Charles's priorities—he really did see France as the root of Europe's problems—and it was also his last campaign. Charles's siege guns battered a breach in Metz's walls, but the duke of Guise,[87] commanding Metz's garrison, had already built an earthen rampart behind this weak spot in the city's defenses. Guise's men withstood the imperial charge, and the onset of winter storms did the rest. As his army melted away, a defeated and dispirited emperor retired to Brussels (January 1553).

Charles abdicated his hereditary lands in favor of his son Philip in January of 1556. After further fighting against France's Henry II, including a major victory in northern France (1557), Philip and the French king signed a treaty of peace (1559):[88] the Habsburg dynasty was confirmed in its possessions, including Milan, while France had nothing to show for sixty-five years of intermittent warfare against Spain and the empire, except for

Figure 8.5. Emperor Charles V as Victor at Mühlberg. Titian (ca. 1488–1576) came from Venice to Augsburg in 1548 to do two portraits of the emperor, one of which shows him as he might have looked after his victory over the elector of Saxony (April 1547): "Charles V as Victor at Mühlberg," 1548. (*Art Resource, New York, NY/Museo del Prado, Madrid.*)

Metz, Toul, and Verdun.[89] Meanwhile, a settlement had already been reached in Germany. Before abdicating, Charles gave Ferdinand full responsibility for negotiating with the Schmalkaldic League. It was clear that Lutheran as well as Catholic princes would be recognized as having the right to determine the religious identity of their territories.[90] The sticking point was how to define the status of the empire's many ecclesiastical principalities, for some had become Protestant and more were likely to follow. Reluctantly, Protestant negotiators accepted the "ecclesiastical reservation" demanded by Ferdinand: except for those who had already made a change of religion,[91] prince-bishops or prince-abbots who became Protestant would automatically lose their position. This issue settled, the Peace of Augsburg was proclaimed in 1555.

In the end, the defeat of Charles V's ambition to reunite a religiously divided Germany reflects a failure on his part to grasp two things: the strength of Protestant religious convictions and the polycentric character of European civilization as it had evolved over the past thousand years. Charles had only the best of motives, or so he thought. He saw Latin Christendom as a body of believers gravely threatened by Ottoman power—why did supposedly Christian powers like France prevent him from devoting his attention to this larger struggle? He was more conscientious about the business of government than most of Europe's crowned heads—who could accuse him of failing in his duties as a Christian prince? He knew better than anyone how precarious his family's hold was on each of its hereditary lands—did anyone imagine he wanted yet more territory for himself? Yet it was part of the normal duties of advisers to appraise new opportunities for the ruler and his dynasty, and it was well known that Charles had eagerly (if ultimately in vain) sought Habsburg expansion in some areas. To many observers the emperor's retention of Milan seemed proof of an insatiable appetite for power. The fundamental problem was that post-Roman Europe had never seen a dynasty whose territories bestrode the continent from the Low Countries to Sicily and from Spain to Transylvania[92]—not to mention Spain's overseas possessions. To Christendom as most people understood it, made up of independent territories that could be enemies in one war and allies in the next, the mere existence of such a colossus was deeply threatening. Charles never understood why his enemies opposed him not just because of the lands they suspected him of wanting to grab, but also because of the lands he had lawfully inherited.

9 | Politics

Wars of Religion, 1562–1648

For European statesmen of the sixteenth century, a prince's natural desire to expand his territory was a familiar motive for war. Religion was not. The practice by which major powers kept permanent ambassadors in one another's capitals had been invented by Italian states of the fifteenth century and transferred across the Alps by about 1500. An ambassador's main job was to prevent his home government from being confronted with unpleasant surprises, and there was no better guide for guessing another government's intentions than a calculation of its long-term self-interest. Hence, experienced diplomats were skilled at discerning the real interests—what Florence's Niccolo Machiavelli (d. 1527) called "reason of state"—that lurked behind a rival government's professions of good will. The assessments produced by Venice's patrician envoys,[1] or by Machiavelli himself,[2] are uncommonly shrewd, but also cynical. Having identified a "reason of state" for a policy or action, they treated it as the sole explanation, not allowing for the complexity of human motivation, even among princes and kings.

This habit of calculating a rival's material interests was employed selectively by states or parties that went to war in the name of religion. Each believed in the sincerity of its professions of religious motive and treated the enemy's as sheer hypocrisy. Thus Habsburg rulers had a keen eye for the secret ambitions of their Protestant foes, while anti-Habsburg states (Catholic as well as Protestant) saw with equal clarity the dynasty's interest in absorbing new territories. The importance of reason of state in these wars was obvious enough to cause sensitive observers to feel disgust at the way great men used religion as an excuse for their quarrels.[3] Yet religion was important enough to help shape the eventual outcome; partisans of the dominant religion could not get the peace treaties they wanted without granting their rivals freedom of conscience,[4] and in some cases limited

145

freedom of worship as well. Thus the wars called "religious" were mainly about politics, but also about religion.

This chapter will consider three series of wars: France's Wars of Religion (1562–1598), the Dutch Revolt (1572–1609), and the Thirty Years' War (1618–1648), fought in Germany but involving armies and subsidies from most European powers. One common thread that links these three very different conflicts is that each involved, at least to some degree, a convergence between Habsburg power and the preservation of Catholicism. In France's religious wars, intervention by Charles V's son Philip II was important, though not decisive, in preventing the victory of a Protestant king. In the Low Countries, Philip and his successors managed to retain for the Habsburg dynasty and the Catholic religion only the southern provinces— the northern provinces became an independent nation, officially professing the "evangelical Reformed religion."[5] During the Thirty Years' War, the descendants of Charles V's brother Ferdinand reasserted Habsburg and Catholic control of their hereditary lands (especially Austria and Bohemia), but a coalition between Catholic France and Europe's Protestant nations thwarted their ambitions to transform the loose federal structure of the Holy Roman Empire into a strong monarchy.

France's religious wars began with the premature death of King Henry II (1559). Sixteen-year-old Francis II died after barely a year, and the queen mother, Catherine de Medici (1519–1589), was not able to gain control of the regency council for nine-year-old Charles IX.[6] This opened the door to a classic power struggle among the three great men of the kingdom: Antoine de Bourbon, the prince of the royal blood who was closest to the throne after Henry II's four sons; Anne de Montmorency, France's hereditary constable and greatest landholder; and Francis, duke of Guise, Henry II's most successful military commander. It was to be expected that the clientele of each of these party chieftains would close ranks behind their leader.[7] What was novel in this case was that factional rivalry took on a religious coloration, owing to the fact that each of the great men had a distinct religious identity. Bourbon and most of his kinfolk were Huguenots. Guise and his brother, the cardinal of Lorraine, were partisans of Tridentine Catholicism. Montmorency, some of whose kin were Huguenots,[8] stood for a pre-Tridentine Catholicism that prized independence from Rome.[9]

Since no one side had the strength to defeat the others, successive wars[10] ended in treaties allowing some freedom of worship for Huguenots, always including Huguenot nobles on their estates.[11] In the towns, scores were settled during the wars, but also during periods of peace. In the great

Figure 9.1. The arrest of Councillor Anne du Bourg in the Parlement of Paris.
Councillor du Bourg was arrested for heresy (later tried and burned) when he
spoke in favor of the Reformation before the Parlement of Paris and in the presence
of King Henry II (upper right): from Alfred Franklin, Les Grandes Scènes Historiques du XVIe Siècle, Reproduction Fac-Simile du Recueil de J. Tortorel et J. Perrissin (Paris, 1886). (*University of California at San Diego Library.*)

city of Lyon, for example, the Huguenot minority seized power just after
the first war had begun (1562) and suppressed Catholic worship; when
Huguenot troops were withdrawn as the first peace was proclaimed
(1563), Catholics regained power and suppressed Protestant worship.[12]
But major fortified cities that remained firmly Protestant (like La Rochelle
in the southwest) anchored the Huguenots' defensive position even when
battlefield results were not encouraging.

After the first war Catherine de Medici sought to build a biconfessional
basis of support for the crown by taking her son on a slow circuit of the
kingdom (1564–1566). But the benefits of this strategy were partly negated
by her meeting in the south of France with her daughter Elisabeth, wife of
Spain's Philip II, who was accompanied by the duke of Alba. Huguenots
suspected some great Catholic conspiracy was afoot, and these fears re-
awakened when Alba marched his 10,000 men along France's borders toward the Low Countries (1567).[13] The Prince of Condé, Bourbon's younger
brother, and Gaspard de Coligny, France's hereditary admiral, organized
a Huguenot plot to capture the person of young Charles IX and pry him

Sainct Iean d'Angely afsiegé par le Roy Charles 9, le 14.Octob.1569.iufques au 2. Decembre 1569.

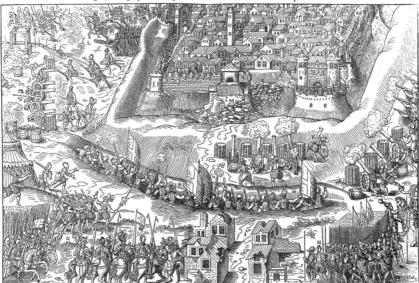

Figure 9.2. France's Religious Wars: a Royalist/Catholic siege. View of the unsuccessful Royalist/Catholic siege of a Huguenot stronghold in southern France, St. Jean d'Angely, December 1569: from A. Franklin, Les Grandes Scènes Historiques (see figure 9.1). (*University of California at San Diego Library.*)

loose from the influence of a council dominated by the Guise family. This ignited a new war, which only brought another inconclusive peace. Still another war began (1568) when the cardinal of Lorraine, encouraged by contacts with Philip II, sought to have Coligny and Condé arrested. Soon thereafter Coligny and Condé signed a treaty of mutual support with William of Orange. Each side now had its allies outside the kingdom.

By 1572, Charles IX had assumed control of the realm in his own name. Coligny, who had won his trust, argued that a war against Spain—France's natural enemy—might heal the kingdom's internal divisions. With the king's permission, Louis of Nassau, Orange's brother, crossed into the southern Netherlands at the head of a Huguenot force and seized two fortified towns (May 1572). The fact that Alba had to gather his scattered units to retake these towns gave the Sea Beggars a precious few weeks to expand their control of towns in Holland and Zeeland.[14] In France, however, this adventure was to have a dire sequel for the Huguenots. During the month of August, Coligny and leading Huguenots were gathered in Paris for the marriage of Henri de Bourbon, Antoine's son and heir, to the king's sister,

Marguerite de Valois. On 22 August 1572, Coligny was the victim of a failed assassination attempt. Historians usually point to Catherine de Medici as the culprit in this plot, though some favor the duke of Guise.[15] What matters is that as tensions mounted in Paris, the royal council, with Catherine and Charles IX present, determined on a preemptive strike against Coligny and other Huguenot leaders.[16] The result, intended by no one, was the grisly massacre of St. Bartholomew's Day (24 August 1572). Thinking they were acting on the king's orders, Catholic Parisians slaughtered some two thousand Huguenots. Similar massacres in other cities claimed three thousand more victims. Reaction among Huguenots was deeply divided. Some, taking this terrible catastrophe as a sign of God's disfavor, presented themselves to the authorities for penitence and readmission to the Catholic Church. Others resumed the struggle with renewed determination and a new theory of resistance: they were fighting not just against the king's evil councillors, but also against a tyrannical monarchy that had forfeited the obedience of its subjects.[17]

On Charles IX's death the throne passed to his brother Henry III[18] (ruled 1574–1589), but there was another brother whose ambitions were not satisfied, the duke of Anjou. In 1576 the king faced a Huguenot army strengthened by Anjou and by 20,000 German mercenaries brought from the Palatinate by John Casimir.[19] In the ensuing peace, Huguenots were ac-

Figure 9.3. The St. Bartholomew's Day Massacre (24 August 1572). François Dubois, "The Saint Bartholomew's Day Massacre." (*Musée Cantonal des Beaux-Arts, Lausanne, Switzerland.*)

corded freedom of worship and the right to build churches everywhere in the kingdom, save in fiercely Catholic Paris. But this Huguenot victory provoked a Catholic reaction. The 1576 treaty included a clause assigning a Catholic city in the north to a Huguenot commander for safekeeping.[20] Local nobles formed a Catholic League among the populace to resist the transfer of power, and their success in this objective led to the organization of a similar league throughout the kingdom, headed by the duke of Guise. Lest he be politically isolated, King Henry III placed himself at head of the league; this caused many partisans to lose interest, and the league may have ceased to exist altogether.

But in 1584 the king's younger brother died; contemporaries immediately concluded that the heir to the throne was likely to be the Huguenot Prince Henry of Bourbon.[21] Among France's Catholic majority the implications of having a Protestant sovereign were ominous—was this not the era of the principle "whose region, his religion"?[22] The Catholic League was quickly reorganized with a much broader popular base, especially among urban guildsmen, and a two-point program: All treaties granting toleration to heresy were to be overturned, and Henry of Bourbon would never be France's king. In some thirty large cities, the league, supported by local notables as well as by the clergy and the guilds, formed a kind of shadow town government. This process was most visible in Paris, where a league committee known as the Sixteen gradually assumed effective control of the city.

Head of the league once more, Guise negotiated a secret treaty with Spain's ambassador to France: Philip promised to recognize the league's

Figure 9.4. A Procession of the Catholic League in Paris. Anonymous, Procession of the Catholic League, departing from the Hôtel de Ville (City Hall) in 1590 or 1593; note that friars bearing arms are prominent in the throng. (*Des Musées de la Ville de Paris, Musée Carnavalet, Paris.*)

candidate for the French throne;[23] Guise promised a hefty subsidy for Philip's war in the Netherlands. Facing the isolation he had always feared, King Henry III oscillated between Bourbon and the league. Meanwhile, the popular duke of Guise was all the more popular after his forces turned back a large Protestant army brought from the Palatinate by John Casimir (1587). The king prohibited Guise from approaching Paris, but Guise ignored the ban. His arrival triggered an uprising (May 1588): Parisians built barricades against a possible attack by royal mercenaries, and the king quietly slipped out of the capital he no longer controlled.[24]

Henry III had his revenge when Guise obeyed a summons to attend upon the king and was cut down by his attendants. League preachers and polemicists, hitherto supportive of royal authority,[25] now acclaimed the right of resistance, the idea that subjects of a tyrant-king had a God-given right to overthrow him, and the sooner the better. Henry III had no choice but to join forces with Henry of Bourbon. His assassination by a fanatical Dominican friar (August 1589) left the league facing its real enemy, the man who now called himself King Henry IV. It seemed the new monarch had inherited a crown, but not a kingdom.

In fact, Henry IV had important assets not limited to his Huguenot following. First, by the traditional rules of royal succession in France, he was undoubtedly the rightful king;[26] this counted for something in a country where legitimacy was a sacred principle.[27] Second, a middle party had been building for some years. The so-called *politiques* ("politicals") were mainly Catholic nobles unwilling to sacrifice the peace and unity of France to the cause of religious purity. Some, led by members of the Montmorency family, had experience in keeping religiously divided parts of the kingdom at peace by observing strict parity in the distribution of offices. This faction rallied behind Henry IV, helping him to gain several victories against league armies commanded by Guise's brother, the duke of Mayenne.

By the late spring of 1590, Henry IV completed the encirclement of the great city of Paris, citadel of the league.[28] Having made no preparations for a siege, the Sixteen turned to Spain's ambassador for help. Philip II ordered his commander, the duke of Parma (see below), to break off the fighting in the Low Countries and march to the rescue of Catholic Paris. Outmaneuvering Henry IV with a feigned attack, Parma brought relief to a starving populace. But Henry IV renewed the siege when Parma withdrew, and the defenders of Paris now faced internal problems. The only plausible alternative to Henry IV had died,[29] opening the difficult question of who should be king. Meanwhile, the league was beginning to fracture along social lines, as parish clergy and the craft guilds, acting through the Sixteen, demanded the dismissal of high-born royal officials thought to be less than resolute in their opposition to Henry IV. When Mayenne and the Spanish ambassador proposed the election of new monarchs—Mayenne's son and Philip II's daughter, to be married for this purpose—only the Sixteen showed any enthusiasm; the Parlement of Paris, bastion of royal official-dom, declared that any transfer of the crown to a foreign prince or princess would violate French law.

This was the moment (July 1593) when Henry IV abjured Calvinism and professed his Catholic belief in a ceremony at the abbey church of St. Denis, outside Paris.[30] Rather than forcing his subjects to change their beliefs, the king changed his own. Skepticism among ardent partisans of the league pro-longed hostilities, albeit at a lower level of intensity. It took several months to arrange Henry's triumphal entry into Paris (March 1594) and three years to subdue scattered resistance among league nobles. The fruit of his victory was the Edict of Nantes (1598), proclaimed by Henry IV and (under pres-sure from the king) accepted by the *parlements* as part of French law.[31] Huguenots were guaranteed freedom of conscience throughout the king-dom and freedom of worship in all the towns they controlled as of 1597 as

Figure 9.5. King Henry IV of France (reigned 1589–1610). Anonymous equestrian portrait, showing Henry IV across the Seine River from the walls of Paris, just be-fore his triumphal entry into the city in 1594. (*Art Resource, New York, NY.*)

well as in noble households; Catholics were guaranteed freedom of worship in Huguenot towns. In a separate royal decree not submitted to the *parlements*, Henry IV pledged royal tax revenues to the support of Huguenot garrisons in roughly half of the two hundred towns the Huguenots controlled. This creation of a Huguenot "state within a state" would cause problems for later monarchs,[32] but it was what had to be done to induce Huguenot nobles to lay down their arms.

The Edict of Nantes did not mean France had become a secular state. In the sixteenth and seventeenth centuries almost no one conceived of the idea that a state could (much less should) be indifferent to the religious practices of its citizens.[33] Henry IV's goal in issuing the edict was the goal of moderate Catholic *politiques* who supported him: France should be reunited in the Catholic faith, but over time rather than all at once, and not by force of arms.[34]

What the settlement did mean was a revival of royal authority. At different times, both the Huguenots and the Catholic League had embraced ideas of monarchy which emphasized the rights of subjects rather than the prerogatives of the crown. The *parlements* that dragged their feet about accepting the Edict of Nantes were defending another version of the theory of limited or constitutional[35] monarchy. *Politique* writers argued that all these theories of resistance served the factional violence that only a strong king could overcome. France needed what other theorists called "absolute" monarchy.[36] This idea gained credibility from Henry's success in ending the terrible civil wars and also from the memory left by his reign—a time of peace, prosperity, and just government, ending only when good King Henry was assassinated by an unrepentant Catholic fanatic (1610).

From 1572 to 1576 the Dutch Revolt was confined to two small provinces, Holland and Zeeland, which were hard-pressed to match Spain's outlay of treasure and troops. The rebels' advantage lay in their control of the sea, which made Philip II[37] incur the added expense of supplying his Netherlands army by the long overland route from northern Italy. On land, however, they had difficulty stopping Spain's seasoned troops—until the Spanish siege of Leiden was broken (October 1574) when waters flowing through nearby dikes began lapping at the walls of the city.[38]

Things changed when the financial problems Philip had inherited from his father came home to roost. In 1575 Castile's monarch declared a kind of bankruptcy, in which lenders were compelled to accept long-term treasury bonds at low rates of interest in lieu of the repayments they had been promised on high-interest loans.[39] This made new loans hard to get, while Spain's soldiers in the Netherlands waited at the end of a long credit pipeline. Spain's fighting men were better disciplined than most, but they were not made of steel. In July 1576, not having seen their regular pay for nearly two years, a number of Spanish units mutinied and brutally sacked a loyalist town near Brussels. When Philip II failed to provide a remedy for this outrage, troops engaged by the States of Brabant placed members of the king's council in Brussels under arrest and Brabant summoned a meeting of the States General.[40] While representatives from the hitherto loyal provinces deliberated in Ghent with deputies from Holland and Zeeland, the mutineers converged on Antwerp, smashed through its defenses, and went on a terrible rampage, leaving 8,000 civilians dead and 1,000 houses burned.

Figure 9.6. William of Orange in his Later Years. Adriaen Thomasz Key, "William of Orange in his Later Years." (*Rijksmuseum, Amsterdam.*)

Within days of this "Spanish Fury" loyalist and rebel deputies concluded the Pacification of Ghent (November 1576), an agreement to expel all Spaniards from the country. The pacification recognized the religious status quo, with Calvinism as the sole authorized religion in Holland and Zeeland and Catholicism in the other provinces, but also called for an end to Habsburg antiheresy legislation. This was William of Orange's great moment. The Netherlands was united in resistance to Spanish tyranny, and religious differences were pushed into the background—or so it seemed. Orange was not able to prevent radical Calvinist minorities in great cities like Ghent and Antwerp from seizing control of town governments by force and closing the churches to all but Reformed worship. This recrudescence of intolerance did not bode well for keeping politics to the fore in the national struggle.

Spain's position was retrieved through the efforts of one man, Alessandro Farnese, duke of Parma (1545–1592),[41] who assumed command of Philip's forces in 1578. Farnese skillfully exploited the divisions between radical Calvinists and the Catholic nobility of the French-speaking provinces, who had joined in the general rebellion against Spanish troops but could not countenance the violent suppression of Catholicism in Ghent and other cities. In 1579 rebel provinces in the north formed a union among themselves to conduct the war against Spain. The Union of Utrecht[42] guaranteed freedom of conscience to all citizens but banned the public practice of any but the "evangelical Reformed religion," and Catholic worship was banned even in private. In response, Parma organized a counter-union among southern provinces, based on Catholicism and reconciliation with the king (Union of Arras, 1579). A brilliant strategist, Parma then began reconquering the major towns one by one. His greatest triumph came with the capitulation of Antwerp (1585), following a siege that involved blocking the Scheldt River with a bridge of boats. Antwerp's Calvinists[43] were given four years to decide whether to convert to Catholicism or sell their goods and move elsewhere.[44]

Protestant powers, especially England, now feared a Spanish reconquest of all the Low Countries. The Revolt's great leader, Prince William of Orange, had been removed from the scene by a Catholic assassin's bullet (1584), and his son Maurits (1567–1625) was as yet young and untried. And could there be such a thing as a republic on the scale of the Low Countries, without any kind of prince at all?[45] In 1585 the States General[46] concluded a treaty agreeing to accept a governor-general sent by England's Elizabeth I. The queen's choice was Robert Dudley, earl of Leicester (1533–1588), who came with an English force meant to help stem Parma's advance. Leicester was hailed by Calvinist ministers and by religious exiles from the southern Netherlands,[47] who hoped that a new English-dominated government would bring stricter enforcement of the laws against popish idolatry[48] and a Reformed church free from control by the town and provincial governments.[49] Aided by his Dutch friends, Leicester dismissed the duly elected magistrates of Utrecht and replaced them with his own supporters.[50] This high-handed behavior plunged Leicester into what proved to be a losing contest with the "regents," or ruling elite of the towns,[51] especially in the populous and highly urbanized province of Holland.[52]

Just now, the regents' party gained an exceptionally able leader, Johan van Oldenbarnevelt, who would serve as chief legal adviser of the States of Holland from 1586 until 1618.[53] Oldenbarnevelt and the magistrates differed from Leicester and his ardent Calvinist backers on several key points. First, like William of Orange, they saw the goals of the Revolt as more political than religious. To be sure, the Reformed religion was the one and only "public church," and the magistrates punished Catholics in particular if they attempted to conduct religious services in public. But many regents saw no harm in allowing non-Reformed Christians, Catholics included, to worship in house-churches discreetly shielded from public view. To keep overly zealous ministers from causing public disturbances on this or other issues, they kept a watchful eye on Reformed congregations in their towns. Further, since their own power base was in the towns and in the provincial parliaments to which the towns sent deputies, the regents were also adamantly opposed to any kind of strong central government, such as Leicester seemed intent on creating.

Thinking that England's help was prolonging the Revolt, Philip II determined on an ill-fated effort to punish Elizabeth I for her intervention in the Low Countries. All of 1587 was devoted to preparations for a great Armada that sailed from Spain the following year; instead of engaging the enemy, Parma was ordered to keep his troops on the coast of Flanders, ready to embark on Spanish ships as they headed for England. Philip's objective was to land an expeditionary force in southeastern England and conquer territory that could be held in exchange for Elizabeth's withdrawal from the Low Countries. But as the Armada sailed into the English Channel, its tight formation was broken up by the superior gunnery of attacking English vessels.[54] Parma's men never had a chance to embark and scattered elements of the Armada, sailing north into unfamiliar waters around Britain and Ireland, were driven against the rocks by storms. This disaster weakened Spain's prestige immeasurably; unlike his father after the calamity at Algiers (1541), Philip II (d. 1598) in his remaining years never repaired the damage by subsequent victories.

In the rebel provinces, Oldenbarnevelt and the regents' party were now firmly in control. Ardent Calvinists were aggrieved when the States of Holland adopted (1591) a church ordinance giving town governments final authority in the appointment and dismissal of pastors.[55] Proponents of

Figure 9.7. Johan van Oldenbarnevelt. Michiel van Miereveld, "Johan van Oldenbarnevelt," Grand Pensionary of the States of Holland, 1584–1619. (*Rijksmuseum, Amsterdam.*)

a stronger central government were disappointed that each separate province remained sovereign in determining how to raise its quota for the war budget managed by the States General. This decentralized system, a puzzle to outside observers, worked surprisingly well, especially in the financial sphere, which was one of Oldenbarnevelt's special domains.[56] Soldiers of the rebel provinces, paid in full and more or less on time, rarely broke loose in the savage mutinies that so bedeviled the Spanish government in the Low Countries.

Oldenbarnevelt and the regents had an important partner. Maurits of Nassau (d. 1625) proved an able strategist and an innovator in military tactics.[57] Following Parma's death (1592), he recovered many towns and secured the new state's boundary against provinces loyal to Spain with a line of new-style fortifications that resisted easy assault.[58] As conditions stabilized in the early 1600s, observers could sense rival patriotisms developing on either side of a battle line approximating the modern border between Belgium in the south and the Netherlands in the north. This equilibrium was ratified when Oldenbarnevelt and the representatives of Spain's Philip III (ruled 1598–1621) signed a Twelve Years' Truce (1609). At least provisionally, the Dutch Republic[59] and the Spanish Netherlands[60] took their places among the nations of Europe.

Philip II could draw on the wealth of highly urbanized provinces as well as a stream of silver from the Americas.[61] The Austrian branch of the Habsburg family was rich only in its titles. Following the battle of Mohàcs (1526) Ferdinand claimed the crown of Bohemia as well as of Hungary.[62] But Bohemia was ruled less by its monarch than by its parliament or estates, in which the nobles had the greatest influence; since most of the nobles were either Lutheran or Hussite,[63] the new monarch, a German and a Catholic, was treated with suspicion. The vast kingdom of Hungary was divided into three parts after 1526.[64] Much of central Hungary was under the direct rule of Sultan Suleyman the Lawgiver. Eastern Hungary was the power base for the Zapolyai family, leaders of Magyar[65] opposition to the German Habsburgs; their claim to the Hungarian crown was backed by the sultan. Ferdinand controlled western and northern Hungary, but its resources did not support the costs of frontier defense. From 1547 on, Ferdinand got Turkish agreement to prolong the truce between the two sides only by paying a humiliating annual tribute.[66]

In the hereditary Austrian lands, including six duchies,[67] Ferdinand presided over a kind of aristocratic confederation. Territorial administrators were appointed by the estates of each duchy, dominated as in Bohemia by the nobles. The nobles, mostly Lutheran, did not allow their ruler much room for pursuing a Catholic agenda. Ferdinand had called members of the new Jesuit order to Vienna (1551) to serve as professors at the university and as preachers at St. Stephen's Cathedral,[68] but he could not prevent Austrian town councils from following the example of the nobles by appointing Lutheran pastors to their churches. Finally, during Ferdinand's reign as Holy Roman Emperor (1556–1564), the balance among Germany's confessional parties tilted toward the Protestant side. Though displaced by Calvinism in the Palatinate[69] and some other territories, Lutheranism was still expanding in ecclesiastical principalities where cathedral chapters that had become Lutheran elected a Lutheran bishop, notwithstanding the so-called ecclesiastical reservation.[70] Ferdinand had insisted on inserting this clause into the 1555 Peace, but he lacked the authority to enforce it. Rather than abandoning altogether the principle that ecclesiastical principalities must remain Catholic, he granted "indults" or exceptions for Lutheran bishops seeking admission to the diet as imperial princes.

Maximilian II (ruled 1564–1576) succeeded his father as emperor, while two younger brothers, Charles and Ferdinand, administered Austrian duchies. Archduke Charles in particular took important steps to roll back the gains of Lutheranism in his lands,[71] but Maximilian as a young man gave every indication of sympathy for Lutheranism. He had to swear an oath in the presence of his father and his brothers never to abandon the Catholic faith in order to avoid being disinherited. As emperor, Maximilian continued Ferdinand's practice of granting to newly elected Lutheran bishops the recognition they sought as imperial princes.

Maximilian's eldest son, Rudolph II (ruled 1576–1611), transferred his capital in 1583 from Vienna to the much larger city of Prague, capital of Bohemia. Rudolph took a somewhat stricter Catholic line—refusing to grant any more exemptions from the ecclesiastical reservation—but politics was not his interest. Instead he devoted himself to his art collection and to the recondite pursuits of the scholars attracted to Prague by his patronage—astronomers (including Johannes Kepler, d. 1630),[72] alchemists,[73] and practitioners of what was called natural magic.[74] Rudolph's indifference to problems in the empire (see below) raised questions about the dynasty's future, all the more so because the emperor never married. His brother Mathias conferred with their cousins about ways of easing the emperor from his throne and managed to have himself elected in Rudolph's place as king of Hungary (1607) and king of Bohemia (1611). As the brothers competed for support that in Bohemia was only to be had by making religious concessions to the estates, both signed the so-called Letter of Majesty (1609), granting full toleration for Hussites, and, by implication, for all other Christian creeds.

Meanwhile, Bavaria and the Palatinate were the focal points for a growing confessional polarization. Bavaria's Duke Albert V (ruled 1550–1579), having beaten back a Lutheran movement among his nobles, put the machinery of state behind Tridentine reform. His "spiritual council" took over direct management of church affairs in 1570, bypassing Bavaria's bishops and their foot-dragging cathedral chapters.[75] Dukes William V (ruled 1579–1598) and Maximilian (ruled 1598–1651) were ready to defend the Catholic cause on a larger stage. In the Palatinate, the championship of Calvinism under Elector Frederick IV (ruled 1583–1610) was guided first by John Casimir, the elector's uncle (d. 1592), then by his chief minister, Prince Christian of Anhalt. Anhalt had great plans for the young Elector Frederick V, whose marriage to Elizabeth Stuart, daughter of England's King James I (ruled 1603–1625), he arranged in 1613.

Twice during Rudolph's long reign Bavaria and the Palatinate almost went to war. In 1582, when Cologne's prince-archbishop publicly married his mistress and converted to Protestantism, the ecclesiastical reservation was upheld by having Duke William V's brother Ernest of Bavaria elected as his successor.[76] John Casimir raised an army to defend the claims of the Protestant prince-archbishop, but withdrew from the field when Lutheran princes, ever distrustful of Calvinists, refused to support him. In 1608 Bavaria's Duke Maximilian, acting on the authorization of the emperor, occupied the Protestant free imperial city of Donauwörth,[77] and supervised its reconversion to Catholicism. Christian of Anhalt organized a union (1609) among leading Calvinist territories as well as a few Lutheran princes and cities, but a lack of broader Lutheran support prevented the union from taking action. Meanwhile, the rivalry between Bavaria and the Palatinate was overshadowed by the interest that powerful states outside the empire took in the disputed succession to a cluster of five Rhineland territories (1606–1614); what threatened to be a European conflagration was prevented only by unforeseen events.[78]

The crisis that did not subside came in Bohemia. The childless Emperor Mathias (ruled 1612–1619) planned for the eldest of his cousins, Archduke Ferdinand of Inner Austria,[79] to succeed him in his various offices, starting with his election as king by the estates of Bohemia (1617). Since Archduke Ferdinand was known for his persecution of Lutherans in Inner Austria,[80] the largely Protestant estates demanded, as an afterthought, that Ferdinand add his signature to the 1609 Letter of Majesty. But Ferdinand named as his governors in Bohemia two deputies whose ardent Catholicism had alienated their Protestant colleagues, and almost immediately there were disputes about the circumstances in which the Letter of Majesty permitted Protestants to build new churches. Tempers flared at a specially called Protestant assembly in Prague (May 1618); those in attendance marched to the royal palace, seized the two governors, and, consciously repeating a revolutionary gesture of their Hussite forebears, dragged them up a marble staircase and threw them out the window.[81]

This defiance meant war. The Protestant assembly formed a new government for Bohemia, raised an army, expelled the Jesuits, and confiscated the lands of Catholics loyal to Ferdinand. Among the adventurers who proffered assistance Christian of Anhalt came to the fore; he saw a chance to have Elector Frederick V chosen as Bohemia's king in place of Ferdinand. Initial fighting in Bohemia went well for the rebels, and in 1619, shortly after Ferdinand was elected Holy Roman Emperor, the states of Bohemia voted to have the Elector Palatine as their king. Frederick was joyously greeted when he arrived, but Hussites and Lutherans were put off when Calvinist ministers acting in the new king's name began removing from the churches the religious images that they too cherished.

Maximilian of Bavaria agreed to raise an army of the empire's Catholic League[82] to join Habsburg forces for an invasion of Bohemia from the south, under the command of Jan Tserclaes, count of Tilly (1559–1632), a seasoned Counter-Reformation warrior from the Low Countries. The Lutheran Elector John George of Saxony (ruled 1611–1656) agreed to invade from the north in return for the right to occupy Lusatia, a border province of the Bohemian crown. Finally, Ferdinand's cousin in Madrid, Philip III, agreed to have an army from the Spanish Netherlands invade the Palatinate.[83] All three invasions went as planned. The climax came when Tilly's men caught up with Anhalt's Bohemian army entrenched on the brow of White Mountain, just west of Prague; charging uphill in the fog (8 November 1620), they routed their enemies. Frederick, a king no more, found refuge with Denmark's King Christian IV (ruled 1588–1648). Bohemia's towns and provinces hastened to submit to Ferdinand.

Following the battle of White Mountain, Bohemia was thoroughly subjected to Habsburg and Catholic rule. Noble families that supported the rebellion were dispossessed, their lands handed over to a polyglot nobility formed from officers in Tilly's army. Some forty leaders of the revolt were beheaded on the main square of Prague (1621), and Bohemia was declared a hereditary possession of the Habsburgs, no longer an elective monarchy. The Letter of Majesty was revoked; Protestant and Hussite pastors were evicted and replaced by Catholic priests. Seldom has a major kingdom been so completely transformed by the fortunes of a single battle.

This great victory evoked dreams of Habsburg grandeur for Ferdinand and for Spain's new king, Philip IV (ruled 1621–1665). Neither Spain's continuing occupation of the Palatinate nor Ferdinand's transfer of the electoral title to Maximilian of Bavaria (1623) were accepted by the diet—both were thus violations of imperial law. But among the imperial princes only Christian IV of Denmark[84] seemed willing to do anything more than protest. Supported by Dutch and English subsidies, Christian IV marched into Germany twice but was twice defeated by Tilly (1624, 1626). Meanwhile, Spain's control of the Palatinate helped provide a safe route of passage for men and supplies traveling from northern Italy to the Low Countries. After hostilities in the Low Countries were reopened,[85] Philip's commanders in Italy secured another link in the "Spanish road" by annexing the Valtellina, a strategic Alpine valley connecting the duchy of Milan to the friendly territory of Switzerland's Catholic cantons.

Count Albert of Wallenstein, a Bohemian military adventurer, now contracted to raise an army on Ferdinand's behalf, without any charge to the imperial treasury—his men would support themselves by pillage. Having raised a force of over 100,000, Wallenstein crunched through the Protestant territories of north Germany that had not yet submitted to the emperor. Despite misgivings about the independent position Wallenstein was carving out for himself,[86] Ferdinand recognized his conquests by depriving the Lutheran duke of Mecklenburg of his land and title and awarding both to Wallenstein (1628). Not since Frederick Barbarossa (d. 1191) had any emperor controlled north Germany's Baltic coast as Ferdinand II now did. But the empire's electoral princes, now including Maximilian of Bavaria, denounced the transfer of an imperial principality to the upstart Wallenstein as a flagrant violation of imperial law[87] and informed the emperor that they would not elect his son Ferdinand as King of the Romans unless Wallenstein were dismissed and deprived of his ill-gotten gains.

Instead, Ferdinand chose to exploit Tilly's and Wallenstein's victories by redressing the empire's political balance in favor of Catholicism. The emperor and his advisers (including his Jesuit confessor) had discussed the idea of reversing all the changes of religion that had occurred in the empire's ecclesiastical territories since the 1555 ecclesiastical reservation, regardless of whether or not the changes were sanctioned by "indults" granted by Emperors Ferdinand I and Maximilian II. The imperial diet would never endorse such a revolutionary step, involving the lands of some fourteen bishoprics and fifty important monasteries or convents; the emperor would have to act on his own authority, in effect daring the imperial princes to react. Ferdinand took the risk, promulgating his Edict of Restitution on 6 March 1629. From the imperial princes came letters of protest, nothing more. Backed by Tilly's and Wallenstein's troops, the emperor's agents began implementing the new decree in one territory after another. Though there was resistance in places, as in Magdeburg, which had been Lutheran for a hundred years,[88] this was the high point of the Counter-Reformation in Germany. Since Ferdinand II was in effect governing the empire by decree, rendering the diet superfluous, it was also the high point of Habsburg claims to hegemony in Europe.

In fact, Ferdinand's success was possible only because potential foes chose not to intervene in imperial politics. England[89] and the Dutch[90] were distracted by other concerns. France, the Habsburgs' ancient enemy, was the key player. Cardinal Richelieu, prime minister[91] for King Louis XIII (ruled 1610–1643), saw the containment of Habsburg power as France's most important priority. But a strong "devout" party in the king's council, backed by popular opinion, wanted France to pursue a "Catholic" foreign policy,[92] which certainly did not include backing the Habsburgs' Protestant foes. Also, royal power in France was seriously challenged when the Huguenot "state within a state"[93] rose in rebellion (1625). Events in Italy played into Richelieu's hands. When the duke of Mantua died without issue, Spain's Philip IV persuaded Ferdinand II to send troops to occupy his lands (1628) rather than allowing them to pass to the French prince who was the duke's rightful heir.[94] Pope Urban VIII (ruled 1623–1644) made no secret of his opposition to this Habsburg land grab in Italy—a circumstance that greatly facilitated Richelieu's contention that an anti-Habsburg policy was not anti-Catholic. Meanwhile, royal troops ended Huguenot resistance by conquering the heavily fortified port city of La Rochelle (1628). Though he did not find it necessary to revoke the Huguenots' civil and religious rights,[95] Richelieu rendered them politically harmless by having royal garrisons occupy their former strongholds. Finally, he gained a clear victory against his foes in the royal council (1630); Louis XIII dismissed leaders of the "devout" party and reaffirmed his confidence in Richelieu. Richelieu was now free to look about for a partner willing to challenge Habsburg supremacy in Germany.

Sweden's King Gustavus Adolph (ruled 1611–1632), already alarmed by imperial successes along the Baltic coast, was incensed when Wallenstein provided 12,000 troops to his enemy, King Sigismund III Vasa of Poland (ruled 1587–1632).[96] After French diplomats arranged a truce in the fighting between Poland and Sweden (1629), Gustavus Adolph landed an army on Germany's Baltic coast, announcing his intention of defending Sweden's interests in the region. Finding that his large force could not gain much by pillaging land already picked clean by Wallenstein's regiments, Gustavus Adolph accepted (January 1631) French subsidies to keep his men on the march. Sensing an opportunity to present himself as the Protestant champion, he hoped to break Tilly's siege of Magdeburg, but north Germany's Lutheran princes, suspicious of the Swedish intruder's intentions, barred the way. Tilly's men stormed Magdeburg (May 1631) and went on a murderous rampage; thousands more perished as fire raced through the city's wooden houses.[97] Elector John George of Saxony now joined forces with Gustavus Adolph, and the combined Protestant army caught up with Tilly's force at Breitenfeld, north of Leipzig (September 1631); Tilly's men turned back the Saxons but broke and fled before the firing by ranks[98] of Gustavus Adolph's well-trained Swedish infantry.

Breitenfeld was the first major defeat for Ferdinand II and a cause of joy for Protestant Europe. But Richelieu was alarmed as Gustavus Adolph marched unopposed into south Germany;[99] to protect French interests along the border with the empire, he compelled the prince-archbishop of Trier to hand over two fortresses on the right bank of the Rhine. While one of his German Protestant allies drove Spanish troops from the Palatinate, the Swedish king ravaged the Main valley and parts of Bavaria before turning back to the north, pursued now by Wallenstein's new army.[100] At Lützen, west of Leipzig, Gustavus Adolph was killed, but his men won another victory (November 1632). The king's chancellor[101] organized the empire's Protestant princes into a new federation under Swedish leadership. But the emperor's son Ferdinand and Spain's Philip IV had not given up the fight. A Spanish army en route to the Low Countries made a juncture with Ferdinand's men and routed the Swedes at Nördlingen in south Germany (September 1634). Within a few weeks, all of the south German lands that Gustavus Adolph and his Protestant allies had conquered were regained by the Habsburgs and the Catholic League. Saxony's John George now arranged a treaty with the emperor's son: the Peace of Prague (1635) nullified the Edict of Restitution, except for ecclesiastical territories reconverted to Catholicism before 1627. As in 1555, Lutheranism and Catholicism would enjoy the protection of imperial law; Calvinism would not. Weary of war, most German princes of both confessions accepted this treaty.

Richelieu could not permit the Habsburgs and their Saxon allies to settle Germany's future. In May 1635 France openly declared war on Spain.[102] While French diplomats arranged another truce with Poland, permitting Sweden to rebuild its forces in north Germany, French commanders occupied most of the imperial province of Alsace[103] and launched campaigns against Mantua and the Valtellina in Italy. For thirteen years more the various combatants marched their armies back and forth across an exhausted Germany. The end result secured France's gains and was somewhat more favorable to the empire's traditional character as a federation of independent states than the Peace of Prague had been. The Peace of Westphalia (1648) transferred to France all rights claimed by the emperor in the imperial province of Alsace;[104] France also retained two key fortresses on the right bank of the Rhine and the bishoprics of Metz, Toul, and Verdun as well as the three cities. The Dutch Republic, somewhat expanded beyond the frontiers of the 1609 truce, won permanent recognition from Spain of its status as an independent nation. The imperial constitution was vindicated by restoration of Frederick V's eldest son to his family's Rhenish lands as well as the title of Elector Palatine, but Maximilian of Bavaria was awarded territory formerly controlled by the Palatinate and kept his electoral title.[105] Elector John George of Saxony was confirmed in its possession of Lusatia, and Sweden received half of the duchy of Pomerania on the Baltic coast; the other half went to a shrewd military enterpriser, Elector Frederick William of Brandenburg-Prussia (ruled 1640–1688).[106]

Finally, the religious configuration of the empire was brought more into balance by moving back from 1627 to 1624 the date from which the religious identity of the ecclesiastical principalities was to be regarded as fixed

Figure 9.8. Cardinal Richelieu. Philip de Champagne, "Cardinal Richelieu." (*National Gallery, London.*)

—re-Catholicization campaigns subsequent to 1624 were thus abandoned. At the same time, freedom of conscience was recognized by limiting the ruler's right to determine the religious identity of his territory (as defined by the 1555 Peace of Augsburg) to matters of external observance; subjects were not to be molested for their private beliefs. But Ferdinand III (ruled 1637–1657) insisted on separating his hereditary lands from the new imperial law on this point; in Austria and in most of the lands of the Bohemian crown, the Habsburg ruler retained the right to determine what his subjects should believe.

But if the Austrian Habsburgs emerged from the Thirty Years' War much stronger than before in their hereditary lands, Ferdinand II's vision of ruling all Germany by decree was shattered once and for all in the grim final stage of the conflict. For the rest of its history, the Holy Roman Empire would remain as the 1555 Peace of Augsburg had envisioned it, a loose federation of independent states. This result was achieved mainly by French subsidies, to a lesser extent by French armies marching into Germany. Richelieu's "devout" critics had warned that the French people would suffer for the cardinal's dreams of glory, and so they did; to pay for the armies that ravaged Germany's peasantry, France's peasants were squeezed to the point of rebellion.[107] But Richelieu's dream was realized, even if the cardinal was no longer alive to see it. France emerged from the Treaty of Westphalia as Europe's preeminent power, a status confirmed by eleven more years of fighting along the Spanish frontier.[108] By contrast, Spain sank to the status of a second-rate power: more than a century of nearly continuous wars (tracing back to the time of Charles V) had exhausted Castile's treasury and distorted its economic development.[109] Under France's King Louis XIV (ruled 1656–1715), Catholic Austria would have to band together with Europe's Protestant powers in a series of coalitions aimed at forestalling French hegemony.

Like Richelieu's campaign against the Habsburgs, wars of the century or so after 1650 were fought for reasons of state; the age of religious wars was over. Yet the conflicts of the period between 1560 and 1650 had left a mark on European society. Paradoxically, wars that were in part motivated by the desire to suppress false religion achieved a result that was nearly the opposite, for each of these conflicts ended by providing Christian minorities a modicum of religious liberty. Ardent Catholics in France were angered by the fact that heretics still controlled two hundred towns in the kingdom. Ardent Calvinists in the Dutch Republic were angered by the fact that town magistrates were not punishing popish idolaters as the law required when they celebrated mass in private houses. In the empire too there was grumbling from zealots on both sides about provisions of the final settlement that limited a ruler's rights over the religious life of his territory to public worship, not private beliefs. In all three conflicts the moderates could take some satisfaction in the outcome: Catholic *politques* in France; Reformed town regents in the Dutch Republic; and, in Germany, Lutheran princes like Elector John George of Saxony, loath to see the empire torn by further war.[110] In all three wars the final settlements made a small but important crack in traditional European assumptions about the proper relationship between the civil and ecclesiastical spheres of Christian society. Government still identified itself with true religion by determining the terms and conditions of public worship. But so long as they did not challenge the government's claim to control the religious use of public space, citizens who happened to hold heterodox beliefs were not to be molested. It was not that the coexistence of different confessions in one society was thought to be a good thing;[111] rather, dogged fighting between armed factions adhering to opposing beliefs had made some kind of compromise a requirement for peace. This limited recognition of the civil rights of religious minorities emerged not from the idea of toleration, but from the fact of religious war.

10 | Politics

The European Reformations

In the history of European state-building the Reformation era was a period of increasing centralization. Taxes that were novelties when first granted to their rulers by parliamentary bodies of the fourteenth and fifteenth centuries became routine, necessitating the creation of new or larger government bureaus for overseeing collection and auditing disbursements. The French idea of a standing army[1] was adopted by all states that could afford it and some that could not, meaning a standardization of expectations as to how soldiers were trained and equipped. Maintaining a permanent force and keeping up with rapid improvements in military technology[2] required more expenditures, even in peacetime. Territorial parliaments accepted additional forms of taxation with the greatest reluctance, in part because they often required compiling information about wealth and business activities that was precious to the ruler and dangerous for his subjects. Meanwhile, the prince's courts were using the natural litigiousness of every European society[3] to extend his authority in another sphere. Unable to abolish the various kinds of courts that competed with their master's tribunals,[4] the prince's judges insisted on appellate jurisdiction, which in the long run encouraged plaintiffs to come to their courts directly.

In some territories the growing strength of the ruler meant that the parliamentary bodies that had been so important in former centuries were rendered powerless or even abolished altogether.[5] But we must not exaggerate the control rulers of this period were able to exercise over the lives of their subjects. Even the most closely governed territory still had enclaves where the ruler's writ did not run, and even the most powerful prince still depended on the collaboration of important men who were strong enough to obstruct his will on issues that mattered to them. At least for western and central Europe, there are now few defenders of the once

169

popular idea that certain kings were able to achieve in practice the "absolute" or unlimited monarchy written about by theorists.[6]

There was, however, an unmistakable trend toward consolidation of princely authority, and it was powerfully abetted by men who served the prince. The actual business of governing, once tended to by nobles and bishops who also had other duties, was by the sixteenth century firmly in the hands of career officials, recruited either from the nobility or from wealthy burgher families. Such men did not forget to look after their own kinfolk, but they saw themselves more as servants of the crown than as defenders of the interests of their native cities or regions. This esprit de corps, combined with university training in the law,[7] imbued professional bureaucrats with a sense of mission. Faced with a labyrinth of local control, manipulated by powerful subjects for their own purposes, the officials had a glimmer of a new and better order in which all would be equally subject to the law that a wise prince imposed all across his territory. As a common French saying has it, these men were more royalist than the king.

In an age when religion was such a volatile and divisive issue, strong-willed rulers and their activist officials could not fail to take interest in the beliefs and practices of the prince's subjects. No one of any consequence disputed the common belief that it was the sovereign's highest duty before God to care for the spiritual as well as the material well-being of his subjects.[8] Besides, how could there be peace in the realm if Christians nurtured fratricidal hatred of one another? And how could public order be maintained without good preachers and teachers to instruct citizens in their moral duties? Usually, decisions about religion were not made by the prince and his officials acting alone; persons of some political weight—nobles and magistrates of important towns—had to be brought into the discussion. But no one gave much thought to the opinions of the illiterate common folk who made up the great majority of the prince's subjects. On a matter of such importance as religion, the people at large were to be governed, not consulted.

To give an idea of how governments attempted to determine the religious lives of their subjects, this chapter discusses three outcomes: the Lutheran settlement in Scandinavia, the Calvinist settlement in the Dutch Republic, and the Catholic settlement in Habsburg Austria. England's many different settlements are discussed in Chapter 11.

Outside of Germany, Martin Luther's teachings became the basis of established churches only in the neighboring realms of Denmark (including Norway) and Sweden (including Finland). Humanist scholars like Paule

Helie (1480–1534) of Copenhagen awakened interest in religious reform, and former Wittenberg students like the Dane Hans Tausen (1494–1561) and the Swede Olaus Petri (1493–1552) spread Luther's message. By the early 1530s there were strong evangelical movements in the largest cities in Denmark, Malmö[9] and Copenhagen, and in Bergen (Norway), a port-of-call for German merchants. But the Reformation in Scandinavia owed its success to the fact that rulers of Denmark and Sweden had a common problem: They needed cash, and the wealth of politically troublesome bishops was an inviting target.

Christian II, last king of a united Scandinavia (ruled 1513–1523),[10] was no friend of the aristocracy. In Sweden he arranged a massacre of leading nobles, provoking a rebellion led by Gustavus Vasa, son of one of the victims, who gained recognition as king of Sweden (1523–1560). The great merchant city of Lübeck—a bitter foe of Christian II[11]—provided Vasa with money for hiring troops, and ships to convey them from Germany. The new king could not ignore Sweden's debt to the Baltic's major naval and financial power, but neither could he find money to pay Lübeck. The property of the church attracted his attention, partly because of his enmity with the former archbishop of Uppsala, ousted on suspicion of complicity in the murders arranged by Christian II, and now demanding restoration, with papal support. At the Diet of Västerås (1527), Vasa pressured Sweden's nobles and town deputies to agree to place the wealth of the church at his disposal. The diet also decreed that clergy were to preach "the pure word of God, without human inventions and fables." This was the Swedish Reformation.[12]

In Denmark Christian's attack on noble privileges, though popular in the cities, led the otherwise fractious bishops and nobles who made up the Council of the Realm[13] to join forces; Christian fled into exile, and the council elected the duke of neighboring Holstein as King Frederick I (1523–1533). Because the bishops had a strong position in the council, Frederick moved warily in matters of religion, despite the presence of Lutheran preachers in his entourage. But Frederick's son and presumed heir, the future King Christian III, was organizing a full-blown Lutheran reformation in Schleswig, the *apanage* he controlled.[14] Thus, Frederick's death ushered in a three-sided civil war, lasting from 1533 to 1536. Emperor Charles V claimed Denmark for one of his nieces, a daughter of his brother-in-law, Christian II, but the troops he was finally able to get shipped to Denmark came too late.[15] Meanwhile, the Lutheran towns of Copenhagen and Malmö were fighting in the name of their old ally, Christian II himself.[16] But since Christian was the worst of all choices for Denmark's noble families, the aristocratic bishops and their kinsmen on the council rallied behind Duke Christian of Schleswig-Holstein, son of the late king. Having made his triumphal entry into Copenhagen, King Christian III (d. 1559) declared the bishops responsible for the turmoil of civil war. The bishops themselves were imprisoned; their property was forfeit to the crown. Denmark too was now Lutheran by decree.

In Denmark the consolidation of the new religion over the next few generations was relatively tranquil. Neither King Christian III nor his son Frederick II (ruled 1559–1588) found it necessary to prescribe the 1530 Augsburg Confession as a binding statement of belief.[17] Instead, efforts were made to keep out heretics (meaning Calvinist or Anabaptists). The so-called Strangers Articles of 1569 were based on the Augsburg Confession, but only "strangers"—foreigners wishing to take up residence—were obliged to swear to believe as the articles prescribed. The intra-Lutheran quarrels between Philippists and Genuine-Lutherans[18] surfaced in Denmark when a prominent professor at the University of Copenhagen was forced to recant his Calvinist teachings on the Lord's Supper and eventually dismissed from his post (1576–1579).[19] Early in the reign of Christian IV (ruled 1588–1648) danger came from a different quarter. Young Danes and Norwegians were crossing the Baltic to attend Jesuit colleges,[20] and some converted to Catholicism before returning home. When a Jesuit graduate who had become headmaster of the Latin school in Malmö openly professed his sympathy for Catholicism, the government prohibited Jesuit alumni from serving as ministers or schoolteachers. In Norway, six crypto-Catholics (including four preachers) were ferreted out and banished. Denmark and Norway, open to the world along long coastlines, were not open to un-Lutheran doctrines.

Sweden followed a different path. Here some years went by before any formal condemnation of Catholic belief and ritual occured; only in 1544 did an assembly of the clergy repudiate such practices as the veneration of saints and the saying of masses for the benefit of souls in purgatory.[21] Unlike Denmark's monarch, Gustavus Vasa's son and successor Erik XIV (ruled 1560–1568) welcomed Calvinist refugees from France and the Low Countries and was suspected of sympathizing with their views, even though he prohibited them from proselytizing. Laurentius Petri, the first Lutheran archbishop of Uppsala (1531–1573), stood for a high church[22] Lutheranism; he was orthodox and anti-Calvinist in matters of doctrine, but he asserted the independence of the church from state control and sought to retain as much as possible of the old ceremonies. The church order written by Petri, not accepted during Erik's reign, was adopted by king and parliament under his brother and successor, John III (ruled 1568–1592).

Influenced by his wife, Catherine Jagellio,[23] the daughter of Poland's King Sigismund II, King John was attracted to Catholicism, but not of the Tridentine variety. This theologically sophisticated monarch envisioned a national church worshiping according to the ancient Catholic liturgy, in the language of the people.[24] He drafted his own liturgy, the so-called Red Book, which Sweden's Lutheran bishops accepted with some misgivings (1577). Jesuit missionaries were allowed to enter the country, and John himself secretly converted to Catholicism. He would make his conversion public if Rome approved three concessions: the laity must be allowed to receive the wine as well as the bread in communion; priests must be allowed to marry; and the language of worship must be Swedish, not Latin. But Pope Gregory XIII (ruled 1572–1585) refused to countenance any such departures from the norms Trent had decreed for the universal Catholic Church. King John expelled the Jesuits and ended his days as a Lutheran.

Meanwhile, Sigismund Vasa, the son of King John and Catherine Jagellio, had been raised a Catholic and was now promoting a Tridentine agenda as king of Poland (1587–1632). Hence, when John III died, his brother Charles persuaded the royal council to convene a church synod, which for the first time adopted the Augsburg Confession as Sweden's confession of faith. Since the synod's decision was endorsed by many of the leading men who made up Sweden's Diet, or Parliament, Sigismund Vasa had to accept it as a condition for his coronation (1593). Several years of friction between the Catholic monarch and his Lutheran estates led to a few military skirmishes, after which Sigismund abruptly returned to Poland. The Parliament deposed Sigismund (1599), and eventually acclaimed his uncle as King Charles IX.[25] We may conclude that over the course of nearly three generations Lutheranism had taken hold in Sweden, certainly among the clergy and the political elite. In 1527, Gustavus Vasa was able to impose a change of religion on the kingdom; in 1593, Sigismund Vasa was not.

The Dutch Republic was the most important European state to adopt Calvinism as its official creed. But only a tiny fraction of the population were members or sympathizers of the Reformed Church.[26] As late as 1586, though the numbers were rising, it was estimated that no more than 10 percent of the Dutch people were adherents of the "evangelical Reformed religion." Moreover, the leaders of the church were in no hurry to change things; to them, quality of membership counted more than quantity.[27] Nonetheless, the "public church" was vested with exclusive control of all churches that still functioned as houses of worship—the others were closed or converted to other uses. Town governments also endowed scholarships for ministerial students in the theology faculty at the new University of Leiden.[28] This was because the Dutch government and the church needed each other. No government of this age could function without invoking God's blessing, and no clergymen could be more fervent than the Reformed ministers in calling upon the Lord to bless those who guided the Revolt against Catholic Spain.

Especially in Holland and Utrecht, urban magistrates were usually Protestant,[29] but not necessarily Calvinist in their beliefs. In these provinces there was something of a marriage of convenience between church and state, and it was rife with friction. The church had a cohesive organizational structure: a church council (pastor and elders) for each parish, a *classis* for each town and its hinterland, and provincial synods to which each *classis* sent deputies.[30] As far as ministers and elders were concerned, town regents had a right to be notified when the *classis* chose a minister, but no right of appointment; and decisions by the synods of the public church ought to be recognized by the government as having the force of law. The regents saw things quite differently. Many would have preferred a broader church in which Christians of differing beliefs could worship together. Remembering the radical Calvinists whose seizure of power in cities like Ghent and Antwerp had fractured the unity of the Revolt,[31] they also mistrusted the south-Netherlands exiles who were so prominent among Reformed ministers and elders. To prevent hotheads among the clergy from causing trouble among the people, it was essential that magistrates keep the church in hand by sending "commissioners" to observe the meetings of the local *classis* and by exercising their rights to appoint or dismiss ministers.

During the 1580s these conflicting principles led in half a dozen cities in Holland and Utrecht to bitter struggles that followed a similar script. A preacher built up a large following, but fellow ministers making up the local *classis* attempted to remove him because he questioned Calvinist doctrine, often in regard to predestination.[32] The preacher then appealed to what he deemed the superior authority of the town magistrates, who gladly maintained him in office, at least until a compromise was reached. Meanwhile, deputies to the provincial parliaments studiously ignored the decisions regarding the governance of the church promulgated by provincial synods or by the national synod of 1584. Instead, the States of Utrecht (1590) and the States of Holland (1591) approved their own plans for church governance, explicitly recognizing the rights of magistrates. In most places these resolutions of their "high mightinesses"[33] were studiously ignored by the church.

In the early years of the new century, a dispute within Leiden's theological faculty turned these issues into a crisis of national proportions. Jacobus Arminius (1559–1609) was trained at Geneva, still the center of Calvinist orthodoxy. During his tenure as a pastor in Amsterdam (1588–1603), his views on predestination were questioned by some colleagues in the ministry, but Arminius's wife was from one of the city's leading families, and he enjoyed the favor of the magistrates. In 1603 he was named a professor of theology at Leiden, despite opposition from another member of the faculty, a south Netherlands refugee named Franciscus Gomarus (1563–1641). Arminius proved a popular lecturer, in part because among the theology professors he alone was a native of the provinces that now comprised the Dutch Republic. In the public debates that Gomarus now demanded, Arminius contended that God's final decree of salvation depended on which individuals freely chose to accept His grace.[34] This doctrine put Arminius squarely at odds with Calvin, and, as he acknowledged, with the article on predestination contained in the Belgic Confession, a statement of faith that church rules required every minister to sign.[35] Arminius proposed that the states of Hol-

Figure 10.1. A Calvinist lampoon of the false doctrines of Arminius. Anonymous cartoon showing the true doctrine of Calvin (and of Gomarus) outweighing the ragbag doctrines of Arminius—a small glimpse of the extensive pamphlet and broadside campaign waged by rival Gomarists and Arminians. (*Rijksmuseum, Amsterdam.*)

land convene a special assembly to consider revising the Belgic Confession—but for Gomarus, a strict Calvinist, such a subordination of matters of doctrine to state authority would be if anything even more of an abomination than Arminius's repudiation of orthodox teaching on predestination. This was the theological equivalent of war.

As graduates trained by Gomarus and Arminius filled ministerial posts, their mutual recriminations percolated through Holland's towns, transforming an academic debate into partisan strife. In the vibrant printing culture of the Dutch Republic, the debate among learned men quickly became a war of pamphlets aimed at a broader readership. City councils and church councils alike divided along factional lines, and preachers built up a popular following by denouncing the heresies or the narrow-mindedness of their opponents. When the *classis* of Alkmaar dismissed a preacher who had refused to sign the Belgic Confession (1608), Arminius's disciples grasped how precarious their position in the church was. In 1610, shortly after Arminius himself had died, forty-four ministers (many of them his former students) presented a "Remonstrance" to the States of Holland, requesting protection from harassment by orthodox Calvinists. This petition was sympathetically received by the states, but the recourse to state authority only intensified the hostilities between those who now called themselves "Remonstrants" (Arminians) and "Counter-Remonstrants" (Calvinists).

Where one faction gained control of a *classis* and filled the pulpits with its own men, adherents of the opposing faction seceded and formed their own church, recognized and supported by fellow-believers in other towns. With Holland in an uproar, the Calvinist party demanded the convening of a national synod of the church, the first since 1584; but Holland had always blocked this idea in the States General.[36] Holland's leader, Oldenbarnevelt,[37] decided the time had come to teach the *dominees*[38] their place. At his urging, the States of Holland convened a theological colloquy and, when this failed to bring agreement, commanded both sides to stop quarreling and live at peace. The outnumbered Remonstrants were quite willing to do so; the question was whether their "high mightinesses" could lay down the law to Holland's Calvinists.

In fact, Oldenbarnevelt badly underestimated the opposition. In some places where Remonstrant preachers were maintained in their pulpits by sympathetic magistrates, worshipers in the local church were outnumbered by secessionist Counter-Remonstrant congregations meeting outside the town walls. Meanwhile, political winds were shifting. Oldenbarnevelt's ideas on lay control of the church had always been strongly supported by deputies from Amsterdam, Holland's greatest and richest city.[39] But now the ruling faction whose members had treated Arminius as one of their own was giving way to a new group who were strong Calvinists and whose overseas commercial ambitions were hampered by the Twelve Years' Truce Oldenbarnevelt had concluded with Spain.[40] Thus Oldenbarnevelt found himself facing powerful opposition in the States of Holland. The final blow came from the prince of Orange, Maurits of Nassau, who was glad to see signs of interest in renewing the war with Spain— the Twelve Years' Truce had been approved over his protest. When Maurits announced his support for the Counter-Remonstrant cause (1617), opposition in the States of Holland to the convening of a national synod began to crumble. As preparations were being made for the Synod of Dordrecht (1618–1619), Oldenbarnevelt was arrested by order of the States General on vaguely worded charges that he had betrayed the fatherland to its enemies. The fact that no proof of treason was forthcoming did not prevent his execution (May 1619). Meanwhile, the Synod had completed its work. The Calvinist doctrine of predestination in its most extreme form was forcefully reasserted;[41] the teachings of the Remonstrants were explicitly condemned. Following the Synod, some two hundred Remonstrant preachers were dismissed and forced into exile.

In some ways the Synod of Dordrecht marked a decisive turn in the religious history of the republic. The theology of the church was now unambiguously Calvinist, and no parliamentary body would ever again challenge the principle that doctrinal decisions were to be made by the church. Moreover, the fact that ordinary believers had some influence on the outcome— voting with their feet if confronted with a preacher not of their liking—reflected a steady growth in church membership.[42] This trend continued through the remainder of the century, partly because the restriction of certain civil privileges to church members was for some an inducement to conversion,[43] and partly because many believers were attracted by the distinctive teachings of Calvinism.

But the victory of Calvinism was not so complete as it seemed. When the political constellation that had made the convening of the synod possible changed, so too did the country's religious climate. Frederick Henry, Maurits's son and successor (1625–1647), let it be known that Remonstrant leaders who returned to their native country would not be persecuted. By the 1630s, Remonstrants were even allowed to build plain-looking houses of worship for their services. In Amsterdam, where a new and less ardently Calvinist ruling faction was taking control, the same courtesy had already been extended to Mennonites and Lutherans, and also to Sephardic Jews from Portugal. Catholics were usually not allowed to build houses of worship—this would have been an affront to Calvinists—but it became less and less likely that illegal Catholic services in house-churches would be raided by the local sheriff. The end result was a paradox. Just when Calvinism was finally becoming the majority religion (around 1650), the place of non-Calvinist communities was becoming anchored in the daily

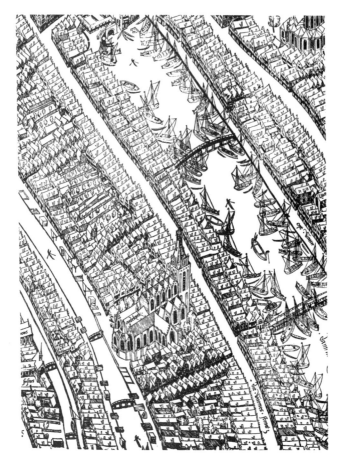

Figure 10.2. Section from a bird's-eye view of Amsterdam (1544). This section of Cornelis Anthoniszoon's view of Amsterdam (1544) shows the Old Church ("Oude Kerk"), one of the city's two parish churches, and Vegetable Street ("Warmoes Straat"), a fashionable area where merchants from the Baltic held the open-air grain exchange. (*Amsterdams Historisch Museum, Amsterdam.*)

life of the republic, if not in its public law. If one may describe as pluralistic a society that recognizes one religion formally and many others informally, this was Europe's first pluralistic society.

In the six duchies that made up the core of the Austrian lands, Emperor Ferdinand I (d. 1564) and his nobles had an informal understanding: They

Figure 10.3. The Synod of Dordrecht, 1618/1619. Frederick Muller, "The Synod of Dordrecht." (*Rijksmuseum, Amsterdam.*)

supported his campaigns against the Ottomans; he did not inquire into their beliefs, which were increasingly Lutheran. By the time of Ferdinand's death only Tirol remained largely Catholic. Upper and Lower Austria along the Danube (the latter having Vienna as its capital) and the three duchies to the south—Styria, Carinthia, and Carniola—all seem to have had Lutheran majorities at all levels of society. In his will Ferdinand provided for a division of the Austrian lands among his sons: Ferdinand (d. 1595) was to have Tirol; Charles (d. 1590) was to have the three duchies of Styria, Carinthia, and Carniola—now called Inner Austria; and Maximilian II (d. 1576), his designated successor as Holy Roman Emperor and king of Bohemia, was to have Upper and Lower Austria. Of the three brothers, it was Archduke Charles in Inner Austria who initiated the Catholic counteroffensive.

By this time the great monasteries of the Austrian lands were moribund, some having only a few monks left.[44] Ferdinand I appointed commissions of visitation that documented these conditions; Maximilian II appointed a "cloister council" to impose discipline on the monasteries, but this was a work of decades, not years. The state of the secular clergy was hardly any better; bishops who visited the parishes of Inner Austria during Charles's reign found many priests who had come here to escape their evil reputations elsewhere. Help could only come from the new orders flourishing in other parts of Catholic Europe. Ferdinand I showed the way by calling Jesuit priests to Vienna (1551) to serve as professors at the moribund university and as preachers at St. Stephen's Cathedral. Starting with but a handful of listeners, Peter Canisius (1521–1597) in a few years' time filled the cathedral—a result that led Lutherans elsewhere to be on guard against the Jesuits. Hence, when Archduke Charles invited the Jesuits to Graz (1572), Styria's capital, Graz's solidly Lutheran town council decreed fines for all who attended Catholic services, prohibited burghers from sending their sons to the new Jesuit school, and ordered local printers not to print its textbooks. But prominent families were not to be prevented from signing up their sons for a first-rate classical education. The school had 200 pupils by 1580 (though mostly not from the area), and according to Jesuit reports the town of some 8,000 people had 1,000 Catholic communicants, as opposed to about twenty in 1570. There was now some basis of support for a more aggressively Catholic policy.

Meanwhile, however, the estates of Inner Austria had compelled Archduke Charles to issue a sworn guarantee of freedom of worship for nobles (1578); he refused to say whether the same guarantee applied to the towns as well, and the nobles who dominated the estates did not press the matter.[45] This concession to Lutheran nobles was protested by the papal nuncio and by Charles's brother-in-law, Duke William V of Bavaria; Charles, though bound by his word to the nobles, agreed to interpret the concession narrowly. In 1580 he began a step-by-step attack on urban Lutheranism. He decreed a ban on Lutheran worship, first in a few newly acquired cities, then in all the cities of Inner Austria, which would have forced Lutheran burghers to attend services on noble estates outside the walls or in rural parishes whose pastors were appointed by the nobles. It is not clear that the archduke's officials were able to enforce this decree, but he kept up pressure on the towns by, for example, promoting the election of Catholic burghers to town councils. In 1586, the flourishing Jesuit school in Graz was recognized by the pope as a university; Archduke Charles's son, the future Emperor Ferdinand II, enrolled as its first student.

Following his father's death, while a regency council ruled Inner Austria in his name, young Ferdinand pursued his studies at the now Jesuit University of Ingolstadt in Bavaria (1590–1595). When he took the reigns of government in his own hands (1596), Archduke Ferdinand picked up the threads of the program of Catholic restoration. He used the receipts of his treasury to endow three more Jesuit colleges in Inner Austria,[46] and he let nobles in the estates know that while he respected their freedom of conscience he did not feel bound by his father's oath to guarantee them freedom of worship. Like his father, Ferdinand decreed a ban on Lutheran worship in the towns. Unlike his father, he enforced it through "reform commissions" made up of high church and state officials, with a mandate to interrogate urban pastors and schoolmasters as to their beliefs; adherents of the Augsburg Confession were dismissed from their posts and ordered to leave the territory within two weeks. Lutheran nobles in the estates protested but took no action, perhaps because the peasant uprising in nearby Upper Austria (see below) made them fearful of challenging the ruler's authority. By 1601 Ferdinand felt strong enough to issue a general mandate prohibiting Lutheran worship throughout Inner Austria; the reform commissions now questioned Lutheran pastors in the countryside who were appointed by local nobles.[47] Additionally, Ferdinand began purging territorial administrations and town councils of Lutherans. Soon Lutheran burghers of key cities like Graz were required either to convert to Catholicism or sell their goods and go into exile. Between 1598 and 1605, some 11,000 Inner Austrian subjects chose exile over conformity.

By the time Archduke Ferdinand was elected king of Bohemia (1617), the re-Catholicization of Inner Austria had been brought to a more or less successful conclusion. But in Upper and Lower Austria, which Ferdinand inherited from his uncle Mathias in 1619, the estates were not minded to accept meekly whatever their new ruler might decree. In both duchies Emperor Maximilian II had struck a bargain with the estates (1568–1571): in return for sizable grants to pay off his debts, he guaranteed freedom of worship for Lutheran nobles. By the early years of Rudolph II's reign, as many as 90 percent of the nobles in Lower Austria were Lutheran. In Vienna, the Landeshaus, the headquarters of the estates of Lower Austria, served also as the city's principal Lutheran church. In Upper Austria the situation was similar. Emperor Rudolph, in Prague, had entrusted the governance of Upper and Lower Austria to his brother, Archduke Ernest (d. 1595), who had hopes of imitating the Counter-Reformation policy of Archduke Charles in Inner Austria. He prohibited Lutheran services in the Vienna Landeshaus. To make it clear there would be rewards for having the correct belief, he dismissed Lutherans from the city council and appointed Catholics instead and ceased appointing Lutheran nobles to posts in the territorial administration. Lutheran and especially Calvinist nobles opposed these measures,[48] but the nobility's dependence on their Catholic rulers was made clear by a peasant rebellion in Upper Austria (1594–1597), directed against new obligations the noble landlords were imposing on their peasant tenants. Peasant armies fought the troops raised by the estates to a standstill but accepted a compromise dictated by Emperor Rudolph II.

Archduke Mathias, who followed Archduke Ernest as administrator of Upper and Lower Austria, pursued the same strategy of giving leading families incentives to convert to Catholicism. But Mathias's plans for easing Emperor Rudolph from his throne forced him to negotiate for the support of the estates, in Austria as well as Bohemia. He guaranteed freedom of worship for the nobles of Upper Austria in 1609 and for the towns in 1610. From this time forward the cause of Protestant nobles in Upper and Lower Austria was connected to that of their confreres in Bohemia.[49] Hence when Bohemia's estates revoked their election of Archduke Ferdinand and chose Frederick V of the Palatinate as their king instead (1619),[50] the estates of Upper and Lower Austria let Ferdinand know that hereditary succession did not mean what he thought it did—he would be their ruler only if they chose to accept him as such. In Vienna, Ferdinand had the fortitude to refuse the estates' demands—including the expulsion of the Jesuits and the building of a Lutheran church in Vienna—even as an army sent by the rebel estates of Bohemia neared the city gates. He was saved from a likely disaster only by the timely arrival of a cavalry troop from Tirol, which bolstered Vienna's defenses.

Ferdinand deputized Maximilian of Bavaria, head of the Catholic League, to deal with Upper Austria. En route to Bohemia, Maximilian, backed by Tilly's army, forced the submission of the rebellious estates in Linz, the capital city (August 1620). Since Maximilian and the league had borne the expense of this campaign, Ferdinand named him interim administrator of Upper Austria. For six years the occupying Bavarian officials collected taxes with great punctiliousness and ousted Lutheran pastors as soon as they could find suitable Catholic priests to serve in their stead. Replacement of a Lutheran pastor was the spark that touched off the last great peasant rebellion of the early modern era (1626–1627). A peasant army defeated Bavarian forces in the field and confined them to Linz and one other fortified town. Mindful of the historical record, their leaders reissued the Twelve Articles of the 1525 Peasants' War[51] as a basis for negotiation. Their specific demands included expulsion of the Bavarians, reinstatement of dismissed Lutheran pastors, and the admission of peasant deputies to the estates of Upper Austria.[52] But the arrival of a new and more skillful Bavarian commander meant defeat once more for the recurring dream of peasant freedom.

Only now did Emperor Ferdinand decree for Upper and Lower Austria (1627) the enforced re-Catholicization he had put in place some years earlier in Inner Austria: all Protestant pastors and teachers were to be expelled from the territory, no matter by whose authority they held their position. Meanwhile, Ferdinand's efforts to change the beliefs of the all-important nobility were beginning to show results, partly because administrative positions were open only to Catholics, and partly because of Jesuit preaching and the quality education offered by Jesuit schools. Under Ferdinand II (d. 1637) and Ferdinand III (d. 1657), burghers in Upper and Lower Austria were given the choice between conversion and exile; between 1620 and 1660, some 50,000 people chose exile. Though small communities of "hidden Protestants" survived into the eighteenth century, especially in the remote mountain valleys of Tirol and Inner Austria, Habsburg Austria was becoming solidly Catholic.

One can see now why Ferdinand III insisted on exempting the Austrian lands from the clause in the Treaty of Westphalia that abrogated the ruler's prerogative (according to the 1555 Peace of Augsburg) of compelling his subjects to profess the religion of his choice. Charles V had fought, ultimately in vain, to prevent the empire's Lutheran princes from exercising the so-called "right of reformation" to determine the religious identity of their subjects. In the years subsequent to 1555 there were certainly Lutheran and also Calvinist princes who made use of the right of reformation to change the confessional character of their lands.[53] But one of the historical ironies of the Reformation era is that no princely dynasty in the empire made better use of this prerogative than the Catholic Habsburgs, in their own hereditary lands.

Scandinavia's monarchs believed it lay within their power to determine the religious belief of their realms; so did Archduke Charles and Emperor Ferdinand II in their Austrian lands. Oldenbarnevelt and Holland's regents believed that wise government could steer the Dutch Republic safely past the storms stirred up by a few Calvinist agitators. Each was in some degree mistaken. Sweden's Sigismund Vasa found he could not bend the will of a political elite grown accustomed to Lutheranism; Ferdinand II found that the peasants of Upper Austria had more stomach for resisting a Catholicism imposed from above than the Lutheran nobles of his territorial estates; and Oldenbarnevelt lost his life by failing to recognize the appeal that Calvinist doctrine had for ordinary believers. Each of these outcomes shows that doctrine and politics are not enough to account for the religious changes of this era—we must also have some sense of how different social groups reacted to the doctrines of the preachers and the actions of their rulers. This point will be strengthened by looking at the religious history of England (Chapter 11), where each successive government found its vision of religious uniformity for the kingdom obstructed by one kind of resistance or another. Part IV (Chapters 12–14) will take up the interests that divided social groups from one another.

11 | Politics

England's Reformations, 1527–1660

Late medieval England had an underground dissenter tradition, tracing back to the condemned doctrines of John Wycliffe (d. 1384), an Oxford theologian. That sixteenth-century Lollards became Protestants is not easy to document, but they prepared the ground for Reformation doctrines by rejecting many Catholic doctrines[1] and by insisting that lay people nurture their faith by reading the New Testament in their own tongue.

Luther was told in 1519 that his Latin works were being reprinted and discussed in England. The earliest known center of this discussion was at Cambridge's White Horse Inn, where regular gatherings of students inspired by the humanist program of biblical study, presided over by an Augustinian friar named Robert Barnes, soon had townsfolk calling the tavern "Little Germany." Imprisoned for his heterodox beliefs, Barnes escaped to Wittenberg, where he studied with Luther. When England repudiated the papacy Barnes became an English agent in Germany, but when he returned home he was burned as a heretic (1540) for preaching the doctrine of justification by faith. Though apparently not connected with the White Horse group, William Tyndale, a preacher and an Oxford graduate, proposed to translate the New Testament directly from Greek into English. Church leaders, however, frowned on this "Lollard" idea. Instead, Tyndale found backing from London merchants while he lived in the Low Countries and saw his English New Testament through the press (1525). He then produced polemical writings of a generally Lutheran inspiration, aided after 1528 by another English refugee, John Frith. Frith was martyred for his beliefs (1533) shortly after returning to England; Tyndale too was eventually caught, tried, and executed, not in England, but by Charles V's government in Brussels (1536). Though Barnes's theology was wholly Lutheran, Tyndale and Frith seem to have adopted some Zwinglian ideas during their years on the continent. Right from the start,

English Protestantism showed signs of the heterogeneous character that was to be its distinguishing feature.[2]

During the first decade of the continental Reformation, England's King Henry VIII (ruled 1509–1547) had no patience for heretics like Barnes and Tyndale. An amateur theologian, he won praise from the pope for a treatise in defense of the Catholic doctrine of the sacraments against Luther (1521). One of his councillors, the humanist Thomas More (1477/8–1535), matched Tyndale's polemics from the Catholic side book for book; as chancellor of England (1529–1532), More presided over a judicial apparatus that sent Anabaptists to the stake, in keeping with antiheresy laws once enacted against the Lollards (1415). Yet in the end, as in Sweden and Denmark, it was the king and not the scholars who made the first of England's many Reformations.

This chapter briefly discusses Henry VIII's separation of the Church of England from the Catholic Church (1534–1547), Edward VI's establishment of Protestantism (1547–1553), the reestablishment of Catholicism under Mary Tudor (1553–1558), the reestablishment of Protestantism under Elizabeth I (1558–1603), the reassertion of episcopal authority and certain pre-Reformation practices under Charles I (1625–1642), and the Presbyterian establishment mandated by Parliament (1646–1649). While England was controlled by Oliver Cromwell (1649–1658), the Congregationalists or Independents sought without success to have an established church according to their liking, while radical sects like the Quakers created their own religious communities.

In 1503 the future *Henry VIII* married his elder brother's widow, Catherine of Aragon, a younger daughter of Ferdinand and Isabella.[3] In light of Old Testament warnings that the man who took his brother's widow to wife would have no issue,[4] Pope Julius II issued a dispensation for the marriage. But Queen Catherine gave Henry no living child save for a daughter, Mary Tudor,[5] born in 1516. Not having a son to carry on his line, King Henry feared he was under God's curse, a fear that took on a new edge when he determined (1527) on marrying one of the queen's young attendants, Anne Boleyn. Did the pope really have authority to dispense anyone from an obligation of divine law, as laid down in the Bible? And could the present pope not retract the papal dispensation of 1503, thus rendering Henry's marriage with Catherine invalid, so he could marry Anne? But this was no time for Pope Clement VII to defy the wishes of Catherine's nephew, Emperor Charles V.[6] Hence, the papal legate who after protracted negotiations finally came to England immediately declared that he was remanding the matter of Henry's annulment to the curia in Rome.

Figure 11.1. King Henry VIII (reigned 1509–1547). Hans Holbein the Younger, "King Henry VIII of England." (*Colección Thyssen-Bornemisza, Madrid.*)

While Clement VII sought excuses for further delay, an angry Henry VIII brought into play a statute of 1393 prohibiting appeals to any court outside of England.[7] The king's chief adviser, who had also been exercising the judicial powers of a papal legate in England, was first to feel the sting of this new turn in royal policy.[8] Henry seized on the fact that royal courts had been suggesting England's ecclesiastical courts were violating the 1393 statute by the mere fact of recognizing Rome's appellate jurisdiction. In return for his gracious pardon for this offense, the king forced a cowed Convocation (assembly of the clergy)[9] to recognize him as "sole protector and supreme head" of England's church (1531). Parliament then approved a suspension of the payment of papal taxes to Rome.[10]

At the same time, a petition purporting to come from members of the House of Commons (actually drafted by one of Henry's ministers) complained that bishops who swore an oath to the pope were not even proper subjects of the king; Henry professed to be shocked. Parliament specifically prohibited appeals to Rome in 1533, just as a new archbishop of Canterbury, Thomas Cranmer (1489–1556), granted Henry the annulment he had sought and solemnized his marriage to Anne Boleyn. The 1534 Act of Supremacy declared the king to be "supreme head of the church in England," and for good measure Parliament made it treasonous to say otherwise. In 1535 a few

Figure 11.2. Sir/Saint Thomas More (1478–1535). Hans Holbein the Younger (1497–1543), "Sir Thomas More," 1527. (*The Frick Collection, New York, NY.*)

brave souls who refused commands to endorse the king's supremacy over the church, including Thomas More, the former chancellor, and Bishop John Fisher of Rochester, were beheaded at the Tower of London.

Since the Latin mass continued to be celebrated as before, the priest vested as before, parishioners had only a dim idea of the great changes afoot. But in 1536 Parliament suppressed England's smaller monasteries and confiscated their property to the profit of the king.[11] This attack on the fabric of church life gave rise to rumors that parish churches too would be closed, which sparked a series of popular uprisings, mostly in northern England, known as the Pilgrimage of Grace (1536–1537). As one of their manifestos proclaimed, the rebels aimed at "maintenance of the faith of God, the right and liberty of his church." Though mobilizing sizable forces in places, they were talked into laying down their arms, and nothing changed. As in other parts of Europe, England's common folk were to be governed in matters of religion, not consulted.

What kind of church was England to have? Two court factions struggled over this question for the balance of Henry's reign. The group that sympathized with the doctrines of the continental Reformers was led by Thomas Cromwell (d. 1540), the architect of the king's Reformation legislation; Archbishop Thomas Cranmer; and Edward Seymour, duke of Somerset (1500–1552), the uncle of Henry's third wife,[12] Jane Seymour. The group that sought to preserve as much as possible of Catholic doctrine and practice was led by Thomas Howard, duke of Norfolk (1473–1554), and Stephen Gardiner, bishop of Winchester (1497–1555). Various credal statements were drafted, sometimes influenced by the 1530 Augsburg Confession and sometimes not. Henry's preferences are evident in the so-called King's Book, adopted by Parliament in 1543, which asserts a Catholic interpretation of the eucharist and specifically defends human free will against the Protestant doctrine of predestination. When the confiscation of chantries was proposed (1545–1546),[13] the measure was defended before a skeptical Parliament not on doctrinal but on fiscal grounds—the king needed money. But in 1546 Howard was accused of treason, and Gardiner's name was dropped from a proposed list of regency councillors for the king's nine-year-old son.

Policy in the reign of *Edward VI* (ruled 1547–1553) was made initially by Seymour, the young king's great-uncle, and after 1549 by a more zealous Protestant, John Dudley, earl of Warwick (1504–1553). It was of great importance for England's subsequent religious history that for Seymour and Dudley, Reformation doctrine came from Zurich and Geneva, not the

Augsburg Confession.[14] The new reign began with a royal decree (1547) banning all emblems of "superstition," including altars,[15] all religious images, candles, and processions. Royal commissioners made a circuit of the kingdom's parishes over the next few years to enforce the decree, though they met a good deal of resistance.

Meanwhile, a committee under Cranmer's direction was preparing an English- language liturgy, with texts for the traditional monastic hours[16] as well as for the mass. *The Book of Common Prayer* was endorsed by Convocation (1549), after Seymour intimidated conservative bishops into abstaining. Introduction of the Prayer-Book liturgy provoked a brief uprising in the west of England, where rebels demanded that every priest at mass pray for the souls of the dead by name, "as our forefathers did." Three years later Convocation approved a credal statement, the *Forty-two Articles*, which repudiated Catholic teaching on the presence of Christ's body in the eucharist but did not endorse the Reformed doctrine of predestination. Under Dudley's influence, Convocation issued a second *Book of Common Prayer* (1552), which confirmed the Reformed understanding of the rite that was now called holy communion, no longer the mass. The legislation of Edward's reign thus amounted to a revolution in belief and worship going well beyond Henry VIII's revolution in the governance of the church. Whether changes of this magnitude could have been successfully imposed on an unwilling populace remains uncertain. When Edward VI died of an illness (1553), England's new ruler was the Catholic daughter of Henry VIII and Catherine of Aragon.

Mary Tudor (ruled 1553–1558) easily overcame a Protestant conspiracy mounted by Dudley,[17] as well as a brief rising in favor of her Protestant half sister, Anne Boleyn's daughter Elizabeth, which was provoked by Mary's marriage to a foreign prince, Spain's Philip II (1554). But her restoration of Catholic worship and of England's ties to Rome evoked no more resistance than Henry VIII's Act of Supremacy in 1534. Some of Henry's conservative bishops—those who opposed a Protestant theology for the new church and were deprived of office under Edward VI—had by now accepted papal supremacy and regained their positions under Mary; Stephen Gardiner and others carried on learned polemics with continental Reformers. To deal with the convinced Protestants whose numbers had grown appreciably during the previous reign, the heresy laws of old were also reinstated. Among the roughly three hundred victims during Mary's reign, many were Anabaptists. Some were leaders of the Protestant wing of England's clergy who had not gone into exile on the continent,[18] like the preacher Hugh Latimer, (1485–1555); they met their deaths as bravely as

Figure 11.3. Mary Tudor. Anthonis Mor, "Mary Tudor, Princess of England."
(*Scala | Art Resource, New York, NY | Museo del Prado, Madrid.*)

More and Fisher under Henry VIII.[19] Meanwhile, churchwardens around
the country brought out altars and statues and restored them to their
places of honor. The fact that these and other church furnishings had been
carefully hidden away, not destroyed, suggests parish leaders were hoping that the changes dictated from on high under Edward VI would not
last. In fact change was only beginning. In 1558 the ailing and childless
Mary recognized her Protestant half sister as her lawful successor.

Elizabeth I (ruled 1558–1603) was recognized by the 1559 Act of Supremacy as "supreme governor" of the Church of England.[20] Insofar as the

Figure 11.4. Protestant Martyrs under Queen Mary. The Burning of Bishops Hugh Latimer and John Ridley, John Foxe, Book of Martyrs (London, 1776). (*Special Collections, University of Minnesota Library.*)

new queen's intentions may be divined,[21] it seems Elizabeth envisioned a straightforward restoration of the *Book of Common Prayer* and the *Forty-two Articles* of 1552. Note, however, that a church governed by bishops was an unlikely spiritual home for the zealous preachers who now returned from exile in the continental centers of Reformed Protestantism.[22] Elizabeth's Reformation statutes also blurred some doctrinal and liturgical distinctions. The 1559 Act of Uniformity reinstated the *Book of Common Prayer* of 1552, but with new language permitting a Catholic as well as a Reformed understanding of the eucharist and an "Ornaments Rubric" requiring clergy to wear the traditional vestments. When thirty-seven London clerics of a Reformed Protestant temper ostentatiously refused to don "popish rags" for their services, Elizabeth insisted on their removal from office. The queen's concessions to Catholic sentiment were dictated by the politics of getting her statutes accepted in the House of Lords,[23] but they also reflect her fears of the kind of popular resistance to radical changes in worship that had been evident in the two previous reigns. If England's people were still in some sense Catholic, Elizabeth and her officials took well-considered steps toward creating a Protestant sensibility.[24] Royal commissioners who now made a circuit of the parishes ensured that altars and statues and other "superstitious" church furnishings were destroyed—not hidden away for future use, as in Edward VI's time. Copies of the popular *Book of*

Figure 11.5. Elizabeth I (reigned 1558–1603), standing on a map of England. Marcus Gheeraerts the Younger (1561/2–1636), "Elizabeth I." (*National Portrait Gallery, London.*)

Martyrs by John Foxe (1517–1587), recounting in particular the gruesome torments suffered by faithful Christians under "Bloody Mary" Tudor, were ordered placed in every parish church, along with a copy of the English-language Great Bible completed under Henry VIII (1539).

Partly in hopes of preserving amity with Spain, Elizabeth was at first loath to see Catholics punished for their beliefs—but not after a series of

Catholic plots against her were sparked by Pope Pius V's declaration (1570) that she was excommunicated and that faithful Catholics must no longer recognize her as queen.[25] In 1574 she authorized the first executions of "seminary priests," trained at a seminary for English Catholic exiles at Douai in the Low Countries. A 1582 statute declared seminary priests and Jesuit missionaries automatically guilty of treason, a crime punishable by death. By the 1580s Catholic "Recusants," willing to accept the penalties for their form of dissent, were a dwindling minority.[26]

Meanwhile, Spanish backing for Catholic plots in England helped persuade Elizabeth to provide highly visible support for the Dutch Revolt. This in turn provoked Philip II to send against England his "invincible Armada" (1588), the defeat of which stoked an English national pride that was by now firmly identified with the Protestant cause.[27] But a Protestant foreign policy was of little consolation for those frustrated by the queen's apparent unwillingness to "complete" England's Reformation. When the new Protestant bishops presumed to endorse a new version of the *Forty-two Articles* (1562–1563) they were sharply reprimanded; only in the queen's good time were the *Thirty-nine Articles* approved, and by Parliament, not Convocation (1571). When groups of devout Protestant clergy and laity formed biblical study groups known as "prophesyings,"[28] Elizabeth ordered the archbishop of Canterbury to suppress these divisive gatherings; when he refused (1576), she placed him under house arrest,

Figure 11.6. The Defeat of the Spanish Armada. Netherlandish School, sixteenth century, Launch of Fireships against the Spanish Armada. *(National Maritime Museum, Greenwich, England.)*

waited for him to die, and found a successor, John Whitgift (1583–1604), who was more than willing to carry out her wishes. To silence those among his clergy who were now calling openly for a presbyterian[29] rather than an episcopal form of church governance, Whitgift required all clergy to swear to the *Thirty-nine Articles,* which included a defense of episcopal authority. Eventually, some three hundred clergy were dismissed for refusing the oath. Such pressures from above provoked a series of bitterly satirical anonymous pamphlets(1588–1589) denouncing the queen's bishops for their betrayal of the Reformation.[30] An angry Elizabeth authorized a roundup of zealous Protestants, of whom a few were executed. The Conventicle[31] Act of 1593 threatened death for anyone (not just Catholics) who refused to attend Church of England services.

By the end of Elizabeth's reign the ambiguities of her religious legislation were causing serious dissension. For example, the *Thirty-nine Articles* took no position on the key question of predestination. Hence a group of young professors and students at Oxford felt at liberty to espouse publicly the doctrine of human free will. To set these errant youngsters straight, Archbishop Whitgift convened a synod that approved the Calvinist doctrine of predestination in its most extreme form (1595).[32] But the queen ordered the withdrawal of this new statement, precisely because it went beyond the *Thirty-nine Articles.* Meanwhile, and without rejecting the authority of their bishops, clerics sympathetic to presbyterian ideas on church governance were forming Netherlands-style *classes* with like-minded colleagues in the same district. Sympathetic lay patrons were endowing preacherships, earmarked for orthodox Calvinists, to make up for a lack of preaching by the poorly paid and sometimes poorly educated parish clergy. The earlier controversy over "popish rags" was not forgotten either. Indeed there was now a more general demand for purging the liturgy of a long list of "popish" elements, like saints' days, candles, the exchange of rings at marriage, prayers at the graveside, and the religious celebration of Christmas.[33] Finally, it grieved many earnest Christians that Sunday, the Lord's day, was mainly given over to such lewd entertainments as drinking, dancing, and plays and that traditional parish festivals continued as before, with the same pagan overtones, like dancing around the Maypole.[34]

Those expressing such sentiments had come to be known as Puritans. But Puritanism in the latter years of Elizabeth's reign was a current of opinion within the Church of England, not a separate church body. Puritans had a distinctive tendency to personalize the doctrine of predestination, searching within their own experience for a moment of conversion at which God's grace had entered their lives. Still, on the doctrinal formula of predestination, and also on a more proper observance of the sabbath, most bishops were of the same mind as the presbyterians with whom they so strongly disagreed on church governance.

Figure 11.7. A godly household in Flanders. Anthonius Claeissins, "A Family Saying Grace before a Meal," c. 1585. (*The Shakespeare Birthplace Trust, Stratford-upon-Avon, England.*)

Also, not all of those who hoped to see the church some day "purified" of episcopacy and popish ritual had presbyterian views on church order. Refusing to recognize any larger church body, Separatists believed decisions on all important matters must be made by each congregation.[35] Searching their consciences for evidence of God's grace in their lives, like other Puritans, Separatists also concluded that baptism must be the expression of the precious experience of conversion—and hence not a ritual suitable for infants. Harassed by Church of England authorities, in part because of their views on baptism, some Separatist or "Baptist"[36] congregations took refuge abroad.[37] Within the broad Puritan current there were thus numerous countercurrents flowing in different directions. The demarcation between defenders of the established church and a Puritan opposition, overly simple for Elizabeth's reign, did eventually become a battle line, but only because of the events of the next two reigns.

King James I (ruled in England 1603–1625)[38] made promises to relax the laws against Catholic Recusants but backed down in the face of pressure from a solidly Protestant Parliament. James was perhaps never more in harmony with his subjects in England than in the months following the foiled Gunpowder Plot (November 1605), in which Guy Fawkes and several other Catholics secreted thirty-four barrels of powder beneath the House of Lords. For Protestants this was not just the act of a few men; it was a diabolical popish plot directed from abroad, with the complicity of people whose foreign allegiance prevented their being true Englishmen. The growing sense of a distinctive English identity included a streak of rabid anti-Catholicism;

Figure 11.8. James I of England (reigned 1603–1625) and VI of Scotland. Daniel Mystens, "James I of England and VI of Scotland," c. 1621. (*National Portrait Gallery, London.*)

England's greatest writer of a later generation could speak of Catholicism not so much as a religion as a "[foreign] priestly despotism under the cloak of religion." The penal laws now multiplied: Recusants were forbidden to practice law, take a university decree, or vote in local or parliamentary elections. A bill for making Catholics wear red hats (as Jews were made to do in papal Rome) was discussed but failed to pass.[39]

In just about every other respect James's reign sowed mistrust of the crown, especially among ardent Protestants. Because of his experience as king of Scotland, he made it clear he was no friend of those who wanted a presbyterian Church of England.[40] As a self-styled political theorist, he believed a king was answerable only to God, not to his subjects—he once shocked the House of Commons by referring to himself as an "absolute" monarch.[41] Under Elizabeth, members of the privy council formed a faction in Commons, helping to guide the House's deliberations; James elevated his councillors to the upper nobility,[42] leaving himself no organized party in the lower House. James's queen, Anne of Denmark, converted to Catholicism, creating at the court an island of toleration for Catholicism, which made Puritans in particular deeply suspicious.

Also, the expenses of James's household much exceeded those of the frugal Elizabeth; critics made no allowance for the fact that Elizabeth did not have a family to maintain in royal state, but they did note that some of the king's largesse went to two handsome male favorites, each in turn raised to a high place in his council. Since Parliament refused to increase the subsidies granted during Elizabeth's reign, James and his council made do with customs revenues, which grew as foreign trade increased. Between 1611 and 1621 James governed without summoning Parliament, save for one brief and contentious session (1614). This was not illegal, but it was unprecedented, and men with experience in Parliament pondered what it meant when the king had no need for his subjects' consent.

The separate issues of religion, governance, and state finance fused together in debates on foreign policy. During the early stages of the Thirty Years' War, there was wide support for the popular Princess Elizabeth, wife of the embattled Frederick V of the Palatinate, but little appreciation of what going to war would cost. Meanwhile, seasoned Spanish diplomats dangled before the king hopes of a Spanish bride for his son and heir, Prince Charles. The idea of a Spanish Catholic match was deeply unpopular, but James had visions of a Spanish dowry that would solve his financial problems. After years of fruitless discussions, Prince Charles and the duke of Buckingham, his father's current favorite, crossed the English Channel and rode incognito across France to reach Madrid, only to learn Spain was not interested in a marriage under conditions England could accept (1623).[43] Summoned the following year, Parliament readily accepted proposals to

Figure 11.9. Charles I of England and Scotland (reigned 1625–1646). Anthony van Dyck, "Portrait of Charles I," 1637–1638. (*National Gallery.*)

break England's treaties with Spain. For a moment, it seemed that James's heir and Parliament would unite behind an anti-Spanish policy.

But *Charles I* (ruled 1625–1646) and Buckingham concealed from Parliament the true costs of an ambitious policy that included subsidies for Protestant armies in Germany and naval expeditions against Spain. This left the new king hungry for money and Parliament puzzled by his need for it. Moreover, none of the ventures that England now undertook or helped sponsor met with success; for example, the English fleet that raided

Cadiz captured the wine stores of the Spanish navy, leading to a few days of merriment during which the Americas treasure fleet slipped into port unmolested. Finally, an anti-Spanish policy was not necessarily a Protestant policy. France's Cardinal Richelieu was promoting anti-Habsburg coalitions well before the time he was free to mobilize France's resources toward this end. It was in this context that Buckingham arranged for Prince Charles to marry Henriette Marie, daughter of France's Louis XIII. Many English Protestants were offended by the new queen's Catholic chapel, and despite the king's denials they rightly suspected from his actions that some relaxation of the anti-Recusant laws had been part of the bargain. When Charles at Parliament's behest ordered stricter enforcement of the laws, Richelieu responded to this breach of faith with one of his own: English ships lent to France for the war against Spain were used instead in the siege of the Huguenot port of La Rochelle.[44] Protestant England was outraged.

Meanwhile, the Parliament of 1626 had raised the idea of having responses to their grievances before voting on the king's fiscal requests;[45] members demanded among other things that Buckingham, the architect of Charles's policies, be impeached[46] before the House of Lords on a long list of treason counts, including a fantastic accusation that he had poisoned the late King James. To save Buckingham from being tried on trumped-up charges Charles dismissed Parliament, without getting approval for the subsidies and customs duties he so desperately needed. Charles presumed the right to continue collecting the usual customs duties, and to make up what was lacking he levied a forced loan on his wealthy subjects.[47] A number of knights[48] and burghers refused to pay, appealing to the king's courts for vindication. But Charles and his councillors pressured judges to make sure no one escaped his quota in the loan. In one instance, the king's attorney general had the court record falsified to make it appear that a case actually decided on procedural grounds had established a precedent allowing the king to imprison his subjects without showing cause. As word of these tactics leaked out, there was widespread public discussion of the king's unprecedented attack on the rights of Englishmen.

When Parliament was again summoned in 1628, Commons refused to vote the requested subsidies until Charles accepted the Petition of Right, stating that no English subject could be forced to pay a loan or tax without approval by Parliament or held in prison without a showing of cause. But Charles's insistence that the customs duties he continued to collect were not a "tax" subject to parliamentary approval led to bitter disputes in the Parliament of 1629; members of Commons also claimed that the king's "Arminianism" in religion (see below) portended a Catholic and Spanish "tyranny" for England. When Charles ordered Parliament dissolved, two members of Commons held the speaker in his chair, while others barred the doors against those wishing to leave, until a resolution was passed declaring that anyone who paid customs duties or promoted Arminianism was a "capital enemy" of England. Charles decided that he, like his father, could govern England without Parliament.

England had by now made peace with Spain, relieving the pressure on the king's budget, while Buckingham's assassination by an unknown hand removed the most obvious target for popular hatred. Charles still needed revenue for the navy (he was properly concerned by the growth of Dutch naval power),[49] but his lawyers contrived a novel means of raising it. By tradition, five cities along the Channel were required to supply ships for the king's needs. Charles now commuted this nearly forgotten obligation to a payment for ships and extended "ship money" from the five ports to the whole kingdom (1634). As in the previous disputes over customs duties and forced loans, this novel practice was denounced in numerous pamphlets and tested in the royal courts. But the combination of ship money and the still increasing customs revenues enabled the king and his council to manage for eleven years (1629–1640) without summoning a Parliament, where Charles would have to confront the opposition to his policies head-on. Indeed, the king might have ended his days without ever calling a Parliament, had it not been for the religious policies that provoked war in Scotland.

Under James, a king who strongly defended episcopal authority against the presbyterian challenge, some bishops presented episcopacy as a matter of divine law, not mere human law; England's bishops were true successors of the Apostles, as were Roman Catholic and Eastern Orthodox bishops.[50] This implied recognition that the Catholic Church was a true church, albeit misguided on some points, was deeply offensive to Puritans, but not to King James. Indeed, he saw the Church of England as a "middle way" or happy medium between the excesses of papal tyranny and presbyterian fanaticism. In keeping with this conception of the church, some bishops and clergy pressed for restoring a solemnity of worship comparable to Catholicism, to complement the traditional Protestant emphasis on preaching. Among other things, they proposed moving the communion table[51] from the center of the church to the east end, where once the altar had stood, and surrounding it with a railing, where those who wished to do so might kneel for reception of communion.

Meanwhile, Puritans also vigorously attacked the doctrine of free will, which had been given a new lease on life by Elizabeth's refusal to sanction the bishops' condemnation of it (1595).[52] They denounced with equal vigor the doctrine of the apostolic succession of bishops and any effort to revive liturgical practices of the pre-Reformation era. Puritan opposition helped

Chapter 11

Figure 11.10. Archbishop William Laud. Anthony van Dyck, "Archbishop William Laud," 1633. (*Courtauld Institute of Art, London.*)

fuse these otherwise disconnected issues into a coherent point of view.[53] By the end of James's reign, Puritans were convinced that "Arminianism" was a dangerous stalking horse for that cesspool of iniquity, "popery" itself.[54]

William Laud (1573–1645), whom James I named bishop of St. David's, was one of a number of influential clerics eager to counter Puritan polemics point by point. Charles I signaled from an early date his backing for this "Arminian" tendency in the Church of England. He protected from parliamentary censure a cleric who wrote against Jesuit tracts but without including the (for Puritans) obligatory denunciation of Catholicism as the religion of Antichrist. The king baffled his subjects by his leniency to Recusants, repeatedly promising Parliament to enforce the penal laws more strictly but not doing so in practice; that some of his aristocratic advisers were known to be Catholics only made things worse. Finally, he promoted Laud through the ranks of the hierarchy, making him bishop of London (1628) and archbishop of Canterbury and leader of the church (1633). Despite increasingly vocal opposition from Puritan clergy and laity, Laud and other like-minded bishops worked to promote liturgical reform throughout England. If churchwardens of former times were badgered for not having gotten rid of their altars, they were badgered now for not setting the communion table "altar-wise" in the east end of the church and surrounding it with a railing at which those receiving communion were to kneel.

Charles and Laud decided that Scotland too must have the benefit of this new order. Under King James a weak form of episcopacy was superimposed on the Scots Presbyterian Kirk in 1570. He later demanded that the Scots conform to certain usages in England's *Book of Common Prayer* (1614) but had the good sense to back down on further changes that evoked opposition. The version of the *Book of Common Prayer* now decreed for Scotland, following perfunctory consultations in the northern kingdom, was slightly modified to suit Scottish sensibilities. But the first use of the new service in Edinburgh's cathedral of St. Giles (July 1637) caused a major riot, which served to galvanize opposition in much of the country. Early in 1638, a National Covenant demanding a General Assembly of Scotland's Presbyterian Kirk was signed with great ceremony by nobles, preachers, and burghers. The General Assembly duly met, voting in large majorities to abolish all changes in worship imposed by James I and Charles I, as well as the office of bishop.

Meanwhile, the Catholic faction among the king's advisers urged him to be bold in facing down the Scots. This was bad advice, but Charles was not accustomed to seek counsel from men who failed to tell him what he wanted to hear. He marched to Scotland with an army, but lacking funds to keep his men in the field he accepted an inconclusive treaty. By refusing in subsequent discussions to abandon episcopacy in Scotland, he in effect prolonged a war for which he had no resources. The so-called Short Parliament (April 1640) was quickly dissolved when Charles found that appeals to English patriotism against the Scots were of no avail; in fact, opposition leaders in Parliament were already in contact with Scottish Covenanters. When the Covenant Army entered northern England, Charles had to agree to buy them off; but the invaders pointedly refused to withdraw until they had their money in hand. Charles had to summon what came to be known as the Long Parliament.

Even now, Charles and the opposition in Parliament might have reached an accommodation had it not been for unforeseen events in Ireland. Since the twelfth century, the descendants of a conquering English aristocracy based in the area around Dublin had gradually extended their authority to the rest of the country, save for the northern region of Ulster, where native Irish chieftains still ruled.[55] The Reformation was officially proclaimed when a docile Irish Parliament created the Church of Ireland (1534). But strong support for the Church of Ireland was not evident until "new English" settlers occupied land that was confiscated from Irish chieftains during Elizabeth's reign and regranted for "plantation" or colonization by English entrepreneurs. By the late sixteenth century, as seminary priests trained in the Low Countries ministered to the "Old English," and bards created a new Catholic literature in Irish,[56] the Counter-Reformation was well underway. From 1594 until 1603 Ulster's chieftains fought an ultimately futile struggle against England's political control of the country; their flight to France in 1607 created an opportunity for more extensive "plantations." In parts of Ulster groups of English or Scottish colonists settled solid blocks of land from which Irish Catholic landholders and tenants were forcibly removed. England's government in Ireland, represented from 1632 to 1641 by Thomas Wentworth, earl of Strafford, did not shrink from stern measures to quash resistance.[57] But in October 1641, Old English nobles and Irish chieftains conspired to seize fortified posts in Ulster; their declared goal was the defense of Irish and Old English rights, not rebellion against the crown—one leader even claimed to be acting in the king's name. This carefully orchestrated rising among the elite sparked a very different kind of rebellion, as local groups of Catholic Irish, often led by women, spontaneously vented their fury on Protestant settlers, leaving perhaps four thousand dead and many more expelled from their lands. This was the desperate violence of the dispossessed, comparable in some ways to Indian uprisings against English settlers in North America.[58] But in Protestant England, things were seen rather differently.

King Charles had found himself virtually powerless as Parliament convened in November 1640. He accepted Commons' condemnation of ship money as illegal, as well as a bill providing that Parliament must meet at least every three years. But Commons also voted to impeach the king's two most detested councillors, Archbishop Laud and the earl of Strafford.[59] Despite solemn assurances from the king that the charges against Strafford were baseless, the House of Lords voted a sentence of death.[60] After an attempt organized by the king to break Strafford out of prison was foiled, a mob outside the palace howled for Strafford's blood; Charles did as he had to, signing an innocent man's execution warrant. Still mistrustful of the king's intentions (not without reason),[61] the opposition leadership forced him to accept a bill providing that Parliament could not be dissolved without the consent of the members.

At this point Charles made a surprise trip to Scotland (August 1641), where he first attempted (again without success) to organize the overthrow of the Covenanters and then accepted a treaty abolishing episcopacy in Scotland. Hoping to return to London with some measure of prestige restored for having made peace with his Scottish subjects, Charles was instead engulfed by a wave of anti-Catholic hysteria touched off by lurid reports of the rebellion in Ireland. By a vote of 159 to 148, Commons passed the so-called Grand Remonstrance, declaring that all the evils England had suffered for many years past were part of a vast popish plot, fomented by Jesuits and bishops, that had now reached its horrid climax in the slaughter of law-abiding English settlers in Ireland. In the House of Lords, twelve conservative bishops declared that angry crowds in the streets were making it dangerous for them to attend sessions. Commons impeached the bishops and placed them under arrest, depriving the king of twelve votes in the upper house. Charles retaliated by presenting a bill of impeachment for six leaders of the opposition (January 1642), but the Lords balked, and Charles's efforts to carry out the arrests himself roused great anger.[62] The king and his entourage soon had to quit a capital he no longer controlled. Negotiations between the two sides continued for several months, but when Charles was presented with an ultimatum that would have stripped him of all effective authority, he chose instead to raise an army, as Parliament did the same. England was at war.

The *Presbyterian settlement* was a consequence of Parliament's victory in England's Civil War. In 1645 Parliament created a New Model Army, based on egalitarian principles: the officer ranks were for the first time opened to men not of noble birth. Though Oliver Cromwell (1599–1658), one of the Army's more successful leaders, was of the lesser nobility,[63] most commanders were commoners. It was not the Parliament but this new and effective fighting force that defeated the king's armies in several crucial battles. The Parliament was made up of respected and propertied gentlemen; the army had a good sprinkling of social upstarts. More important, Parliament had legitimacy, but the army had power.

Most members of the Long Parliament, by now Presbyterians, favored an alliance with the Scottish Covenanters (concluded in 1644) and a national Presbyterian church, free of bishops, similar to Scotland's. A national synod of Presbyterian clergy (the Westminster Assembly, 1645) adopted an orthodox Calvinist creed,[64] but it was only in 1646, after the king's armies had been decisively defeated, that Parliament abolished episcopacy and created a Church of England governed along presbyterian

lines. Puritan austerity in worship and Puritan morality were the new orthodoxy. Churchwardens were now badgered if they failed to bar the
church door on Christmas day, lest parishioners sneak in for Christmas
carols and other popish ceremonies.

But the army's leading officers, Cromwell included, were Independents,
not Presbyterians; they favored congregational autonomy for the church,[65]
and toleration for the Protestant sects (like the Anabaptists) condemned as
heretical by the Presbyterians. This diversity of opinion was important for
the army, because Anabaptists could make good officers, and so could the
adherents of political factions like the Levellers, who demanded abolition
of the monarchy and a broadening of the franchise for parliamentary elections.[66] But once Charles I surrendered (1647), Presbyterians viewed the
army and its heretical friends as a liability; Parliament voted to dismiss the
army without pay. Instead, the army occupied London and dictated the
impeachment of eleven Presbyterian leaders. Following a confusing year
(1648) in which Charles I escaped from captivity and opened discussions
with a Parliament that now feared the army more than the king, the army
triumphed once more. Charles was recaptured, roughly a hundred Presbyterians were purged from the Long Parliament, and the members remaining agreed to try the king and order his execution as a traitor (1649).
Monarchy and the House of Lords were now abolished.

From 1649 until the restoration of monarchy in 1660, England was a *Commonwealth,* not a kingdom. Lavish revenues from the seizure of church lands
and the properties of the late king's supporters now supported ambitious
campaigns by the army. In Ireland, where leaders of a reorganized rebellion
had now joined forces with royalists, Cromwell's campaign of 1649–1650 was
decisive. At Drogheda and Wexford, he calmly sanctioned the slaughter of
defeated soldiers and civilians alike, for in his eyes this was God's retribution
on the Irish, "tainted" with the blood of English victims in 1641. In 1650–1651
he turned back two armies loyal to the late king's son, whom Scotland had
acclaimed as King Charles II. But neither the "Rump" of the Long Parliament
(finally dismissed by Cromwell in 1653) nor the "Parliament" whose members were handpicked by the Independent or Congregationalist churches
(1653)[67] was able to agree on a form of government for the now kingless England. In 1654 power was returned to the army, and in a constitution written
by leaders of the army, the Instrument of Government, Cromwell was named
Lord Protector of the Commonwealth. But when the Parliament elected according to this new constitution refused to accept the supremacy of the army,
it too was dissolved by Cromwell (1655). The next Parliament (1656–1659) offered the crown to Cromwell; he declined, but he did designate his son

Figure 11.11. Oliver Cromwell. Robert Walker, "Oliver Cromwell, Lord Protector of England," c. 1649. (*National Portrait Gallery, London.*)

Richard to succeed him as Protector, as Parliament had also suggested. But when Oliver Cromwell died (1658), the new Protector had little support either in Parliament (which he dissolved) or in the army. As leaders of the army conducted contentious discussions with members of the recalled Rump Parliament,[68] royalists and Presbyterians joined forces to raise an army in Scotland that marched south and entered London. A newly elected Parliament (including a revived House of Lords) negotiated the terms by which Charles I's son returned to England as King Charles II (ruled 1660–1685).

During the Commonwealth years the army leadership also had plans for a new order in England's religious life. Cromwell favored a unified national Protestant church, with full toleration for all of the disparate tendencies that might loosely be grouped together as Puritan. To an important degree, toleration of this kind already existed. The abolition of episcopacy (1646) meant that the episcopal courts that had traditionally exercised censorship over the publication of religious tracts no longer existed. The expulsion of the Presbyterians from Parliament (1649) undermined the authority of the orthodox Calvinist clerics who now filled most pastorates. Hence under Cromwell there was an explosion of sectarian opinions such as had not been seen anywhere in Europe since the early years of the German Reformation.[69] The Congregationalists or Independents were Calvinist in their theology of predestination and the sacraments, but not in their conception of church order. The Baptists or Separatists had by now split into two warring camps over the interpretation of Christ's redeeming death.[70] Other Separatists, known as Seekers, were not so much an organized sect as a loose grouping of believers who rejected any organized worship, gathering instead in small groups to read the Bible and seek illumination from the Spirit of God moving within them. The Seekers in turn gave rise to still other groups. One was the Ranters, whose preachers derided the idea that there was any such thing as "sin" for those truly possessed by God's grace. Another, popularly known as the Quakers, developed from the life and teaching of George Fox (1624–1691), an itinerant cobbler who believed that Christ had commissioned him to "turn people to that inward light, spirit and grace . . . that divine Spirit which would lead them all into Truth." The Friends (as Fox's followers called themselves) gathered in silence, waiting until someone among them was led by the Spirit within him or her to offer a word.

Figure 11.12. A Quaker Meeting. "Reunion of Quakers," seventeenth-century engraving from the school of E. Heemskerk. Note that it is a woman who speaks as worshipers listen. (*British Museum, London.*)

This proliferation of conflicting opinions about the ultimate nature of reality was as alarming to many seventeenth-century Englishmen as it had been to many Germans of the sixteenth century, all the more so because radical preachers were often (like George Fox) of humble background, and some called for an overturning of the social hierarchy as well as the hierarchy of the church.[71] Yet Cromwell remained a consistent advocate of toleration within the limits that he envisioned.[72] The Rump Parliament agreed (1650) to a Toleration Act abolishing the requirement to attend services of the national church,[73] but it also tightened existing laws against blasphemy and adultery, a reflection of Congregationalist fears about the unheard-of sects (like the Ranters) that now seemed to be sprouting like mushrooms. In fact, Congregationalist churches were just as eager to suppress the heretical doctrines of the Separatists as the Presbyterians had been to suppress the heretical doctrines of the Congregationalists. Cromwell persuaded the Congregationalist Parliament of 1653[74] to pass legislation enabling each parish to name "Tryers and Ejecters" to test the doctrine and qualifications of current or would-be pastors; this measure strengthened the generally Puritan character of the pastorate, but did nothing to still the imprecations that different groups hurled at one another. In 1656 Parliament thumbed its nose at Cromwell's desire for toleration by insisting on trying and severely punishing a Quaker leader named James Nayler for "blasphemy."

In the end, toleration for Protestant Dissenters was promised in the terms that Charles II agreed to (1660), though not in fact implemented for some time. Some 1,750 Puritan clerics were dismissed from their posts and replaced over time by clergy who accepted the authority of the restored bishops. In the so-called Clarendon Codes of 1661–1665 Dissenters as well as Recusants were banned from taking part in elections or attending universities and subjected to heavy fines for nonattendance at Church of England services. But the king's Act of Indulgence (1672) authorized dissenting Protestant congregations to purchase from the crown licenses to worship as they chose.[75] Puritan preachers of various persuasions, including many dismissed from office when Charles II came to the throne, could now function as pastors of regularly organized churches rather than underground conventicles. After so many vicissitudes, after so many versions of Christianity had each had its hour on the stage of power, England too was a nation that recognized one religion formally and many others informally.

✦

A moment's reflection on England's history between 1527 and 1672 corroborates two important points. First, politics and religion cannot be separated. It was not religion that made Henry VIII anxious for a male heir or gave him the force to cow his bishops, nor was it politics that made him reject the theological advice of the Protestant councillors who were the most natural supporters of England's break with Rome. The halfway house between Protestant and Catholic ideas of the church that Elizabeth I created for reasons of political prudence became, for King James I and Archbishop Laud, a principle of theology that allowed England to navigate safely between the contrary errors of Rome and Geneva. Charles I might conceivably have ended his reign without another Parliament, but Scottish Presbyterian resistance to the *Book of Common Prayer* forced him to confront the opposition in England. Again, the constitutional conflict between king and Parliament might possibly have been resolved short of war, except for the superheated English Protestant reaction to the rebellion in Ireland. Finally, the major Protestant parties involved in these conflicts seldom challenged the medieval principle that there must be only one law of belief for all of England. As in France, Germany, and the Dutch Republic, the limited toleration finally made available to Protestant dissenters was dearly bought. It was based not on a belief that subjects of the crown ought to be free to believe as they wished, but on recognition of the fact that all efforts to achieve by force the laudable goal of uniformity had failed.

Second, politics and religion by themselves do not provide a sufficient explanation for the flow of events. This is especially true for the years between 1640 and 1660. The respectable Presbyterian gentlemen of Parliament, much as they opposed Charles I, found a king more to their liking than the army and its lowborn clientele; it was the humbler folk who filled the army's ranks who wanted monarchy abolished altogether. Ireland's gentry, with a stake in the existing order, modulated their rebellion, but the dispossessed peasantry did not. Neither religion nor politics can be understood without an appreciation for the conflicts that divided people of differing wealth and status and for the visions of social harmony evoked to bridge such differences. This is the topic of Part IV.

IV SOCIETY AND COMMUNITY

The words "society" and "community" have a shared range of meaning.[1] But "society" usually refers to all who live in a given territory, while "community" usually refers to a smaller unit within the social body.[2] Also, "society" describes the complex of social relations in a morally neutral way; "community" describes a unity that surmounts individual or interest group conflicts. The people of a community are thought capable of achieving harmony because they make up a relatively small, face-to-face group. Was the medieval town or village a community in this ideal sense of the term? Or was it merely a less complicated version of our own market-driven society? For most of the twentieth century, social theorists have debated whether the idea of community indeed describes an earlier phase of human social evolution or simply expresses a nostalgia, on the part of thinkers unhappy with modern life, for a harmonious past that never existed.[3] Niccolo Machiavelli offered another alternative. He believed there could be a true community even in a large city like Florence, but only under two conditions: There had to be an external danger strong enough to overshadow normal tensions between haves and have-nots, and the common people had to have some share in political power.[4]

While differing about whether to define society according to class (as understood by Marx) or merely according to status groups,[5] Reformation historians have sought to explain religious choice in terms of economic conflicts. But the results have been mixed. Any social group one can name will be Lutheran in some areas, Catholic or Calvinist in others, and in still others impossible to classify as tending one way or the other. Literacy sometimes seems more important than economic status, as do political conflicts, like that which pitted the independent-minded magistrates of Toulouse against the judges of the Parlement of Toulouse, who naturally took the king's side in any dispute.[6] In two other large French cities, Lyon

211

and Rouen, what counted was not whether one was a rich master crafts-
man or a poor journeyman, but whether one's guild was new to the city or
long established.[7] Yet a great number of local studies, by authors espousing very different views of society, have found group rivalries of one kind
or another taking on a confessional coloration. There seem to be social explanations for religious choice, if not necessarily economic ones. In fact,
early modern Europeans survived by the aid of their fellows—kindred,
neighbors, members of the same guild or the same political faction. In a
matter as complicated as religion, it was a mark of good sense to do as
one's fellows did. This pattern of collective action has led scholars to ask
what the different forms of group solidarity may have meant for the Reformation. "Society" and "community"[8] have to be looked at together.

Chapter 12 describes the *society* of late medieval Christendom, defined
by myriad interest group conflicts, as well as the ideal of *community*, as represented by the family, the parish, the village, and the town. Chapter 13
then examines interest group conflicts in the German and Swiss Reformation, together with Lutheran and Swiss Protestant ideas on how conflicts
were to be surmounted in a true Christian community. Chapter 14 considers the same questions for the Calvinist and Catholic Reformations outside the empire and concludes with a look at a few of the religiously mixed
urban societies that represent the greatest break from medieval conceptions of the social order.

12 | Society and Community

Late Medieval Background

SOCIETY

Christendom in the late Middle Ages was predominantly rural, and its slow growth beyond the limits of subsistence farming was mainly due to incremental changes in agriculture. Yet the fraction of its people that lived in towns created the market conditions that helped stimulate innovation in the countryside.[1] Town and countryside are often contrasted—townsmen certainly thought of their rural neighbors as mere bumpkins—but both were shaped in the medieval centuries by the same economic and social processes. Priests and the members of male and female religious orders were an even smaller fraction of the population.[2] There are indications that lay people of the late Middle Ages were more willing than ever to follow the guidance of the clergy,[3] but there is also evidence of growing resentment, in some parts of Europe more than others, of the privileges that set the clergy apart from lay people. This survey of structural conflicts in late medieval society takes up, in order, the countryside, the towns, and relations between clergy and laity.

From roughly 500 if not earlier, much of Europe's arable land was parceled out into large manors or estates, organized for the profit of great landowners who eventually came to be seen as Europe's *nobility*. Nobles liked to think of themselves as a superior breed of human stock,[4] descended from valiant ancestors of the distant past, able to face unafraid the shock of battle that made ordinary men quake. Though the origins of these families were in fact quite heterogeneous,[5] so long as success in war depended in part on a ruler's ability to deploy large numbers of the fighting-age landholders

213

who alone could afford to equip themselves as heavily armed horsemen,[6] the nobility's dominant place in Europe's social order was secure. But the advent of new infantry tactics in the fourteenth century diminished the military importance of mounted warriors,[7] just as men from burgher families, fortified by university degrees, were moving into judicial and administrative posts formerly monopolized by nobles. In many parts of Europe, these new men acquired titles of nobility, much to the disgust of the old nobility.[8] Like their burgher cousins, who also invested in land, the new nobles were often better estate managers, introducing new crops, devising new ways to squeeze income from their peasants (see below), and making loans to spendthrift traditional nobles, which not infrequently led to foreclosure.

The one sphere in which the nobility doggedly maintained its dominance was the church. The great bulk of the church's landed income came from donations by rulers and especially by the nobility.[9] Noble families endowed many of Europe's parish churches; they also alienated parcels of land to monasteries and convents, often presided over by their younger sons and daughters. Would-be reformers of the clergy had long demanded observance of the canon law requirement that a certain percentage of important positions be set aside for non-noble clerics with university degrees in canon law or theology. But the nobility fought off the reformers; in Strasbourg, for example, members of the cathedral chapter, from which bishops were often chosen, had to have sixteen quarters of nobility.[10] Having made the church rich, noble families regarded the church's places of honor as the birthright of their surplus children. In a city like Strasbourg, the Reformation was in part a burgher protest against a church dominated by the rural nobility.

Peasants made up the pool of labor for the great estates.[11] Until about 1150 most peasants had the legal status of unfree persons, or *serfs*. Serfs could not be sold by their noble or ecclesiastical lords, but in other respects their status was no different from that of slaves.[12] Serfs could not leave the patch of ground tilled by their ancestors; they could not testify against a free man or woman; they had to marry their daughters as dictated by the lord. Lords were free to demand from serfs extra labor on the lord's demesne land[13] or a higher portion of the harvest, over and above what was theirs by custom. This was not an agrarian economy that generated a large surplus. Serfs produced for their families and for the lord's portion; what was left they bartered for goods they needed. Money had not been widely used in transactions among rural folk for centuries. But after about 1150, the growth of cities (see below) generated a new, cash-based economy. Needing workers for their crafts, towns offered freedom to serfs.[14] To avoid the trouble and expense of fetching back runaways, some lords granted their serfs freedom in return for annual lease payments in cash. To provide more grain for an expanding population, other nobles developed newly cleared land; to attract settlers, they offered inducements, including freedom for serfs. The great population catastrophe of the fourteenth century, due to famines as well as plagues like the Black Death,[15] was a good time for Europe's remaining serfs, as lords converted demesne lands to leaseholds for former serfs, rather than having to keep their serfs from running off to better opportunities elsewhere.

But other responses to the agrarian labor shortage were also possible. In the early fifteenth century, the prince-abbots of many south German monasteries forced peasants, under threat of arbitrary imprisonment, to sign documents acknowledging their status as serfs. This was the part of Germany marked by a series of rural uprisings, beginning in the 1440s. Some rebellions opposed departures from "old law," the customs regulating what landholders could demand. Others demanded "godly law," meaning that serfdom and other customs, no matter how old, were evil and must be abolished.[16] The close connection between the enserfment of the fifteenth century and the great Peasants War of 1524–1526 is indicated not only by the geography of the revolt, but also by where it did not occur. Though there were centers of the revolt to the west and east of Bavaria, there was no rebellion in the duchy itself, apparently because there had been no enserfment. Bavaria had a tradition of strong government— monasteries and nobles were simply not permitted to treat peasants in a way that curtailed their ability to pay taxes to the duke. After 1526, monasteries and other lords in the areas affected by the revolt made agreements with peasants recognizing the abolition of serfdom; this much was achieved by the rebellion.

Serfdom still had a future farther east. Beginning about 1450, Europe's population began a long period of recovery, until population levels of the pre-Black Death era were surpassed in most areas by about 1600.[17] To cash in on the growing demand for grain during this period, noble proprietors in east-central Europe compelled hitherto free peasants either to become serfs or to accept the burdens of labor-service associated with serfdom.[18] Rulers had a natural interest in protecting peasant wealth for purposes of their own taxation. But just as there was no superior to tell Germany's prince-abbots how to treat their peasants, rulers in Poland, Bohemia, Hungary, and the Austrian lands had little control over what nobles did on their estates. In some areas the nobility's normal contempt for the peasantry was enhanced by language differences: thus Polish peasants were enserfed by German lords in northern Poland, Ukrainian peasants by Polish lords in southeastern Poland, and Slovak peasants by Hungarian lords in Habsburg Hungary. Czech peasants in Bohemia were enserfed by the polyglot aristocracy that won the battle of White Mountain.[19] Thus by about 1650 there was a new line of division in rural Europe. West of the

Elbe River, peasants might be poor or rich, but they were legally free and not bound by labor service. To the east, peasants were either unfree or bound by labor service.

Some peasants owned their land,[20] but in most places they were a small fraction of those tilling the soil. As serfdom disappeared from Europe west of the Elbe, on different timetables in different areas, the *tenant farmer* became the "common man" of the countryside. Tenants leased their land, usually for lengthy periods, like seven to nine years. Their living standards varied enormously, depending on many different circumstances. One was the size of the holding; another was security of tenure. In Lombardy,[21] lords had an incentive to renew their tenants' leases, because local law required a lord not renewing the lease to pay for improvements put in place by his tenant. In England, by contrast, tenant farmers faced eviction wherever the major landowners of a village determined on "enclosure," meaning that scattered fields[22] were either consolidated or converted to pasture. This process began in the fifteenth century, as dwindling grain prices in an era of depopulation made the coveted wool[23] of England's sheep a better crop, and continued into the nineteenth century.

Terms of the lease were another important consideration. As grain prices rose again after about 1450, tenant farmers prospered in the Low Countries and northern France, where tenants owed landlords only the annual rent, but less so in much of Italy, where sharecropping was the common arrangement. Lords could demand higher rents as leases expired but not if tenants had the option of moving on to a better arrangement elsewhere. In southern France, for example, rents increased significantly only after about 1600, when there was no more new land to be opened for cultivation by contractors and their tenant farmers. Demography and inheritance customs played a role as well. Especially in regions of partible inheritance,[24] abundant families meant a splintering of tenancies that left the new generation without enough land to scrape out a living. Finally, beginning in the fourteenth or fifteenth century, depending on the area, the prince's tax collectors were a veritable scourge—peasants sometimes had to borrow at high rates to make the cash payments. More than anything else, it was the steadily increasing levels of taxation that drove peasants in late medieval and early modern Europe to take up arms against the existing order.

Despite all the vicissitudes that left a few men rich and their fellows not far from poverty, tenant farmers had an honorable status. They were the managers of the rural economy. Looked down on by their social betters, they were the solid citizens of the village communities to be discussed below. The people on whom tenant farmers could look down were the hired hands, known in England as *cottagers*. These relative new-

Figure 12.1. A Peasant Feast. Pieter Bruegel the Elder (ca. 1525–1569), "Peasant Wedding." (*Kunsthistorisches Museum, Vienna.*)

comers to the local scene supplemented the wages they received from landlords or from wealthy tenant farmers by growing what their could on tiny patches of ground attached to their cottages. Their time of opportunity was during the agricultural depression of the late Middle Ages, when labor was at a premium. Despite laws enacted in response to the clamor of landholders, wages could not be kept at pre-Black Death levels. According to scholars who have examined records of the meals provided to day laborers in some areas, the rural working man had a richer diet in the late fourteenth century than at any time until the twentieth century. But as rural population rose again, especially after about 1500, wages were locked in while prices for basic necessities steadily rose. Soon there were too many working folk for the rural economy to support. Mercenary warfare was an option for young men, especially in Switzerland and south Germany, the favored recruiting grounds for military entrepreneurs. Other options were to wander the roads as vagabonds (see Figure 12.2) or to migrate to the nearest town. Cities in this era were hothouses of disease, never able to maintain their population by natural increase. They gladly opened their gates to the rural poor, so long as it was understood they must fend for themselves.

Figure 12.2. A Poor Vagabond. Hieronymus Bosch (d. 1516), "The Prodigal Son." (*Museum Boijmans-van Beuningen, Rotterdam.*)

Until the eleventh century *cities* functioned mainly as administrative centers. The county, a Roman political unit preserved by medieval rulers, was ruled by the count from a castle in his major *civitas* (city). Towns were but a shadow of what they had been in late Roman times, for social upheavals and barbarian invasions had repeatedly devastated urban life between roughly 250 and 850.[25] As ecclesiastical rulers of dioceses that often perpetuated the boundaries of Roman administrative units, bishops too occupied fortified urban centers; within the boundaries of the Holy Roman Empire, they often ruled their cities as prince-bishops.[26] Counts and bishops governed with the help of a sparsely documented local elite. Some of these "better sort of people"[27] were merchants grown prosperous in local or even long-distance trade; others were lesser nobles who settled in town without cutting their ties to the rural economy. Between about 1050 and 1150, earlier in Italy than elsewhere, the better sort of people set up town governments of their own, the so-called *communes*, relegating the count or the bishop to the background.[28] The cities of northern and central Italy were generally larger than those north of the Alps, and their communes were stronger, often asserting economic and military control of the entire county; communes in Germany in the Low Countries were fortunate to master more than a mile or two of territory beyond their city walls.

The commune was a sworn association of male citizens.[29] In Italy and southern France, citizen assemblies elected a two-man team of consuls[30] each year. In Castile, annual town meetings in which women as well as men participated (this was unusual) chose officials whose titles reflected centuries of Muslim rule.[31] In Germany and the Low Countries and northern France, councils of aldermen[32] chose their own successors, permitting members of the same families to rotate in and out of office. After about 1100, new towns were usually chartered as cities by a local ruler and endowed from the outset with the kind of communal government now familiar in older cities. The ruling elite were often known as "magnates" in Italy. Elsewhere they were simply "the families," but historians have dubbed them *patricians*.[33] They governed many cities north of the Alps for roughly two hundred years, others for many centuries more.

Even before the communes were organized, grievances that the "better sort of people" lodged against their rulers hinted at a commercial awakening in Italy.[34] The Crusades (1096–1293) encouraged maritime cities like Venice and Genoa to tap into the caravan trade bringing silks and spices from faraway Asia to various eastern Mediterranean ports. Deposit banking got its start in the thirteenth century, stimulated by the papacy's need for a means to transfer funds. Meanwhile, new instruments of credit facilitated payments in distant markets, and Italian bankers gained privileged access to commodities like England's wool exports through large loans to rulers. The availability of high-quality English wool fueled the manufacture of top-grade woolens, especially in Florence, which now competed in European markets with England's other customers, the woolen manufacturers of Ghent and Bruges in Flanders. By the 1270s merchant firms in Venice and Genoa had agents moving back and forth along the "silk road" to the fabled capital of China's Mongol emperors.[35] Italy's "commercial revolution" drew migrants to cities in need of workers and stimulated trade elsewhere, as in the south German cities of Augsburg and Nuremberg. From around 1300, when Venetian and Genoese galleys began plowing the waters of the Atlantic,[36] Bruges became a clearinghouse where merchants trading with Italy could settle accounts. This in turn prompted the Hanseatic League, based in Baltic cities like Lübeck and Gdansk (Danzig), to make Bruges its obligatory trading station for the Low Countries. Europe's major trade routes were beginning to form an integrated network.

The Hanseatic League (in German, Hanse) was an unusual variation on the *merchant guilds* that began to appear around 1150. In large Italian cities some family firms had the resources to deal on nearly equal terms with Europe's crowned heads.[37] Smaller firms, the great majority, found security in banding together with other merchants of the same town. The German word *hanse* originally meant an association of merchants from one city traveling together for their own safety. By about 1300, the word had come to refer to a super-federation aimed at protecting the collective interests of north German towns with merchant guilds. In the sophisticated economies of large Italian cities like Florence, there were several so-called greater guilds, including one each for goldsmiths, bankers, and silk manufacturers and two for woolen manufacturers.

Merchant guilds traded in the precious commodity of legal privileges. In a society in which nobles and clergy were set apart by privileges, like exemption from most forms of taxation, merchants demanded privileges of their own, like freedom from tolls or exclusive rights in the trade of certain commodities. Where cities were ruled by a prince, the simplest strategy was to make a financial offer the prince could not refuse; for example, the count of Holland was persuaded to mandate (1289) that goods moving up and down the Rhine had to be off-loaded for sale at Dordrecht, a privilege that Dordrecht fiercely defended against rival towns (sometimes by force of arms) for more than two centuries. In Italy, where there was no accepted authority to referee bitter economic rivalries, towns took whatever they could get with citizen militias or (after about 1350) mercenary armies. For example, Florence realized a long-term ambition by conquering Pisa in 1406: Pisa, at the mouth of the Arno, had for centuries obstructed the ocean-bound trade of its upriver rival.[38] The whole purpose of the Hanseatic League, focused on exclusive trading stations like Bruges, was to keep traffic in and out of the Baltic in the friendly hands of member cities. But the Hanse had its own internal conflicts: Gdansk, angered by Lübeck's insistence on off-loading for its own markets all merchandise headed from the Baltic to the North Sea, helped open the Baltic to non-Hanseatic intruders from Amsterdam and other ports in Holland.[39]

The fact that towns went to war for their trading interests may look unsurprising to a twentieth-century reader, but it has few demonstrable historical precedents. The mercantile interest had never previously had so much influence with town governments as in medieval Europe. In ancient times, Athens dominated the sea but did not employ naval power to advance its trade. Venice and Genoa, in their contest for domination of the eastern Mediterranean, made economic warfare an art to be emulated by great powers of the future.[40]

The fact that merchant guilds were effective pressure groups does not mean merchants controlled the town governments. Where merchants as a

Figure 12.3. The Image of Respectability. Petrus Christus (1410–1472), "St. Eligius as a Goldsmith," 1449. (*Metropolitan Museum of Art, New York, NY.*)

group did gain power, they did so in alliance with *craft guilds* formed by skilled artisans who prospered from the revival of trade. These self-governing and self-regulating associations of tradesmen emerged earliest in northern Italy, south Germany, and the Low Countries.[41] In some places, guilds were preceded by an era of town-government regulations forcing practitioners of the same craft to live in the same neighborhood, so that city

overseers could better supervise the quality of production.[42] Guilds sometimes formed in the teeth of repressive legislation enacted by magistrates
and their wealthy constituents to thwart the formation of such associations, especially for industrial production, like the manufacture of woolen
cloth.[43] In France, where craft guilds formed relatively late, often in the
fourteenth century, they were promoted by the crown, which was happy
to sell certificates confirming the status of master craftsmen. Like the merchant guilds, fully developed craft guilds demanded privileges of their
own; in particular, no one not a member of the guild was allowed to practice the trade within the limits of the city's jurisdiction. Craft and merchant
guilds eyed one another suspiciously, especially in cloth towns, but they
also had reasons to join forces against the ruling patrician families.

In northern and central Italy, the guilds' principal grievance was the ar-
rogant behavior of the magnates, combined with the violence of their en-
demic clan feuds.[44] Merchants and craftsmen together formed (1200s) a
new sworn association based on guild membership, usually called the
popolo.[45] When the *popolo* assumed control of the commune, magnates were
excluded from public office, and governance was in the hands of boards of
guild members, chosen by lot to avoid factionalism. But the new regime
fell victim to the same clan feuding that bedeviled the old, and by about
1300 most towns had accepted the rule of a city-lord who claimed to keep
the factions in check.[46] Florence was the only major city that preserved the
guild-based regime of the *popolo* for as long as a century and a half, from
1289 to 1434.[47] Here, the recurring tension was between the craft guilds
and the greater guilds.[48]

North of the Alps, patrician rule was harder to displace. In north Germany, southern France, and most of the northern Low Countries (including Holland), the traditional ruling elites either did not allow craft guilds to
form at all or thwarted their efforts to gain a voice in the governance of the
city. Armed uprisings by guildsmen often made the difference in south
Germany and in the southern Low Countries. In south Germany, the patri-
cian-dominated city council was renamed the small council, with some
seats now reserved for guild members, especially the merchants; on important matters, the small council had to convene a large council representing the craft guilds. In the southern Low Countries, including Flanders
and Brabant, the patrician council often became one chamber in a multi-
cameral urban legislature, with separate chambers for the merchants and
for a variously defined association of craft guilds. Such arrangements were
not as egalitarian as they may seem, for wealthy guild members—craftsmen or merchants—had common interests and influence far beyond their
numbers.[49] Friction between the guilds and the patricians was a lingering
issue in south Germany, but not in Flanders and Brabant, where the real

battles were among the guilds. Late medieval Europe's bitterest urban civil wars pitted Ghent's weavers, small-scale entrepreneurs, against the fullers,[50] their wage-earning employees.

Most towns were hard-hit by the depopulation of the post-Black Death era, and the scale of economic activity declined proportionately. Connections between Italy and China along the silk road broke off,[51] and bankers were more wary of the risky business of lending to princes. A relative lack of customers for luxury goods pinched the woolen industries of Flanders and Florence alike; new beginnings had to be made in products with wider appeal, like lighter woolens and fustian.[52] Master craftsmen sought security for their families by making it difficult for anyone but their own sons and sons-in-law to become full members, thus converting the hitherto fluid relationship between journeyman and masters[53] into a fixed hierarchy that generated new social tensions.[54]

The trading economy that revived with the slow growth of population after 1450 had new centers of gravity. Portuguese voyages of exploration down the African coast reached a long-sought goal when Vasco da Gama, having rounded the Cape of Good Hope, sailed on to Calicut in southwest India (1498). Portugal now had direct access to the spices and silks of the East, cutting out the "Moorish" (Muslim) enemies of Christendom[55]—not to mention their Venetian trading-partners. Captains of Portugal's "State of India" did in the Indian Ocean as Venice had done in the eastern Mediterranean: chokepoints controlling key straits were conquered and fortified, forcing local merchants to respect the rules laid down by Portuguese warships. This strategy was not completely successful, and the mainly Muslim[56] merchant skippers of the Indian Ocean still found the means of moving their merchandise, some of which found its way to the Mediterranean ports where Venice had outposts. During the sixteenth century, however, the bulk of Asian silks and spices reaching Europe went through Lisbon to the Low Countries for distribution. The entrepôt the Portuguese chose was not Bruges but Antwerp (Brabant), which had been gaining ground by trading with central and south German merchants not welcome in Bruges, since their towns were not members of the Hanseatic League. Augsburg and Nuremberg in particular were seeking outlets for the copper and silver that came from a technology-based revival of the mining industry[57] in regions like Saxony, Tirol, and Slovakia. The demand in Antwerp for copper and for bronze (an alloy of copper and tin) increased dramatically because of the overseas requirements of Portugal's maritime empire: copper was one of the few commodities Europeans could trade advantageously in India,[58] reducing the need for sending out silver to buy spices. Armbands and other bronze artifacts were prized trade goods in West Africa, where the Portuguese had begun the long and dismal history of Europe's African slave trade.

If Bruges had been the nodal point of a European trading network, Antwerp was the nodal point for an incipient world network. The possibilities of these multiple connections are illustrated in the careers of Augsburg's Jakob Fugger (d. 1525) and Antwerp's Erasmus Schets (d. 1544). The Fuggers began as fustian-weavers in the late fourteenth century. A hundred years later they were trading with Venice and making loans to rulers, like the Habsburg archduke of Tirol. Jakob Fugger parlayed his partnership with a key mining engineer and the Habsburg mining rights[59] he gained as collateral for his loans into a dominant position in the mining industry in Tirol, later extended to Slovakia by the firm's next generation. To satisfy Portugal's demands, huge quantities of Fugger copper were carted over the Carpathian mountains, shipped down Poland's Vistula River to the Baltic, thence to Amsterdam and along the Low Countries' inland waterway system to Antwerp.

Erasmus Schets married into a family that owned a mine for calamine, a key mineral in the new copper-smelting technology. As a young man he traded from Lisbon, shipping bronze armbands to West Africa, and formed connections with men bound for a new country that Portugal's mariners had accidentally hit upon as they arced west[60] across the south Atlantic toward the Cape of Good Hope—the land known as Brazil. Brazil's first sugar mill was set up by one of Schets's agents. Back in Antwerp, Schets bid against agents of the Fuggers for the three-year monopoly contract to distribute Portugal's spice cargo. If Jakob Fugger had provided a good part of the huge loan Charles V needed to bribe the empire's electoral princes in 1519,[61] Erasmus Schets and the agents of Jakob's nephew Anton Fugger (d. 1560) sometimes competed for the honor of financing Charles's wars. These men combined great wealth and access to power to a degree not hitherto seen in Europe. This was precisely why ordinary guildsmen harbored the darkest suspicions about what such "great purses" were up to.

Firms like the Schets and the Fuggers were in fact the leading edge of a merchant capitalism that was transforming the economy in ways profoundly threatening to the small-scale enterprise characteristic of the guilds. In Tirol, later in Slovakia, miners who had been independent operators became, under Fugger control, wage-earning employees, and not by choice. All over sixteenth-century Europe, investors found among the surplus population of the countryside a willing pool of cheap labor for new rural industries. The bans on rural brewing or clothmaking that towns sometimes secured from their princes were not very effective. In some places urban guildsmen who were now being undersold vented their fury on the competition, like the men of Chemnitz in Saxony, who marched out to smash the linen looms of a nearby village

Figure 12.4. Rembrandt's "Beggars receiving alms at the door of a house." Rembrandt van Rijn (1606–1669), 1648. (*Rijksmuseum, Amsterdam.*)

(1522). But the economic logic that supported a displacement of low-skill enterprise to the countryside was inexorable. Even within urban guilds the traditional safeguards against having a few rich men monopolize the trade were crumbling. Masters who could afford to do so ignored regulations about how much capital equipment or how many workers a single shop might have. Small-scale brewers in Delft (Holland) complained of such practices to the magistrates, as did furriers in Strasbourg. But the magistrates were friends and partners of the men of wealth. In Strasbourg, for example, rich members of the craft guilds were often members of the social club formed around the merchant guild, Strasbourg's wealthiest guild.

Though their livelihood might be imperiled, guildsmen were still the solid citizens of Europe's proud cities. Like tenant farmers in the country-side, the urban "common man" had people to look down on. Guildsmen were always burghers (citizens) of the town.[62] People who were not born in the town or who could not afford the substantial fee for purchasing rights of citizenship were classed as "inhabitants"—the journeymen who often wandered from town to town in quest of advancement and espe-cially those who had neither a skill nor steady work. Guildsmen viewed such people as riff-raff, but they were simply the *urban poor*, transplanted from the countryside. In rare cases the urban poor resorted to arms to seize a place for themselves in the social pecking order, like the wool-carders of Florence, who for a time (1378–1382) gained for unskilled workers in the wool industry the right to form guilds and play a role in city government. Mostly they strove to do as others like them had been doing for centuries, to find a niche where hard work might lead to the respectability of guild membership and town citizenship. But around 1500 such newcomers were more numerous than before, and they found fewer possibilities for ad-vancement. They could take to the roads, swelling the ranks of the vagabonds that towns increasingly complained about during these years, or they could stay put, somehow making do on seasonal employment and the occasional handout. Thus at a time when a few families scaled the heights of wealth, in cities across Europe a larger proportion of inhabitants than ever before, ranging from 30 to 50 percent, were classed as too poor to pay taxes. This era of growing social polarization was also the era of the Reformation.

Clergy[63] and religious (members of religious orders) were a microcosm of Europe's social divisions. Chantry priests[64] barely eked out a living; pastors lived comfortably. Members of cathedral chapters enjoyed a living standard like that of the noble families from which most of them came. There were convents whose modest entrance fees met the needs of guild families seek-ing an honorable place for a surplus daughter, others that demanded not only a rich dowry but sixteen quarters of nobility as well.[65] By and large, however, tensions among the men and women of the church came not so much from differences in family background as from corporate self-interest. Monasteries and convents were corporations, so were cathedral chapters and parish churches.[66] How were the competing claims of such bodies to be sorted out? For example, how was the bishop to share authority with his cathedral chapter in governing the diocese? And what rights did the bishop have over convents and monasteries that claimed to have papal exemption from his jurisdiction? Escalation to the level of armed combat was unusual in such matters, but not unknown. The bishop of Brixen (Tirol), at odds with his chapter, ruled that local shepherds be allowed to lease a mountain pasture. The owner, an allegedly exempt convent of noble ladies, said no. The chapter sided with the convent, and so did the archduke of Tirol, who raised troops and drove the bishop from his diocese.[67]

Franciscan and Dominican friars saw themselves as showing the ill-disciplined parish clergy by their good example how to preach the gospel to urban layfolk. But parish priests resented competition from the churches of the friars,[68] and some resented even more the friars' claims to moral superiority; if a priest's own parishioners did not mind his having a "second-class wife," what right did self-righteous friars have to thunder from their pulpits against "fornicating" priests?[69] Franciscans and Dominicans were not the best of friends either. The two orders' principal theologians had disagreed over the question of whether Mary, the Blessed Mother of Jesus, was conceived without the stain of original sin; in later generations each order denounced the other for "heresy" on this point.[70] Finally, within the different orders, there were bitter fights about how strictly the founder's rules were to be applied, especially among the Franciscans. Most of St. Francis of Assisi's spiritual descendants believed the one-paragraph directive he had left behind needed amplification, but not the Spiritual Franciscans of the late thirteenth century, the Observant Franciscans of the fifteenth century, or the Capuchins of the sixteenth and seventeenth centuries, all of whom insisted that the deliberate simplicity of the original rule was necessary to guard against corruption by wealth and physical comfort. The clergy and religious of the pre-Reformation era were not a solid body marching to the same tune, but a loose collection of corporate cells, each marching to a music of its own. In this way too they resembled the larger society from which they sprang.

Despite all their differences, clergy and religious were set apart by their enjoyment of common privileges, in some cases dating back to Roman times.[71] Townsfolk paid a sales tax for the wine or beer they purchased; priests and religious houses did not. In the countryside, landholders and their tenants were taxed for the land they farmed; pastors and monasteries were not. When lay persons accused of a felony stood trial before a town court, death sentences were common for crimes like theft (not to mention murder). Clerics and religious could only be tried before the bishops' courts, which had no right to sentence anyone to death and were known for their leniency. Moreover, these church courts also had jurisdiction over lay people in matrimonial disputes and in cases involving wills and other statements attested by oath.[72]

During the later Middle Ages there is evidence for a growing resentment of clerical exemptions from rules binding ordinary people, partly because of the growing sense of solidarity (see below) in lay communities. Why should a thieving or murderous priest get off with a few years of confinement, instead of being strung up by the town executioner, like a proper felon? Or what right had the local Dominicans to disregard an ordinance requiring all edifices upriver from where the town got its drinking water to cease discharging their sewage into the river? Why should the Franciscans be allowed to pay no excise tax on beer sold in their tavern,[73] meaning that honest tavern-keepers had to charge more? Why did church courts punish good Christian folk for falling behind on debts to "Jewish usurers" or the tithes they owed rich priests who bought these church incomes as an investment?[74] And why must dairymen in the Cologne region suffer the monopoly for making a local cheese that the prince-archbishop had granted the nuns of a poor convent, under pain of excommunication?

This rising tide of anticlericalism is surely related to the Protestant Reformation that followed. Yet the depth and intensity of anticlerical sentiment varied greatly from place to place. For both England and France, scholars disagree about how widespread it was and whether it did or did not prepare the ground for Protestantism. In rural south Germany and Switzerland, sharp differences between one locality and another may reflect the history of relations between important monasteries and the peasantry.[75] To take the two extremes of the debate, the sources for late medieval and sixteenth-century Germany are rife with a global critique of the clergy that is almost entirely lacking in contemporary sources for Castile. Was this because the reforms imposed on the clergy in Castile by Queen Isabella and Cardinal Cisneros had made a difference? Or because the mere presence of the Inquisition discouraged Castilians from adverse comment about their priests?[76] Or was Germany rather than Castile the outlyer, possibly because the empire's prince-bishops and prince-abbots wielded authority in a heavy-handed way that was not permitted to bishops and abbots in lands governed by strong rulers? And how important was this apparent difference in starting point for the differing outcomes, a Germany more than half Protestant, and a Castile more solidly Catholic? There are no agreed-on answers to these questions. All we can say is that the good local histories of the Protestant and Catholic Reformations are those that take into account the previous history of relations between clergy and laity.

COMMUNITY

In all societies the *family* is the basis for the idea of community. In terms of family structure, scholars now speak of a distinctive "European marriage pattern." In other parts of the globe parents commonly arranged marriages for their teenage children, who then lived with one set of parents. In the European pattern, couples deferred marriage until their mid- or even late twenties then immediately established independent households. That young people delayed marriage until they were in a position not to have to live under someone else's roof suggests a strong desire for autonomy. The temporary withholding of women from the reproductive pool had the effect of limiting natural population growth, and it seems couples limited it further by spacing their children.[77] For northwestern Europe—England, the Low Countries, northern France, and Scandinavia—this pattern can be traced back at least to the fourteenth century.[78]

Yet a 1427 wealth-census in Florence, perhaps Europe's best-documented city, shows a very different pattern. Here the average age of marriage was thirty for men, seventeen for women. Since there are usually fewer thirty-year-old men than seventeen-year-old women, rich dowries were needed to attract a respectable husband.[79] Florentine writers of this era insisted on the importance of the patrilineage—the male line of the clan was what counted; women were viewed as temporary residents in their families of marriage. In many regions, like northern Italy and northern Spain, the organization of fifteenth- and sixteenth-century households seems to echo the Florentine sense of the larger, patrilineal family. Scholars are agreed that the Catholic Church's long-standing insistence that marriage be based on the free consent of both parties was a necessary condition for the emergence of the European pattern, but it was clearly not a sufficient one, since fifteenth-century Florence was no less a Catholic society than England was. But by the end of the seventeenth century, the "European" pattern seems to have become common for all of Latin Christendom, even in the east, where it had been the custom for teenage couples to live with one set of parents.

The change in family structure had important implications for the social standing of women, for the European pattern implied a full-scale partnership between husband and wife, as opposed to the idea (as in Florence) that marriage meant joining the family of one's husband. To be sure, family elders throughout the late medieval and early modern centuries had definite ideas about suitable husbands for their daughters, but the mere fact that women married in their twenties rather than in their teens suggests greater freedom in the choice of a life-mate. Moreover, the period when the European pattern was establishing itself north of the Alps was also the era when, in the cities, craft production was concentrated in small shops where husband and wife worked side by side, even if at different tasks. But as the world of small-scale production came under threat from mercantile capitalism, it began to make more sense for an artisan's wife to concentrate her energies on the household.[80] Simultaneously, artisans and journeymen, animated by a stronger sense of male honor, began restricting the limited opportunities for guild membership that had previously been available to women. In these new circumstances a woman's contribution was no less necessary than before to the survival of her family, but it was increasingly relegated to a lesser status as household or "women's" work.

Both in the choice of a mate and in the allocation of responsibilities between husband and wife, women often found themselves as the center of an age-old tension between private desires and family responsibilities. The focus of scholarly discussion about the origins of individualism has now shifted from Renaissance Italy to medieval Europe.[81] In these bygone centuries, understanding oneself as an autonomous individual did not necessarily mean being in conflict with one's family. Prospective brides seem mostly to have found a way to satisfy their wishes as well as those of the elders, just as wives found ways to create an acceptable division of labor within the family economic unit under changing circumstances. This delicate balance within the family, between personal choice and group pressure, seems fundamental for an understanding of the other models of community to be considered here—the parish, the village, and the town. If it is plausible to speak of individual self-consciousness in Europe as early as the thirteenth century, this may be because European society threw up so many kinds of tightly organized groups and thus so many occasions for individuals to play out the game of deciding who they were.

The *parish* system was distinctive to Christendom, east and west. No other great religion covered the ground with an unbroken network of cells of activity, each precisely bounded and centered on its house of worship. In this the early medieval church imitated the ancient empire, whose writ ran to the remotest valley. In some areas rural parishes were not well developed until the ninth or tenth century. In later times new parishes formed as towns grew too big for one main church, and villages lobbied successfully for a parish of their own. It was thus a work of many centuries to create the landscape one still sees in many parts of rural Europe, where a visitor standing on a knoll can often make out village church spires in each of the four cardinal directions.

The parish was a grouping of believers, defined not by social status or personal affinity, but solely by geography. This promiscuous unity was subject to a process of fissuring by which the actual multiplicity of society reasserted itself. Noble landholders could keep private chaplains, so as not to have to worship with their peasants. Country people in the far corners of a parish preferred wayside chapels where a priest might come a few times each month. In the towns, the parish mass said at the main altar in the chancel[82] competed for attention with the many private masses said in side chapels,[83] often by chantry priests. Literate folk set themselves apart at mass by reading the prayer books that were common from the fourteenth century. Others among the devout regularly attended mass at a Franciscan or Dominican church or at a chapel built around a local shrine, rather than in the parish where they lived. The wealthy donated stained glass windows adorned by their family coats of arms; guilds provided windows featuring their patron saints. Pews, an invention of the fifteenth century, allowed people of quality to reserve spaces for themselves toward the front of the nave,[84] where they would not be disturbed by the idle chatter of lesser folk or the beggars who commonly tugged at the sleeves of churchgoers, demanding alms. Parishes also spawned confraternities, at least a few in country churches, dozens in a large city parish. There were also age-specific groups, as in rural England, where candles were kept burning before the altar by young men yoked to a plow (threatening to plow up the gardens of noncontributors) and young women who organized dances.

Was there a shared sense of purpose, beneath the buzz of separate activities, despite social distinctions that were as visible inside the church as outside it? Certainly the priest's elevation of the consecrated host was a solemn moment for all, as noted in an earlier chapter. Though most people did not receive communion more than once a year, it was a custom on Sundays to pass around the *pax*,[85] a small wooden or silver plate with an image of the crucified Christ, to be kissed by all as a symbol of their unity. It was also considered one of the priest's principal duties to reconcile those among his parishioners who had become enemies. God's blessing for the parish was invoked in vernacular prayers during the Latin mass and also in the Rogation Day processions in which many parishioners followed the priest in his vestments as he made a circuit of the parish boundaries.

The parish's collective will was expressed in another way through a system of governance that appeared in most areas during the thirteenth century. The pastor was expected to use his income to maintain his part of the church, the chancel, but upkeep of the nave now fell to the parishioners. Churchwardens, chosen by the local landowner or sometimes elected by the parishioners, spent as needed the income from portions of the church's endowment set aside for their use; they also provided church furnishings, including statues, mural paintings, chalices, and altar cloths. Other respected parishioners oversaw the relief of the parish poor. In France from the thirteenth century, so-called Tables of the Holy Spirit distributed bread to the needy from the church porch on stated days. In the Low Countries, somewhat later, parish officials had regular days and routes for bringing food to "the poor living at home." It was not unknown for a large urban parish to maintain a school for children, a hospital for the sick, and homes for elderly men and women. Some scholars have been impressed by the apparent capacity of late medieval parishes to build a sense of solidarity among their members. Others warn against judging on the basis of the kind of documentation that survives, mainly telling what should happen rather than what actually did happen. If we think in terms of the standard by which people measured themselves (whether they lived up to it or not), there seems less room for argument. Parishioners saw it as their responsibility, not just the priest's, to make their small bit of society a community.

Village is an aggregate name for many different kinds of cultivator settlements, the earliest of which trace back to the agricultural revolution of the fifth millennium B.C.[86] Villages across the world vary enormously in size. In medieval Europe they could have two thousand people or more, larger than some agglomerations officially recognized as towns, or less than a hundred, no larger than the small, unorganized settlements known as hamlets. Villagers had regular ways of cooperating among themselves even during the centuries of serfdom. For example, if a landlord chose to convert his demesne land to leaseholds for his serfs, the serfs took on the task of deciding which crops to plant where, formerly handled by the lord's estate manager. Even though they were subject to the criminal jurisdiction of the lord's bailiff, serfs often had a court of their own for minor altercations inside the hedge or the fence that marked the village boundary. At some point, as early as the twelfth century in western Europe, villages secured recognition as organized bodies that we may for the sake of simplicity describe as communities (*gemeinde* in German, *commune* in French and Italian). In more developed rural communities of the fourteenth century or later, villagers held an annual assembly that approved regulations to govern village life and elected members of a village council or nominated them for approval by the lord's bailiff, who usually presided at council meetings. As in urban communities, villagers were expected to renounce their feuds with one another in order to participate in the assembly; henceforth the village council, not family patriarchs, would be arbitrators of justice.

By the fifteenth century, villages functioned as corporate entities at law, for example in contracting debts. Since village councils were able to levy small taxes, these receipts were used as collateral for loans, to build a grain mill, repair a dike, or even to surround the village with a brick or stone defensive wall, as many rural communities did in Germany and France. The village often had a history and a siting quite separate from that of the parish church that served its people, but where the agrarian and the ecclesiastical communities overlapped, the village council might gain the authority to appoint the churchwardens, or borrow money to make repairs that could not be paid for from the church's endowed income, like rebuilding the roof after a fire. The church itself became the village hall, for the annual meeting and other purposes. In Switzerland and south Germany, village governments petitioned church and territorial authorities for the right to name their own pastors, as villages in a few areas already did. As towns did, some villages found the means to purchase land from local nobles or fund utilities like mills and baking ovens. By the era of the Reformation, larger villages had enough business to require a full-time secretary and a full-time legal adviser.

The way villagers lived their lives is never documented as well as it is for many towns, where fat volumes of council proceedings permit scholars to trace the history of quarrels great and small. Villagers placed a high value on being "neighborly"; tenant farmers greeted one another as "neighbor," as a sign of their essential equality. But rural neighbors, like urban guildsmen, were becoming less and less equal. After about 1450, some peasant proprietors and some tenant farmers were able to profit from the rising demand for grain by expanding their holdings significantly. These "village roosters" (to use the French term), often literate, took a lively interest in the wider world, sometimes in new ideas for religious reform. Small-scale tenant farmers were being squeezed down into the ranks of the hired hands, who had never been addressed as "neighbor," not even in the bygone days of rough equality among tenant farmers. Some local studies based on the period after 1600 find villages seething with conflict. For the pre-Reformation era, it seems likely that villagers sensed a growing disparity between the "neighborliness" everyone theoretically owed one another and the reality of division between the haves and the have-nots.

Superficially, Europe's *cities* were never more unified as communities than in the hundred years or so before the Reformation. In many parts of Europe, larger towns built wider circuits of walls during the fourteenth or fifteenth centuries, enclosing settlements outside the old wall within high and seemingly impregnable fortifications.[87] To give defenders a free field of fire, settlement outside the new walls was discouraged; the separation between town and countryside was, however, not quite so stark as it appears to be on the many engravings and bird's-eye views of cities that begin to be common

Figure 12.5. A Man and his Wife at Work. Quentin Metsys (1465/66–1530), "The Money-lender and his Wife." (*Musée du Louvre, Paris.*)

around 1500. The walls were often manned by guildsmen, whose training in "shooting guilds"[88] gave them civic importance even in towns where they did not have a voice in local government. Scholars recounted glorious urban histories, like the one that boasted (1517) of Toulouse's first charter as a city in 439, older than the French monarchy itself. It was not that the kingdom did not matter, but it mattered less; for townsmen of this period, as one French scholar has said, "foreigners" began at the city gates.

Meanwhile, town governments enacted into law the principle that the community was responsible for the well-being of all its people, inhabitants as well as citizens. Parish institutions like schools, hospitals, and homes for the elderly were taken over by the magistrates for better oversight and supported if need be from city revenues. Charitable institutions founded by private bequests were sometimes treated in the same way, though many continued to be governed as provided for by the founder, like the Fuggerei,[89] a veritable city for the poor of Ausgburg built by Jakob Fugger (1519). Since the city was answerable to God for how burghers behaved, magistrates mandated civil penalties for blasphemy, banned styles of clothing deemed suggestive, and forced prostitutes to ply their trade only in the less respectable parts of town. In this official urban morality, sins against God's law and sins against the social order seen as willed by God were not clearly distinguished. Sumptuary laws, which helped preserve the visible boundaries between status groups, were justified as a means of preventing folk from wasting their substance on frivolity.[90]

The church too was subject to regulation. Taking note of how much property was already in the hands of tax-free monasteries and convents, magistrates prohibited further alienation of land for religious purposes; they took over administration of the properties of religious houses, especially those marked by scandal, and applied every pressure they could to secure the removal of unworthy men from pastorates and other church positions. For many people, these long-term efforts to make a city one community under God found their logical conclusion in Reformation-era laws forcing clergy to become citizens, subject to the same laws as everyone else.

At the same time, however, new opportunities were steadily prying wealthy burghers loose from their social moorings in the urban collective. Florentine statesmen of the early fifteenth century no longer thought of themselves as representatives of their guilds, but as members of an elite naturally fitted to govern. Even before he came to power in Florence, Cosimo de Medici (ruled 1434–1464) built a palace such as no private citizen had ever built, rather as Jakob Fugger did in Augsburg a few generations later. Families like the Medici and the Fuggers also set the fashion for building rural villas for summer recreation. In Siena, near Florence, wealthy testators left fewer and fewer bequests for the urban poor, but more and more for private chapels to glorify the family name. North of the Alps, town magistrates were coming to have more in common with their brothers and cousins in princely service than with their fellow burghers. In the Low Countries, and in many German and Italian states, demands by rulers for higher subsidies to fight their wars did not seem so unreasonable to magistrates who had learned to profit from cooperation with the prince by providing credit at favorable rates or participating in revenue-raising state monopolies. In France the king's imperious need for money allowed ambitious merchants, bankers, and lawyers to climb into the ranks of the nobility, merely by purchasing one of the many royal offices put up for sale after about 1520. Elsewhere, rich dowries for impecunious nobles enabled burgher families to form connections among the lords of the land. In south Germany urban statesmen saw themselves as the equals of the nobility; they too demanded to be addressed as "lords" by their subjects, that is, by their fellow townsmen. In the Low Countries, magistrates who served as deputies to the provincial states were now styled "high mightinesses."

Figure 12.6. View of a Village. Pieter Bruegel the Elder (ca. 1525–1569), "A Village and its Fields," from Max Friedlaender, Pieter Bruegel (Berlin: Propylaen, 1922), p. 91. (*University of Minnesota Library.*)

If the ruling elite understood the "community" as a corporate body all of whose members were bound by the decisions of its rulers (themselves), the "the common man" understood the "community" as the whole body of citizens, whose interests were often disregarded by the magistrates in their all-too-friendly negotiations with princes. Thus resistance to higher taxation came from the guildsmen, whose loyalty was to the town itself and who felt the pinch of urban excise taxes[91] more keenly than their social betters did. The guild had always been the common man's last line of defense, but now rich guildsmen were setting the rules at naught (see above) to become richer still. Hence the common man's growing alienation from the ruling institutions of the town was loud enough to be heard, so much so that magistrates used it to their advantage in negotiations with higher powers. In the Low Countries, Charles V's officials listened with sympathy when spokesmen for the towns, pressed as to why they refused to authorize higher subsidies, blamed the fact that "the common man" (*de gemene man*) demanded taxes be kept as they were. When magistrates of south German towns were pressed by Charles's officials in Germany as to why they tolerated a "gospel" contrary to the teachings of the church, they

Figure 12.7. Amsterdam's Orphanage. The Amsterdam Orphanage ca. 1614, from Joannes Pontanus, Beschrijvinge van Amsterdam (see figure 10.1), p. 108. (*Special Collections, University of Minnesota Library.*)

had an equally plausible reply: "the common man" (*der gemeine Mann*) demanded it.

The "common man" in south Germany's towns did in fact take a special interest in gospel doctrine, but so did people from many levels of society. Appeals for a "reformation of the community" were heard from village councils, from wealthy town magistrates, and from officials and clergymen who sought to make a whole territory a "community," as defined in the religious confession (Catholic or Protestant) espoused by their prince.[92] Can such grand schemes for changing the selfish ways of ordinary people possibly have succeeded? The stream of complaints by official visitors, who found little or no change in the ingrained and not very edifying habits of rural folk in particular, gives ample reason for skepticism. Nonetheless, the next two chapters will argue that generations of preaching and indoctrination eventually did bring about a new kind of society, if not the true community devout Christians longed for. Pre-Christian magical beliefs about the world gradually lost their grip, even as the witchcraft craze that had begun in the fifteenth century reached a crescendo during the century from about 1550 to 1650. Children more commonly learned how to read, so they could read their catechism lessons. Adults seemed more willing to heed the injunctions of their pastors, even in matters of sexual behavior. The rich were more apt to take some responsibility for the poor, if only as a matter of their own self-esteem. Finally, dissident religious groups, fired by their own preaching and indoctrination, gave the lie to the age-old Christian belief that only the orthodox could lead good lives. All but the last of these changes reflected in some way the aims of the reformers. For the future character of European society, however, this last change was the most important of all.

13 | Society and Community

The German and Swiss Reformation

This chapter explores the connections between social tensions, group solidarities, and confessional identity, from the beginnings of the German and Swiss Reformation to about 1600. Discussion of the social background of religious choice focuses on the "common man" in general and the cities in particular. Next, there are the blueprints for a true Christian community crafted by preachers of the Lutheran and Zwinglian Reformations: To what extent did they adjust their presentation of the gospel message to the special wishes of the groups where they found most support? Finally, there is the question of results: To what extent were these fond hopes for a more Christian society realized?

THE COMMON MAN

The German and Swiss Reformation was a communal movement. Lay people embraced the new doctrine not only because of its promise of individual salvation, but also because it seemed to point the way to a true community, under God.[1] In the towns, better documented than the countryside, the strongest support for the new teachings came from the guilds, the natural home of the "common man" who so closely identified his wellbeing with that of the community. The communal character of the Protestant message is already implied by the pulpits from which the urban Reformation was so often proclaimed. Some preachers of the new gospel were members of religious orders,[2] but more often they were secular clergy. A surprising number occupied one particular niche in the parish hierarchy: they were holders of the endowed preacherships created by civic-minded benefactors, starting in the early fifteenth century. Since pastors and vicars often did not preach, it had become customary for preaching friars, like the Franciscans, to made a regular circuit of parishes within reach of their monasteries.[3] Parish preacherships were an alternative to mendicant sermons. The endowments required preaching in the language of the people and sometimes called for "the pure gospel." In the early sixteenth century, theology graduates who had studied the biblical languages usually did not have the family connections needed for high positions in the church, as pastor of an important parish or a member of a cathedral chapter. But their humanist theological training gave them impressive qualifications as exponents of "the pure gospel." Huldrych Zwingli, "People's Preacher" at Zurich's main parish from 1519, was only one of many humanist clerics who used his endowed pulpit to launch a Protestant movement. In fact, during the 1520s church authorities in Swiss and south German cities had trouble finding suitable preachership candidates who were not "tainted" by Reformation doctrine. The preacherships thus became, in one scholar's phrase, a "bridge" between the communal religion of the fifteenth century and the Reformation of the sixteenth.[4]

That ordinary people interpreted Protestant teaching according to communal values can be shown from the outpouring of vernacular-language pamphlets during the early years of the German Reformation.[5] The educated few wrote most of these pamphlets, including some that claim to speak for "Farmer Jack."[6] But scholars have sorted out the ones that seem to have been penned by men or women of relatively little learning, just as they have been able to detect, in rural petitions drafted by village pastors, the ideas of the peasants themselves.[7] In these documents the "common man" of the 1520s left a record of his thoughts not matched in any previous time, not found again until the nineteenth century. The predominant theme was the gospel: The priests taught mere human opinion, but no one could be saved without the pure gospel.

What did the gospel mean? There were echoes of Luther's "by faith alone," but more commonly the gospel was the rule by which Christians live. This view resembled Zwingli's belief that the gospel was a kind of law,[8] except that the emphasis of the pamphlets and the petitions on "love of neighbor" was closer to the good-works Catholicism of the late Middle Ages. Christians were saved by being neighbors to one another—in other words, by building a true community. The demand that everyone be on the same footing before God shows the wide appeal of Luther's "priesthood of all believers," but it also reflects communal values. In one scholar's findings, only the pamphlets written by artisans expressed fears about the Christian community breaking up into "sects" instead of maintaining its unity.[9] This may have been one of the reasons why artisan pamphlets and peasant petitions alike were harshly critical of monasticism, which might be seen as splitting Christians into rival factions.[10] No monasteries or convents were needed, only one priest for each parish, chosen by the civil community. Likewise, baptism and communion were the only sacraments needed; noble pamphleteers envisioned alternative forms of the sacrament of confession, but artisans wanted it abolished altogether. Thus the popular understanding of the Reformation was a blend of three elements: the teachings of Luther and Zwingli; the ideal of the community; and the life experience of working men and women who saw themselves as the backbone of "neighborliness."

The Reformation movement was communal also in the sense that it was usually the common burghers who demanded its implementation. Members of the urban elites, inherently suspicious of all novelties, were doubly cautious about religion: They rightly saw any change as an implied threat to social stability, and their own kinsmen often had high posts in the local church hierarchy. Their hesitation about accepting the new ideas gave citizens stronger reasons for distrusting the magistrates. As noted in the last chapter, "community" seemed to many people of the middling sort to be breaking down: What had the magistrates done to prevent the rich and successful from growing ever more powerful, while hard-working guildsmen struggled to stay in place? Were they now going to stand in the way of the gospel as well? In almost every city where the Reformation triumphed, it was because popular opinion centered in the guilds pressured reluctant magistrates to dismantle the Catholic religious establishment step by step: First clergy were instructed to preach "according to the gospel," then some churches were opened to Protestant worship and some monasteries were closed.

In some towns support for the new doctrines seems to have varied according to socioeconomic rank: the less wealthy guilds harbored the most ardent Protestants, while the magistrates preferred to change as little as possible—for them, Lutheranism was better than Zwinglianism.[11] Constance and Zwickau are exceptions that prove the rule of popular support for the Protestant cause. In Constance, a city whose patrician magistrates actively supported the Reformation,[12] the less wealthy guilds showed clear signs of loyalty to Catholicism. In Zwickau, a Saxon mining town, patrician magistrates, frightened by the radical doctrines of Thomas Münzter and his disciples,[13] sought as an antidote a preacher who had the blessing of their Lutheran prince.[14] At least initially, however, guildsmen showed no interest in the religion chosen by their patrician magistrates. On Easter in 1524, only twenty people received communion according to the Lutheran rite.

In these and other cases, religious disagreements often followed preexisting lines of division between magistrates and burghers. But there was also a second pattern of preexisting conflict, pitting cities as corporate bodies against their princely rulers, and conflicts of this sort also found a religious expression. Territorial princes had been demanding higher taxes to subsidize their wars;[15] they were also weaning members of the burgher elite away from their urban loyalties by offering them posts in the territorial administration. Cities ruled by the princes had to accommodate their rulers, but they endeavored to do so without giving up their hard-won rights of self-rule. Even the fully self-governing Swiss cantons and the empire's free imperial cities felt pressures from above. If most Swiss cantons allied with France in its wars against Charles V, one reason was that the Habsburg dynasty was the traditional enemy of Swiss liberties.[16] By contrast, the free cities of south Germany formed close connections with the Habsburgs under Maximilian I (d. 1519), because the growing power of the territorial princes threatened their independence as well as the emperor's authority.[17]

These time-honored political strategies ran into a brick wall as soon as social tensions within the cities were further stirred up by Reformation preaching. Of the sixty-five free imperial cities important enough to send representatives to the imperial diets, only a dozen remained Catholic all through the sixteenth century, despite all the influence Charles V and his agents in Germany could bring to bear.[18] Even as the magistrates took steps to appease the common man's demand for the gospel, they knew they were alienating the emperor, who measured his friends according to their orthodoxy. The imperial cities that became Protestant included most of the empire's commercial centers, with the interesting exception of

Figure 13.1. A View of Magdeburg. Fom Matthaeus Merian, Martin Zeiller, Topographia Germaniae (see no. 32), vol. XIV, following p. 166. (*University of Minnesota Library.*)

Cologne, which had a city council that kept clerical privileges well under control and a staunchly orthodox university whose theology professors were well integrated into the city's churches.[19] In the many territorial cities with Catholic rulers, magistrates had to choose between preserving the goodwill of the prince and making concessions to the growing evangelical movement among their burghers.

The outcome of this three-way struggle depended in good part on local political alignments. In cities governed by politically aggressive prince-bishops the transition from Catholicism to Lutheranism seems to have been almost seamless. The prince-archbishop of Bremen, preoccupied for more than a decade by his efforts to conquer new territory, suddenly found himself confronted (1522) by magistrates and burghers united behind a new Lutheran preacher. In Magdeburg, whose prince-archbishop was a notorious collector of bishoprics, the story was much the same.[20] But most episcopal cities remained Catholic. There were often Lutheran movements among the burghers, especially among the more prominent members of the craft guilds, but they were not able to withstand the civil power wielded for confessional aims by strong-minded prince-bishops in the latter part of the sixteenth century.

Among the secular princes, Henry of Brunswick-Wolfenbüttel (ruled 1514–1542) was if anything a more determined defender of Catholicism than William IV of Bavaria (ruled 1514–1550). But William's key advisers were laymen and natives of the duchy; the steps they took to curtail the privileges of the clergy probably helped keep Bavaria's towns Catholic. Henry's advisers were either clerics or laymen from other territories; their attempts to use control of religious policy as a means of advancing ducal authority helped provoke Lutheran movements led by the magistrates of his cities, first in Brunswick, then in Goslar, whose appeal to the Schmalkaldic League led to Henry's expulsion from his territory.[21] Here too there are exceptions that prove the rule. The few secular princes who eagerly embraced the Reformation at an early date sometimes faced Catholic opposition movements in their towns. In Brunswick-Lüneburg, Lüneburg's salt-master patricians saw Duke Ernest's Reformation as a ploy by which the ruler meant to gain control of the city's vital salt trade.[22] Their loyalty to Catholicism was shared by guilds active in the salt industry but not by other craft guilds, which had their quarrels with the patricians and found the duke's Lutheranism more to their liking.

The urban Reformation usually culminated in the abolition of Catholic worship throughout the territory controlled by the city. This was a grave matter, all the more so in episcopal cities, where mass was prohibited also in the cathedral of the city's prince-bishop. The magistrates preferred not to assume all responsibility for such decisions. In south Germany and

Protestant Switzerland, where the guilds had a formal voice in town government, guilds were consulted on this key issue through the large council, most of whose members were chosen by the guilds.[23] In some towns the guilds were not content with traditional rules of consultation. In Basel, the victory of the Reformation put in place (for a time) new voting rules giving the guilds more authority and the patricians less.

In north Germany, where exclusively patrician town councils still ruled much as they had done for centuries, the community in a wider sense often played a role in the final triumph of the Reformation, even if craft guilds as such did not. Lübeck is instructive, because this great maritime city's patrician regime was resolutely Catholic. The magistrates were troubled that some members of the merchants' guild, just below the patricians in Lübeck's social hierarchy, were known "Martinians."[24] Their strength was displayed in the "song war" of December 1529: a group of men and women singing Luther's hymns, joined by others as they processed along a main street, peaceably occupied one of the city's parish churches. But this was not the decisive event. What tipped the scales was the fact that Lübeck could not pay off debts contracted during Sweden's civil war[25] without new taxes; the patrician government was not able to impose new levies without summoning an assembly of the community. The committee of burghers chosen to draft needed fiscal legislation insisted in its report, also in December 1529, that there would be no new taxes without new preachers. The city council had no choice; Lübeck too became Lutheran.

What of the urban poor, and their view of the new doctrines? The short answer is that we know too little. There are no pamphlets specifically traceable to journeymen, and it would be unusual to find unskilled workers who even knew how to read, much less write. The angry crowds that often stormed and sacked urban monasteries during the 1520s certainly included lesser folk, and journeymen and day laborers are also found among men and women arrested for individual acts of desecration directed against statues and other symbols of Catholic belief. Yet later evidence from the Low Countries suggests that support for the new doctrines did not come from the lowest levels of society. According to religious censuses conducted in towns recaptured for Spain by Parma in the 1580s, Calvinists were most often found among the middling sort of folk, including members of the craft guilds, but both the rich and the poor were mainly Catholic.[26]

Münster offers one final variant on the ways guild members attempted to shape their city's religious life. Following the conquest of the Anabaptist kingdom (1535), Münster's prince-bishop prohibited all forms of Protestant worship and attempted to govern his depopulated capital city through an appointed council.[27] Pressed by the imperial diet, he agreed to restore Münster's rights of self-government (1541), but only partially. Restoration of the rights of the craft guilds came only in 1553, when the prince-bishop needed funds for war. Tensions now developed between the traditional communal aspirations of the city and the prince-bishop's growing bureaucracy, for whom Münster was simply the capital of a sizable territory. By the 1580s these two visions of Münster's place in the world found expression in two different forms of Catholicism. On one side were members of the new Jesuit order, authorized by the prince-bishop to convert his cathedral school into a university. From other parts of Germany, even from other countries, Jesuit teachers promoted High German, the common literary language, rather than the local dialect of Low German.[28] For lawyers and other officials of the prince-bishop's territorial administration, often members of the Jesuit sodality,[29] the Jesuit fathers were agents of a needed transformation, bringing Münster into step with the universal culture of Catholic reform. But for guild members to whom High German was a foreign language, the Jesuits were foreign priests. The burgher assembly dominated by the guilds first attempted to prevent the Jesuits from taking up residence in the city then barred them from teaching in city schools. The assembly also took up the cause of Protestant burghers, who could not bury their dead in church cemeteries, because the prince-bishop (backed by the Jesuits) had forbidden it. Members of the assembly noted pointedly that they did not tolerate Protestant worship in the churches, but their Catholicism was not good enough for the prince-bishop, whose forceful intervention (1612) ended the participation of the guilds in political decision-making. In their losing struggle, Münster's guilds were late witnesses to the belief that a city's religious life must be controlled by its own people. In earlier decades this communal ideal more often found a Protestant form of expression. Where the Reformation was not made by the princes, it was made by the common man.

TRUE COMMUNITY

Those who wrote and preached on behalf of the Reformation knew their audience. Vernacular-language publications appealed in a hundred different ways to the common man's anticlericalism. Broadsides[30] might depict a grotesque Carnival procession, with fat priests, lecherous monks, and sleek cardinals led by the devil himself. Luther's scatological rhetoric set the tone for this kind of propaganda: since the papacy was the Antichrist, the worst imaginable perversion of the gospel, no human language could be filthy enough to describe it. But hatred of the clergy was good only for tearing down the old order. When the elector of Saxony authorized the first visitation of rural parishes, visitors were taken aback to find peasants who knew the pope was the Antichrist but had never heard of justification by faith. Luther again pointed the way toward a new order when he invoked the priesthood of all believers, a principle expressed also in his doctrine of the sacraments. Baptism and communion, shared by all believers, were the only true sacraments.[31] Did the new form of worship imply a new and truer form of Christianity community? Some have argued that Luther's insistence on the total depravity of human nature due to original sin[32] limited his interest in any project for the moral betterment of society.[33] The idea that scripture is a guide for Christian living[34] comes instead from Zwingli, himself a burgher and familiar with how the "common man" felt about Christians working out their salvation as members of a community. This view makes too sharp a distinction between the free cities of Switzerland and south Germany and the territorial cities of the north, and between the Zwinglian and Lutheran Reformations. Lutheran preachers, no less than Zwinglians, envisioned a community of men, women, and children living more truly according to God's law. These blueprints were the theological counterparts of the common man's sense of the gospel. The following pages touch on five specific measures of a more Christian society: the reform of worship, religious indoctrination, poor relief, marriage law, and the campaign against witchcraft.

Worship. The pre-Reformation parish church was a place where one had access to the power of the holy. It was already a protection against evil to dip one's finger in the holy water fount and make the sign of the cross[35] upon entering church. People took small containers of the holy water blessed by the priest, or palm fronds blessed by the priest on Palm Sunday,[36] to guard their homes against the power of the devil. Most of all, the priest had power to offer the sacrifice of the mass. For Catholics, the mass was a re-presentation of the sacrifice by which Christ had offered Himself on the cross to atone for the sins of humankind. Reverence for the miracle of transubstantiation did not prevent people from walking about or carrying on conversations in church, but the moment when the priest raised the wheaten host and the chalice of wine for the adoration of all was the high point of Sunday worship.

For Lutherans, the church was a place to hear God's Word. For rituals marking the stages of human life, Luther's German-language texts simplified the Catholic order of worship, so as to bring out the Word more clearly. Engaged couples were to have their unions blessed by a clergyman, not just in front of the church, but before the altar, so they might hear God's commands to married folk in texts that grew more elaborate as the sixteenth century progressed.[37] In the baptismal rite, the exorcisms[38] —prayers calling on God to free the person about to be baptized from the power of the devil—were reduced in number, but not eliminated. Luther believed in the reality of the devil's power in human life, but he wanted Christians to trust solely in God to ward off the Evil One.

The mass required more serious alteration. To speak of it as a sacrifice offered by the priest was an "abomination" to Luther no less than Zwingli, a derogation from the honor due to God alone and a blasphemous corollary to the false Catholic belief than human works could be holy in the sight of God. Yet since God's Word did indeed assure believers of the comfort of Christ's presence in the sacrament of the altar, Luther's German mass retained most of the prayers and gestures from the Latin rite, purging only what related to the idea of sacrifice. [39] He even kept the custom of lifting up for all to see the bread in which the Lord's body was present; to avoid the suggestion that this miraculous testimony of God's favor depended on the clergyman's recital of Jesus' words at the Last Supper, Luther transferred the elevation to a different part of the mass.[40] Without explicitly acknowledging that ordinary believers grasped the meaning of religion most easily through symbolic actions, the Lutheran Reformation allowed people to carry forward into the new order much that was comfortable and familiar from Catholic practice. But the medieval custom of having the priest celebrate mass with his back to the people[41] was altogether unacceptable. In Lutheran lands, altar tables were set in front of the high altar,[42] so the minister could face the people and speak to them, in their own tongue, the Word of God's promise.

To Zwingli, Reformed worship demanded more thoroughgoing change. If Luther found prayers, gestures, and church furnishings acceptable if they did not contradict scripture, Zwingli found them unacceptable if they were not prescribed by scripture.[43] Image-covered walls were to be whitewashed; statues of all kinds, even crucifixes, were "idols" to be removed and destroyed. Luther composed hymns of great beauty, and the long tradition of Christian organ music reached its greatest heights among Lutheran composer-organists.[44] Zwingli, though himself a lover of music, found in scripture no justification for congregational singing, except for the Psalms; since scripture did not mention organs, they too had to be removed. Luther is reputed to have helped popularize the Christmas tree in family celebrations, but for Zwingli there was no Christmas: scripture commands believers to make holy the Lord's day, only the Lord's day. Baptism did not free the recipient's soul from the power of the devil, it simply incorporated him or her into the body of believers, much as the Jews of old did by circumcising male infants as a sign of their covenant with God.[45] Instead of rushing newborns to church lest they die without the grace of baptism,[46] parents should pick a suitable date for having their infants baptized as part of the Sunday service. To avoid superstition, the tra-

ditional parish baptismal font, silently tolerated by Luther, must be replaced by a simple basin, and the "magical" exorcism prayers (as Martin
Bucer of Strasbourg described them) must be eliminated altogether. Without explicitly identifying the spoken word as the only medium through
which faith could validly be expressed, the Zwinglian Reformation required worshipers to cast off utterly a deep-rooted religious culture of
symbols, gestures, and songs. The Sunday service was built around scripture and the sermon. Since bread and wine were blessed only on days set
aside for communion, there was no need for a fixed altar table.[47] The pulpit, as in Zurich, could thus claim the place of honor in the chancel, the better to show that one came to church only to hear God's Word.

Indoctrination has become an evil word in a century marred by totalitar-
ian attempts at thought-control. It was not so in the era of the Reformation.
The fundamental Protestant charge against the Catholic Church was a failure of indoctrination, from top to bottom. Despite universities scattered
across Europe, Latin schools in the towns, and vernacular-language schools
in not a few villages, the faithful did not know the doctrine needful for salvation, because they had been wrongly taught by their priests. The new
Protestant liturgy, in both its Lutheran and Zwinglian versions, was part of
a grand program of Christian indoctrination. Luther led the way by re-

Figure 13.2. A Mennonite Pastor in the Dutch Republic. Rembrandt van Rijn,
"Pastor Ansloo and his Wife," 1641. (*Bildarchiv Preussischer Kulturbesitz, Berlin.*)

forming Wittenberg's theology curriculum, setting aside the scholastic authors, and requiring study of the biblical languages as well as the church fathers. The theology faculty now began forming earnest young men willing to preach the gospel wherever they were needed; with their wives and children, these new pastors would also be models for a sober and righteous evangelical household. Luther urged towns that did not already have Latin schools to establish them, for the preparation of pastors and territorial officials. Philip of Hesse's church ordinance of 1526[48] created a new Protestant university at Marburg and called for establishment of schools of the appropriate level in every village and town. Elector John of Saxony issued a similar decree in 1528, the same year that visitors made their first full circuit of rural parishes. The visitors found many long-time pastors or vicars paying only lip service to the new doctrines, to keep their jobs. Many among the faithful were seduced by the ranting of radical preachers or grasped little about the Reformation beyond Luther's denunciation of the papacy, as noted above. The few recent theology graduates who had taken rural churches complained bitterly that church incomes rightfully theirs had either been appropriated by others or were painfully inadequate to support a wife and family. Revenues set aside for starting new schools were also insufficient, at least according to village officials. Territorial officials now grasped for the first time how much of a struggle it would be to find the resources for pastors with families and for new schools.

Luther had cherished the belief that scripture itself should be the content of basic Christian education. Now, having seen from the visitors' reports how "the gospel" could be interpreted by ordinary folk in wildly differing ways, concluded that children must have the essential teachings of scripture presented to them in handbook form, for memorization.[49] In 1529 he penned a *Large Catechism* for the instruction of preachers and a *Small Catechism* whose language was simple enough to be conveyed directly to children. Luther followed the format of well-known fifteenth-century catechisms,[50] but, as he did in revising the liturgy, he gave them a new direction by highlighting key doctrines. The *Small Catechism* in particular quickly became the basis of instruction in Lutheran primary schools. While princely officials worked to ease out the old pastors and find a decent living for their successors, the new pastors pressed villagers to erect schools and carefully checked the doctrinal orthodoxy of teachers. The story was much the same in Reformed areas. Zwingli's *Short Introduction to the Christian Religion* (1523) may be compared to Luther's *Large Catechism;* others in Zurich or Strasbourg wrote catechisms for the young. Pastors trained at Zurich's theological academy cultivated a sense of solidarity perhaps not found among Lutheran clergy, owing to continuation of the regular meetings or colloquies begun by Zwingli. All over Protestant Germany, university-educated pastors gradually filled the pulpits, and schools were established where none had existed before. But did rural folk let their children attend these schools? And did children who had the precepts of evangelical doctrine drummed into their heads grow into adults knowledgeable about religion and devout in their faith? Answers to these questions must for the moment be deferred.

Poor relief illustrates the connection Reformers drew between correct doctrine and building true community. In Germany as in Europe generally, the misery of the urban poor made the gap between social reality and Christian ideals painfully evident. The resources of privately endowed and parish institutions like hospitals and homes for the elderly, even if taken under the supervision of the city council,[51] could not keep pace with the needs of a growing indigent population. Sermons, especially those of the mendicant friars,[52] exalted the poor for their detachment from worldly comforts, while excoriating the rich for grasping after still more wealth and for shirking their duty, before God, to be charitable to the less fortunate. But did the friars by their praise of poverty obscure the real wretchedness of indigence? And did they by their own begging encourage others to look for handouts rather than looking for work? This was also the era of a nascent capitalist ethos hostile to that of the friars. A famous Italian humanist condemned the Franciscans as useless drones buzzing at their prayers and had seeming words of praise for the merchants whose quest for riches created work for their fellow citizens.[53]

Juan Luis Vives (1492–1540) complained bitterly of the files of filthy and ulcerous beggars importuning respectable burghers from both sides of the church door on Sunday mornings. Vives, a Spanish humanist living in Bruges, penned an influential treatise on poor relief (1526).[54] Poverty such as was now to be seen in Bruges, he warned, was a breeding ground for an insurrection against the rich. For their own good and that of the city, magistrates must consolidate the funds of all existing private and parish charities to provide relief for those duly enrolled as deserving poor, that is, genuinely unable to work. Others must be made to work for their upkeep or be expelled from the city; begging must be banned altogether, and strangers sent back to their own cities. A few months earlier, the nearby cloth town of Ypres had incorporated many of the same ideas into a statute for the poor, later revised (1531) to include added points suggested by Vives. The 1531 Ypres poor law was endorsed by the theology faculty in Paris, a bastion of Catholic orthodoxy, and later by Emperor Charles V. But other theologians, especially among the mendicant orders, condemned legislation of this kind as an assault on traditional Catholic beliefs about the holy state of poverty; in their view, caring for the poor was the responsibility of the church, not of civil society. Reflecting this conflict of values within the

Catholic world, many towns that had enacted poor laws revised them to permit begging by the friars and to recognize the autonomy of church-sponsored charitable organizations such as confraternities.[55]

Luther and the Reformers came to similar conclusions about helping the poor, without any of the hesitations one finds in Catholic writers like Vives.[56] According to the new theology, giving to the poor was not a "good work" meritorious in the sight of God, nor was there any basis for the claim (by members of religious orders) that all who freely chose a life of poverty lived a more perfect Christian life.[57] The Wittenberg town council's "Ordinance of the Common Chest," issued after consultation with Luther (1522), expelled the mendicant orders, prohibited begging, and mandated weekly collections in the churches for a civic fund for the poor. The following year Luther helped draft a common chest ordinance for the nearby "community" of Leisnig,[58] in which the civic fund was to be replenished from confiscated church properties and an annual tax for relief of the poor. Leisnig's magistrates resisted both of these provisions but eventually gave in to pressure from Saxony's territorial government. The idea spread quickly, for example to Nuremberg and Strasbourg, even before these towns formally adopted Protestant worship.

The fact that similar institutions were created at about the same time in Catholic as well as Protestant territories indicates that poor-law reform was more a social than a religious process. The prohibition of begging, conspicuously including the friars, points to a specifically antimendicant strain in urban anticlericalism.[59] Certainly the "common man" was pleased to see action at last taken against the "sturdy beggars" whose piteous pleas were well-crafted to deceive honest folk. There may also have been, as some have argued, an element of calculation on the part of large-scale employers, who benefited from having laborers they needed only occasionally supported by the city the rest of the time. Yet there also had to be religiously sound reasons for changing a system based on religious conceptions of the poor as favored by God and of the Christian duty of charity. Whether Catholics who saw charity as a work pleasing to God donated more or less than Protestants who saw it as something expected of believers[60] is not possible to say. The more important difference lies in the fact that Protestant poor relief was less ambiguous than its Catholic counterpart in shifting responsibility for the poor from the church to the state. Protestant town governments often accommodated separate systems of church poor relief, especially where it was organized by Calvinist diaconates.[61] But it was the magistrates who made the key decisions and launched major new initiatives, like the civic workhouses where the working poor were confined, the better to instill proper discipline.[62] This was an important step farther in the process by which the town itself, not the

Figure 13.3. Amsterdam's Workhouse. The rasping of wood at which inmates were frequently employed gave the institution its Dutch name (Rasphuis): the Amsterdam Workhouse ca. 1614, from Joannes Pontanus, Beschrijvinge van Amsterdam (see Figure 10.1), p. 133. (*Special Collections, University of Minnesota Library.*)

semipublic religious bodies to which citizens belonged, assumed the main burden of making society a community.[63]

Marriage in Christian thought was shaped from the beginning by St. Paul's statement that "it is better to marry than to burn" (with sexual desire). Marriage was an institution—the only one—within which the primal and spiritually dangerous urges of the body could safely be confined. During the medieval centuries the Catholic Church developed a marriage law of its own, similar at many points to Roman law, but reflecting also a conception of married life as a state of life sanctioned by God, albeit a less worthy state than the life of those who renounced their sexuality in the service of God.[64] Ancient Germanic law treated marriage as a contract between two families. By contrast, the church's canon law treated marriage as a contract between the parties, to which the free consent of both—including the young bride—was essential. Over time, this view prevailed; for example, "betrothal" came to mean a ceremony involving the parties, not an exchange of gifts between their families. Episcopal courts claimed jurisdiction over disputes involving promises of marriage, leaving it to secular courts, like those of the towns, to punish adulterers for violating the obligation of marital fidelity. From at least the twelfth century the church also viewed marriage as a sacrament, a ritual by which God imparted his grace in a very special way; it was for this reason that the bond of marriage could not be broken—church courts recognized various grounds for separation, including impotence and infidelity, but not even the injured party was free to remarry. Sacraments had to have "ministers," but in this case the ministers were the couple themselves.[65] Parental consent was encouraged, so was the blessing of a priest and publicizing the marriage through the so-called banns,[66] but neither was strictly necessary for a canonically valid marriage.

One unintended consequence was clandestine marriage: couples forbidden to marry by their parents could present them with a fait accompli. By the sixteenth century, marriages of this kind were a sore point among propertied families. Fathers were increasingly anxious lest a daughter's foolishness give some no-account adventurer a claim to a share of the family patrimony. The Council of Trent addressed these concerns by requiring (1563) a church ceremony and the presence of witnesses (if not consent of the parents) as conditions for a valid marriage. The same concerns were addressed earlier and more fully by the new Protestant understanding of marriage.

The Reformers elevated the spiritual dignity of marriage by eliminating monastic life as a choice for Christians. For men and women alike, the married state was now the Christian state pure and simple, in which the Lord willed that believers serve his will. Luther's own marriage (1526) to a former nun[67] consolidated a shift begun by more radical preachers as early as 1522. Not celibates, but married people, especially the pastor and his wife, were to be models for Christian life. At the same time, because there were no sacraments instituted by Christ except for baptism and communion, marriage was a purely human bond and could for certain reasons be dissolved. Luther recognized three grounds for divorce with the right of remarriage (impotence, infidelity, refusal of sexual congress), and Zwingli added others, including abandonment. Since the claims of episcopal courts to regulate marital disputes were no longer recognized, new courts had to be created, combining the competence of the old episcopal courts and the marital jurisdiction hitherto exercised by town courts. As in Basel (1533), these new courts moved fairly quickly to give marriage a more social dimension by requiring parental consent and the blessing of a clergyman as necessary conditions for a valid marriage. Protestant marriage courts stressed publicity more than consent as a condition for the validity of marriages, and they also interpreted a husband's responsibilities more broadly, to include material support as well as sexual fidelity. Preachers were as vigorous as their Catholic rivals in denouncing as sinful all forms of sexual contact except for vaginal intercourse, but they did not call on couples to refrain from marital relations during Lent. The common thread of novelty seems to be that marriage in the Protestant view was more consistently seen as a social institution. Couples were not just individuals answerable to God for their vows to each other, they were the cells that made up the larger body of the Christian community.

Despite the differences in theology there were parallel changes in the Catholic understanding of marriage. In the Catholic duchy of Bavaria, as in Protestant lands, notions of social propriety helped shape a marriage law suitable to the self-understanding of honorable folk. Town courts took a strong interest in restraining "profligacy," meaning extramarital sexual relations. At the same time, they made it more difficult for a young man and woman to marry if they lacked financial means. The honorable state of matrimony, foundation stone of the social order, was only for couples able to support themselves as independent households, without being a charge on the public treasury.

The campaign against *Witchcraft.* Hexing[68] is an age-old practice found all over the world. In the early Middle Ages folk beliefs about the casting of spells were not seen by church officials as a diabolical threat. One document advises priests that women who say they have flown through the night air by the power of "Diana"[69] are to be treated as deluded—God does not grant evil spirits control over nature. But the great scholastic theologians opened the door to a dark future by entertaining the possibility that God could allow Satan to compass the "evil deeds"[70] traditionally attributed to witches. By the fourteenth century, inquisitors warned of heretical groups consorting with the devil, and the fifteenth century saw the first witchcraft panics: accusations snowballed as persons charged with doing "evil deeds" by the power of the devil named others in hopes of exculpating themselves. Two German Dominican friars gave witchcraft belief its classic formulation in a 1486 manual for prosecutors.[71] A witch, usually a woman, was one who consigned her soul to the devil in return for powers to fly through the night and cause evil deeds at will; witches gathered in "covens" of thirteen for obscene rites, sometimes including intercourse with the devil.

Although the two Dominicans had trouble selling this new theory of witchcraft to some church officials, the great European witch-hunt was by now well underway. Between 1450 and 1750, between 100,000 and 200,000 people, mostly women,[72] were tried for the crime of witchcraft, mainly by secular courts;[73] tens of thousands were executed. Among the multiple explanations of how the craze got started, two are worth mentioning here because they tie the rise of witchcraft belief to beliefs about the community, albeit in different ways.[74] One scholar argues that people no longer willing to be charitable to older female neighbors projected their own sense of guilt on these women by accusing them of witchcraft.[75] Another sees witchcraft belief as rooted in fears that the community has become polluted, contaminated as if physically by the intrusion from without of a frightful evil.

Regional variation across Europe was enormous. Seventy-five percent of

Ein erschröckliche geschicht/ so zu Derneburg in der Graff-
schafft Reinstepn/ am Hartz gelegen/von dreyen Zauberin/vnnd zwayen
Mañen/ Jñ ertlichen tagen des Monats Octobris Jm 1 5 5 5. Jare ergangen ist.

D Je alte Schlang der Teüffel/dieweyl er Got/vnd zäuoran den Sun Gottes/vnsern Herrn Jesum Christum/vnd das gantze menschliche ge
schlecht/fürnemlich vmb vnsers Haylands Christi willen hasset/hat er sich bald im anfang/vnd türglich nach der erschaffung vmb dz weibß
bild/als vmb die/welcher same seinen topff zertretten solt/angenomen/dieselbigen durch sein hinderlist vnd lugen/zũ dem jämerlichen fal/deß vñ
glaubens vñ vngehorsams wider Got gebracht/Darauß das gantz menschlich geschlecht/in ewige verdamnuß vñ verderben komen were/so Chri
stus vnser Hayland/den zorn des Vatters nicht weck genomen/vnd das gericht wider vns auffgehaben het/Nu behelt der alte Feind gleichwol al-
ten haß wider Christum/vnd vns/für vñ für/vnd het auch sein alte weyse/er setzet sonderlich dem weiblichen gschlecht hart zu/als dem schwecheren
werckzeug/damit es sie von Christo wegtrey sse/vñ in ewige verdamnuß füre/vñ wie er zũ Eva sprach/sie wurden werdẽ wie die Götter/Also bläßt
er noch das gifft in der weyber hertzen/let sie zaubern/auff das er sie klüg mache/das sie mehr wissen dann andere leüt/vnd also den Göttern ge
leich werden/damit macht er sie jm anhengig/vnd zũ Teüffels dienerin/ja auch zũ Teüffels beüten/wie dise jämerliche geschicht/welche warhaff
tiglich also wie vnden angezaiget/am Hartz ergangen ist/Die derhalben also gemalet vñ geschriben/im druck auß gangen/Auff das doch die rohe
lose welt/zũ Gottes forcht erweckt werde/damit macht er sie jm anhengig/vnd von den Gotlosen wesen abgeschreckt werden/Dann Gott der allmechtige derhalben solche Exempel
vns setzen lasse/ja damit vnsere harten hertzen durch dise erschröckliche exempel / zur forcht Göttliches gerichts/vnd straffe erweckt/man mag
es malen/predigen/singen vnd sagen/vñ wie man jmer kan den leüten einbilden/damit der laydige hauffe ein wenig zũ Gottes forcht/gehorsam/
vnd zucht gezogen werde/besonder zũ disen letzten zeyten/in welchen der listige Sathan/dieweyl er merckt/das der tag des gerichts sich nahet/gar
rassend toll vnd vnsinnig ist/vnd bede durch sich vnd seine gelider/grewlicher weyse/wider Christum vnd sein armes heüfflein wüttet/Die ellende
welt aber dargegẽ so frey sicher in allem mũtwillen dahin lebt/als ob der Teüffel vor langst gestorben sey/vnd kain Got/kain gericht oder straff/
verhanden were/Der Almächtig Got vnd vatter/vnsers Herrn Jesu Christi/wölle dem grimigen seinde wehren/sein armes heüfflein vor jm vnd
seinen glidern schützen vnd handthaben/seinem vnd der seinen wütten vnd toben/einmal ein ende machen/durch Jesum Christum Amen.

¶ Folget die geschichte / so zũ Derneburg in der Graffschafft Reynstein am Hartz
gelegen/ergangen ist/ Jm October des 1 5 5 5. Jare.

A Vff den Dinstag nach Michaelis/den ersten Octobris/seind zwõ Zauberin gebrandt/die eine Gröbische/die ander Gißlersche genant/ vñ hat
die Gröbische bekandt/das sie Aylff jar mit dem Teüffel gebület habe/vñ man dieselben Gröbischen zũ der Feuerstat gebracht/vnd an die
saul mit Ketten geschlagen/vnd das Fewr angezündt/ist der büle/der Sathan komen/vnd sie in lüfften sichtiglich vor jederman weckgefürt/Am
Donerstag/nach dem die Gröbische vñ die Gißlerschin am Dinstag zãuor seind gerichtet worden/das ist den 3, Octobris/seind dise bede Frawen auff
den abend in der Gißlersche hauß komen/vnd die Gißlerschen man zur thür hinauß gestossen/das er nider gefallen vnnd gestorben ist/welches ain
Nachbaur gegen vber gehöret/vnd zũ gelauffen ist/durch die thür gesehen/das zway weyber bede estel sewrige/vmbs sewr gedantzet/der Gißlerschin man aber/lag vor der thür vnd war todt/Am Sonnabende nach Dionisi/das ist der 12, Octobie/ist der Gröbischen man gerichtet worden/
vmb der vrsach willẽ/das er bey seines schwester geschlaffen hat/welche er zũ einem wey be gehabt/vñ darnach die Gröbischen genomen/
Des Montags darnach/das ist der 14, Octobie ist ain weyb die Serck'schen genandt/auch verbrandt worden/der vrsach/das sie des Herrn Atha-
cius von Veldthaym des Stiffts Halberstat hauptmans weybe vergeben hate/vnd ainem mañ zũ Derneburg ain Krotten vnter die Schwöllen
gegraben/daruon der man erlamet/vnd jm das vibe vmbkomen ist.

C Wie sicher man wañ der Teüffel an ainem ende einnistet/vñ begundt zũ Regieren/wie wüst er mit seinem gifft vmb sich frisset/vnd wie vil personen
komen die vmb/in wenig tagen/vnd soll vns solch grewlich exempel billich rayzen zur büß/vnd zur forcht Gottes/auff das wir vns mit dem wort
Gottes vnd gebette/wider den gemelten seynd schützen/vnd mag dise Histori den sichern gotlosen Epicurern vnnd Zaubern/wol ain erinnerung
sein/dieweyl sie sehen/das der Teüffel noch lebt/vnd das das Hellische sewr noch nit erloschen ist/Der Almechtig Got wölle sie auch zur büsse brin-
gen/vnd vns alle inn/vnd bey seinem raynen wort erhalten/vnd mit seinem hayligen Gayst regieren/auff das wir leben in aller Gottseligkayt/
Zucht vnd Erbarkayt/zũ ehren seinem hayligen Namen/Durch vnsern Herren Jesum Christum/ A M E N.

¶ Getruckt zũ Nürnberg bey Jörg Merckel/durch verleg Andres Zenckel Botten.

Figure 13.4. The Burning of Witches. Contemporary broadside describing the burning of witches at Denerburg in the Harz Mountains, 1555. (*Germanisches Museum, Nuremberg.*)

all the trials took place within the boundaries of the Holy Roman Empire. In England, few people were executed, because England's common law, unlike the continent's Roman law tradition, did not permit the use of torture to obtain confessions for capital crimes. Spain had few trials for witchcraft, because the Spanish Inquisition held on this point to a prescholastic theology that denied the devil any agency in the world. The wave of trials ended soonest in the Dutch Republic (1590s) and continued longest in parts of eastern Europe. Some have contended that the idea of witchcraft lost credibility as the scientific view of the world slowly took hold, but the legal profession's standards of proof and due process seem to have been more pertinent; after a certain point in time, high courts (as in France and Denmark) routinely overturned all convictions for witchcraft in lower courts. Conversely, the courts of small, autonomous territories in the empire, not subject to any appellate jurisdiction, pursued the hunt for witches well into the seventeenth century and often had the highest rates of execution for those convicted.

The Reformation did not initiate the campaign against witches, and may in some ways have retarded it. For all his belief in the reality of the devil's power, Luther, like the inquisitors in Spain, rejected the whole idea that God would allow the devil to do "evil deeds" in the physical world. During the early decades of the Reformation, from 1520 to 1560, the number of known witchcraft trials across Europe dropped somewhat. But it rose again after 1560 and peaked in the period from about 1580 to 1650, which was also the period of the most intense religious conflicts, especially between armies pledged to causes Catholic or Calvinist. It seems that proponents of the rival visions of reform competed with one another in their zeal to cleanse the world of witchcraft, perhaps more so in Catholic and Calvinist than in Lutheran territories. In parts of the Holy Roman Empire where territories have been studied comparatively, Lutheran lands had fewer trials and lower rates of execution than Catholic lands. Calvin's Geneva burned[76] remarkably few witches, but smaller Calvinist territories had some of the highest rates for trials and executions, comparable to those of small Catholic territories.

Comparative studies of social standing suggest that the accused were relatively poor and isolated, while their accusers were somewhat better off and more likely to play leadership roles in the local community. In the end it was the accusers, even more than the theologians or the trial judges, who drove the baleful engines of prosecution forward. Especially in a climate of religious reform, people of goodwill had to take the Bible's words to heart: "Thou shalt not suffer a witch to live."[77]

We may conclude that the German and Swiss Reformation was communal also in its blueprint for a more Christian life. The Protestant reform of worship aimed at centering the Sunday gathering of the people on God's Word, to the relative or (for Zwingli) total exclusion of all possible distractions. The reform of instruction, top to bottom, sought to harness existing forms of schooling to the dissemination of the Word. Protestant poor relief made the civil community responsible for achieving this vital dimension of moral community, just as Protestant marriage set each couple more clearly in its place as a living cell of the body social. Witchcraft trials may seem a jarring exception to this focus on community, but they were not. Like all things human, the ideal of community had its dark dimension. The flip side of solidarity with one's neighbors was a suspicion of everything "foreign" and a downright loathing for anything by which the community might be polluted. For sixteenth-century Christians, a town or village was polluted—rendered liable to God's wrath—by its toleration of false worship, even more by its toleration of devilish witchcraft. Hence many of those who clamored for the gospel clamored also for the exclusion of popish idolatry from all houses of worship within the city walls. Hence too, in many towns and villages, the same middling sort of folk who embraced ideas of reform might also come forward to accuse others (often outsiders in the town or village) of commerce with the devil—it was their Christian duty. Thus for those accepted as members, the community could be a wonderful source of strength; for those extruded from the charmed circle, it could be a nightmare.

Success or failure. Did better preaching and better indoctrination make for better Christians? The Reformers were soon disabused of the idea that the pure Word of God would by itself work wonders among the faithful. Accordingly, the Reformation became a campaign to use all appropriate means to bring the people to that standard of righteous living that the Catholic Church in its long history had so manifestly failed to achieve. Reform of the clergy was the first task. Properly trained preachers graduated in increasing numbers from universities that had become Protestant or new ones created to advance the reform.[78] If only a fraction of the Catholic parish clergy at the beginning of the sixteenth century had attended universities, by the end of the century all but a fraction of the Protestant clergy had degrees. Regular meetings, like the synods established by Zwingli in Zurich, created an esprit de corps among the clergy, abetted by the fact that Protestant clergy were over time increasingly likely to be the sons of clergymen. By around 1600 the Catholic Church too was filling its pulpits with a better class of men, graduates of the seminaries mandated for each diocese[79] by the Council of Trent, or Jesuits or Capuchins, often foreign-born; the order priests set a new standard of learning and decorum for Germany's Catholic clergy, among whom the rule of celibacy was more and more strictly enforced. One way or another, the clergy was becoming an elite corps, conscious of its mission to elevate the ignorant laity to a higher moral and spiritual plane.

Paradoxically, however, this process of professionalization, the proud achievement of religious reformers and territorial governments working together, probably made it more difficult to reach the larger goal of changing Christian society for the better. The new ministers and priests were too educated to have any sympathy for the mind-set of ordinary folk and too conscious of their dignity to consort with parishioners at the local tavern. They had much more to say than their medieval predecessors, but would people listen?

Zealous Protestant pastors had in fact many errant sheep. Some had never come to church anyway, not even when threatened with excommunication by the Catholic Church. Others rejoiced in the overthrow of priestly authority but scorned the new clergy's pleas for attendance or showed up for Sunday services occasionally, giving nary a hint of inner engagement. Still others clung stubbornly to some radical doctrine or resorted in time of illness to the nearest Catholic shrine. By the second half of the sixteenth century, reform-minded clergy of all major confessions were agreed on two essential points: the people needed to be disciplined and no real progress could be made unless those who scoffed at God's truth were cowed by the power of the state.

Within this framework of consensus there were many different ideas about how to get people to take Christian teaching to heart. In Zwingli's Zurich, all coercive authority rested with the Christian magistrates. Anabaptists and other spreaders of false teaching were punished without pity, and Sunday church attendance was ensured by the simple device of levying large fines for noncompliance. Strasbourg's magistrates claimed the same authority but were not nearly so zealous; this was why Martin Bucer tried various means of instilling virtue in the people, including the formation in each parish of circles of the devout meant to serve as a leaven for the whole.[80] As Strasbourg gravitated toward a Lutheran rather than a Reformed orientation in its theology, the city's religious leaders remained at odds with the magistrates, but they had different means for forming a Christian conscience among believers, such as individual confession of sins to the pastor.[81] Yet church leaders in the nearby Lutheran duchy of Württemberg had more confidence in the duke's church council—made up of theologians and civil officials—than in the parish clergy: the church order of 1559 vested the key power of excommunication in the church council.[82] Similarly, most of the twenty-odd German territories that became Calvinist put in place a state-centered approach to the control of morals, rather than the parish-centered consistory of Calvin's Geneva.

In Catholic Germany the old tradition of clerical independence of the state was deeply compromised by rulers like the dukes of Bavaria, who merely kept Rome informed as they governed the church through a church council, more or less as their Protestant peers did. Rulers all over Germany backed the clergy in bringing the wayward to heel: Marriages had to be blessed by the clergy in order to be lawful, teachers had to have their religious orthodoxy certified, and nonconformists were subject to expulsion. By the seventeenth century, civil officials were requiring persons moving to a new place to have their good character attested to by the clergyman of their former residence—a usage appropriated by immigrants to the United States in more recent times.[83] Historians now use the term "confessionalization" to describe this collaboration of state power and clerical authority to achieve a reformation of morals. But subjects are never so pliable as rulers want them to be, least of all in matters of the mind and heart. The heavy hand of the state, like the professionalization of the clergy, may actually have made it more difficult to elicit the inner consent of the people to the process of reform.

Roughly speaking, scholars have judged the urban Reformation a success in changing the minds of the people and the rural Reformation a failure.[84] Strasbourg's transition from a Reformed to a Lutheran version of Protestantism was dictated by the magistrates' grasp of political imperatives.[85] Once the change was made, however, popular opinion proved decisive in the city's adoption (1591) of the Formula of Concord,[86] despite the magistrates' preference for a measure of ambiguity in confessional matters. Calvinist Emden was the capital of the county of East Friesland. When Emden became the rule of an ambitious Lutheran count, its preacher and a city council chosen by the people blocked his attempt to impose Lutheranism (1595–1599). In Lemgo, capital of the county of Lippe, magistrates who bowed to the count's demand for Calvinist preaching were overthrown in a popular uprising (1609) that kept the city Lutheran. In 1614 Brandenburg's Elector Johann Sigismund (ruled 1608–1619) announced his conversion to Calvinism. But when a would-be Calvinist pastor mounted the pulpit of Berlin's cathedral, "the common mob . . . shouted curses and blasphemies, and ran out" (1614). With crowds throwing stones at Calvinist preachers in Berlin and other cities, the elector backed off: The dynasty would be Calvinist; Brandenburg remained Lutheran. This kind of popular support for a specific creed does not necessarily mean that people have changed in their heart of hearts. It does indicate, however, that the people have become "confessionalized": this creed, and no other, was now henceforth a part of their identity.

We should also be wary of assuming that preachers had simply implanted their ideas in the minds of listeners. People paid little heed to the novel idea that engaged couples should refrain from sexual relations. They saw no good reason to curtail the merriment of their festivals, and even in Zurich, dedicated to the proposition that the Word alone sufficed for man's spiritual needs, they practiced obscure rituals, like digging up the bones of ancestors to recite the traditional prayers for the dead. The Reformation took hold only through a process of appropriation, making it the people's religion, not just that of the preachers.[87]

For evaluating the success of the Reformation in rural Germany, scholars depend on the reports of officially sanctioned clerical "visitors" who made regular circuits. Visitors followed printed forms with questions for the pastor and his parishioners, so that answers can be compared over time. Country people were no doubt intimidated by these prying, citified strangers, but not enough to give the right answers. Even if taught their catechism as youngsters, they were seldom able to recite the Apostles Creed or the Ten Commandments, and they had only the vaguest ideas about how sinners were saved from damnation. Pastors complained again and again about the many who jumped up to leave as soon as the sermon began, or stayed away from church altogether, and about village officials who silently obstructed the mandates of godly princes for a reformation of festivals and other popular customs. There seems little difference between the visitors' reports from Lutheran and Calvinist territories or between Catholic and Protestant territories. Rulers who applied the full force of their authority could achieve some results—people did generally go to church where they were fined for nonattendance—but compulsion does not make for inner conviction. Yet the picture is not uniformly bleak. In some rural districts that have been studied, there is evidence that people attended Sunday services regularly, worried less than their ancestors did about evil spells or other threats from the realm of magic, and used the disciplinary procedures of the new church to resolve conflicts among themselves. In one corner of Catholic Germany where no ruler had the power to impose either Protestantism or a Tridentine form of Catholicism, the process of appropriation is a bit clearer: by the eighteenth century, villagers attended Sunday mass more regularly, but they still preferred the pastors they knew—never mind whether or not these priests had concubines—to austere and learned Jesuits representing an alien faith. Rural folk whose religious identity had once been decided by princely fiat eventually did create for themselves a religious culture based on the new beliefs, but only over a very long period of time.

The principle that separates the relative success of urban Reformations from the painfully slow implantation of new religious ideas in the countryside was grasped by the great Muslim historian Ibn Khaldun: "One cannot expect [prophets] to work the wonder of achieving superiority without group feeling."[88] Ibn Khaldun was referring to the Prophet Muhammad and the "group feeling" of Arab tribes. But one can apply his reasoning to the civic solidarity that powered the urban Reformation and made it difficult for princes to reverse a religious choice once accepted by townsfolk. In this sense, too, the Reformation in its most successful form was a communal movement.

14 | Society and Community

Reformations across Europe

Calvinism and Tridentine Catholicism were the two forms of Christianity that competed most aggressively for the allegiance of early modern Europeans (Chapter 7). Most of the leaders willing to use war as a means of achieving religious objectives were found among militant Calvinists or militant Catholics (Chapter 9). This chapter focuses on the fact that Calvinism and Tridentine Catholicism were also conspicuous in their zeal for the reformation of morals, albeit in very different ways. As in Chapter 13, the discussion here will consider the social basis of each movement, its vision of a more Christian community, and its successes and failures as measured against this objective. Like German Lutheranism, Calvinism and Tridentine Catholicism were able to engender a sense of confessional identity strong enough to enable both faiths to withstand the pressures of minority existence in societies dominated by other creeds. The Catholic preachers who tried to convert Huguenot La Rochelle after its conquest by Richelieu (1628) did not have much success; neither did Calvinist ministers the Dutch Republic sent into northern Brabant (also in 1628) after conquering a territory that by then had two generations of Counter-Reformation preaching. Thus if the various Reformations changed European society through the creation of better-disciplined communities of believers, they changed it even more by making such communities strong enough to cohabit with one another, even if against their will. The time when religious pluralism would be accepted as a positive good lies beyond the chronological limits of this book. But it will be appropriate to end our survey of the Calvinist and Catholic Reformations with a brief look at a few urban societies where political circumstances made pluralism a fact of life.

CALVINISM

The *social basis* of Calvinism was to be found in the towns. Calvin's creed held few charms for peasants. In west Flanders, where the new textile industry was centered,[1] the towns had many Calvinists, but surrounding villages had none. In France, Nîmes and La Rochelle, Calvinist for generations, bought grain from and had vineyards worked by Catholic peasants. The rural areas where Calvinism had success[2]—marked by cottage industry and unusually high rates of literacy—are exceptions that prove the rule.

If Lutheranism readily identified with movements for local control, Calvinism had a special appeal for those with broader horizons. Calvin himself welcomed to Geneva the refugees of many nationalities,[3] and he and his successor, Theodore Beza, kept up a voluminous exchange with correspondents from most corners of Europe.[4] Leaders of the movement knew what it was to choose exile for their beliefs. While in exile, in Geneva, London, or Emden,[5] they rubbed shoulders with coreligionists from distant lands. Calvinism's ability to rise above the limits of a local outlook seems to have been one of the sources of its appeal for the twenty or so German princes (starting with the count Palatine)[6] who converted Lutheran territories to Calvinism between about 1560 and 1620. This so-called second Reformation was backed by bureaucrats who grew beyond identification with their native towns by serving the prince. For these reformations from above, parochial loyalties were merely obstacles to be overcome. Something similar can be seen in the French-Pyrenean principality of Béarn, where a Huguenot military victory (1569) permitted Jeanne d'Albret (d. 1572),[7] lady of the ruling house, to impose Calvinist reforms that the largely Catholic estates of her land had hitherto resisted.

Calvinism's international flavor may also help to explain its appeal for Europe's cosmopolitan nobility.[8] In France, it is estimated that around 1560 some 10 percent of the population[9] were Calvinist but 50 percent of the nobles were. It was rare in Protestant churches elsewhere, but not in France, for clergymen to come from noble families. Scotland's Reformation was largely made by the nobles. Nobles were prominent also in early stages of the protest movement against Philip II's repressive religious policy in the Netherlands, though not in the Dutch Reformed Church after 1572.[10] In Hungary, Calvinism, backed by many of the kingdom's great magnate families, became the majority religion in the largely Magyar-speaking central region ruled by the Turkish Sultan after 1541.[11] Politics had something to do with these choices. In France, clients of the Bourbon family often followed their chieftain's religious lead.[12] Scotland's Protestant nobles were linked to the pro-English faction, and Hungary's magnates no doubt shared anti-German feeling directed against the Catholic Habsburgs.[13] But Reformed religion was also a matter of conscience, certainly for literate and strong-minded noblewomen who converted their male kinfolk.[14] Merchants involved in long-distance trade were on the whole no more likely than their neighbors to turn to Calvinism. There were few Protestants among leading families in Europe's great banking centers—Antwerp, Lyon, Genoa, and Augsburg.[15] Antwerp's merchant community was prominent among local Calvinists in 1566–1567, when it seemed that Catholicism in the Low Countries was about to collapse,[16] but underrepresented in earlier years, when churches "under the cross"[17] faced persecution. In Lyon, wealthy businessmen who rallied to the Reformation were mostly émigrés, like the master-printers; the native elite remained largely Catholic.

Guildsmen were the backbone of urban Protestantism in France and the Low Countries, though with some distinctions that may not apply for Lutheran Germany. In the 1550s, Calvinism had a powerful appeal for "proletarian"[18] guild workers in the new textile industries of west Flanders, but none at all[19] for those protected by well-established guild regulations in the centers of traditional woolen production, like Ghent. In Antwerp at roughly the same time, guildsmen were disproportionate in number among those persecuted for their Protestant beliefs. In Utrecht of the 1580s, orthodox Calvinism[20] had its strongest support from the guilds, including craftsmen with shops along the city's main canal. La Rochelle, where Calvinism was quickly embraced by the wine merchant and vineyard owner elite, was perhaps an exception for France, rather like Constance in Germany.[21] Elsewhere, guildsmen were the most reliable Calvinist constituency, even though often outnumbered, as in Dijon, by guildsmen who remained Catholic. Those most likely to hearken to the new doctrines came from the high end of the scale of craft skills, where literacy was common or even required:[22] in Lyon, printers, goldsmiths and jewelers, and silk-workers; in Rouen, bonnet-makers; in Antwerp, diamond-cutters and silversmiths, and, in the textile industry, braid- and trimmings-makers. Many of these highly specialized craftsmen were outsiders seeking opportunity in centers like Antwerp and Rouen, where, as in Lyon, they found in underground Calvinist communities a haven for newcomers frozen out of established parish hierarchies. Urban Calvinism in France and the Low Countries was, it seems, a religion not of the common man in general, but of the discriminating common man, able to read scripture in the vernacular and conscious that his superior skill was not matched by superior status.

There may also have been a Calvinism of the unskilled. The spread of Reformed Protestantism was punctuated by iconoclasm, a venting of anticlerical fury stoked by incendiary preaching. In many cases, this violence was attributed by contemporaries to the lower orders of urban society.[23] In La Rochelle, where Calvinist magistrates sought to keep passions under

Figure 14.1. Interior of Amsterdam's Portuguese Jewish Synagogue. Emmanuel de Witte, "The Portuguese Synagogue in Amsterdam," 1680. (*Rijksmuseum, Amsterdam.*)

control, some 300 people from the poorer quarters broke away from a huge outdoor communion service to smash each of the city's churches, threatening death to the mayor who bade them cease (1562). During the previous year, actions of this kind, including killings of priests, comparable to the murders of Huguenots in Catholic riots, were especially common in the region around Agen, between Bordeaux and Toulouse.[24] The preacher whose sermons lay behind some of these incidents was dismissed from his post; in La Rochelle, preachers and consistory alike rebuked all who presumed to destroy churches without the consent of the magistrates. In the turbulent early years of the Dutch Revolt, most preachers and consistories denounced those responsible for attacks on Catholic churches and priests.[25] Calvin had set the tone by rebuking his erstwhile colleague in Geneva, Guillaume Farel, for resorting to violent methods.[26] Preachers who followed Calvin's lead could not altogether prevent violence against the "idolatrous" Catholic worship their sermons so roundly condemned. But their conscientious effort to keep pure religion from being contaminated by mob passions was surely a part of Calvinism's appeal to Europe's aristocracy.

✛

True community. Proponents of Germany's "Second Reformation" distinguished between Luther's reformation of the individual conscience and the reformation of society promised by Geneva's example. Reminders of the Catholic belief that divine grace can work through material objects were tolerated under Lutheran regimes but not in the new Calvinist order. There must be no altars,[27] no baptismal fonts, no statues, no paintings. Likewise, the common folk must renounce long-held beliefs against which Lutheran preachers had campaigned (or so it was thought) with insufficient zeal. Unlike popish priests, the ministers of God's Word claimed no spiritual power that could touch people's daily lives. There was no need to bless crops or fishermen's boats, for all things were in the Lord's keeping. There was no sacrament of the dying,[28] only pious laymen deputed to attend upon the dying and read from scripture.[29] There was no holy water to take home for warding off evil spirits, no fronds or branches blessed by the priest on Palm Sunday: the only religious object a Christian home needed was the Bible.

The same demands were made on the inhabitants of territories influenced by Zwingli's teachings, but Zurich had no consistory to impose them on church members.[30] The lay elders who served with pastors on Geneva's consistory were cut from the same cloth as members of the city council—both were chosen in the same annual elections. After 1555[31] the two groups collaborated closely: those excommunicated by the consistory were exiled by the council.

Larger territories that adopted Calvinism recognized a distinction, not found in Geneva, between members of the church, eligible to participate in the Lord's Supper, and those who merely attended services.[32] To become a member, one met with the pastor (bringing two character witnesses) and swore to uphold the church's confession of faith and submit to its discipline. Names of prospective members were read aloud to the congregation, in case anyone had something unsavory to report that would bar admission. In churches ruled by consistories,[33] members might also be visited in their homes by one or more elders just prior to a celebration of the Lord's Supper.[34] There could be probing questions about beating one's wife, gambling parties, or the sudden bursts of anger that so often led to

FOEMINA HONESTA GENEVENSIS.

Figure 14.2. A Woman of Calvin's Geneva. "Foemina Honesta Genevensis" ("A Virtuous Woman of Geneva"), from H. Weigel, *Habitus Praecipuorum Populorm* (Nuremberg, 1577). (*Bibliothèque Publique et Universitaire de Genève, Geneva.*)

unseemly violence. Elders knew what to ask because dutiful church folk kept them informed: The husband's visit to the brothel had been noticed, and the respectable merchant's wife had been heard by many when she shouted insults on the open street like a fishwife. The reason for this scrutiny was to keep the Lord's Supper unstained by the pollution of sin, or even public rumor of sin. A Dutch tax-farmer charged with malfeasance convinced his elders he was not guilty, but he was nonetheless excommunicated from the church because he could not prove his innocence beyond all doubt. Members declaring bankruptcy might be excommunicated automatically, on the assumption that only spendthrifts and wastrels were unable to maintain their credit among honest folk.[35]

Some cities were able to approximate the identity between church membership and membership in the civil community for which Geneva was the model. In Emden, a Reformed church built by a Polish refugee preacher and scholar took hold among the people over two generations and successfully resisted a change of religion ordered by its Lutheran prince.[36] The Calvinist movement in Nîmes started among teachers at the Latin school, drew inspiration from conversions among local mendicant friars, and gained the allegiance of most magistrates by about 1561; adhesion of the populace was signaled by a riot in which about 100 Catholic notables were massacred (1567). In later years, among some 12,000 there were at most 400 Catholics, mostly of the lower orders.[37] But in La Rochelle, where houses of Reformed worship were established only in the central wards where the elite lived, the consistory was openly mocked by a self-styled "carnival king," and it was nearly two generations before the new beliefs took hold among artisans.

Changing the outlook and behavior of an entire kingdom, like Scotland, was even more difficult. Calvinist preachers in the Gaelic-speaking Highlands were forced to accommodate local culture: No one confused the locally prized gift of "second sight"[38] with damnable witchcraft, and the Reformed liturgy included a blessing for fishermen's boats. In Béarn, Jeanne d'Albret's determination to impose Calvinism on a "rude and ignorant" populace brought a warning from her leading preacher, Pierre Viret (d. 1571):[39] "A small flock of sheep and lambs is better than a large flock that has more wolves and pigs than sheep and lambs."

The Dutch Reformed Church[40] opted for a solution similar to what Viret had proposed. Civil authorities tolerated no other form of worship, but church membership was voluntary, not constrained. In cities where magistrates put their weight behind it, the church came to embrace most of the population; in cities where they consistently fought against it, the church claimed only a fraction of the citizenry.[41] For the republic as a whole the choice for exclusive membership had consequences. On one hand, not much could be done to reform public morals. Visiting English Puritans were shocked to find that in a professedly Calvinist country dancing and theatrical shows flourished in the towns, and peasants worked as needed in their fields on Sundays.[42] On the other hand, it was all the more urgent for believers who freely gave their allegiance to the church to form a truly Christian community, a miniature Geneva shining its light among the ungodly.

Broadly speaking, then, Calvinist ministers worked in one of two kinds of setting. Where the work of pastors was sustained by a shared sense of community, whether on a civic basis (as in Geneva, Emden, or Nîmes), or on a voluntary-church basis (as in the Dutch Republic), they preached to willing and enthusiastic congregations. As in solidly Lutheran German cities like Strasbourg, preachers and congregants together developed a strong sense of confessional identity. But where the Reformed religion had little popular support, as in Béarn or the Scottish Highlands, it was an uphill battle to make godly folk of the indifferent, just as it was for rural pastors in German territories that had become Lutheran by princely fiat. But can Calvinists can be distinguished from Lutherans or Catholics in their behavior? Did consistories really make a difference?

Success or failure. Examination of court records before and after the Reformation bears out the Calvinist claim that Reformed Genevans were less quarrelsome, more sober in their habits, and more honest in acquitting public responsibilities than their Catholic forebears had been. What were the secrets of this transformation? Calvin's followers attributed great things to the cumulative influence of his preaching over the years. No doubt they exaggerated his impact. But the Calvinist sermon, featuring an hour or more of detailed scriptural exegesis with some "punishing of the papacy"[43] sprinkled in, gripped the minds of early modern folk in ways that are now difficult to fathom.[44] The behind-the-scenes work of Geneva's consistory, locked up for centuries under the indecipherable handwriting of official secretaries,[45] is just now beginning to be better understood. The tribunal's aim was to reconcile sinners to the church; excommunication, the extreme sanction, was seldom employed. The typical person summoned might be a young bachelor cited for fisticuffs, a married man who treated his wife harshly, or an old woman overheard mumbling her Our Father in popish Latin instead of proper French. Forms of behavior control associated with Puritanism[46] were of less concern than offenses against the family unit or the public peace. Being a good Christian meant being a good spouse and a good citizen. This focus on community building appears also in other urban churches that tried to copy Geneva's success.

Emden's church leaders campaigned against inebriation for generations, but to no avail; consistory records corroborate the gossip of nearby towns—Emdeners carried a deserved reputation for drunkenness into the eighteenth century. There was, however, a slow but perceptible decline in the number of citations for out-of-wedlock pregnancies, physical violence, and the kind of verbal abuse that led to fights. Young women who conceived apart from marriage were being shamed,[47] and men as well as women were developing stronger inhibitions against violence. At Nîmes, the consistory made headway in curbing prostitution and in protecting the virtue of servant girls living in households headed by older men. Festivals and merrymaking could not be curbed, despite such dramatic actions as the smashing of violins and carnival masks by repentant church members. Banned in Nîmes, dances were still held in surrounding Catholic villages. In an age when combative notions of a gentleman's honor were spreading from Italy into France, the church's great success lay in inducing many of its male members to lay aside the quarrels that so often led to duels. As in Emden, the consistory strove to preserve the family unit and the public peace.

In Scotland and the Netherlands, discipline was exercised by church councils at the parish level[48] rather than by citywide consistories. Most people cited before Scottish church tribunals during the first fifty years of the Reformation era were accused of sexual offenses like adultery or fornication. This focus on the more obvious sins suggests a church not yet strong enough to attack other sources of public disorder in a society known for its protracted feuds. In the university town of St. Andrews, the church council, strongly backed by the magistrates, could boast of a sharp and fairly rapid decline in the number of sexual cases considered, especially for fornication. The Scots *kirk* employed a method that may help explain this success: confessed fornicators had to sit for three successive Sundays on a "stool of repentance"[49] and hear themselves denounced from the pulpit by the minister.

By comparison with St. Andrews (about 4,000 people), Amsterdam was a metropolis, rising from around 40,000 souls in 1580 to around 200,000 in 1650. Despite this difference in scale, Amsterdam's church councils resembled similar bodies elsewhere both in their priorities and in their successes and failures. In a city where most people were not Reformed, the councils had to abandon the usual Calvinist prohibitions against dancing and theatergoing. But over time the church instilled in its members new standards of sexual conduct: by the late seventeenth century, the relative numbers for persons cited for fornication were dwindling. In the shaming of unwed mothers, records indicate that parish elders and the "neighborhood folk" who kept them informed shared the same values. The councils gave great attention to fights and shouting matches, expending much time and effort to induce contending parties to give each other "the hand of friendship." That they had some success in changing the way people reacted to insults is indicated by the many members who, if slandered by a neighbor, seemed content with the satisfaction they received by having a church council publicly certify their good reputation.[50]

In sum, while popular amusements were relatively immune to ecclesiastical censure, it seems that people who accepted the discipline of the church learned over time to moderate their sexual urges and to contain their angry impulses. If seventeenth-century Europeans were indeed less prone to random sexual adventures and spontaneous outbursts of violence, religion was certainly not the only reason,[51] but it is a part of the explanation, perhaps especially so in strongly Calvinist church communities like those just discussed. Presuming that Calvinism could and did reach into the human psyche to discipline the instincts, scholars have speculated about the historical significance of this inner transformation. One view is that Calvinism prepared the way for capitalism, in part by training its followers to curb their spendthrift appetites, the better to accumulate capital. But merchant capitalism was a well-established fact of life before the Reformation began,[52] and the relative economic ranking of European regions of Catholic and Protestant background looks very different now than it did nearly a century ago, when this theory was propounded.[53] Another view is that Reformed Protestantism's repression of aggression had the effect of turning it inward, creating a potentially destructive self-scrutiny, as is suggested by Zurich's rising suicide rate during the late sixteenth century. Even if this argument is correct, however, it need not apply to the Calvinist form of church discipline, in which members discussed their spiritual lives with pastors or elders, a psychological safety-valve comparable in some ways to the Catholic practice of confession. Could a Calvinist "reformation" of the instincts have produced a conscience that was finely honed, without being self-punishing? This is a fascinating question, but consideration of materials that might yield answers[54] would take us too far afield. The surest conclusion is one that leads back to the social dimension of religion to which this section of the book is devoted: Calvinist consistories worked hard to build a Christian community among their members, and they clearly had some degree of success.

CATHOLICISM

The Catholic and Protestant Reformations had many of the same objectives. Germany's new Protestant universities were matched by Catholic foundations,[55] and the seminaries gradually put in place by Catholic bishops bear comparison with the theological academies of cities like Geneva and Nîmes. When educated clergy of any denomination took a country parish, they carefully avoided tavern-drinking and other indecorous pastimes; they were not to be members of the community, but beacons of instruction, standing above it.[56] The *classes* in which Calvinist preachers met regularly provided fellowship for these lonely professionals, as did the revived rural deaneries for Catholic pastors.[57] To catechize the people, the basic points of true religion (different for each confession) were boiled down to simple statements, to be repeated in sermons for adults and drilled into the heads of schoolchildren. For children not attending school there were weekly catechism classes. As in Protestant lands, however, Catholic young people were not eager to devote Sunday afternoons to religious enlightenment. This was an area in which civil governments might intervene. In some German Calvinist territories, parents were fined for not sending their children to catechism classes. In Spain, people of the centrally located diocese of Cuenca learned their catechism well, as determined by questioning persons held in prison by the local inquisition.[58] Yet in the diocese of Ourense in remote Galicia, a region of distinct culture,[59] not even monetary fines induced parents to send children to catechism classes. In staunchly Catholic Lille, the magistrates organized Sunday religious instruction at sites throughout the city. Elsewhere in the Spanish Netherlands, the idea of monetary "attendance prizes" was bruited about, but neither parish boards nor village councils wanted to put up the money; complaints from clergy eventually induced the government to issue the needed instructions—village councils fell into line, and children started coming.

Yet there was a fundamental difference. Much as they yearned for a purer Catholicism, Catholic reformers could not condemn as Protestants did the religion bequeathed to them by earlier ages. Rather than attacking the tyranny of the clergy, they accepted the structure of the church hierarchy as fundamentally sound. Rather than castigating ordinary believers for their superstition, they sought in the religious culture of the people valid elements on which to build. This conservative stance frames the distinctive features of Catholic reform: its social dimensions reflected the contrast between pre- and post-Tridentine Catholicism; its vision of a more Christian society depended on rebuilding the church hierarchy; and its successes and failures were measured by attempts to modify rather than replace the religious culture of the people.

Social basis. As noted above, in France neither peasants nor members of the more traditional urban guilds (e.g., butchers and bakers) showed much interest in Calvinism. In Lyon, most people who were not newcomers seemed to find contentment in customary arrangements that ensured a place in the city's civic and religious hierarchy for each guild and each confraternity.[60] People who change their religion may be presumed to have reasons for doing so, but those who persist in the same belief could be acting from inertia more than conviction. When Catholicism in France seemed to be threatened by the Protestant Henry of Bourbon's emergence as heir apparent to the throne, guildsmen in towns all over France, especially in the north, rallied to the militant program of the Catholic League.[61] In the Low Countries, however, people of presumably Catholic sympathies stood passively by as ruffians hired by fanatical Calvinist ministers looted churches and smashed the symbols of their belief.[62] One weakly governed area in Germany suggests what kind of religion ordinary Catholics might choose for themselves when the moral authority of seminary-educated priests was not backed by the coercive power of the state.[63] Seventeenth-century villagers attended Sunday mass more regularly, but they balked at changing the way they kept their festivals and refused to discriminate against the occasional fellow-villager who happened to be of the wrong persuasion. They eventually did accept Catholicism as an identity that separated them from the Lutherans and Calvinists of nearby villages, but this "confessionalization" of the people was not complete until the eighteenth century.

Tridentine Catholicism had a more sharply defined social profile. The Protestant Reformation rejected the idea that men and women could be holy—there was no such thing as sainthood. The Catholic Reformation, especially through its many new religious orders, resembled the great ascetic movements of the past in demanding a heroic renunciation of self.[64] The call to holiness is never answered by large numbers, but many of the men and women who now did respond came from the upper levels of society. Teresa of Avila (1515–1582) was the daughter of a New Christian[65] cloth merchant who had purchased a title of nobility. Joining a convent in 1535, she began around 1555 to have the intense spiritual experiences, including seeing visions, that brought her a sense of personal union with God and a determination to work for the reform of her Carmelite order. Facing down opposition, she founded a new branch of the order, based on strict poverty and strict enclosure;[66] its spread beyond Spain was aided by the growing fame of her spiritual writings. Ignatius Loyola, founder of the Jesuits, was a nobleman. Two of his early companions in Paris had been shepherds in Savoy,[67] but another was Francis Xavier (d. 1552), the Spanish nobleman Ignatius sent as a missionary to Portugal's outposts in India.

In the generation after the end of the Religious Wars (1598), France witnessed an extraordinary surge of religious energy. Barbe Acarie (1566–1618), widow of an ardent Catholic Leaguer connected with the Paris Sixteen,[68] sought to live a quiet life of prayer, but reports of her ecstatic experience brought men and women eager for her guidance. Inspired by a vision of Teresa of Avila, she founded the first French house of the reformed Carmelites. Francis de Sales (1567–1622), son of a noble family in Savoy, was a popular spiritual writer[69] whose earnest but noncontentious preaching won many converts in the diocese of Geneva, of which he was titular bishop. With Jeanne Françoise de Chantal, the widowed daughter of a leading royal judge in Burgundy, he founded the order of the Visitation, whose members, though later compelled by church authorities to live in convents and dress as nuns,[70] initially wore lay clothes as they went two by two visiting the sick poor. Jacqueline Arnaud (1591–1661) joined the convent of Port-Royal (outside Paris) at eleven and became its abbess at thirteen,[71] thanks to the influence of her father, a leading magistrate of the Parlement of Paris. Long restive in a life she had not chosen, she experienced a conversion through the Lenten sermons of a Capuchin friar and pushed through a reform of convent discipline that initially shocked her family.[72] Soon the convent was not big enough for those demanding admission. The new Port Royal (1626), built in the suburbs of Paris, became a focal point for devout lay men and women, like the male "solitaries" who abandoned promising careers, gave away the proceeds of their property, and started a school for poor children. Pierre Bérulle (d. 1629), son of another member of the Paris Parlement, was influenced by Madame Acarie, who came to stay with his family when her husband was sent into exile (1594). He founded the French branch of an Italian order, the Oratory of Divine Love, which under his guidance opened secondary schools and taught in many of the new diocesan seminaries. Vincent de Paul (1581–1660), an immensely popular preacher who was born of a peasant family, founded an order of priests, the Congregation of the Mission, to preach "missions" (see below) in rural areas. The networked confraternities he created to distribute food and clothing to the poor were known as "Charities."[73] He encouraged Louise de Marillac (d. 1660), a niece of Cardinal Richelieu's political rival,[74] to found an order of nuns, the Daughters of Charity, to coordinate and extend the work of the "Charities."

Vincent de Paul was not the only Counter-Reformation saint[75] to come from humble people. The peasant-born John of the Cross (1542–1591), one of the great poets of mystical experience, was inspired by a meeting with Teresa of Avila to extend her Carmelite reform to the male branch of the order. Philip Neri (1515–1595), from a poor family in Florence, gathered a group of followers in Rome and in effect refounded the Oratory of Divine Love[76] as an order of priests, later established in France by Bérulle. But the prominent background of the others mentioned here is not the only indication that Reform Catholicism depended on people of wealth and position. Jesuit secondary schools mainly attracted the sons of noble and wealthy burgher families. These "colleges" were the main recruiting ground for the society, which had over 8,500 members by 1600, and also for the Jesuit-guided lay confraternities known as sodalities. Members were encouraged to pray according to the rules of Ignatius's *Spiritual Exercises*.[77] Jesuits initially formed sodalities among the top students at colleges, priests holding important positions in a diocese, or leading members of lay society. Jesuit spirituality was not restricted to any one level of society, but there was a conscious strategy of working through those who set the tone for others. In northeastern Italy, noble sodality members accompanied Jesuit fathers in preaching missions to the countryside, to show the peasants an example of devotion.

The status group solidarity of Europe's noble families was growing stronger during the sixteenth and seventeenth centuries. All churches had to accommodate this trend, for example, by reserving front pews for the better sort of people, who paid a rental fee.[78] But Protestant reformers insisted on the unity of the worshiping community: there must be no privileges of rank, no special groups meeting to pray apart from the rest. To prevent members of a large congregation from forming divisive attachments to individual preachers, Dutch churches made a practice of not announcing who would be preaching at which Sunday service. By contrast, Catholic reform capitalized on the popularity of preachers like Vincent de Paul, encouraged the formation of special groups like confraternities, and gave existing divisions of society the sanction of religious approval. All across Catholic Europe nobles sought to form confraternities or sodalities of their own, breaking the tradition that these religious associations were to be a meeting ground for all respectable people.[79] With the blessing of the clergy, they did so, and merchants and artisans soon followed their example. In far-off Mexico, where confraternities initially included Indian converts, Spaniards demanded their own associations, and so did Indians. In a native society brought low by conquest and ravaged by European diseases,[80] Indian confraternities became cells for rebuilding. This affirmation of existing social and even ethnic distinctions has parallels in other aspects of Catholic reform.

True community. The Protestant Reformation drastically simplified the church hierarchy. Once Luther undercut the whole idea of a sacramental priesthood, Lutheran clergy married and became citizens subject to local taxes. In Calvinist lands clergy also shared the dignity of the ministry with lay elders. After the closing of monasteries and the repudiation of the papal and (in most areas) episcopal authority, what remained was a tiny band of ministers more or less equal in rank. Before the Reformation, the diocese of Geneva had a prince-bishop, 110 parishes, and 53 monasteries; by 1546, this structure was replaced by a mere 31 Reformed pastors.

By contrast, the Catholic vision of reform reinforced the distinctive spiritual authority of the priesthood at every level. In Rome, new committees of cardinals known as congregations worked to make the papacy's su-

Figure 14.3. The Corporal Works of Mercy among the Incas of Peru. "A Good Work of Mercy" (Burying the Dead), from the work of an Inca scholar, Felipe Guaman Poma de Ayala (flourished 1613), El Primer Coronica I Buen Gobierno, p. 613, facsimile manuscript with an introduction by Richard Petschmann (Paris, 1936). *(James Ford Bell Collection, University of Minnesota Library.)*

premacy effective. The Congregation of the Inquisition (1542) claimed supervision over heresy trials in church tribunals. For more than sixty years this claim was rejected by Venice, where magistrates were accustomed to giving orders to inquisitors and other local church officials. With help from Spanish Milan, the papacy finally went to war and forced the republic to submit (1605–1608). There were also papal commissions for special topics, like correction of the calendar inherited from ancient Rome. In 1582 Pope Gregory XIII promulgated a reform that required dropping eleven days that year in order to make human dating match celestial time.[81] But Italy's greatest scientist, the Florentine Galileo Galilei (d. 1642), ran afoul of the Roman inquisition when he insisted on describing the heliocentric theory as a fact, rather than a mere hypothesis.[82] Meanwhile, papal nuncios traversed Europe pressing rulers to cooperate with Catholic reform, and overseas missions were placed under the authority of a new Congregation for the Propagation of the Faith (1622).

The Council of Trent gave bishops greater powers to supervise all aspects of religious life. Zealous prelates like Milan's Archbishop Carlo Borromeo (ruled 1565–1584), later canonized as a saint, set an example by visiting even the remotest parishes and holding regular synods to instill higher standards among his priests. At the parish level, the seminary-trained clergy who took over in most places during the course of the seventeenth century were generally faithful to the church's rule of celibacy. New-style priests were instructed to take under their watchful supervision any new confraternities, as well traditional lay bodies hitherto bereft of clerical oversight.[83] No one was to have any doubt that spiritual authority lay in the pastor's hands.

But Counter-Reformation Catholicism, like the church of medieval centuries, was also energized by order priests not subject to episcopal authority. Every sphere of church activity was marked not just by a plurality of jurisdictions, but by multiple understandings of the devout person's role in Christian society. The Confraternities of Christian Doctrine, formed under the influence of Bologna's reforming bishop,[84] had pastors send trained laymen into the streets to round up children as best they could for catechism classes. The Capuchin fathers were a branch of the broad Franciscan movement, based on imitation of Jesus' life as described in the Gospels. If Jesus prayed and fasted forty days in the desert, preachers too must break off for long periods of prayer and solitude. If Jesus had come to preach the gospel to the poor, Capuchins must seek out the poorest quarters wherever they established themselves. Capuchin-founded confraternities took a special interest in the poor, and, as the friars themselves did, they embraced the traditional ascetic practice of disciplining the sinful flesh. Like flagellants[85] of old, hooded confraternity members processed through the streets on solemn occasions, scourging one another. In the Jesuit sodalities, corporal discipline, if deemed necessary by one's father confessor, was to be practiced in moderation and never in public.

These differing approaches were often complementary, as with the "missions" to rural areas poorly served by the existing parish structure. Members of orders active in Catholic Europe's overseas missions sometimes expressed the belief that people of the continent's remote corners

Figure 14.4. St. Vincent de Paul and the Daughters of Charity. Anonymous, "St. Vincent de Paul and the Daughters of Charity," ca. 1740. (*Musée de l'Assitance Publique, Paris.*)

needed Christianizing as much as the heathen of Asia or the Americas.[86] Often chosen for their oratorical skills, mission priests traveled two by two—Jesuits, Capuchins, or members of St. Vincent de Paul's Congregation of the Mission. Following the example of late medieval circuit preachers,[87] they preached for several weeks in a given parish, striving to instruct the ignorant and rouse devotion.

But the mere existence of many different models of the Christian life, each supported by its own order or other institutions, also meant that controversy was inevitable. One example may suffice. From about 1550, the strongly orthodox theology faculty at Louvain (near Brussels) developed a serious interest in the writings of St. Augustine, in order to refute Luther's claim to stand in the Augustinian tradition.[88] In the early seventeenth century Louvain's Augustinian theology spread to France through graduates like the abbot of Saint-Cyran, an influential theologian and a champion of the Port-Royal movement. More important, Augustine's dour views on human nature fitted the life experience of a new generation of urban-born and seminary-trained pastors, confronting surly rural folk who seemed to think about religion no more often than they thought about bathing, that is, once a week. Hence the *Augustinus* (1638), a posthumously published exposition of Augustine's theology by a bishop and Louvain graduate named Cornelis Jansen, found an audience in France as well as the Spanish Netherlands. But Jesuit defenders of human free will[89] pounced on the book for espousing a doctrine of predestination hardly distinguishable from Calvin's heresies. In turn, Saint-Cyran and others linked to the austere convent of Port-Royal denounced the Jesuits as purveyors of an easy morality suitable to their friends among the high and mighty.[90] Cardinal Richelieu, angered by criticisms of his war policy[91] among the Port-Royal circle, had already given Saint-Cyran a taste of prison. This heavy-handed act of state, coupled with reactions to Jansen's book, touched off a long and many-sided struggle over "Jansenism" in Catholic Europe.

Every church of this era had its unseemly internal quarrels. But in the Catholic Church squabbles of this kind were an inevitable consequence of the fact of plural ministries. Just as Tridentine Catholicism accepted and built on existing social divisions, it also accepted and built on a pluralism of religious perspectives not unlike that of the late Middle Ages. Paradoxical as it may seem, Europe's most clerical form of Christianity was also the one most characterized by multiple and often conflicting centers of wide-ranging initiative.

Success or failure. Catholic reform sought to correct rather than to eradicate traditional belief. In pre-Reformation Europe, the understood way of professing that a given town or village stood under God's judgment was through a procession in which all participated. In time of plague, citizens of Renaissance Florence processed to a nearby village to bring back and carry around the city a reputedly miracle-working statue of the Virgin Mary. In Paris, when a locally revered statue was decapitated by Protestant iconoclasts (1528), King Francis I organized a procession of penitence in which the citizens joined. Each guild, each parish, each confraternity had its assigned place, making the order of march a walking diagram of urban society.[92] This habit of collective religious display found little scope in Protestant Europe, but Counter-Reformation clerics saw it as needing only pruning here and guidance there. Priests were instructed to take the lead of processions they had not led before. Processions associated with rural festivals were to be made truly religious by inducing villagers to abandon boisterous habits (like shooting off their weapons) and march quietly behind the eucharist carried aloft by their priest. Like Venice's magistrates, who carefully refashioned the republic's great civic processions during the same era, Catholic reformers believed ideas could be conveyed by ritual, not just by words.

Many Protestant preachers (if not always their people) accepted Calvin's dictum that the age of miracles was long past.[93] The healing shrines at

Figure 14.5. A Counter-Reformation pilgrimage site in Bavaria. Altoetting, from Dorothy Alexander and Walter L. Strauss, The German Single-Leaf Woodcut, 1600–1700: a Pictorial Catalogue (2 vols., New York: Abaris, 1977), I, 52. (*University of Minnesota Libraries.*)

which country people sought cures for their ailments were blasphemous at best and more likely clerical frauds —if not outright sorcery practiced by devilish priests. Even in strongly Catholic lands like Bavaria, visits to wonder-working shrines tapered off during the middle decades of the sixteenth century, no doubt as an echo of Protestant critique. From the latter part of the century, however, pilgrimages to some shrines revived and even surpassed earlier levels. Counter-Reformation priests examined the history of these shrines and the documentation for the relics of the saints they contained. Some local cults they rejected as spurious; others they promoted through their sermons and by writing learned treatises and popular pamphlets. The age of miracles was not over, and people could prove it for themselves by bringing their humble petitions to approved shrines of Catholic saints.

People feared the devil as much as they hoped for miracles. In the later sixteenth century, the upsurge in witchcraft trials[94] was paralleled by a dramatic increase in cases of alleged demonic possession, in which the minions of hell were believed to have forcibly taken over the body of an innocent person. The classic indicators of possession—people speaking in unaccustomed voices or languages and racked by convulsions or showing unbelievable strength—were observed and carefully described not just among Christians of this era, but also among Jews.[95] Since ancient times, the Catholic Church had employed exorcism to deal with such phenomena. Most dioceses had rules requiring examination of the person or persons involved to determine whether the symptoms could be explained by natural means. If not, a priest with a reputation for probity was chosen for the solemn ritual in which the possessing demon was abjured, in the name of Christ, to depart from the victim. Most Protestant theologians accepted the possibility of demonic possession and believed that "dispossession" was possible through prayer and fasting; Luther himself attempted a dispossession late in his life. Some later writers, citing Calvin's belief about miracles, argued that the age of possession and dispossession was also past. But all Protestant writers condemned Catholic exorcism as fraudulent, and this made the church's traditional rite, like miracle-working shrines, a test of Catholicism's credibility. In 1570 Peter Canisius, the celebrated Jesuit preacher,[96] caused a sensation by expelling several demons from a young noblewoman in a publicly announced ceremony held in Augsburg's cathedral. The devil's power was real, but no match for the power of Christ, mediated by the rites of the church.

What was the relationship between the Catholicism of the elite and that of the lowly? Scholars working on French history have found a gradual withdrawal of elites from participation in what had hitherto been a common culture, extending to beliefs as well as amusements. One may distinguish between the refined preoccupations of better-educated people—including Catholic Reform—and what may now be termed popular culture and popular religion. But for scholars working on Spain the only meaningful distinction is that each locality had beliefs and practices not current elsewhere.[97] Between high personages and the humble Spanish believers there was no real difference. When either Charles V or Philip II met a priest bearing the eucharist through the streets to a sick person, he knelt on the spot, heedless of the puddle at his feet.

One may envision a spectrum of attitudes whose range was not necessarily the same for all Catholic lands. At one end, devout Catholics shared the beliefs of common folk but always saw room for improvement: not every alleged case of demonic possession was genuine, nor was every shrine to be maintained. At the other end, those who shared the skeptical temper of an Erasmus might wonder whether miracles were worked at any shrine or any person was truly possessed by the devil, without rejecting the possibility that such things could occur. Post-Reformation Catholicism had room for levels of belief, just as it did for the social solidarity of rival status groups and for competing centers of clerical initiative.

As a communal movement, the Reformation in its Lutheran and Calvinist forms struggled to overcome this confusing multiplicity, ultimately medieval in origin: all Christians were to profess the same gospel truth, submerging their differences in a unified community. This was a noble dream, but it collided with the natural human tendency to form associations based on interests and affinities of various kinds. Post-Reformation Catholicism, precisely because of its backward-looking rootedness in medieval multiplicity, may have been better adapted to a European society that was, after the Reformation as before, characterized by a nearly endless multiple of corporate bodies, each ready and willing to defend its lawful turf against all comers.[98] Yet Protestantism as a whole was multiform in a different way: There were different ways of being Protestant, and members of rival churches usually did not whole regard one another with quite the same hostility that Catholics and Protestants did. This opening toward a tacit acceptance of diversity of creeds was lacking in Catholicism, which remained medieval also in its more determined repression of dissenters. French Protestants had more freedoms than Dutch Catholics in the first half of the seventeenth century, but not in the second. Catholics in England and Scandinavia had a less difficult life than Protestants in the Spanish Netherlands or Austria, not to mention Spain. What neither Protestants nor Catholics of this era could accept was the idea that civil society was

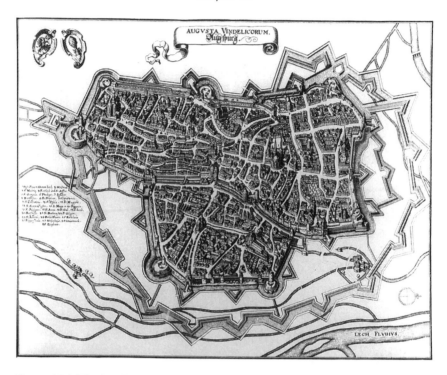

Figure 14.6. The free imperial city of Augsburg. A full image of the view of Augsburg from which figure 3.4 is taken. (*Special Collections, University of Minnesota Library.*)

best not founded on a specific creed. Where different faiths were practiced, the dominant party viewed this state of affairs as something to be overcome through a combination of patience, proselytizing, and social pressure. There were, however, places where people of different denominations lived together long enough to begin to think of religious division as permanent, if not desirable—places like Augsburg in Germany, Haarlem in the Netherlands, and the tiny walled town of Layrac in France. These were the places that pointed to a new conception of society.

DE FACTO RELIGIOUS PLURALISM

Augsburg grew from around 20,000 people in 1500 to around 40,000 in 1600. On the eve of the Reformation, the guilds controlled five-sixths of the seats on the small council responsible for daily concerns and all seats on the large council convened for major decisions. Zwinglianism predominated among the craft guilds, Lutheranism among the so-called greater guilds, whose members took the lead in city politics, and Catholicism among patrician banking families like the Fuggers. The large council voted by a sizable majority for a Zwinglian Reformation (1534). But with a watchful eye on the Catholic princely territories that surrounded it, Augsburg did not prohibit Catholic worship altogether until a year after it had joined the Schmalkaldic League in 1536. In 1548, residing for several weeks in the Fuggers' great mansion, Charles V personally imposed the hated Interim on the city for which it was named and also decreed new electoral rules to strip the guilds of power: patricians henceforth had three-fourths of the small council seats, commoners only one-fourth. The new patrician government, mainly Catholic, then replaced the guilds with trade associations headed by council-appointed leaders. The 1555 Peace of Augsburg recognized only Lutheranism and Catholicism as lawful in the empire, which induced Augsburg's Zwinglian majority to choose Lutheranism. But it also provided that in filling lesser city offices a one-for-one parity must be observed among the two denominations. The Catholic minority's control of the small council was balanced by the predominance of Lutheranism among middling-to-rich tradesmen who made Augsburg thrive. Catholics had more churches, but in some of them Protestants retained control of the pulpit and the nave, leaving only the sanctuary to Catholics.

Within these parameters imposed from above the two communities groped their way toward a new sense of urban citizenship. The city's Latin school was founded (1552) by Protestant humanists who kept doctrinal disputes in the background; Catholic pupils were welcome, even after the Jesuits founded a school of their own (1579). After 1555 the mostly Catholic small council appointed mainly Lutheran "alms lords" to administer the unified (1522) civic charity that controlled the city hospital and many other activities; contributions came from the wealthy, especially the Fuggers. When an influx of starving poor from the countryside prompted Augsburg to open Germany's first orphanage (1572), the "orphan-father" and most of his small clients were Lutheran, but Catholic children were raised in the religion of their parents. The military vicissitudes of the Thirty Years' War encouraged first one party, then the other, to reach for exclusive control of the city. But the 1648 peace restored a balance here as in the empire at large, and it was not disrupted when each confession created an orphanage and a hospital of its own. It was by now understood that the two communities still made up one urban society, even if they created separate institutions to replace the common civic institutions of old.

Layrac had about 1,100 people in 1600, most of them Huguenot. Its four annually elected consuls and the "sworn men" who advised them were solidly Huguenot by 1580, when Layrac expelled its Benedictine monks and abolished Catholic worship. After the Edict of Nantes in 1598, Huguenot consuls, though grumbling that there were no two Catholics of appropriate wealth and status, were forced to make their college biconfessional. Following a revolt against the crown in which many of southern France's Huguenot towns joined (1620–1622), royal orders excluded Huguenots from the consulate. Yet the principle of parity was still observed; the Huguenot schoolmaster received a larger share of city funding because he had more pupils. When a new Catholic pastor (armed with a doctorate in theology) and those who joined his new confraternity pressed for a more zealously Catholic policy, most Catholic magistrates stood with Protestant colleagues in resisting. They opposed his attempts to increase the level of the tithe and refused to bar Protestant burials in the city cemetery. Beginning in 1644 Huguenots were readmitted to the consulate, despite the objections of militant Catholics. This small victory for a common civility reflects a common sociability; Layrac's leading families shared in business dealings, civic processions, and (despite the fulminations of the Huguenot pastor) carnival festivities. Even more, it reflects the fact that it was the job of urban magistrates in France to help siphon off a certain amount of wealth through taxation, for fighting the king's wars. In a town like Layrac this was not possible without Huguenot cooperation. Layrac's confessional coexistence ended only when troops backing Louis XIV's Revocation of the Edict of Nantes (1685) forced its Huguenots into exile.

Haarlem made its definitive choice for the Dutch Revolt in 1578. The initial agreement with the rebel States of Holland called for freedom of worship in the city, but violent disruption of Catholic services by fanatical garrison troops (including the killing of a priest) led to a Calvinist takeover of Haarlem's parish church. A new agreement of 1581 provided for freedom of conscience but allowed none but Reformed worship, "to avoid confusion." Meanwhile, a stream of mainly Protestant émigrés from the southern Netherlands was already flowing in, helping Haarlem to grow from around 15,000 people (1564) to around 40,000 (1622). The Flemish linen-workers who now revived the local industry were often Anabaptist, or, as the Dutch now said, Baptist-minded.[99] Baptist-minded congregations frequently split over disputes as to how strictly church rules for "shunning"[100] sinners were to be applied, but they claimed as many as one-seventh of Haarlem's inhabitants. In the relaxed climate of the Twelve Years' Truce with Spain (1609–1622) they built an unmarked meeting house (1616), later divided in two to accommodate a schism among the members. Haarlem's Lutherans, mainly German immigrants, built their unmarked house of worship at about the same time. Other refugees from the south, including cloth-workers, formed the backbone of Haarlem's Reformed congregation; there were 400 adult members in 1580, 4,000 in 1617, or about one-fifth of the population.

The old religion was kept alive in the city and in the prosperous and still Catholic villages near Haarlem by priests of the Holland Mission, chartered by Rome in 1592. Illegal "assemblies" were frequently broken up by the sheriff so long as it seemed that Catholicism meant loyalty to Spain. But the allegiance of most Catholics to the republic (and bribes to the sheriff) led officials to look the other way after about 1600. Informal communities of religious women taught catechism classes, tended the sick, and knocked on doors to give the time and place for Sunday mass. By 1625 Haarlem's Catholics were said to have eighteen "hidden churches," usually in the upper stories of large houses.

A sense of confessional identity was taking hold, apparently among all of Haarlem's denominations; workers sought employers of the same faith, and employers did the same for employees. At the same time, many Haarlemmers seem to have been content to profess no particular religion. Though some churches gained over time, notably the Calvinists and to a lesser extent the Catholics, the existence of many options apparently left room for some people to choose none. Meanwhile, magistrates, Protestant but not necessarily Calvinist in sympathy,[101] kept alive the idea of a civic culture not tied to confession. Haarlem's Latin school and its unified system of poor relief were under their control so that efforts in these areas by confessional bodies were at most supplementary. If Haarlem's relative toleration did not extend to non-Christians, it was because the Portuguese Jewish congregation whom magistrates encouraged to settle here (1605) received a better offer from nearby Amsterdam (see Figure 14.1).

Seventeenth-century Haarlem approximated the religious pluralism of later centuries in fact, if not in theory. Few individuals espoused the principle that civil society should not be built on confessional foundations, but in practice this was a civil society whose confessional foundations were kept in the background. Rather than attempting to permeate civil society, as in the past, religion had come to play the role of enabling believers to form within the larger society smaller communities according to their own liking. This resolution of the ancient tension between community and society was an outcome no reformer had foreseen or desired. It came about because of an unpredictable coalescence of religious fervor with political ambitions and social reality. In Haarlem as elsewhere, this was the combination of circumstances that reshaped society in the era of Europe's Reformations.

15 | Conclusion

Europe's Reformations in Global Perspective

The era of the Reformation was also the era in which Europe reached out to the rest of the world, not only with merchants and gunboats, but also with missionaries. In the period covered by this book the missionaries were mainly Catholic, not Protestant. The Catholic nations of Iberia established overseas colonies well before the Protestant English and Dutch did, and Calvinist theology of the time also had hesitations about carrying the gospel to pagans. The English were at first uncertain whether North American Indians were worth converting, while the Dutch in what is now Indonesia[1] reasoned that if these heathen had not become Christians after so many centuries, it must be God's will.[2] If, by contrast, members of the new Catholic religious orders were eager to make converts abroad, it was partly because they saw in mission lands a spiritual harvest to offset the souls lost to Protestant heresy in Europe. In effect, the Counter-Reformation exported to Asia and the Americas both the dynamism of the new forms of spirituality and the disagreements that divided them.

A second reason for missionary enthusiasm among Catholics was that they sought and found imagined homologies between their own beliefs and those of Asian and American peoples. One of many strands in Portugal's push toward the Indian Ocean was the hope of finding legendary Christian peoples said to dwell on the far side of the hostile Muslim world.[3] In the wake of Hernan Cortés's conquest of the Aztec empire for Spain (1522), Franciscan friars identified the unexpectedly civilized Mexicans with the so-called Lost Tribes of ancient Israel,[4] whose return to true religion would betoken Christ's return to earth to establish his everlasting kingdom. Inspired by Renaissance humanist conceptions of a universal human nature, both Franciscan and Jesuit missionaries sought at various times to build Indian utopias,[5] where the generous qualities of America's native peoples, secluded from European greed, could flourish under the guidance of faith. In China, as in Europe, Jesuits sought to win the minds and hearts of those who set the tone for others. Permitted to reside at the emperor's court in Beijing, they lived and dressed as scholar-officials. They studied Chinese literature, looking for points of contact between Confucian and Christian teaching, and concluded that the concept of "Heaven" (T'ien), so venerated in the Chinese classics, could properly be translated as "God." They slowly made converts among the empire's bureaucratic elite. Was it a problem if Chinese Christians made obeisance to the emperor as Son of Heaven, as court ritual required?[6] No, reasoned the Jesuit fathers, this was a civil ceremony, not an act of worship. But Franciscans aimed, in China as in Europe, at bringing the gospel to the poor. They dressed in their European habits, sought out the common people neglected by the Jesuits, and violated Chinese law by preaching their alien doctrine in the public streets. Frequently imprisoned for their pains, as Jesuits seldom were, they denounced the Jesuits for allowing their converts to participate in idolatrous court ceremonies and demanded action from Rome.[7]

It is easy at a distance of centuries to see how the missionaries were wrong in the comparisons they made between European and Asian or American beliefs, but they were not wrong in looking for analogies. Contrary to the common saying, history does not repeat itself. Historical understanding demands that ideas be grasped in a context that is unique to a given period and region, a concatenation of circumstances that in the vast span of human time occurs only once. This means (I would argue) that although historians may borrow from sociology or economics, history itself is not a social science. To a historian, the historical event or process is of interest in itself, not as a case study useful for validating or disproving some conceptual model of human behavior in general. Yet the uniqueness of a given historical situation does not preclude comparison to others that are somewhat similar.

Indeed, for European historians in particular, a growing awareness of Europe's connectedness to the rest of the world—in the past as well as at present—requires that we give some thought to how a particular process unfolding in Europe may compare with or relate to the histories of other areas of the globe. In the case of Europe's Reformations, the religious concerns that this book has discussed may be seen to bear some resemblance to the concerns that have animated reform movements in other traditions. For this concluding reflection on the global context of Europe's Reformations, I have chosen reform movements that show some analogies with distinctive features of the Protestant Reformation as discussed here: (a) the Neo-Confucian recovery of the Confucian scripture, (b) the Wahhabiya purification of worship in eighteenth-century Arabia, (c) the holy community of Hasidic Judaism in eighteenth-century

Figure 15.1. A German Jesuit, Adam Schall, at the imperial court in Beijing.
Schall in his mandarin garb as court astronomer and President of the Board of
Rites, responsible for determining the astrologically auspicious dates for Confu-
cian court ceremonies: from Athanasius Kircher, S.J., E Societatis Jesu China Mon-
umentis Illustrata (Amsterdam, 1667), among the illustrations following p. 112.
(*Special Collections, University of Minnesota Library.*)

Poland-Lithuania, and (d) the Iconoclast purification of worship in the seventh- and eighth-century Byzantine Empire.

The Neo-Confucian recovery of the Confucian scripture. China stands out from every other region of the globe because of its cohesion through the millennia as a political entity. Starting around 1500 B.C. with the Shang Dynasty, China has been ruled for most of the past thirty-five centuries by imperial dynasties that followed one another either directly or, in some cases, after a period of "warring states" lasting a century or two. The emperor was styled "Son of Heaven," meaning that his rule enjoyed celestial approval and that he was responsible for correct observance of the traditional rituals by which China maintained a proper relationship with the higher powers of the cosmos. From 221 B.C. until 1939, when the last emperor of the last dynasty was deposed by Japanese invaders, emperors were assisted in governing their vast realm not by a military aristocracy, as was common in Latin Christendom, but by civilian officials who prided themselves in their learning. Emperors of the T'ang Dynasty (618–907) inaugurated a system, revived in later centuries, in which entry to the ranks of officialdom was based on competitive examinations that required a polished literary style and a command of the Chinese classics.

By common consent, the greatest of the classical authors was the sage known in Western languages as Confucius (551–479 B.C.), who lived during one of the warring-states periods. Among his many interests, Confucius was a moralist, framing ethical precepts to guide the private life of a thinking man; for the public good, these same precepts were all the more necessary should one be called upon to serve the state as an official. His thought also had a religious dimension, since duties to Heaven[8] counted among the obligations whose fulfillment was the measure of a man's true worth. But by the time the examination system took root, poetry was getting more attention from scholars than the ethical teachings of Confucius and his disciples—"the Way," as adepts called it.

Also, other doctrines now competed for allegiance. Buddhism, having come by way of Central Asia in the sixth century A.D., soon sprouted monasteries for men and for women all over China, propagating the ideal of withdrawal from the worldly occupations for purposes of interior self-cultivation. T'aoism, building on traditional Chinese beliefs about communication with the world of spirits, offered yet another set of precepts for cultivating the soul within. The reformulation of the Way that historians describe as Neo-Confucianism focused on the element of self-cultivation in Confucius's thought, so as to satisfy the taste for "rectification of the mind-and-heart"[9] without abandoning the traditional Confucian emphasis on duties to the ruler and to society.

The scholar-official Ch'eng-i (d. 1107) credited his brother Ch'eng-hao

(d. 1085) with a momentous discovery: by diligent study of Confucius's writings, he was able to "pick up the threads of what had not been transmitted for a thousand years" and "illumine the Way" by clearing away "overgrowth and weeds" obstructing the correct path. One might compare this sense of the recovery of lost meaning to the feeling of European scholars and theologians who, for the first time in many centuries, pored over scripture in its original languages.[10] Ch'eng-hao had rediscovered what he saw as the neglected moral core of Confucian teaching, contained especially in a treatise called *The Great Learning*. "Rectification of mind-and-heart" meant rigorous control of selfish desires and vigilance against the corrupting influence of false doctrines (such as Buddhism and T'aoism, according to Ch'eng). This interior renewal was the sole basis for a renewal of human society. Hence it was the scholar-official's highest duty to lecture the emperor on the truth of the Way, at the risk of losing his position. Chu-Hsi (d. 1200), who codified the ideas of the Ch'eng brothers in his *Commentary on the Great Learning*, was arrested as a spreader of false doctrine.

Later generations would see things differently, after China was incorporated into the vast Mongol Empire founded by Genghis Khan (d. 1227). Genghis's grandson Khubilai Khan (d. 1294) was impressed by the teachings of Neo-Confucian masters brought from south China to his capital in Beijing, so much so that he established an Imperial College devoted to the study of Confucius's writings as interpreted by Chu-Hsi and the Ch'eng brothers. Starting in 1313, this curriculum, somewhat simplified to make it accessible to officials of Mongol as well as Chinese origin, became the basis for a revived system of competitive examinations. Under the Mongol or Yuan emperors and the subsequent Ming Dynasty (1368–1644), scholar-officials inspired by the example of Chu-Hsi held public lectures to impart the Way to the emperor's subjects. The Yuan Dynasty needed a unifying belief system to bridge differences between Mongol conquerors and the Han or ethnic Chinese population. Neo-Confucianism had many attractive features, including the linkage it made between personal integrity and service to the empire. Thus the once-despised doctrine of a few dissident scholars became, by stages, the favored religion of a great empire.[11]

The Wahhabiya purification of worship. Within a century of the Prophet Muhammad's death (632), Islam spread with astonishing rapidity, to the Pyrenees mountains of northern Spain in the west and the Himalayas in the east. The new creed was uncompromising in its worship of Allah, the one and only God, and straightforward in its demands. The faithful were to pray five times a day, fast during the month of Ramadan, give alms, make war on the infidel, and make a pilgrimage to Mecca,[12] the ancient holy city of Arabia, whose capture by the Prophet had marked Islam's first great triumph.

Mosques served as gathering places for daily prayer, often with a sermon by the prayer leader on Friday, the Muslim holy day.

God's Word as revealed to Muhammad in the Koran included a comprehensive code for living. Some religious scholars devoted themselves to the study of the Koran itself or to the authentication of the *hadith* ("traditions"), collections of sayings attributed to the Prophet and his companions. Others turned to Arabic translations of the writings of Plato and Aristotle, seeking to reconcile the revealed truth of the Koran with the pagan wisdom of ancient philosophy, a pattern to be followed by certain Jewish thinkers as well as by scholastic writers of the Christian Middle Ages.[13] Still others built up a body of legal opinions by which the teachings of the Koran and the *hadith* could be applied to disputes arising in daily life. In time, legal scholars organized themselves into several distinctive schools of thought; one school, the Hanbalis, differed from the others by its reluctance to take *hadith* or previous legal opinions into account; if at all possible, only the Koran itself should be counted as authoritative—an idea not the same as Luther's *sola scriptura*,[14] but not entirely different either.

Some among the faithful were not satisfied by external observances, for the Koran also described how the soul could experience ecstatic union with God. Teachers called Sufis[15] developed regimens of prayer aimed at enabling devout Muslims to achieve this exalted state. Religious brotherhoods grew up around magnetic Sufi leaders, who often designated successors to carry on after their deaths. For devotees, the tomb of the holy founder became the shrine of a saint, a site for pilgrimage, and a source for stories of miraculous cures, much like the tombs of martyr-saints in early Christianity. Thus by the tenth or eleventh century, Islam had developed a rich religious culture, in which many of the faithful who gathered for Friday prayer at the town's chief mosque might sort themselves out for the rest of the week into smaller groups pursuing interests that were distinct and even conflicting.

For some, however, this great variety of practice and belief betokened a lamentable departure from the Prophet's austere simplicity. Taqi al-Din Ibn Taymiya (d. 1328), a legal scholar of the above-mentioned Hanbali school, was so rigorous in his condemnation of the tomb-cults of Sufi saints that he would not countenance any special honor being paid to the memory of the Prophet: no man, only Allah, deserved the worship of the faithful. Owing to his denunciation of popular local cults, Ibn Taymiya spent much of his adult life in the prisons of Cairo and Damascus. But later scholars preserved and continued to discuss his writings. At a school in Medina, not far from Mecca, Ibn Taymiya's works were read and recopied by Muhammad Ibn Abdul Wahhab (1703–1791).

Ibn Abdul Wahhab, a Hanbali scholar like his father, began preaching

Figure 15.2. A Sufi Preacher. Madjalis al-'Ushshah (a sixteenth-century Persian artist), "A Sufi Preaching." (*Bodleian Library, Oxford, MS Onseley Add. 24, fol. 55 v.*)

in public shortly after his father's death in 1740. Like Ibn Taymiya, he denounced all the elements of the tomb-cults of Sufi saints: kissing the tomb-
stone or other acts of reverence, leaving candles or other gifts, and praying for the saint's intercession with God. Like Ahmad Ibn Hanbal (d. 855),
founder of the Hanbali school, he told of how the Prophet himself had
prayed, "O God, make not my grave into an idol that is worshiped." On
the basis of travels through Arabia, Ibn Abdul Wahhab was familiar with
the practice of the Islamic religion, and he did not like what he saw. If
Zwingli and Calvin believed that the veneration of saints among Catholics
was a continuation of ancient polytheism,[16] Ibn Abdul Wahhab believed
that superstitious practices among Muslims of his day represented a recrudescence of the ancient paganism of pre-Islamic times. He and his followers described themselves by a term meaning "those who confess that
God is one," while referring to their enemies as "cupola people," an allu-
sion to the domed mausoleums of Sufi tombs.

His attacks on usurers as oppressors of Islam earned respect among
common people, if not the rich, but he made enemies by denouncing religious scholars who opposed him as "pagans." By 1744, Medina had become unsafe, but he found refuge with a warrior chieftain, Muhammad
Ibn Sa'ud. The two men made a pact: inhabitants of the lands to be conquered by Ibn Sa'ud would be required to practice the pure form of Islam
preached by Ibn Abdul Wahhab. Wherever the armies of Ibn Sa'ud succeeded, his Wahhabi followers in their zeal for pure worship leveled the
Sufi mausoleums that had dotted the landscape of Arabia for many centuries. Like the Calvinist Reformation in certain princely territories, such
as the Palatinate, Ibn Abdul Wahhab's austere and uncompromising
monotheism only became the norm for all believers when it was backed by
the power of the state.

By 1804, the Sa'udis, having taken Mecca and Medina, were masters of
all Arabia. But the Ottoman Turkish sultan in Istanbul, whose empire included the Arabian Peninsula, sponsored a counterattack. For over a century the Sa'udis had to be content with something like their former status.
Meanwhile, Wahhabi doctrine carried by wandering preachers took root
in various parts of the Islamic world, notably in West Africa. During the
First World War Sa'udi ambitions were rekindled by Britain's need for an
ally against the Turks. When the house of Sa'ud entered Mecca in triumph
for a second time (1924), the Wahhabi version of Islam became the state religion of what has since been known as Saudi Arabia.

The holy community of Hasidic Judaism. Among Christians and Muslims,
Jews were a readily identifiable and despised minority. In bad times their
settlements were assaulted by angry mobs, and even in good times they
were subject to a regimen of restrictions imposed by the ruler. Mob vio-

lence was more frequent in Muslim lands, but the restrictions were more severe in Christian countries. As people do when living in a hostile environment, Jews protected themselves with a panoply of community institutions. Even fairly small communities had a synagogue (house of prayer) with a cantor to lead the congregation in song and a rabbi learned in the Hebrew Bible. Larger communities boasted schools for organized study of the scriptures and of the Talmud[17] and governing councils made up of prosperous men and leading religious scholars.

In the Muslim kingdoms of Spain,[18] where the Jewish population had been large and influential since Roman times, scholars had the luxury of branching out. Some pored over Arabic translations of pagan philosophers like Plato and Aristotle, seeking, as Muslim and Christian scholars did, to reconcile the truth of faith with the conclusions of human reason. Others delved into a collection of Hebrew writings known as the Kabbalah, purporting to show how the holy words of scripture could be made to disclose hidden truths about the nature of the world, to heal the sick, or to enable the soul to rise to an experience of union with God.

As Christian kings conquered formerly Muslim lands, Spanish Jews were subjected to further restrictions. More important, Christian mob violence of the years following the terrible plague known as the Black Death (1347–1349)[19] had a quite unexpected result: many Jews, often led by their rabbis, presented themselves for Christian baptism. Integration of these "New Christians" into Spanish society was actively promoted by high officials of church and state, but resentment lingered among "Old Christians" who saw them succeeding in occupations that had formerly been barred to them as Jews. Many Spaniards of New Christian heritage would play an important role in Spain's Catholic Reformation, but many others continued to practice Judaism in their homes. Queen Isabella of Castile launched the Spanish Inquisition (1478) to ferret out heresy among the New Christians.[20] Spanish Jews who had not accepted baptism were now expelled from the peninsula, in 1492 from Castile, somewhat later from the neighbor kingdom of Aragon. The refugees, known in Hebrew as "Sephardim" (the westerners), proved that communities having a high degree of complex organization could be scattered by a sudden blow, but not extinguished. They rebuilt their lives in Muslim North Africa; in Italy, where restrictions on Jews were generally less severe than in other Christian lands; and especially in the Ottoman Turkish Empire. Down to the twentieth century, a form of Spanish known as Ladino was still spoken among descendants of Sephardic Jewish exiles in cities like Saloniki (modern Greece) and Izmir (modern Turkey).

This sequence of persecution and rebuilding is found also in the history of the Ashkenazic ("eastern") Jews of Poland. Poland-Lithuania, created by a dynastic marriage in 1389, was a vast and relatively undeveloped eastern outpost of Latin Christendom, encompassing what is now Poland, Lithuania, Latvia, and Estonia as well as Belarus and western Ukraine. Poland's kings welcomed the refugees who, after the persecutions of the fourteenth century, looked eastward for a new home. Poland's major cities—taking a cue from craft guilds that feared competition—enacted laws that prevented Jews from settling within their walls. But the kingdom was dominated by its nobles, great and small, who were busy planting new villages and eager to have estate managers, craftsmen to supply their peasants with goods, and more peasants to till virgin soil. Thus Jewish settlements took root in royal or aristocratic lands, a process that accelerated during the sixteenth century as neighboring Bohemia expelled its Jews.

The Jewish population of Poland-Lithuania is estimated at 30,000 in 1500, 450,000 in 1648 (about 4.5 percent of the population), and 350,000 in 1660, after a terrible slaughter of Jews during a Cossack-led rebellion that attached western Ukraine to the Russian crown. Though Jews came from many lands, as far away as Spain, they spoke Yiddish ("Jewish"), a German dialect influenced by Hebrew. As the Catholic Reformation took root in Poland, from the late sixteenth century, the church demanded stricter enforcement of traditional restrictions against Jews. But Poland's rulers protected Jewish subjects, as is indicated by their firm stand against the hoariest of anti-Semitic legends, the "blood libel" that had Jews sacrificing Christian children in secret rites.

Though the threat of persecution was always present, Jewish communities had room to breathe. A community's governing council (*kahal*) was often controlled by managers of noble estates, and the rabbi often owed his appointment to the local noble (bribes were not unknown). Estate managers and religious scholars joined in lending at high rates to poor peasants, Jewish as well as non-Jewish. But as in contemporary Christian cities, where the growing wealth of elite families set them more and more apart from their fellow burghers,[21] the prosperity of a few took a heavy toll on the traditional sense of solidarity within the Jewish community. *Kahal* leaders took to wearing gentile (non-Jewish) clothes; they threatened poor Jews with expulsion from their lands for nonpayment of debt and haled them before Christian courts to make good their threats.

Such practices were condemned in sermons by synagogue-preachers who came from poor families themselves. Unlike the rabbis and the Talmudic scholars, these poorly paid men, wandering from one community to another, often drew their inspiration from writings based on the Kabbalah. Their message was that the spiritual and moral renewal of a sinful and unjust world depended on achieving the blessed state of union with God and that this in turn was only possible for the man who renounced gentile ways and lived as a devout (Hasid), Law-observing Jew in every detail of his life. In some communities, circles of the devout (Hasidim) formed around a charismatic leader, often a preacher, known to his followers as a *zaddik*, a just man.

Such was the wandering preacher known as the Baal (Healer) Shem Tov (1700–1760), whose name implies that he practiced a form of faith healing. He urged listeners to "set the world aright" through prayer and devotion. Rural Jews understood that his call for "ransoming Jewish captives" meant freeing Jewish peasants from back-rents owed to Jewish estate managers. The Hasidim who rallied to his teaching were few in number at the time of the Baal Shem Tov's death, but their numbers grew under the men recognized as his successors, Dov Baer (d. 1772) and Rabbi Nachman of Bratislav (d. 1810), a grandson of the Baal Shem Tov.

The Hasidim came to be characterized not merely by their punctilious observance of the Law and their study of the Kabbalah, but by ecstatic and tearful prayer as a sign of joy in the Lord and by the use of the folk tale as a medium for religious instruction. These practices were denounced in a celebrated pronouncement by the leading religious scholar of the important city of Vilnius (Lithuania) but to little avail, since the traditional religious elite had already lost the allegiance of many Jews. By the early nineteenth century, what had begun as a dissident movement among the less fortunate was well on its way to embracing the majority of eastern Europe's[22] Jewish population.

The Iconoclast purification of worship. For early Christians, religious images had dangerous associations with contemporary paganism. In Greek and Roman worship, deities were believed to be present in and acting through their images, especially statues. Thus, as one fifth-century bishop of Sardinia put it, once images were held up to the veneration of Christians, "pagan customs do the rest." The objects of devotion for Christians of the fourth and fifth centuries were the relics of martyr-saints and images of the cross on which Christ the Redeemer had been crucified; both were carried in processions calling on God to ward off evil; both were believed to have miracle-working powers.

Only in the sixth century did the religious panel paintings known as icons (images) begin to be produced in the Byzantine or East Roman Empire, especially in certain important monasteries. Paintings on the interior walls of churches date from the same era, as do the splendid religious mosaics of a style that would become known in the West as Byzantine. Icons were soon receiving the same cult worship previously bestowed on the cross and on relics of the saints—they were carried in procession in times of danger, and stories circulated about icons that had delivered a city from Muslim or pagan invaders or cured the sick.

It is not unlikely that some Christians were alarmed by this departure from tradition, but signs of such a reaction are hard to detect in the scattered sources available for the seventh century. It is possible, but not certain, that a few bishops of Asia Minor were censured by the patriarch of Constantinople for having ordered the removal of images from their churches early in the eighth century. On the whole, it seems that the iconoclastic (image-breaking) reform of Christian worship was promoted from the top down, by a series of emperors: Leo III (717–741), his son Constantine V (741–775), and Leo V (813–820).

Leo III apparently took a great earthquake centered on the Aegean island of Thera (726) as a sign of God's wrath, directed against idolatrous icon worship. After some preliminary moves against images in the capital city, he decreed that wall paintings be covered and icons be removed from all the churches of the empire. Some of his advisers seem to have recommended casting out only the images of the saints, not those of Christ the Savior or Mary, the Mother of God, but the emperor made no such distinction: all the images must go. What support there was for these measures came from members of the parish or secular clergy, while monastic writers took the lead in opposing them. As if recognizing the relative novelty of icon worship, Leo III at the same time actively promoted devotion to the relics of the saints, and especially to fragments of the True Cross[23] on which the Savior had hung.

Leo's son Constantine V continued his father's policies, convening bishops of the Byzantine world in 754 in a council that proclaimed that the only true image of Christ was to be found in the consecrated bread and wine of the eucharist and the only true image of the saints in their virtues. Constantinople's patriarch opposed this proclamation, but Constantine had him deposed and replaced by a more pliant successor. Beginning in 760, leading monks who continued to oppose the reform of worship were imprisoned or forced into exile. But when Constantine's son and successor died after a short reign (780), the Byzantine world learned that his wife the Empress Irene, now ruling in the name of their young son, was an "icondule," or devotee of images. She convened a council of bishops to revoke the iconoclastic decrees (786–787) and was not deterred when the first session of her council was broken up by soldiers from the imperial guard, who apparently identified the iconoclastic faith of Leo III and Constantine V with the military successes of that era, sorely missed in Irene's age. Despite signs of opposition from secular clergy and even from some monasteries, the campaign to restore the icons to the churches gained momentum under Irene and in the years immediately following her death (802). There was a temporary reversal under Leo V, who convened in 815 a synod of bishops that reinstated the iconoclastic decrees of 754. By this time, however, image worship was a subject for intense debate among the faithful, not easily controlled by imperial or ecclesiastical decrees. Popular admiration for the monasteries that were centers of the cult of icons began to make a difference, as did the arguments of icondule writers who maintained that if God Himself had become incarnate in the man Jesus, there was nothing inherently problematic about icons or other material objects being a vehicle or instrument for divine power. At a council of bishops meeting in 843, the iconoclastic decrees of 754 were again set aside, this time for good.

These sketches may suffice to suggest how reform movements in quite different traditions can resemble one another. The Ch'eng brothers' rediscovery of the essential meaning of the Confucian Way, lost from sight for "a thousand years," bears comparison with Luther's rediscovery of the meaning of the gospel, lost from sight, as he believed, since the days of the early church. Both Ibn Abdul Wahhab and Byzantium's iconoclast emperors sought to purify the worship of the faithful by eliminating false accretions, as did the Protestant Reformers, especially Zwingli and Calvin, who altogether banned the religious veneration of images or other material objects. The weeping and joyful singing of Hasidic congregations represents a different spiritual impulse, comparable to Islam's Sufi brotherhoods rather than to the austere simplicity of Calvinist Christianity or Wahhabiya Islam. But the Hasidic movement also bears a resemblance to the community-based character of urban Protestantism: in Christian Germany as in Jewish Poland-Lithuania, the middling sort of people who embraced the new doctrine were to some extent also rebelling against the overweening authority of their social betters. The position of the Catholic clergy in medieval Europe had no real counterpart in the Jewish or Islamic traditions, but both the Wahhabiya and the Hasidic movements represent a withdrawal of allegiance from religious elites that is not wholly unlike Christian anticlericalism. Finally, the triumph of Neo-Confucianism in China and of the Wahhabis in Arabia, like the temporary triumph of iconoclasm in the Byzantine Empire, shows the decisive importance of the same state power that so often made the difference in the ultimate triumph of Protestantism or reformed Catholicism.

These irreducibly different histories resist being classified as instances of some general model of religious reform, but they are nonetheless somewhat alike, if only because human beings living in very different times and places still have something in common. Living in our own time and place, we make sense of the history of any other time and place by making comparisons to what we find more familiar—implicit analogies, similar to those made explicit here. This book has been devoted to the unique features of a sixteenth-century Latin Christendom that will be vaguely familiar to some readers and quite strange to others. But analogies allow us to see that the European Christian tradition, like all others, is not completely unique. For example, it has no monopoly on the human yearning for a deeper understanding of the ultimate truths about our existence or on the human proclivity for building states that draw legitimacy from and hence demand conformity with certain religious beliefs. It is by way of such analogies that a history that must necessarily be the history of only some of us can stand for the history of all of us.

Notes

PART I

1. Latin was used for Christian worship in the western half of the Roman Empire, Greek and other languages in the Eastern Empire, centered on Constantinople, formerly called Byzantium. In the West, the last emperor died in 476, and the empire gave way to kingdoms founded by invading barbarian tribes. The East Roman or Byzantine Empire survived until 1453, when the Ottoman Turks conquered Constantinople, henceforth known as Istanbul. The religious division between Roman Catholicism and Eastern Orthodoxy dates from 1054, when the pope and the patriarch of Constantinople excommunicated each other, in what was more a cultural conflict between "Latins" and "Greeks" than a doctrinal dispute.

2. Town and often village governments were corporate bodies, so were territorial parliaments, monasteries and convents, artisan guilds, parish churches, and, in some sense, even families.

CHAPTER 1

1. The Holy Roman Empire of the German Nation lasted from 960, when the German king Otto I had himself crowned emperor by the pope in Rome, until 1806, when Napoleon dissolved it in order to redraw the map of Europe. In theory, the empire embraced all or large parts of the countries now called Germany, Switzerland, Italy, Slovenia, Austria, the Czech Republic, Poland, Belgium, the Netherlands, and eastern France. In practice, after about 1250, the emperor often did not control much more than the hereditary lands of his own family.

2. "Canon" is a Greek word for law. Canon law is the law of the church.

3. By about 900 A.D. Catholic Europe was covered by a network of parishes, each with a church served by a priest who was its pastor. Parish clergy were "secular" (worldly) in that they lived among lay people, not secluded from the world in a monastery.

4. "Ecumenical" comes from a Greek word meaning the "whole civilized world." The Roman emperor Constantine convened the first ecumenical council of the church by summoning bishops from the whole Christian world to Nicaea, near Constantinople, in 325.

5. For Christians, a sacrament is a ritual by which believers receive the grace or favor of God. The eucharist—also known as communion, or the Lord's Supper—commemorates Jesus' Last Supper with his apostles. Among Catholics, the wafer of unleavened bread is called a host (from a Latin word meaning "victim") because it is believed that the bread and wine consecrated by the priest at mass become the body and blood of Christ, the victim by whose sacrificial death on the cross the human race was redeemed from sin. From the thirteenth century on, lay people were allowed to receive in communion only the consecrated host.

6. In earlier centuries, rulers in east-central Europe bestowed special privileges on German burghers who agreed to come and found cities in their lands. In many towns, as in Prague, Germans retained their favored position long after they had come to be outnumbered by Czechs, Poles, or Hungarians.

7. King Sigismund I of Bohemia, the Czech heartland, was also the Holy Roman Emperor who had convened the Council of Constance.

8. Utraquist comes from the Latin word meaning "both," referring to the demand that lay people be allowed to receive both of the consecrated elements in communion, the wine as well as the bread.

9. The first printing press using movable type was invented in Mainz, where Johannes Gutenberg started his printing business in 1446. Over the next two generations, the earliest printers in other countries were usually German.

10. Tridentine refers to the more disciplined form of Catholicism that slowly took shape under the influence of the Council of Trent ("Tridentum" in Latin) and the new religious orders.

11. What is called Reformed Protestantism (to distinguish it from Lutheranism) began with Huldrych Zwingli (d. 1531) in Zurich and continued with John Calvin in Geneva. The two had much in common, despite the differences between them discussed in Chapter 6.

12. Many villages had a "cunning" man or woman who practiced "white magic" by using potions or incantations to remove the evil spells widely believed to cause illness. A witch practiced "black magic" by casting the evil spells. From the fifteenth century on, such people were seen as invoking the power of the devil to work their evil purposes.

13. The most important sectarian movement of the Reformation era was Anabaptism, to be discussed in Chapter 6.

14. A church may be described as fully established if it has legal control of all church buildings in active use, no other form of worship is tolerated, and inhabitants of the territory are expected to be members.

15. Followers of Cornelius Jansenius (d. 1638), a theologian whose espousal of St. Augustine's doctrine of predestination (see Chapter 3) was denounced by the Jesuits as heretical.

16. So called because of the informal "colleges" in which they met, Collegiants, like the Pietists, stressed devotion more than doctrine and had particular questions about Calvin's doctrine of predestination (see Chapter 6), a touchstone of orthodoxy in the Dutch Reformed Church.

17. For idealists, ideas and beliefs are the mainspring of human action. For the founder of German idealism, G. F. W. Hegel (d. 1831), history as a whole is guided

by the divine Spirit in ways that are opaque at the time but discernible after the fact by human reason.

18. Starting in the twelfth century, teachers at cathedral schools formed *universitates* (corporations) to govern themselves independent of the local bishop. Students began in the faculty of liberal arts, focused on works of the Greek philosopher Aristotle. Following the bachelor's degree, some pursued advanced study in faculties like theology or medicine. Professors followed methods derived from Aristotle's logic but formed competing schools of thought—hence the term "scholastic" philosophy or theology.

19. First put forward by ancient Greek and Roman writers, the doctrine of natural law posits universal principles of right and wrong that are "written in the human heart" or accessible to reason. This doctrine was widely accepted by the scholastics.

20. Luther could accept the religious authority of a bishop (in Latin, *episcopus*) who professed the new doctrines, but Calvin believed the church of New Testament times was jointly ruled by preachers and lay elders, not by bishops (see Chapter 7).

21. I was hired (1966) when the History Department at the University of Minnesota decided to teach Reformation history.

22. A guild was a self-governing association of merchants or craftsmen practicing the same trade or closely related trades. Between roughly 1200 and 1350, urban craftsmen in many parts of Latin Europe, though not all, organized themselves into guilds.

23. For an interesting combination of the two notions of individualism—its modernity and its destructive quality—see Jacob Burckhardt, *The Civilization of the Renaissance in Italy* (New York, 1958), first published in German in 1860, but still worth reading. Burckhardt argued that northern and central Italy "swarmed with individualism" around 1300, marking the end of medievalism and the beginning of modernity. But individualism in its purest form was found in amoral city-tyrants who murdered their own kin to gain power. This book launched the idea that "the Renaissance" was not just an artistic style, but a distinct period in European history.

24. Marx's materialist interpretation of history inverts the idealism of Hegel (see note 17): society is divided into classes, each having a different relationship to property, and the mainspring of human action is not ideas, but class interest.

25. "Bourgeois" in French means the same as "burgher" in English, that is, a citizen of a burgh or city. Not all inhabitants had rights of citizenship, and not all citizens had the right to participate in local government.

26. The term "patrician," drawn from the history of ancient Rome, where only "patricians" could sit in the senate, is used by historians to refer to the office-holding elite among burgher families.

27. In Marx's view of history, the revolution that overthrows the domination of capitalism will only come when skilled workers are pressed down into a mass of unskilled workers, a "proletariat" (people whose only property is their children) that realizes its true interests and is ready to throw off its chains.

28. Agreeing on infant baptism, Catholics and Protestants called those who re-

jected it (on the ground that true baptism required faith, only possible for adults) "re-baptizers," or Anabaptists.

29. "Ecumenical" in the twentieth century has come to have the added meaning of a movement for greater understanding among Christians of all denominations.

30. See *Reason in History*, a translation of the introduction to G. F. W. Hegel's *Philosophy of History*: I do not believe that acceptance of this principle implies acceptance of the rest of Hegel's philosophy (see note 17).

31. Most of us find it easier to discern the selfish interests that are behind causes we oppose than the selfish interests that are behind causes we support.

CHAPTER 2

1. Salvation means the sinner is saved from eternal damnation in hell and gains admission to God's presence in heaven. Justification means the sinner is made just (or treated as just) by God. These different meanings do have a significance in theological debate, but for the sake of simplicity I will mainly use the term "salvation."

2. This was a minority opinion in Luther's day. That the pope is infallible (cannot err) when making pronouncements on matters of faith or morals did not become a doctrine of the Catholic Church until the Second Vatican Council (1870).

3. Augustine is discussed in Chapter 3, Luther in Chapter 4.

4. What set humanists apart from the scholastics was a love of the classical Latin of the age of Cicero (d. 34 B.C.), which compares to medieval Latin rather like Shakespeare's English to ours. Contrary to an older view, Renaissance humanism was not a philosophy of life, espousing secular rather than religious values. See Chapter 3.

5. The migration of Greek scholars to Italy began even before the fall of Constantinople in 1453 (see Part 1, note 1).

6. See Figure 2. 2.

7. For the literate, there were over a hundred partial or full translations of the Bible in various German dialects printed between the Gutenberg Bible of 1455 and the beginning of the Reformation.

8. Flagellants ("scourgers") processed in a circle, each person whipping the person in front. Church authorities often sought to suppress these displays of penitence, but with little success.

9. The rules of most religious orders required seven "hours" of daily prayer, based on scripture (especially the Psalms) and the writings of the Fathers. Simplified manuscript versions of the hours, translated into the vernacular for the laity, were often graced by beautiful miniature paintings of scenes from daily life.

10. Since the second century, fragments of bone or pieces of clothing from the martyrs and other saints were venerated as relics in which something of the holy person's power still inhered. Gold- and silversmiths made elaborate reliquaries to house these precious objects. Canon law required each parish church to have a relic set into the altarstone that rested on the main altar.

11. "Oligarchy" comes from a Greek word meaning "rule by the few."

12. There were similar conflicts between the Byzantine emperor and the patriarch of Constantinople (see the discussion of iconoclasm in Chapter 15), but for a variety of historical reasons the patriarchs never had the same degree of independence from secular authority as the pope in Rome did.

13. Male monastic houses were headed by an elected abbot (father), female houses by an elected abbess (mother).

14. They punned on his Latin name (Lutherus) by calling him "Eleutherius," Greek for "liberator."

15. See Chapter 8.

16. When Swiss pikemen twice defeated Burgundy's Duke Charles the Bold (d. 1477, see Chapter 8), the more populous cantons and their smaller neighbors almost went to war in a dispute over how to divide the booty——Was each canton to have an equal share, or should those that sent more troops have more of the spoils?

PART II

1. In Latin, *"Lex orandi, lex credendi,"* "the rule of prayer is the rule of belief."

CHAPTER 3

1. See the brief discussion of Jewish history in Chapter 15.

2. "Pagan" comes from a Latin word for country people, a reference to the fact that as Christianity took hold in the cities, country people clung to the old beliefs. "Heathen" is an Anglo-Saxon word having the same dual meaning.

3. Meaning that his name might be inserted in the canon or main part of the mass, among the saints to whom the faithful prayed for intercession. Around 1300, the canonization process, hitherto informal, was centralized at the papal court. Spanish Franciscans named a California mission (now a city) for San Bernardino.

4. The Roman Empire had been divided into administrative units known as dioceses. In early Christian times the bishops came to be recognized as rulers of the faithful in ecclesiastical dioceses, usually having the same boundaries as civil dioceses.

5. The Latin words *magister* (master) and *doctor* both mean "teacher." At medieval universities, one holding the degree of master of arts was qualified to teach students in the faculty of liberal arts who were studying for the bachelor's degree. A doctor of theology (or of the other advanced subjects, like law and medicine) was qualified to teach in the higher faculties.

6. In contrast to the Christian doctrine of God's creation of the world, Aristotle believed that the cosmos had no beginning.

7. "Nominalism" refers to only one of the points on which "the modern way" differed from "the ancient way" of Aquinas and Scotus. Aquinas and Scotus believed that the general concepts we have in our minds (e.g., the idea of "tree") are true representations of the property or "form" of tree-ness that inheres in an individual tree and makes it to be a tree. William of Ockham (d. 1349), recognized as

the founder of the "modern way," argued that our knowledge that a tree is a tree is more certain than any theory of such knowledge we can possibly construct. Hence the general concepts we have in our minds are mere names (*nomina*) and do not represent anything actually existing in the thing itself.

8. Exod. 20:1–17, Mark 12:28–34.

9. Aquinas and Scotus accepted the common view that the heavenly bodies exert some influence on the lives of human beings. Other thinkers went farther, asserting that each person's destiny is written in the stars, leaving little or no room for divine providence or human free will.

10. Scholars now think Augustine overstated Pelagius's view of what man could accomplish by his own will, without the aid of grace.

11. See Gen. 3:1–24. Augustine had an important part in formulating this doctrine, according to which the consequences of the sin of Adam and Eve pass on to their descendants, so that each person is born in a state of alienation from God and worthy of condemnation to hell, absent God's saving grace.

12. *Gratia* in classical Latin meant "favor," in the sense in which we now speak of being in someone's good graces. Divine *gratia* was understood by scholastic theologians as a quality infused by God into a person's soul.

13. E.g., Eph. 1:5.

14. "Cathedral" comes from a word meaning the "chair of honor where a bishop sits," always housed in his home church. The congregations of priests attached to cathedrals (and to some other important churches) were called chapters, and the priest-members were called canons. These well-endowed positions were highly sought after, with membership sometimes being restricted to sons of noble families. The higher ranks of the clergy were permeated by noble conceptions of caste: preaching to illiterate commoners was beneath the dignity of an important man.

15. According to canon law, the holder of an ecclesiastical position was required to be resident. But the abuse most often denounced by would-be reformers of the late medieval church was "pluralism": well-connected men obtained multiple positions in different locations and (for an added fee to the papal court in Rome) a dispensation excusing them from the duty of residence.

16. A vicar was a stand-in for the pastor, often because the pastor was a priest with multiple appointments (see previous note) who chose not to live in his country parish. Most vicars were of low social status and not much education. They received only a small fraction of the endowed income set aside for the pastor.

17. The angelus is a prayer to be recited each day at noon, with verses alternating with the Hail Mary. The rosary is a string with beads of different size for reciting Our Fathers and Hail Marys.

18. The commandments of the church included receiving communion once a year, confessing one's sins to a priest once a year, abstaining from meat on Fridays, and fasting as required during the forty days of Lent leading up to the celebration of Christ's resurrection from the dead at Easter.

19. In orthodox Christian belief, the Holy Spirit (or Holy Ghost) is one of three divine Persons making up the Holy Trinity: God the Father, God the Son (who became incarnate in the man Jesus), and God the Holy Spirit. The doctrine that there

are three Persons in one God was formulated by ecumenical councils between 325 and 451, amid much controversy among Christians.

20. Among the Franciscans, for example, the first order (founded by St. Francis of Assisi) was for men, the second (founded by St. Clare) for women, and the third, not involving vows, for layfolk.

21. Those able to read and having some income could purchase the vernacular-language books of hours mentioned in Chapter 2; others might attend the singing of the hours that was coming to be common in urban parishes, funded by pious donations.

22. Dante imagines himself a pilgrim permitted to travel through the three realms of the afterlife, hell, purgatory, and heaven.

23. "Chantry" was the English term for these endowments, referring to the chanting of masses for the soul of the benefactor.

24. In modern law, usury means taking interest on loans at a rate deemed excessive. In medieval canon law, based on Old Testament precepts, usury was defined as taking advantage of another person's need by claiming any interest at all for loans. Canon lawyers took several generations to adapt their teachings to the business practices that had become common, especially in Italy, since the "commercial revolution" of the thirteenth century (see Chapter 12).

25. The "Fuggerei" (Figure 3.4) was rebuilt after the Allied bombing of Augsburg during World War II. According to Jakob Fugger's rules, admission is only for married couples who are honorably poor (i.e., have not thrown away a fortune). Residents must pray for the founder's soul at least once a year, and their annual rent is one German mark. The Fugger bank is discussed in Chapter 12.

26. In early Christian times, the idea that a baptized person could commit a serious sin and still be forgiven by God was slow to take hold. To be readmitted to the fellowship of the faithful, sinners had to make a public confession of their guilt and accept the penance or punishment assigned, which might mean years standing in sackcloth and ashes outside the Sunday assembly of the faithful, calling on God's mercy. In time, the clergy began granting "indulgences" or remissions of rigorous ecclesiastical penances. In later centuries, as the doctrine of purgatory came to be accepted, the idea of remitting the time of punishment was transferred from sinners on earth to the souls in purgatory.

27. A family was shamed when a daughter married beneath her social station. Having a dowry was the price for a respectable husband.

28. Meaning that the dying person made a final confession of his or her sins to a priest and received the sacrament of the dying.

29. Rubrics are the "red" letters written or printed in mass-books, telling the priest what actions he must perform when saying the words.

30. Logic aimed at convincing proof or demonstration, oratory, or (using a word of Greek origin) rhetoric, aimed at persuasion. These two, together with grammar (meaning the study of literature), counted among what were known since antiquity as the seven liberal arts, the others being music, astronomy, geometry, and arithmetic.

31. The collection of ancient Roman legal texts known as the *Codex of Justinian* (named after the Byzantine emperor [d. 565] who ordered its compilation) served

as the basis for civil law in much of medieval and early modern Europe and was the subject of instruction in university faculties of civil law.

32. Bordering on the Papal States to the north, the kingdom of Naples was one of the major powers in Italy. See Chapter 8.

33. Needless to say, scholastics accused humanists of being mainly interested in displaying their own rhetorical skills.

34. He employed what is now called the principle of the harder reading. If the manuscript evidence offers several possible readings for a given term, the reading most likely to be genuine is the one which may offend in some way the religious sensibility of Christian readers. The assumption underlying this principle is that scribes copying and recopying the sacred text over the centuries were likely to "correct" readings they found problematic.

35. Though not a strict pacifist, Erasmus believed that most contemporary wars were neither just nor necessary, and that preachers and theologians usually told princes what they wanted to hear, rather than calling them to account for expending so much blood and treasure for trivial reasons.

36. E. g., Luke 3:8. The Greek (μετανόετε) is rendered in the Vulgate as *penitentiam agite*. *Penitentia* was the Latin word for the sacrament of penance, or confession.

37. Erasmus had a special animus against the friars, perhaps in part for family reasons. He complains of their excessive zeal in denouncing from the pulpit secular priests who (like his own father) had women who were wives in all but name.

CHAPTER 4

1. One was Johannes Bugenhagen (d. 1558), prior of the Carmelite Friars at Belbuck in Pomerania, who subsequently became a professor of theology at Wittenberg and a Lutheran reformer in north Germany.

2. Adherents of what historians style the Protestant movement called themselves evangelicals, meaning "followers of the gospel."

3. Luther says the experience took place in the tower of the Augustinian Friars' cloister at Wittenberg.

4. As in many religious orders, some houses of the Augustinian Friars were affiliated with a "reform" congregation or grouping of monasteries that sought to follow the rules more strictly.

5. Much of what is known about Luther's life before 1517 comes from dinner-table reminiscences copied down by students living in the Luther household and published as *Dr. Luther's Table Talk.*

6. Whether or not it sufficed to be sorry for one's sins because one feared the pains of hell was an unresolved question. Both opinions were defended by respected theologians.

7. Monks and nuns took three vows: poverty, chastity, and obedience to their superiors.

8. When describing the state of mind in which he contemplated the impending wrath of God, Luther in his Latin works prefers the German word *angst*, which (like the Latin *anxietas*, to which it is etymologically related) conveys the idea of "narrowing" as well as the dread one feels when "hemmed in."

9. Meaning that He chooses to treat as righteous a man who in fact remains as much a sinner as ever.

10. See Chapter 2, p. 27.

11. The Catholic doctrine of purgatory distinguishes between the guilt incurred by sin and a debt of punishment that remains even after the guilt is forgiven by God. Indulgences applied only to the debt of punishment in purgatory. But Luther's parishioners were not the only ones to find this distinction difficult.

12. The posting of the theses on the door of Wittenberg's castle church is not reported until after Luther's death in 1546. Scholars now believe he merely mailed a copy of the theses to Archbishop Albert of Mainz, ruler of the territory where his parishioners had obtained the indulgence.

13. In addition to the more general point about Germany being "the pope's cow," German humanists had their own grievances against papal Rome; see Chapter 5.

14. These dates mark the conquest of Jerusalem by armies of the First Crusade and the fall of the last town in Palestine held by Christian forces.

15. The Mamluk sultans of Cairo had previously ruled eastern North Africa, Egypt, Arabia, and much of the Middle East. All of these lands now came under Ottoman rule.

16. "Diet" ("day") was the term for a meeting of the estates of the Holy Roman Empire, described further in Chapters 6 and 8.

17. The duke and the elector of Saxony were cousins, each ruling roughly half of a larger territory once ruled by their grandfather.

18. Chapter 1, p. 5.

19. Rev. 13:1–10, 17:1–7.

20. Popes were believed to be successors of St. Peter, the first bishop of Rome.

21. Ordination was one of the Catholic sacraments that Luther rejected. In the view of medieval theologians, it conferred on recipients a special imprint or character that enabled a priest and only a priest to consecrate the bread and wine offered to God in the mass, so that it became the body and blood of Christ.

22. Baptism, the confirmation ("strengthening") of baptized persons, communion, confession of sins to a priest, marriage, ordination (see previous note), and the anointing of the sick and dying. Luther retained as respected rituals, but not sacraments, confession, marriage, and the laying on of hands (ordination) for a designated minister of the gospel.

23. E.g., Luke 22:19–20.

24. *Bulla* was an ancient term for a document to which a ruler affixed a wax impression of his great seal, the symbol of his authority. Bulls are referred to by the opening phrase of the Latin text.

25. Excommunication meant excluding a person from the communion or society of the church. For Reformation debates over how this ancient practice was to be used, see Chapters 8 and 16.

26. For Charles and the lands he inherited, see Chapter 9.

27. Monarchy in Europe at this time was usually hereditary, with the crown passing to the king's eldest son. The Holy Roman Empire was an important exception to the rule.

28. Some of Charles's key advisers were keen students of medieval arguments (see Chapter 1) to the effect that the emperor, not the pope, was the true head of Christendom.

CHAPTER 5

1. The German of Luther's Bible is the ancestor of modern German. His Bible was the key event in a process by which one dialect among many came to be regarded as the national language.

2. In 1526 Luther married a former nun named Katherine von Bora.

3. At Marignano (1515), French gold induced men from some cantons to change sides at the last minute and attack other Swiss units, giving France the victory. See Chapter 8.

4. In Switzerland, unlike most of Europe, town councils had the power to hire and fire pastors and preachers in local churches.

5. For Luther, the demands of God's law (e.g., "love thy neighbor as thyself") served only to convince sinners of their utter inability to fulfil the law. Zwingli accepted this first or "pedagogical" use of the law, as well as a second use of the law also put forward by Luther, namely, to set some bounds (e.g., "thou shalt not kill") to the evil proclivities of the unrepentant mass of humanity. He differed from Luther in espousing a third use of the law, as a guide for how true Christians must live. Luther's view was that those to whom God imputed righteousness did not cease to be sinners in their hearts.

6. Crosses with a statue of the crucified Christ.

7. Excluding Jewish dietary laws.

8. Most inhabitants of Switzerland's cantons spoke a form of German, but there were also speakers of French, Italian, and other, less well-known, languages derived from ancient Latin.

9. This was a partisan reading of the papal–imperial conflicts discussed in Chapter 1. There was deep resentment in Germany of papal claims of supremacy over the empire, symbolized for some by the engraving of a pope placing his foot on the bowed neck of Emperor Frederick I (d. 1190).

10. For Maximilian's interests in Italy, see Chapter 9.

11. Arminius was briefly described in the *Germania* of the Roman historian Tacitus, published first by an Italian scholar and then in Germany (1515) by Ulrich von Hutten (1488–1523), a humanist and robber baron who carried on his own war against the clergy.

12. This was Martin Bucer (d. 1551), soon to become leader of the evangelical movement in Strasbourg.

13. As an honorary member of Charles's council, Erasmus was entitled to, though seldom received, a handsome annual salary.

14. During their controversy, only part of which is discussed here, Luther forced Erasmus to recognize that statements favorable to free will he found in Augustine's early works are retracted in the later works. But Augustine (unlike Luther) always maintained he was not denying human free will, even when it seems he does.

15. Especially Rom. 9:9–23, where Paul compares a lump of clay shaped by the potter as he wills to human creatures shaped by the hand of God as He wills.

16. In what was called Hither Austria, not far from Strasbourg.

17. For details, Chapter 13.

18. E.g., the famous painter, Albrecht Dürer, who penned a moving tribute when Luther disappeared from public view after the Diet of Worms, a fact that Dürer and others took to mean Luther had been done away with by his enemies.

19. I.e., the original sin believed to be inherited by all descendants of Adam and Eve. See Chapter 3, note 11.

20. Zwingli taught that baptism was not a means of grace, as in the Catholic view, but a sign of membership in the Christian covenant. He retained the baptism of infants because he saw in this practice an analogy to the Old Testament covenant, in which the circumcision of male infants served the same purpose.

21. Matt. 6:34–35.

22. Acts 2:4.

23. Matt. 6:38–39.

24. Acts 2:44.

25. See above, note 5.

26. In medieval German law, serfs could not be bought and sold (unlike slaves), but they were not free to leave the land they tilled or marry without their lord's permission. See Chapter 13.

CHAPTER 6

1. Free cities are discussed in Chapter 14.

2. For Charles V's wars, see Chapter 8.

3. Church ordinances were adopted by evangelical governments and became part of that territory's civil law. Hesse's was drafted by François Lambert, a French refugee and former Franciscan friar.

4. When some bishops did convert to the new doctrines, starting in the 1530s, Luther welcomed episcopal authority in these areas as an alternative to princely control of the church.

5. In the early Middle Ages, peasants were required by church law to contribute a biblical tenth ("tithe") of their crops to the local parish. By now, as peasants knew, tithes had become investment vehicles, divorced from their original purpose.

6. Uri, Schwyz, and Unterwalden. Switzerland (in German, Schweiz) takes its name from the canton of Schwyz.

7. Johann Oecolampadius.

8. The traditional Alpine economy was pastoral—Swiss cheese has a long history.

9. Scholars agree the man himself (Otto von Pack) forged it.

10. While their armies were mobilized, they threatened to invade the lands of the prince-archbishop of Mainz unless he renounced claims to ecclesiastical jurisdiction in their lands. He did.

11. Valdes (1500–1532) corresponded with Erasmus.

12. The two men corresponded.

13. This dispute centers on the interpretation of Matt. 16:16–19, a conversation between Jesus and the apostle Simon Bar-Jona, henceforth known as Peter. Following Simon's profession of faith in Him, Jesus says: "thou art Peter [in Greek, the word means "rock"], and on this rock I will build my church." Was Jesus referring to Peter himself, or to the faith he had just professed?

14. For the creation of this court in 1495, Chapter 8.

15. Notably Rom. 13:1–2.

16. Strasbourg's Martin Bucer was instrumental in arranging the 1536 Wittenberg Concord, in which Strasbourg and other south German cities that joined the Schmalkaldic League in 1535 accepted Luther's teaching on the Lord's Supper with slight modifications. Swiss cities that held to Zwingli's view of the sacrament were excluded from this discussion and never became league members.

17. Chapter 1, 5.

18. See Chapter 8.

19. Following G. H. Williams (see bibliography), many scholars use the term "Radical Reformation" to encompass these various movements.

20. Luther had said exactly this in his 1523 treatise *On Governmental Authority*, but he added a proviso that some radical reformers (like Konrad Grebel) rejected: In order to serve those who needed the state to restrain them, true Christians must willingly participate in the exercise of state power wherever they might be needed, e.g., as hangmen. For Grebel, state power—which included the power to make war—was inherently evil, and true Christians must neither pay taxes nor serve the state.

21. Arius, an Egyptian priest, taught that Christ was the highest of creatures, but not God. To condemn this error, the Council of Nicaea (325, see Chapter 1, note 4) framed the Nicene Creed, asserting that Christ as the Son of God is "consubstantial" with the Father. But since this term is not found in the New Testament, many bishops recoiled. The controversy ended only when the Nicene Creed was confirmed by the Council of Constantinople (381).

22. Calvin's city had the honor (as it was thought) of burning Servetus, but Catholic governments would gladly have done the same.

23. Especially Lelio Sozzini, or Socinus (1525–1562), and his nephew Fausto Sozzini (1539–1602). In the seventeenth century, Unitarians were commonly called Socinians.

24. Albeit not for the reasons Zwingli gave. Schwenkfeld's argument was that if Christ's body and blood were truly present in the bread and wine, all who received the sacrament would live as true Christians—as many obviously did not.

25. Others on the Reformation's radical wing who argued for toleration were Sebastian Franck (1499–1542), Sebastian Castellion (1515–1563), and Dirk Volkertszoon Coornhert (1522–1590).

26. The movement gradually died out in Silesia and South Germany but survives in Pennsylvania, to which 500 Schwenkfelders emigrated in 1734.

27. Rev. 19:11–21 and 20:1–10.

28. Conflict took place with Denmark and then Lübeck, leading to blockage of the sea lanes by which grain was shipped to the Low Countries from the eastern Baltic region.

29. People in Münster spoke a form of Low German that resembled the Netherlandish dialect spoken in Holland.

30. Some three thousand were intercepted by authorities in the Netherlands; many others completed their journey.

31. Notwithstanding such suspicions, there was a sharp distinction between Anabaptists who insisted on a strict, literal interpretation of the New Testament ("resist not evil") and Münsterites who alleged bloodcurdling visions instructing God's elect to take up the sword against their enemies. Both versions of the Anabaptist gospel may be seen (for example) in the statements of Anabaptists rounded up in Amsterdam (1535) after local Münsterites staged a nighttime assault on city hall.

32. Some of their descendants later migrated from Moravia to Slovakia, thence to Transylvania, thence to the Ukraine, and in the 1870s to North America, where Hutterite communities are still to be found in the Dakotas and in Canada's prairie provinces.

33. Many modern Christians who trace their spiritual roots to the Anabaptist movement do so by way of Menno Simons. The schism between the Mennonites and the stricter Amish dates from the era of the latter's principal leader, Jacob Ammann (1644–1730).

34. See Chapter 3, p. 44.

35. From the thirteenth century, each diocese had an official known as the inquisitor, responsible for prosecuting in the diocesan court persons accused of heresy. Those found guilty were handed over to the secular courts for punishment; civil courts had the power to impose death sentences, church courts did not.

36. See Chapter 5, note 5.

37. It was Farel (1489–1565) who persuaded Calvin, passing through Geneva, to remain and join him as a preacher.

38. Voting members of the diet—princes and free cities.

39. Charles's enemy, the king of France, was finding it easy to make allies among Protestant princes of the empire. See Chapter 8.

40. As a concession to the south Germans, who were moving closer to Luther's view of the Lord's Supper (above, note 16), the text was changed to say that Christ's body and blood are present "with" rather than "in" the bread and wine.

41. Melanchthon and Eck, representing the two sides, agreed to a joint statement of the doctrine of original sin.

42. As a young man anxious for the state of his soul, Contarini had a sudden experience of God's grace, convincing him that God gives salvation freely, not as a reward for human efforts.

43. See above, note 21.

44. See the recent (1998) joint statement by the Lutheran World Federation and the Vatican's Congregation for the Doctrine of the Faith.

45. For the *Index of Forbidden Books*, see Chapter 7. Some books were forbidden altogether for Catholics, others on the so-called *Expurgatory Index* were declared permissible only after objectionable passages were excised. Erasmus's works were at first banned entirely, but the protests of Catholic rulers like Ferdinand of Austria (Holy Roman Emperor 1555–1564) led to their transfer to the *Expurgatory Index*.

46. Pope Paul III called a council for 1538, but an outbreak of war between France and the empire forced him to dismiss the bishops who had come.

47. At times they used language to which the conferees at Regensburg (1541) had agreed.

48. For the war, Chapter 8. The Interim was so called because it was meant to have effect only until the Council of Trent resumed and completed its deliberations.

49. See Chapter 8.

50. The pithy Latin phrase often used to summarize the Peace of Augsburg—*cujus regio, ejus religio* (whose region, his religion)—dates from the seventeenth century.

51. Ducal Saxony had been ruled until his death in 1539 by Moritz's staunchly Catholic uncle, Duke George. Moritz was the son of George's younger brother and successor, Duke Henry, a Lutheran. Some Catholic advisers remained on the council from George's era.

52. The Greek term was *adiaphora*.

53. Using a Greek term, they called themselves "Gnesio-Lutherans."

54. Genuine Lutherans objected to wording in the revised Augsburg Confession of 1540 (above, note 40) describing the body and blood of Christ as present "with" (rather than "in") the bread and wine.

55. Written by two of Melanchthon's disciples but more favorable to Genuine Lutheran views.

56. In 1538, Jacopo Sadoleto, bishop of nearby Carprentras, published an open letter urging Genevans to return to Catholic unity. The council was impressed by Calvin's *Answer to Sadoleto*.

57. Men and women who had pulled up stakes elsewhere for the sake of their beliefs were usually strong backers of Calvin's vision of a godly commonwealth.

58. See Chapters 13 and 14.

59. Calvin died in 1564.

60. Jerome Bolsec (1524–1584).

61. Both Bullinger and Luther espoused "single predestination," meaning that God chooses whom He will for salvation and passes over the rest of sinful humankind. This was also St. Augustine's teaching. During the fourteenth century Gregory of Rimini, Father General of the Augustinian Friars and a leading theologian of the modern way (see Chapter 1), had espoused double predestination.

CHAPTER 7

1. The Basques are a people of northern Spain and southwestern France. Theirs is Europe's oldest tongue, having no demonstrated relationship to any other language.

2. Tales of King Arthur and the Knights of the Round Table are an early example of this genre, famously satirized in Miguel de Cervantes's *Don Quixote de la Mancha*.

3. An ancient genre in Christian literary history. Medieval saints' lives contained admiring recollections of the holy man or woman, with a generous admixture of legend.

4. The title of the *Exercises* alludes to military training—this was a book for training men to be soldiers of Christ.

5. See Chapter 15.

6. See Chapter 9.

7. See below, note 11.

8. Chapter 6, p. 89.

9. One slogan of the Counter-Reformation was *"Aut murus aut maritus"*—"Either a [cloister] wall or a husband," meaning that adult women needed the supervision either of a husband or a male convent chaplain.

10. Medieval religious art often depicted the so-called seven corporal works of mercy (tending the sick, visiting the imprisoned, burying the dead, etc.) as well as the seven spiritual works of mercy, which included instructing the ignorant.

11. Gian-Pietro Carafa (d. 1559), a cofounder of the Theatine order in the 1520s. As Pope Paul IV (1555–1559), he promulgated the first *Index of Forbidden Books* (1559).

12. The order that had once numbered Luther among its members.

13. Lainez attended as a theological expert. Only bishops and the heads of religious orders had voting rights at the council, but each bishop was entitled to bring a theological expert, and experts as well as bishops could speak in the debates.

14. Despite Trent's decrees, many Catholic theologians remained loyal to Augustine's views on predestination, as is clear from the Jansenist movement of the seventeenth century (see Chapter 14).

15. Bishoprics and other high positions in the church were a good way for rulers to reward the younger sons of loyal noble families.

16. True also for bishops holding administrative positions at the Roman Curia, as reform-minded writers had long complained.

17. A conciliarist (see Chapter 1) party among the bishops argued that the obligation was a matter of divine law, implying that bishops received their authority directly from God. The papalist party argued that the obligation was merely a matter of human law.

18. The patron was often a layman whose family had given the land on which the church was built some generations previously.

19. By paying a prescribed fee to officials in Rome, monasteries and convents obtained dispensations exempting them from control of their bishops, rather in the way that many towns in Germany became "free cities" (see Chapter 12) by purchasing from the emperor an exemption from control by their territorial princes.

20. E.g., as chantry priests (see Chapter 2) or vicars.

21. The Latin *seminarium* means "seedbed."

22. See Chapter 14.

23. *Nuncios* were accredited to a particular ruler; legates were papal diplomats having a wider brief.

24. See Chapter 11 (Austria) and Chapter 14 (Brandenburg).

25. For the Reformation in Scandinavia, see Chapter 10.

26. Guillaume Farel, later Calvin's fellow preacher in Geneva, had in his early years a reputation for violence. On one occasion he and some companions vanquished "idolatry" in a village church by rushing forward when the priest elevated the host, knocking him down, and trampling on the host. Calvin strongly and consistently opposed any use of violence in spreading the gospel.

27. At a recent conference in Amsterdam, comparing the French Wars of Reli-

gion with the Dutch Revolt, scholars posed a question that is still in search of answers: Why did Low Countries Catholics stand passively by in the face of iconoclastic outbreaks similar to those that provoked a violent reaction from their French confreres?

28. From the Apocalypse, another name for the Book of Revelation.

29. These prognostications originated in Germany, where they had been taken quite seriously by some of the Reformers (e.g., Melanchthon, but not Luther).

30. See Chapter 10 for royal centralization.

31. At times, Francis I eased up on French Protestants in hopes of cementing an alliance with Germany's Schmalkaldic League.

32. The jurisdiction of the fiercely Catholic Parlement of Toulouse included Protestant centers in southeastern France. Raymond Mentzer (see bibliography) counts 1,170 heresy trials for the period 1521–1560, including 684 for 1551–1560. Sixty-two persons were sentenced to death. Most of the accused were convicted, but usually with lesser sentences, such as a public ceremony of atonement or a prison term.

33. The derivation and meaning of this term are uncertain.

34. See Chapter 10.

35. This Christian idea may be compared to the Chinese practice of referring to the emperor as "son of Heaven" (see Chapter 15).

36. For Spain's "New Christians," see Chapter 15. It is clear that far more people—especially "Judaizers"—were haled before the Inquisition in its early decades, even if records are lacking for this period. Henry Kamen (see bibliography) finds that the Toledo tribunal tried 5,400 persons for religious offenses between 1485 and 1501, with 200 sentenced to be burned and 500 others burned in effigy (they had died or escaped before sentencing). For the years 1575–1601 there were 904 such trials, with eleven persons burned and fifteen others burned in effigy. By this time the Inquisition was more concerned with moral offenses, like blasphemy, superstition, and solicitation for sex (including by priests in the confessional). For Spain as a whole, some 49,000 cases were tried from 1540 to 1700; about 40 percent were for religious offenses: 5,007 accused as Judaizers, 11,311 "Moors" (Moriscos) accused of practicing the Islamic beliefs of their ancestors, and 3,489 accused as Lutherans.

37. E.g., participation in "conventicles" or private services.

38. The French *parlement* and the English "parliament" have the same original meaning (a "parley" between the king and his chief nobles), but in England "parliament" became a representative assembly, while the *parlement* in Paris became France's chief law court. Other *parlements,* like that of Toulouse (above, note 32), were created for different parts of the realm.

39. See William Monter (bibliography).

40. A clandestine Protestant group, known to have had fifty-five members, was uncovered in Valladolid in 1558. Following trial by the Inquisition, twenty-six were executed.

41. Isabella compelled many of Castile's religious orders to accept, willy-nilly, the stricter rules of their observant congregations. In this she was supported by her confessor, Francisco Jimenez de Cisneros (1436–1517), who later founded the University of Alcala (1508) for the education of the secular clergy. It has been argued

that these reforms gave Castile a clergy that was better-educated and better-disciplined than elsewhere, helping to account for the scant appeal of Protestantism in Spain.

42. See Chapter 10.

43. The Edict of Nantes. See Chapter 10.

44. Towns rarely allowed more than one Christian confession to be practiced publicly within their walls. Chapter 14 discusses some exceptions to this rule.

45. At its peak c. 1560, the Huguenot movement may have claimed 50 percent of France's nobility, as opposed to some 10 percent of the population at large.

46. Jeanne's mother was the sister of King Francis I, a major religious poet, and the most important patroness of Lefèvre d'Étaples: Marguerite d'Angoulême (1492–1549), Queen of Navarre through her marriage to Henry d'Albret. Her works included *The Mirror of a Sinful Soul*.

47. According to the French monarchy's rules of inheritance, the crown could pass only through a king's male descendants. The Bourbons were descended from a younger son of King Louis IX (d. 1270), later canonized as St. Louis.

48. The author was Jean Morely (1524–1594), who had for a time been a refugee in Geneva. This dispute about congregational autonomy recalls Luther's rejection of Hesse's church ordinance (Chapter 5), and foreshadows the division among English Puritans between Presbyterians and Congregationalists (Chapter 11).

49. A knightly sport in which two lance-bearing combatants converged along a defined path, each seeking to knock the other from his horse.

50. Antoine de Bourbon, a cautious man, was not involved.

51. For example, Holland had been granted by earlier rulers the privilege of not having Hollanders tried outside the limits of their province, no matter what the charge.

52. Three Augustinian friars, members of Luther's order, became the Reformation's first martyrs, burned at Antwerp (Brabant) in 1523. Other Lutherans, driven into exile, became leaders of the Lutheran Reformation along Germany's northern coast.

53. Those who denied that the body and blood of Christ were truly present in the eucharist.

54. In Friesland, armed Münsterites stormed a cloister and held it for several weeks. In Holland, another group stormed and briefly held Amsterdam's city hall, and two similar plots were uncovered elsewhere. For background see Chapter 6.

55. During his term as inquisitor (1545–1566) Titelmans handled an average of a hundred cases per year; of those he convicted of heresy, 264 were executed, mostly Anabaptists.

56. See Chapter 14.

57. The belief that it is cruel to punish people for their beliefs may not seem to require explanation. But the execution of criminals was in this era a spectator sport all over Europe, and the burning of heretics was a popular spectacle in Spain. Earlier scholars would have described the Low Countries outlook as "Erasmian," but the newer view is that Erasmus's own relatively tolerant views reflect the outlook of his countrymen.

58. Women convicted of heresy were usually drowned.

59. Margaret of Parma, regent from 1559 to 1567, was Charles V's illegitimate daughter.

60. William's father was count of Nassau, a princely state of the empire. Upon the death of his cousin (1544) he inherited the possessions of the family's Netherlands branch, including lands in Brabant and Holland and the autonomous principality of Orange in southern France. Charles V summoned young William to the court in Brussels and supervised his upbringing as one of the "great men" on whom government in the Low Countries had always depended.

61. Antoine Perrenot, lord of Granvelle (1517–1586), bishop of Arras. It was widely (though incorrectly) believed that he had concocted the plan to advance himself to the archbishopric of Mechelen, to which Philip had him appointed in 1561.

62. Alba (Don Fernando Alvarez de Toledo, 1507–1582) began his march from the duchy of Milan, a Spanish possession, so as to avoid crossing the territory of France, often at war with Spain.

63. The concept of due process was also deeply ingrained among Spaniards. Alba would not have expected his fellow countrymen to suffer being treated as he proposed to treat the Netherlanders.

64. A. L. Verheyden (see bibliography) gives the names of 12,203 persons who were condemned to death or various other penalties by the council of troubles between 1567 and 1573. The most famous victims were the counts of Egmont and Hoorn, executed in Brussels in 1568—they were loyal Catholics, but their offense was that it was they who had presented Philip in Spain with the council of state's petition for a relaxation of the heresy laws.

65. Equivalent to the "colloquies" of French Huguenot pastors. *Classis* in Latin can refer to many different kinds of groups, including a fleet of ships.

66. Facing the four hundred nobles who demanded relaxation of the heresy laws, one of Margaret of Parma's entourage had referred to them contemptuously as "beggars." This term became a badge of pride for the rebels.

67. Alba could scarcely have designed a tax more likely to provoke opposition: The provincial parliaments claimed they had not approved it; people wanted foreign troops to leave, not stay; and trade-conscious Netherlanders feared the consequences of a permanent sales tax. Hostile national stereotypes common to this era also entered in, since the tax's Spanish precedents made it smack of "tyranny" for Netherlanders.

68. Dutch Catholics formed underground churches not unlike the underground Protestant churches of earlier years. See Chapter 14.

69. For the Dutch Calvinist distinction between members and sympathizers, see Chapter 10.

70. The Hundred Years' War (1337–1453).

71. The battle of Flodden (1513); King James IV was killed.

72. She was sister of the duke of Guise mentioned above. For the Guise family, see Chapter 10.

73. Also known as Mary Queen of Scots.

74. See Chapter 11.

75. In this period the oared galleys known in the Mediterranean since ancient

times were also used in Atlantic waters, often manned by criminals, including those convicted for religious offenses.

76. Mary succeeded her half brother, King Edward VI (ruled 1547–1553), under whom England's government espoused a distinctly Protestant theology. Mary's and Edward's father, Henry VIII, wanted a church separate from Rome, but not necessarily Protestant in doctrine. See Chapter 11.

77. His return was delayed by misgivings about his *Treatise against the Monstrous Regiment of Women* (1557). Knox was attacking Mary of Guise and her daughter, but England's new queen did not appreciate his contention that it was "monstrous" for men to be ruled by a woman.

78. Her husband, King Francis II of France, died in 1560.

79. Mary was the great-granddaughter of England's Henry VII, through his daughter, Margaret Tudor. Elizabeth I, daughter of Henry VIII and the second of his wives, Anne Boleyn, was Henry VII's granddaughter.

80. From Henry VIII on, England's Protestant Church was governed by bishops appointed by the crown.

81. See Chapter 11.

82. The name of the territory comes from an old title held by the rulers, as counts of the (emperor's) palace. The dukes of Bavaria were another branch of the Wittelsbach family.

83. German princes typically had a privy council for matters of state as well as specialized councils for finance and warfare. The church council was a new administrative department.

84. Both treatises circulated in manuscript form for some years before they were published (1589–1590).

85. The Thirty Years' War (1618–1648), a conflict in which religion was only one dimension. See Chapter 10.

PART III

1. See Chapter 15.

2. See Chapter 3.

3. Some convents accepted only daughters of the aristocracy, and having one's daughter accepted as abbess of such a house was a great honor for a noble family.

4. Both claims date from the thirteenth century, when the papacy endeavored with some success to centralize the governance of the church. Before this time, bishops were elected by the cathedral chapters of their dioceses, not appointed by the pope, and heads of male and female religious houses were elected by the members.

5. From the eleventh century, the college of cardinals was the body that elected the pope. The Latin *collegium* meant any corporate body of equals having its own rules, including the "colleges" or dormitories endowed by medieval donors as a way of regulating the unruly habits of teenage university students.

6. For urban society, Chapter 12.

7. These bodies are a distinctive feature of Latin Christendom, appearing in every major territory (and many of the minor ones) between roughly 1100 and 1400. In some lands the clergy sent representatives to a separate assembly, but

more commonly, the higher clergy and the nobility and representatives of commoners (usually limited to delegates from important towns) made up the "three estates" of the realm, as in France.

8. The slogan of the American Revolution, "No taxation without representation," expresses a common reality of medieval kingdoms.

CHAPTER 8

1. Renaissance art, humanist scholarship, the conventions of modern diplomacy, and business techniques like maritime insurance and double-entry bookkeeping are just a few examples of innovations that came to the rest of Europe from south of the Alps.

2. The Kingdom of the Two Sicilies, formed in the twelfth century by a dynasty of adventurers from Normandy (France), broke apart in 1288, when Sicily rebelled against its ruler, a French prince, and submitted to the house of Aragon in Spain. In 1453 the king of Aragon (and Sicily) claimed Naples, reuniting both realms.

3. Proud of their putative Roman origins, fifteenth-century Italians began referring to other Europeans as barbarians, descendants of the tribes Rome had civilized.

4. The valley of the Po River is called Lombardy after the Lombards, an invading Germanic tribe of the sixth century A.D. that had extensive settlements here and whose kingdom for a time included the entire peninsula.

5. The commune was a sworn association of burghers claiming certain rights in the governance of their town, often in defiance of their ruler (in this case, Milan's archbishop, who was also a prince of the Holy Roman Empire). See Chapter 12.

6. Though often referred to by historians as "tyrants," these rulers in their own day were known simply as *signori,* meaning "lords."

7. The Visconti. Milan's Alfa-Romeo automobile firm uses their heraldic emblem, a red man being swallowed by a green viper.

8. Genoa did not rank among Italy's great states because incessant feuding among the great families often led the Genoese to give control of the city to outsiders, like Milan or France.

9. Venice was built on a chain of small islands off the coast.

10. Each new duke had to reconquer the towns that rebelled when his predecessor died.

11. The area around Rome had come to be ruled by Rome's bishops when the authority of the Roman Empire in the west effectively disintegrated during the fifth century. An important section of territory extending to the northeast as far as Bologna was granted to the papacy by Charlemagne's father Pepin (d. 774) in return for papal recognition of Pepin as king of the Frankish lands, replacing the dynasty for which Pepin's family had been chief administrators.

12. See Chapter 1.

13. Erasmus, who watched Julius II enter Bologna as its conqueror (1506), later wrote a savage lampoon (published anonymously) about the pope who acted more "like Julius" [Caesar] than like St. Peter.

14. Many Europeans of this era considered it right and proper that those to whom God gave the gift of power should think of their friends and relatives. Popes

also claimed that only their relatives could be trusted to administer conquered lands—but this meant their successors often had to conquer the same lands again.

15. In a levy known as the *devshirme*, villages in Christian districts were made to provide so many boys and girls each year.

16. The use of such titles was common. France's rulers had for some time styled themselves "most Christian kings."

17. Particularly concerned that justice be fair, not partial, she once got on her horse and rode all night to correct a verdict tainted by favoritism.

18. See Chapter 7.

19. The arquebus, a predecessor of the rifle. Even after this weapon was introduced most men in the unit were still armed with the traditional pike or sword.

20. At issue was the claim by England's King Edward III (ruled 1327–1377) that he and not France's Philip VI (ruled 1328–1350) was the rightful king of France. Though much smaller in area and population, England won important victories by employing tactics (like the armor-penetrating longbow) to which France's aristocratic cavalry was slow to adjust.

21. See Part III, note 7.

22. Notably for assessing what each locality owed. In provinces that had no estates these decisions were made by royal officials.

23. Medieval armies were raised and paid only as needed.

24. Vassals (from an ancient word meaning "servant") provided counsel and military assistance to their lord in return for support, often in the form of grants of land. Historians used to speak with confidence of a medieval "feudal system" linking lords and vassals at various levels together, but some scholars now argue that a "system" existed only in the minds of medieval lawyers trying to make sense of local customs that varied greatly.

25. Sixteenth-century debates about sovereignty are discussed in connection with France's wars of religion (Chapter 10).

26. The count Palatine of the Rhine, the elector of Saxony, the margrave of Brandenburg, and the king of Bohemia.

27. The prince-archbishops of Cologne, Mainz, and Trier.

28. This long and relatively quiet reign may have accustomed Germany's princes to Habsburg rule. At each election the electors could have chosen a prince from another family, and sometimes there was real competition, but, until the empire was abolished by Napoleon (1806), the Habsburg candidate was always chosen.

29. *Hanse* was a German word meaning "merchant guild." The leading members of the Hanseatic League were Lübeck and Hamburg, on either side of the peninsula of Jutland (where Denmark meets Germany), and Gdansk (formerly Danzig), commercial hub of the eastern Baltic.

30. Others (like the free imperial knights) could have attended or sent representatives but usually did not.

31. It was also at the imperial diets that complaints were raised about Germany being "the pope's cow" (see Chapter 2) because of the flow of tax revenue to Rome.

32. The emperor had a court to which feuding princes or towns might have appealed, but few did, since there was no reason to believe that its verdict would be accepted by the losing party.

33. This was how some free imperial knights supported themselves. But the contrast implied here between decentralized Germany and a more centralized country like France represents a difference in degree only. The fact that a whole kingdom was protected by the king's laws did not necessarily mean that merchants traveled safely.

34. Or Nether-lands, a translation of the Dutch "Nederlanden."

35. After about 1300 the leading route from Italy to northern Europe went by sea along the coast, with its terminus at Bruges; another major sea route came from the Baltic, terminating also at Bruges, a major trading station for the Hanseatic League.

36. See Chapter 13.

37. Burgundy made its peace with France in 1435, but the turning point of the war came a few years earlier, when the dauphin, the eldest son of the late king, had himself crowned as King Charles VII in Rheims, the coronation city (1429). Joan of Arc (d. 1431), an illiterate peasant girl, reported hearing voices of the saints tell her she was destined to save France. Somehow persuading French commanders to give her an army, Joan captured the fortified city of Orléans, thus opening the path to Rheims for the dauphin. Later captured by the English, Joan was turned over to the Burgundians, still England's allies, who burned her at the stake as a witch.

38. Including the brothers Jan and Hubert van Eyck, pioneers in the technique of oil painting. See Figure 2.6.

39. Duke John the Fearless (ruled 1404–1419) earned his sobriquet in the last of the Crusades, in which poorly led Christian forces were crushed by the Turks at Nicopolis (1393). At a great banquet in 1457, his son Duke Philip the Good (ruled 1419–1467) swore a never-fulfilled vow to lead yet another Crusade.

40. Provinces consented to taxation through their separate states or parliaments, but Charles forced them to accept decisions made at a national level by the States General his father created.

41. Taxes were now approved by the provincial states; the States General (note 40) served only as a forum for announcing decisions made by the local parliaments.

42. Meaning, born in the country.

43. Piero di Lorenzo (ruled 1492–1494), the son of Lorenzo the Magnificent (ruled 1470–1492).

44. In earlier centuries, a branch of the French royal family, ruling as kings of Naples, had headed Italy's Guelph faction (pro-papal and anti-imperial), ardently supported by the Florentines.

45. King Ferrante of Aragon, Ferdinand of Aragon's illegitimate cousin.

46. An earlier duke of Orleans was married to the daughter of a city-lord of the Visconti dynasty (see above, note 7) who was ousted by his cousin in a cleverly staged coup d'etat in 1385.

47. France's Louis XI (d. 1483) repossessed the duchy of Burgundy, the patrimony of Maximilian's first wife, Mary. When Maximilian's intended second wife, Anne of Brittany, was en route to the Low Countries, Louis's son Charles VIII (d. 1498) intercepted her, married her himself, and claimed her duchy for France.

48. The smaller part of Navarre on the French side of the Pyrenees retained its independence. This was the Navarre ruled by Jeanne d'Albret (Chapter 7).

49. This was by agreement with the new pope, Leo X (ruled 1513–1521), himself of the Medici family.

50. Italian members of the anti-French coalition insisted Milan be restored to the Sforza, the city-lords who ruled prior to 1498.

51. This battle made Huldrych Zwingli, a chaplain for the men of his town, a strong opponent of mercenary warfare (Chapter 5).

52. For the Fugger of Augsburg, see Chapter 12.

53. The revolt of the Comuñeros in Castile and of the Germania in Aragon.

54. By tradition, the emperor was acclaimed by the diet in Germany but had to be crowned by the pope. See below for Charles's coronation in Bologna (1530).

55. Valois was the name of the branch of the royal family that ruled France from 1328 to 1589.

56. Part of Charles's Burgundian inheritance was Franche-Compté, the so-called Free County of Burgundy, an imperial territory running along France's eastern border.

57. This era was marked by a dawning sense of patriotism or loyalty to one's kingdom (not just one's town or province).

58. Restored again to the Sforza (note 50), until the last male of the family died without issue (1535), thereafter under direct Spanish rule. Charles's claim was based on the fact that medieval emperors had at times controlled Milan.

59. After further Turkish victories in 1541, much of Hungary was controlled directly or indirectly by the Ottomans. Mary of Hungary, widow of Hungary's King Lewis, was a sister of Ferdinand and Charles. The couple was childless, and their marriage treaty stipulated that if Lewis died without producing heirs, his kingdoms would pass to Ferdinand.

60. "Hegemony" is a Greek word meaning "leadership." In military and diplomatic terms, a power may be said to have hegemony if it is strong enough to make other states do its bidding, even without going to war.

61. For a campaign of this kind, Charles borrowed from south German or Genoese bankers, who made sums of money available at points along the army's route of march and collected (with interest) from crown revenues pledged to their agents in Castile. This long-distance chain of credit was easily interrupted by rumors of the crown's insolvency due to previous borrowing.

62. Governments in the age of print were keenly aware of the need to get their view of things before the public quickly—preferably before the other side could mobilize its pamphleteers.

63. Some of Charles's councillors promoted an exalted idea of the emperor's place in Christendom, drawn in part from pro-imperial tracts during medieval conflicts with the papacy (see Chapter 1).

64. The Treaty of Cambrai, negotiated on Charles's behalf by his aunt, Margaret of Austria, regent of the Low Countries.

65. Like his cousin, Pope Leo X (ruled 1513–1521).

66. One of the sources of friction between papacy and empire lay in the expectation that an emperor could properly be crowned only by the pope. The precedent for this custom—when Charlemagne knelt before the pope but then took the crown and placed it on his own head (800)—nicely illustrates the ambiguous relationship between the two "heads" of Latin Christendom.

67. Ferdinand's acceptance by the imperial princes as King of the Romans would mean that he, not Charles's son Philip (born in 1527), would succeed as emperor.

68. Charles of course assumed that other interests were at stake, and he was not entirely wrong.

69. Despite occasional campaigns back and forth across the Ottoman/Habsburg frontier, this was the policy that Ferdinand followed, with Charles's steady encouragement.

70. In an attack timed to coincide with Charles's and Ferdinand's campaign in Austria, Andrea Doria landed Spanish troops at the port of Coron in southern Greece, which they held from September 1532 to April 1534.

71. The violence-prone Duke Ulrich was ousted by the Swabian League (1519), which entrusted Württemberg to Habsburg governance. The Schmalkaldic army installed as duke Ulrich's son Philip, who brought Württemberg into the Protestant and Schmalkaldic camp.

72. Chapter 6, p. 89.

73. Widow of the king of Hungary who was killed at Mohaès (1526), sister of Charles and Ferdinand, Mary was regent of the Low Countries from 1531 until 1555.

74. Charles asserted a long-standing claim by conquering Guelders in 1528 and ousting the ruling duke, a bitter foe of the Habsburgs. The duke of Cleves was this man's kinsman, and his occupation of Guelders had support from local nobles and townsmen.

75. Mary organized the resistance so well that both armies were turned back— she did everything but don armor and ride into battle, something her advisers would not permit.

76. Goslar in particular claimed to be a free imperial city, meaning it did not need the duke's approval to make changes in religion. Henry did not agree.

77. The duke had been experimenting with religious reform, but he now had to promise not to introduce any changes in religion.

78. The Peace of Crépy.

79. There were often dual versions of treaties and of ambassadorial instructions; only one was to be made public.

80. See Chapter 6.

81. Philip insisted on having the girl; her mother insisted on marriage. Citing polygamy in the Old Testament as a precedent, Luther and Martin Bucer approved a second marriage (1541), provided it be kept secret to avoid scandal. All agreed to this plan except the new bride's mother, who spread the news.

82. Charles was then in Bavaria (1546); one did not keep a prince's friendship by marching an army across his territory.

83. Moritz told John Frederick he was having trouble mobilizing his troops and would join him on the march.

84. The same duke of Alba whom Philip II later sent to the Netherlands: see Chapter 7.

85. The boundary between France and the Holy Roman Empire had nothing to do with language. French diplomats were beginning to promote the idea that France was the successor state to the ancient Roman province of Gaul, whose eastern border was the Rhine and which had included German-speaking Alsace as well as French-speaking Lorraine.

86. See Chapter 9.

87. For the Guise family's role in French affairs, Chapter 9.

88. The Treaty of Cateau-Cambrésis.

89. From England, France also captured Calais (1558), the last of English possessions in France dating from the Hundred Years' War.

90. As noted in Chapter 6, Calvinism was not given the same recognition.

91. Ferdinand promised in writing that the inhabitants of such territories would not be molested for their beliefs, but this clause, unlike the "ecclesiastical reservation," was not incorporated into the language of the treaty.

92. Transylvania, now in Romania, was a part of the kingdom of Hungary claimed both by Ferdinand, Charles's brother, and by a Hungarian prince named Janos Zapolyai (d. 1540), whose claim was backed by the Ottomans.

CHAPTER 9

1. After completing tours of duty in foreign capitals, ambassadors (usually from leading patrician families) were required to make a long report to the Senate about the affairs of their host country. Many of these are preserved; some are published.

2. It is ironic that Machiavelli, an ardent republican and foe of the Medici, is best known for *The Prince*, a treatise he wrote in the vain hope of gaining a post in the Medici regime that was restored in 1512. His *Discourses* lay out amoral rules for the political survival of a popular government, similar at points to *The Prince*'s description of what a prince must do to stay in power.

3. See the comments on France's religious wars in the *Essays* of Michel de Montaigne (1533–1592), a Catholic "politique."

4. Following a Twelve Years' Truce (1609–1621) and further fighting after 1622, the independence of the Dutch Republic was recognized in the 1648 Treaty of Westphalia.

5. This was the Dutch description of the Calvinist creed of the "public" or state church.

6. Catherine was a politically inexperienced foreigner. A daughter of Florence's ruling house, she wed the future Henry II in 1533, but he kept her in the background; his mistress, Diane de Poitiers, presided at court functions.

7. In the customary patronage system, many positions were given upon recommendation by the king's favorites. Throughout the kingdom those who owed their place to the same great man were natural allies. Patronage is one of the continuities historians have noted between the aristocratic parties of this era and the political parties of more recent centuries.

8. One of his nephews was Gaspard de Coligny—see below.

9. What the French called "Gallicanism" (in reference to Gaul, the ancient name for France) was a version of the fifteenth-century doctrine of Conciliarism (see Chapter 1), which envisioned each national church as governing itself.

10. Between 1562 and 1598 there were eight wars in all, only some of which are mentioned here.

11. This shows the strength of the nobles in the Huguenot party.

12. The early truces allowed no freedom of worship in the towns, save in the suburbs of one town in each administrative district.

13. Huguenots assumed Alba was planning to invade France.

14. Chapter 7, pp. 113–114.

15. Catherine feared Coligny's rise in her son's esteem (the Bourbon marriage was also his idea) meant that she was losing her influence, and she dreaded the consequences for France of another long war with Spain. Duke Henry of Guise believed Coligny was complicit in the assassination of his father, Duke Francis (1563).

16. The council was aware that Coligny's brother commanded a force of 4,000 Huguenots camped outside the city.

17. Whether subjects might lawfully resist the tyranny of their rulers was much discussed by ancient and medieval authors. For a disagreement within the Reformed tradition, Chapter 7, p. 118.

18. He was the third surviving son of Henry II and Catherine de Medici and the last to rule as king.

19. See Chapter 7, pp. 118.

20. Towns held in safekeeping provided the minority Huguenot party with a military guarantee.

21. The king, who sometimes dressed as a woman and enjoyed partying with his male favorites, was widely (though incorrectly) believed to be homosexual.

22. Chapter 6, note 50.

23. Henry IV's uncle, Cardinal Charles of Bourbon (d. 1590), held captive by his nephew, was recognized by the league as Charles X.

24. Henry III had 4,000 Swiss mercenaries stationed throughout the city. In consultation with the Spanish ambassador, Guise timed his approach to Paris so that both Henry III and Henry of Bourbon would be distracted while Spain's Armada (see below) sailed into the North Sea, toward England.

25. Huguenot polemicists made a similar adjustment to new circumstances: instead of urging resistance to the crown, they now argued that everyone must obey the king and his lawful heir, i.e., Henry of Bourbon.

26. In the Bourbon branch of the royal family, Henry was the eldest son of an eldest son, his father Antoine; the cardinal of Bourbon (note 23), Henry's uncle, was a younger son.

27. Constitutional theorists in France spoke of "fundamental laws" that could not be violated, including the rules of royal succession.

28. With some 300,000 people, Paris was the largest city in Christian Europe and by far the largest north of the Alps.

29. See note 23.

30. This was the burial church of French kings.

31. No royal edict could be enforced as law in French courts unless accepted by the *parlements*, and registered in the official statute-book kept by the Parlement of Paris.

32. See below for the Huguenot rebellion of 1625–1628.

33. One exception was the Dutch spiritualist thinker Dirk Volkertszoon Coornhert (1522–1590); another was Amsterdam's Jewish philosopher Baruch Spinoza (1632–1677).

34. Subsequent rulers pursued this goal by, e.g., offering financial and other inducements for Huguenot nobles to convert.

35. Constitutional not in the sense of a written document, but in the sense that the king was considered to act unlawfully if he failed to observe traditional rules and procedures. The *Parlement* of Paris's claim to scrutinize the legality of the king's edicts before accepting them (above, note 31) illustrates the idea of lawful limits on the king's freedom of action.

36. Meaning that the king's authority was not subject to control by any human institution, such as a representative assembly (the Estates General) or law courts (the *parlements*).

37. Like his father, Philip ruled by virtue of separate titles in each province, e.g., count of Flanders, duke of Brabant. There was no title for the Low Countries as a whole.

38. Openings were cut in the dikes at William of Orange's express command, despite the furious opposition of the peasants whose fields were flooded. Riding on the waters came a Dutch relief force in shallow boats.

39. Philip had previously declared a "bankruptcy" of this kind in 1557. Charles V was urged to take this step, but refused.

40. See Chapter 8, notes 40, 41. The States General took over financial management of the war with France during the early years of Philip's reign, but he subsequently ordered that no meeting of the States General was to be called. Instead, his government in Brussels dealt separately with the states of each province.

41. Farnese's mother was Margaret of Parma, illegitimate daughter of Charles V and regent of the Low Countries from 1566 to 1580. His father was Ottavio Farnese, a son of the cardinal who later became pope as Paul III (ruled 1534–1549).

42. Nucleus of the later United Provinces or Dutch Republic.

43. Guido Marnef (see bibliography) estimates that at this time some 55–60 percent of Antwerp's 80,000 people were Catholic, 26–30 percent Calvinist, 13–15 percent Lutheran, and 2 percent Anabaptist.

44. Many thousands of people, not all of them Protestant, migrated to rebel towns like Middelburg (Zeeland) or Amsterdam (Holland), helping to lay the foundations of Dutch prosperity.

45. Initially, the rebel provinces of Holland and Zeeland fought under the pretext that they were obedient to the king's duly appointed *stadtholder*, or provincial governor, William of Orange. The Union of Utrecht renounced allegiance to Philip in 1581 but was looking for a "prince" to take his place.

46. Made up of deputies sent by the states or parliaments of provinces adhering to the Revolt—minus those conquered by Parma since the 1576 meeting in Ghent.

47. As was the case in Calvin's Geneva (see Chapter 7), people who had pulled up stakes because of their Reformed beliefs tended to back a more strongly Calvinist policy.

48. Under the leadership of priests of the Holland Mission (see Chapter 13), Catholics in the rebel provinces were beginning to build house-churches whose all-too-audible Latin hymn-singing on Sunday mornings was often ignored by the local sheriff.

49. The Dutch debate—between Calvinist ministers and their lay supporters on the one side and urban magistrates on the other—resembles the dispute (see

Chapter 6) between Geneva and Zurich about the proper relationship between church and state.

50. The city of Utrecht was the capital of the province of the same name. Leicester's associates also purged the leadership of the provincial states.

51. Leicester was recalled to England late in 1586 for consultations on another matter, and when he returned in 1587 seeking negotiations with Spain (according to Elizabeth's instructions) he alienated his former supporters.

52. Holland, one of the most urbanized regions of Europe, was only one among seven rebel provinces that eventually gained independence from Spain, but it contributed roughly 60 percent of the war budget managed by the States General.

53. His official title was grand pensionary. In this capacity, he worked for consensus among voting members of the States of Holland (eighteen cities and a college of nobles) and served as Holland's spokesman in the States General. The States of Holland and the States General met on different floors of the same building in Holland's capital, The Hague.

54. Geoffrey Parker (see bibliography) has shown that England's ships, unlike Spain's, had gun carriages permitting cannon to be retracted and reloaded once fired. It seems many of the cannon on board Spanish vessels were fired only once.

55. Not accepted by most Reformed churches.

56. Financial decentralization worked because of the close local connection between the collection and disbursement of funds. The same local tax-farmers who collected the receipts were responsible for direct payments to the garrisons of their towns.

57. It has been argued that he invented the tactic of firing by ranks, which permitted a well-trained unit to keep up an unremitting volley.

58. So-called bastion trace fortifications, developed by Italian military engineers in the early 1500s, were designed to withstand artillery bombardment. The high curtain walls of medieval towns and castles gave way to low ramparts surrounded by triangular cannon-platforms (the bastions) meant to keep besiegers at bay.

59. The new state that came into being during the Revolt, made up of seven provinces, can be called the United Provinces or the Dutch Republic.

60. These provinces were transferred to the Austrian branch of the Habsburg family by the 1713 Treaty of Utrecht. The Austrian Netherlands were under French control (1795–1815) during the French Revolution; they were united with the Netherlands by the Congress of Vienna (1815) and became Belgium after the Belgian Revolution against Dutch Rule (1830).

61. The richest mines were at Zacatecas in Mexico and Potosi in the Viceroyalty of Peru (now in Bolivia), both discovered in 1545–1546. Castilian law entitled the crown to one-fifth of the silver shipped from Spanish America.

62. Chapter 8, pp. 135–136.

63. For the Hussite movement, Chapter 1.

64. Besides modern Hungary, the kingdom included the present countries of Croatia, Bosnia, and Slovakia as well as the province of Voivodina (northern Serbia) and portions of western Romania.

65. "Magyar" is the ancient name for the people now called Hungarian, whose language is related to Turkish. Hungarians still refer to themselves and their language as Magyar, pronounced Mah-jar.

66. According to age-old diplomatic usage, Ferdinand by paying tribute acknowledged the sultan as his superior.

67. The duchies and capital cities: Lower Austria (Vienna), Upper Austria (Linz), Tirol (Innsbruck), Styria (Graz), Carinthia (Klagenfurt), and Carniola (Lubljana, known in German as Laibach). The first five are in modern Austria; the last is modern Slovenia.

68. For the work of the Jesuits in Austria, see Chapter 10.

69. See Chapter 7.

70. Chapter 8, p. 143.

71. See Chapter 10.

72. Kepler's careful astronomical observations did much to confirm the heliocentric theory first proposed by the Polish astronomer Nicholas Copernicus (1473–1543), that is, that the earth rotates around the sun. In the traditional view, a stationary earth was at the center of the universe.

73. Alchemy purported to investigate the hidden properties of matter, including formulas for transmuting base matter into gold.

74. Natural magic, an ancient Greek doctrine resurrected by Italian humanists, held that seemingly disparate things, such as a particular plant and a particular mental or emotional state, shared secret affinities because of their connection through a "world soul" animating the cosmos much as individual bodies were animated by individual souls. Early modern beliefs about magic may be glimpsed in the "Faust legend" as treated by Christopher Marlowe (1564–1593) and Johann Wolfgang von Goethe (1749–1832).

75. This council was comparable in its operations to the church councils of Protestant territories (see Chapters 6 and 7). Cathedral chapters, conscious of their privileges, were centers of resistance to the Tridentine reforms.

76. Gebhard Truchsess von Waldburg was the archbishop who announced his conversion. Ernest of Bavaria was a man of dubious morals and already held three other bishoprics, but the promise of Bavaria's help in keeping Cologne Catholic led Rome to support him.

77. In consequence of a conflict between the city and a monastery that had survived the Reformation, Rudolph II placed Donauwörth under the ban of outlawry and entrusted Duke Maximilian with enforcement of the ban.

78. Notably the assassination of King Henry IV (1610), which cut short French plans for intervention. The five territories were divided between two claimants: Cleves, Mark, and Ravensberg passed to Elector John Sigismund of Brandenburg, a recent convert to Calvinism, while Duke Wolfgang William of Neuburg, a recent convert to Catholicism, received Jülich and Berg.

79. The son of Archduke Charles.

80. See Chapter 10.

81. This was the second "Defenestration of Prague." The first occurred (1415) when King Sigismund sent emissaries to negotiate with angry followers of the now martyred Jan Hus (see Chapter 1). These two men were killed, but Ferdinand's governors landed on a dung-heap and survived.

82. Formed in 1609 in opposition to Christian of Anhalt's Protestant Union but hitherto relatively inactive. Maximilian was to be rewarded by transfer of the electoral title from the Palatinate to his branch of the Wittelsbach family.

83. There was no fighting in the Low Countries because of the Twelve Years' Truce (1609–1621).

84. He was a prince of the empire not as king of Denmark, but as duke of Holstein.

85. Following expiration of the Twelve Years' Truce, both sides were ready for more war.

86. He used the profits of war to buy extensive lands in Bohemia.

87. Maximilian was an inconsistent defender of the imperial constitution, but his elevation to the electoral dignity was less startling than raising an adventurer like Wallenstein to a dukedom.

88. Magdeburg was a territorial town that became Lutheran despite opposition from its then Catholic prince-archbishop. Following the Edict of Restitution, the by now Lutheran administrator of the archbishopric was deprived of his office, and one of the emperor's sons was named archbishop, but the city of Magdeburg shut its gates against him and prepared for a siege.

89. See Chapter 11.

90. When hostilities reopened after the Twelve Years' Truce expired, Spain won some victories, but by the time peace was concluded (1648) the Dutch Republic had extended its territories to the south and east, rounding off the modern borders of the Netherlands with Belgium and Germany.

91. The "first minister" prepared the agenda for meetings of the royal council and presided in the king's absence. Armand Duplessis de Richelieu, cardinal-bishop of Lodeve, served as first minister from 1628 until his death in 1642.

92. Members of this group were often descended from families that had been prominent in the Catholic League. Their view of French foreign policy was mirrored by the English Parliament's demands (see Chapter 11) for a "Protestant" foreign policy.

93. Above, p. 153.

94. Since Mantua was technically a dependency of the empire, Ferdinand declared it sequestered, meaning it was under his control until he decided who the ruler should be.

95. This would be done by King Louis XIV (ruled 1656–1715), whose Revocation of the Edict of Nantes (1685) was an expression of religious intolerance plain and simple.

96. Upon the death of Sweden's King John III Vasa (ruled 1568–1592), friction between the Lutheran estates and John III's Catholic son Sigismund, already king of Poland-Lithuania, led to Sigismund's deposition in favor of his uncle, Charles IX, the father of Gustavus Adolph. See Chapter 10.

97. Most houses in cities north of the Alps were still made of timber.

98. See above, note 57.

99. France had agreed to support Gustavus Adolph in a campaign against the emperor in north Germany, not against the Catholic League in south Germany or Bavaria, with which France had a separate treaty.

100. Wallenstein was dismissed by Ferdinand II in 1630, but reengaged in 1632. Following not-so-secret negotiations with various Protestant leaders, Wallenstein was again dismissed by the emperor and murdered by his own men (1634).

101. Axel Oxenstierna (1583–1654).

102. Three months earlier Richelieu had concluded a secret alliance against Spain with the Dutch Republic.

103. See chapter 8, note 85.

104. The question of exactly what these rights were was fertile ground for future wars.

105. The so-called Upper Palatinate, adjoining Bavaria on the north. There were now eight electoral princes instead of seven.

106. Frederick had built up his army in order to stake a claim for new lands when peace was finally concluded. He thus laid the foundation of future greatness for his Hohenzollern descendants. In 1870 the king of Prussia became the first emperor of a newly unified Germany, Kaiser Wilhelm I.

107. In France as in the rest of Europe, taxation fell most heavily on the peasantry.

108. The Peace of the Pyrenees (1659) recognized French sovereignty over two contested border provinces.

109. Sensible Castilians poured into the treasury bonds that made up the kingdom's war debt money that might otherwise have gone to commerce and agriculture.

110. One may also distinguish on the Catholic side between the unremitting zealotry of Emperor Ferdinand II and the relative pragmatism of Maximilian of Bavaria and Emperor Ferdinand III. Ferdinand II at one point toyed with the idea of offering Alsace to France if France would agree to preserve the Edict of Restitution; Ferdinand the younger, who vetoed this plan, preferred keeping Alsace for the empire and giving up the Edict of Restitution.

111. In fact, it was argued that reason of state required religious uniformity, to prevent potential enemies from having a fifth column within one's own borders.

CHAPTER 10

1. Chapter 8, p. 129.

2. Like the siege artillery used by the French in Italy in 1494 (Chapter 8, p. 133) and the bastion-trace style of fortification developed by Italian military engineers to withstand bombardment (Chapter 9, note 58).

3. There may have been parts of the world where people were not eager to use the slightest pretext for bringing the law down on their adversaries. If so, Europe was not one of them.

4. Church courts, town courts, and courts for districts directly ruled by the nobles. A good lawyer could advise clients which courts might be most receptive to their arguments.

5. In France, once the king had permission to levy taxes without the consent of his estates (Chapter 8, p. 129), the Estates General were hardly ever summoned, and the provincial states were involved only in local assessment of tax quotas decided on by the king. In 1558, Duke Emmanuel Philibert of Savoy-Piedmont abolished the parliaments of both his territories and soon raised taxes by 500 percent.

6. Chapter 9, pp. 162–167. For Russia, especially under the reign of Tsar Ivan IV (the Terrible, 1530–1584), the debate about absolute monarchy is still quite vigorous.

7. In earlier centuries, only those lacking the pedigree of noble birth needed university degrees to qualify for administrative posts. In this era even noble officials tended to have some university training, if not always an actual degree.

8. Chapter 9, note 33.

9. Malmö was the metropolis of Scania, now part of Sweden, but then under the Danish crown.

10. Three Scandinavian crowns (Norway, Denmark, and Sweden) were joined in the 1397 Union of Kalmar. Sweden (with Finland) regained its identity as an independent kingdom in 1523.

11. The issue was control of traffic in and out of the Baltic through the Øresund, the strait separating Copenhagen from Malmö.

12. To force the diet's hand, Vasa resigned his kingship, assuming the crown once more only after the legislation he wished was passed.

13. In addition to the frequently meeting council, Denmark also had an irregularly meeting assembly of lords, but not a parliament in the usual sense of the term, because neither had representatives of the towns or other commoners.

14. *Apanage* ("for bread" in French) means the territory whose revenues and governance are assigned to a junior member of the ruling house. Schleswig was part of the lands of the Danish crown; Holstein (Chapter 9, note 84) was a principality of the empire.

15. The troops came on ships from Holland, leading seafaring province of the Habsburg Netherlands, which delayed the effort in every way possible, so as not to imperil its shipping lanes to the Baltic by being drawn into war with Denmark.

16. After eight years of living in exile in the Netherlands, his wife's home country, Christian had invaded the lands of the Danish crown by sea in 1531, only to be captured and imprisoned in Norway. After an internal revolution, Lübeck, formerly Christian's great foe, added its support to his cause.

17. The Church Ordinance of 1537–1539 merely prescribed that each pastor was to possess certain texts by Luther and Melanchthon.

18. Chapter 6, p. 93.

19. Niels Hemmingsen (1513–1580), a Melanchthon student.

20. E.g., at Vilnius, in Lithuania, and the more distant Olomouc (in German, Olmütz) in Moravia, part of the crown of Boehmia.

21. See Chapter 3, p. 41.

22. A later term for those who understood the Church of England as it had been envisioned by Archbishop Laud (see Chapter 11), with a strong idea of episcopal authority and an admiration for the Catholic liturgy.

23. Jagellio was the name of the originally Lithuanian dynasty that ruled the kingdom of Poland-Lithuania (see Chapter 15) from 1385 until the death of Sigismund II in 1572.

24. He was a particular student of the writings of Joris Cassander (1513–1566), an irenic Catholic theologian who was familiar with the plans for church reform in Cleves that were cut short by Charles V's invasion of 1543 (Chapter 8, note 77).

25. Hence the conflict between Gustavus Adolph (Charles IX's son) and Sigismund Vasa, which French diplomats sought to mediate (Chapter 9, note 96).

26. Sympathizers attended weekly services but had not presented themselves

for admission to the communion table, which required examination by the minister and a confession of faith.

27. For competition between the Calvinists and the strict-living Mennonites, Chapter 7, pp. 114–115.

28. The republic's first university, founded in recognition of Leiden's resistance to the Spanish (1575, Chapter 9, note 38).

29. Town regents were not necessarily church members; in the early years of the Revolt, some were even Catholic, despite the fact that Catholics were barred from holding office.

30. Chapter 7, p. 113.

31. Chapter 9, p. 155.

32. Chapter 6, p. 95.

33. The current honorific term for deputies to the states.

34. Thus in the debate between Erasmus and Luther (Chapter 6), Arminius would have agreed with Erasmus, not Luther.

35. Published in French (1561) and Dutch (1562), adopted by Low Countries synods of 1571 and 1581 as the official statement of Reformed belief.

36. On issues deemed to be important—of which this was one—the States General did not act without the unanimous agreement of delegations representing all seven provinces.

37. Chapter 9, pp. 156–158.

38. "Dominee" is a Dutch word meaning "preacher" or "minister."

39. For Amsterdam's extraordinary growth after 1585, see Chapter 14.

40. Portugal and its overseas possessions were under Spanish rule from 1580 to 1640. Hence the truce with Spain limited the extent to which the newly founded (1603) Dutch East India Company could make headway by attacking Portuguese outposts in Asia. Several members of Amsterdam's new ruling faction were leading shareholders.

41. That is, Calvin's doctrine of double predestination (chapter 6, p. 95), supplemented by the view of Theodore Beza (and Franciscus Gomarus) that God's eternal decrees predate the foundation of the world, and thus the fall of Adam and Eve. In respect of an imagined vertical time line, this view was called "supralapsarian" (above the fall), and the alternative view "infralapsarian" (below the fall).

42. In several Holland towns there was broad support for the Remonstrants, but more often popular sentiment ran the other way.

43. According to law, only church members could serve as public officials, or own stock in the Dutch East India Company (note 40).

44. In contrast with more urbanized regions, like Italy and the Low Countries, the mendicant orders were not as important as older monastic orders like the Benedictines.

45. Recall that even in France, where Huguenot nobles and towns developed a habit of collaboration, the treaties ending successive religious wars (Chapter 9) always granted freedom of worship to nobles, but to cities only as the outcome of the war dictated.

46. Ljubljana, Klagenfurt, and Görz.

47. In many cases, the noble was the "patron" of the parish church according to

canon law, meaning that his ancestors had endowed the parish by a gift of land and that he was therefore entitled to appoint the pastor.

48. In Upper Austria the opposition to Habsburg re-Catholicization efforts was led by a few Calvinist nobles, especially Georg Erasmus von Tschernembl (1567–1626).

49. Bohemia's 1609 Letter of Majesty (see Chapter 9, p. 159) was the precedent for Mathias's religious concessions to the Upper Austrian estates.

50. Chapter 9, pp. 160–161.

51. Chapter 5, p. 70.

52. Parliamentary bodies rarely included representation for the peasantry, but the estates of the northern part of the Habsburg-Austrian duchy of Tirol was one that did.

53. For example, in the Palatinate (Chapter 7).

CHAPTER 11

1. E.g., they denied that the body of Christ was truly present in the consecrated host.

2. Open to ideas from Wittenberg, but also Zurich and later Geneva as well.

3. Juana of Castile, Charles V's mother, was Catherine's older sister.

4. Lev. 18:16, 20:21; but contrast Deut. 25:5.

5. Henry VIII's father, Henry VII (ruled 1485–1509), was the first king of the Tudor dynasty.

6. Following the 1527 Sack of Rome, the pope was eager for reconciliation with the emperor (Chapter 8, p. 137).

7. Enacted during a period of conflict between the English crown and the papacy: for the general context, Chapter 2, p. 27.

8. Thomas Wolsey (1472–1530), cardinal archbishop of York and chancellor of England, was now replaced as chancellor by Thomas More.

9. Note the difference from the three-estates parliamentary organization common on the continent, where bishops and other representatives of the clergy were one of three separate chambers or estates. England's Parliament was made of up the higher nobles, in whose number the bishops were counted (House of Lords), and representatives of the towns and shires (House of Commons).

10. The so-called "annates," equivalent to a percentage of the annual income of bishops appointed by the pope.

11. The process of dissolving all of the country's monasteries was completed by 1540.

12. Under circumstances that remain obscure, Anne Boleyn, the mother of the future Queen Elizabeth, was arrested on charges of sexual impropriety. Ten days after her execution (1536) Henry married Jane Seymour, who died giving birth to the future King Edward VI (1537). Henry had no children by his three subsequent wives, Anne of Cleves, Catherine Howard, and Catherine Parr.

13. Actually enacted in 1547, under Edward VI. For chantries, Chapter 3, p. 41. Henry VIII in his own will (1547) left endowments for masses for his soul and for Jane Seymour's.

14. Influential Reformed theologians who sojourned in England include Poland's Jan Łaski (1548–1553), Strasbourg's Martin Bucer (1549–1551—see Chapter 6, pp. 87–88), and Peter Martyr Vermigli (1547–1553), an Italian refugee professor in Zurich. John Hooper, a bishop in Edward VI's reign, had studied in Zurich.

15. Altars, symbolic of the Catholic understanding of the mass as a representation of the sacrifice of Christ on the cross, were to be replaced by communion tables, placed in the center of the church rather than at the east end, where the altar had been. For the Zurich precedent, Chapter 2, pp. 23–24.

16. The basis for Morning Prayer and Evensong services in the modern Anglican liturgy; for the monastic hours, Chapter 2, note 9, and Chapter 3, note 21.

17. In contravention of 1544 Act of Succession, naming Mary as Edward's heir in case he had no issue, Dudley persuaded the dying king to name as his successor Dudley's daughter-in-law, Jane Grey, a descendant of King Henry VII.

18. Among the so-called "Marian exiles" to Geneva and other Protestant centers was John Knox (Chapter 7); just as Knox returned to Scotland after 1558, many others returned to England to play leading roles in the Elizabethan Reformation.

19. Also burned at the stake were John Hooper (above, note 14) and Archbishop Cranmer, who had at first recanted in the vain hope of saving his life.

20. A concession to Protestant arguments that no human being could be "head" of Christ's church.

21. Elizabeth guarded her opinions and intentions very well.

22. In the Reformed tradition (Chapter 6) the office of bishop was deemed a corruption of New Testament norms; Zwingli and Bullinger envisioned a church governed by godly magistrates, Calvin a church governed by consistories. It was not uncommon for Lutheran churches to be governed by bishops (as in Sweden), but there were no Reformed churches with bishops save in Scotland, where the bishops King James VI had insisted on keeping (see below) coexisted uneasily with a presbyterian form of church governance.

23. The two acts, initially rejected by Lords (where the Catholic bishops of Mary's reign still had seats) after being easily passed in Commons, were accepted by one vote in the upper house after Elizabeth agreed to some changes in wording and placed two of the bishops under arrest, preventing them from voting.

24. Some argue (notably Eamon Duffy—see bibliography) that the English nation was not Protestant in sentiment until around 1580.

25. The plots were often in favor of the Catholic Mary Stuart (Chapter 7, p. 117). In fact, Catholics were sharply divided between those who remained loyal to Elizabeth and those who sought the help of foreign Catholic powers (notably Spain) to overthrow her.

26. "Recusants" were those who "recused" the legal obligation to attend Church of England services once a month, as required by a 1581 statute aimed against Catholics; the penalty was a fine of twenty pounds, not a small sum at the time. In 1585 all persons found guilty of harboring a Catholic priest were declared liable to loss of life and property.

27. Chapter 10.

28. Based on a practice begun by Zwingli: Chapter 6, p. 75.

29. For Calvin's critique of episcopacy, Chapter 6, pp. 87–98. I use "presbyter-

ian" for the Calvinist conception of church governance, and "Presbyterian" for a church organized along these lines, as in Scotland and later in England (see below).

30. Known as the Marprelate Tracts—they were published under the fictitious name of "Martin Marprelate," or "Martin, the enemy of prelates [bishops]."

31. A conventicle is a small, unauthorized religious gathering.

32. Supralapsarianism: Chapter 10, note 41.

33. The austere Reformed conception of worship barred anything not mandated by scripture; thus Christians were to keep the Lord's day holy (second commandment), but there was no license for special feast days or any songs but the Psalms.

34. A vestige of pre-Christian fertility rites.

35. A view similar to that of Jean Morely: Chapter 7, note 48. For presbyterians, each pastor was part of a larger body (like the Dutch *classis*), and important issues required the convening of a synod. See below for England's Assembly of Westminster.

36. Baptists (including the many Baptist churches in the United States) thus have a different spiritual lineage than Anabaptists, despite their common rejection of infant baptism.

37. Including the Pilgrims, who migrated to the Dutch Republic (1607) and lived there for a time before establishing their colony at Plymouth, Massachusetts (1620).

38. He was also King James VI of Scotland (ruled 1567–1625); through his mother, Mary Stuart (Chapter 7, note 79), he was the great-grandson of Henry VII of England.

39. Antonia Fraser (see bibliography) discounts the suspicions of the Venetian ambassador and other Catholic diplomats that the plot was concocted by James's chief minister to whip up sentiment against Catholics. There was indeed "a terrorist conspiracy spurred on by resentment of the King's broken promises," but with no support from the clergy or the nobles families who were the leaders of England's Catholics, or from abroad. The quote (cited by Fraser) is from John Milton (1608–1674), author of *Paradise Lost*.

40. See below for James's policy in Scotland. His maxim was, "No bishops, no king"—those who question the authority of bishops were implicitly questioning the king's as well.

41. For French theories of royal absolutism, Chapter 9, p. 153; James was author of a treatise expounding this doctrine, *The Trew Law of Free Monarchies* (1598).

42. Making them eligible for the House of Lords and ineligible for the Commons.

43. Spain's objective was to keep England from supporting its Protestant foes (the Count Palatine and the Dutch Republic) by holding out the prospect of a bride for Prince Charles.

44. Chapter 9, p. 163.

45. The formula used by speakers in Commons was "redress before supply." The more usual parliamentary practice, not just in England, was that the deputies voted subsidies and left the ruler to respond to their grievances at his good pleasure.

46. In the English practice, on which the pertinent articles of the U.S. Constitution are based, impeachment was a two-stage process in which the lower house

voted to bring charges that were then examined and decided on by the upper house.

47. Meaning that subjects having property valued at more than a stated amount had to deliver to crown officials a percentage of their wealth, registered as a loan subject to repayment. This was a centuries-old practice, though less common in England.

48. Members of the lower nobility, usually country gentlemen. The House of Commons included members from the rural gentry as well as from selected towns.

49. The naval war of 1652–1654 was the first of several Anglo-Dutch conflicts.

50. The doctrine of apostolic succession holds that bishops are part of an unbroken chain of spiritual authority, handed down since the time of the Apostles by the laying-on of hands in which new bishops were consecrated by other bishops.

51. See above, note 15.

52. Elizabeth's views on predestination are uncertain. James I urged the Synod of Dordrecht (see Chapter 10) to adopt the now-orthodox supralapsarian doctrine of predestination.

53. For example, James I espoused both supralapsarianism in predestination (note 52) and divine-right episcopacy.

54. This use of the term is distinctive to England. In the Dutch Republic, Arminius and his followers (Chapter 10) had no interest in reviving the episcopal office or in Catholic ceremonies.

55. The Irish language is similar to Scots Gaelic; both are related to other Celtic languages still spoken in parts of Wales and the French province of Brittany.

56. In traditional Irish society, bards had an honored place as poets, scholars, and keepers of the collective memory.

57. A former critic of Charles's policies in the House of Commons until elevated to high office, Wentworth earned the wrath of Puritans by forcing Scottish Presbyterian settlers in Ulster to swear an oath not to adhere to the Scottish Covenant of 1638.

58. Seventeenth-century English writers frequently compared the "wild" Irish to the "savage" natives of North America.

59. See note 57.

60. Most sensational was the charge that Strafford and the king had planned to use the Irish troops he formerly commanded against Protestant Englishmen. In fact, there was talk of bringing the Irish army to Scotland, not England.

61. Michael B. Young (see bibliography) sees Charles's unwillingness to be bound by his promises as his "fatal flaw."

62. Bills of impeachment came from Commons; there was no precedent for accepting a bill from the king.

63. Cromwell was granted exemption from the so-called Self-Denying Ordinance of 1645, by which all currently serving officers had to resign their commissions.

64. Comparable to that approved by the Synod of Dordrecht in the Dutch Republic (Chapter 10).

65. See above, note 35.

66. Not even the Levellers disputed the common belief that a man of no prop-

erty was a man whose vote could be bought by the rich and the powerful. Hence, they kept the idea of a property qualification for voting but set it at a lower level. There was no discussion of female suffrage.

67. Mockingly nicknamed the Barebones Parliament after one of its members, whose Puritan parents had named him Praise-God Barebones.

68. Dismissed by Cromwell in 1653, see above.

69. Chapter 5.

70. General Baptists held that Christ died to atone for the sins of all men (this implied human free will), Particular Baptists held that Christ died only for the sins of those elected to salvation (this implied Calvin's doctrine of double predestination).

71. For example, the "Digger" movement led by Gerrard Winstanley, whose effort to have landless men till common land owned by two villages was broken up by local authorities (1649).

72. It was Cromwell who ended (1654) the ban on Jewish settlement in England, which dated back to the 1290s.

73. From 1646 to 1649 the national church was Presbyterian.

74. Above, note 67.

75. The legal status of Protestant Dissenters was further improved by the Toleration Act of 1689, following the so-called Glorious Revolution in which King James II (ruled 1685–1688), Charles II's Catholic son, was overthrown in favor of James's Protestant sister Mary and her husband, Prince William of Orange.

PART IV

1. The Latin *societas* is an abstract noun formed from *socius*, meaning "ally." The Latin *communitas* is an abstract noun formed from *cum* ("with") and either *munio* ("fortification" or "city wall") or *munus* ("office" or "function"). In other words, the root meaning is "being walled in together" or "sharing the same responsibilities."

2. In medieval political discourse the whole kingdom was said to make up a community. In England, for example, Parliament was seen as representing the *communitas regni*, the community of the realm.

3. For the German sociologist Ferdinand Tönnies (1855–1936) and his 1912 essay on *Gemeinschaft und Gesellschaft* (*Community and Society*), see Werner Cahnman in the bibliography.

4. Pocock (bibliography) chronicles the subsequent history of Machiavelli's belief that the chances for a popular form of government are better where the army is an army of the people.

5. People form a class in Marx's sense if they have a common relationship to the "means of production" (e.g., land in an agrarian society). They form a status group if recognized by contemporaries as having the same rank in the social pecking order.

6. Judges were firmly Catholic, magistrates often Protestant. For politically based religious division in Switzerland, see Chapter 6.

7. See Natalie Davis, Philip Benedict (bibliography). New guilds like the printers (Lyon) or the bonnet makers (Rouen) were the ones attracted to new religious doctrines.

8. The German word was *gemeinde,* formed from the adjective *gemein* ("common"). In the sixteenth century there was no word for "society" in the modern, impersonal sense of the term.

CHAPTER 12

1. In urbanized regions like Flanders and Lombardy from 20 to 40 percent of the people lived in cities; in Poland and parts of Germany the figure was as low as 5 percent. Many of the agricultural innovations of this period—such as the enhancement of soil fertility through mixed farming—were pioneered in the urbanized regions.

2. Cologne, Germany's most important religious center, was quite exceptional in that as many as 10 percent of its estimated 40,000 people around 1500 were priests or members of religious orders.

3. See Chapter 3.

4. In literature by and for the nobles, comparisons with horse-breeding were common.

5. Some indeed had ancestors among the landholding families of Roman times or high-ranking members of the various German tribes that established kingdoms in Europe, but most were descended from upstart adventurers of more recent centuries.

6. The words for armed horsemen also meant lesser members of the nobility: *equites* in Latin, *chevaliers* in French, *caballeros* in Spanish, *Ritter* in German, *knights* in English.

7. Pioneered by Swiss pikemen and by the archers who won England's victories in the Hundred Years' War.

8. The French distinguished between the old or "sword" nobles and the new "robe" nobility (cf. the judge's robe of office).

9. Endowments were made by gifts of land; the beneficiary was entitled to whatever revenue came from peasants working the land.

10. Meaning they could document the noble pedigree of all their ancestors going back four generations.

11. The French word *paysans,* from which the English word comes, means "those who dwell in the *pays,*" meaning "the countryside."

12. The Latin *servus,* from which the French (and English) word serf is derived, means "a slave."

13. The demesne was the portion of the estate farmed for the profit of the lord; serfs cultivated the demesne as well as their own parcels of land.

14. Hence the German proverb, "city air makes free"—many towns undertook to protect serfs who lived within their walls for more than a year against the claims of former lords.

15. The plague occurred 1347–1349; in areas that have been studied as much as one-third of the population perished within the space of a few months.

16. Thus Zwingli's teachings on "godly law" (Chapter 5) unintentionally echoed an existing tradition of peasant protest.

17. Jan De Vries (see bibliography) estimates the population of Latin Christendom at 75,000,000 to 80,000,000 in 1347, 60,900,000 in 1500, and 122,200,000 in 1600.

18. The Czech word for labor service was *robot*. The perfunctory quality of un-free labor gave rise to the word's modern meaning.

19. Chapter 9, p. 161.

20. Known as "yeomen" in England, *laboreurs* in France.

21. Chapter 8, p. 125.

22. In the so-called open-field system, common all across the plains of northern Europe, each cultivator was assigned small strips scattered across the manor's fields. This made economic sense in the early Middle Ages, when peasants had to pool their resources to buy a plough team, but not in later centuries.

23. By woolen manufacturers in Flanders and Italy.

24. Meaning that each child was entitled to an equal share; alternatives were pri-mogeniture (the first son gets the major share) and ultimogeniture (the last son gets the major share).

25. At Bordeaux in southwestern France, the walled city of the early Middle Ages occupied approximately one-thirtieth of the area once enclosed by the Roman wall of the third century.

26. On the empire's prince-bishops, see Chapter 1.

27. The Latin term is *meliores.*

28. Some communes, like Milan's, grew out of conflicts between local religious reformers and the city's prince-bishop during the era of the investiture controversy (Chapter 1, pp. 3–4).

29. In some Swiss and south German towns, male citizens were required to re-peat the founding oath on an annual "swear day."

30. "Consul" is a term of Roman origin.

31. *Alcalde* (mayor) is of Arabic origin.

32. "Aldermen" is an English term. The equivalent term in other languages (Dutch, French, German) comes from the Latin *scabinus,* meaning a man important enough to have a cushion to sit on.

33. In ancient Rome, men of "patrician" families were automatically members of the senate; all other free citizens were known as "plebeians."

34. For example, the ruler's refusal to grant local merchants freedom from tolls.

35. Chapter 15; Marco Polo's *Travels* tell the story of a young Venetian who made the trip in the 1270s.

36. Unlike sailing ships of the era after about 1450, oared galleys usually stayed within sight of land.

37. The Florentine banking house of Bardi and Peruzzi, which went bankrupt after England's King Edward III defaulted on his debts in 1341, was richer by far than the later and more famous Medici.

38. Pisa rebelled in 1494; Florence conquered it again in 1509.

39. Penetration of the Baltic (1400–1450) was the first great step in the growth of Holland's merchant marine.

40. See Chester Starr (for Athens) and K. N. Chaudhuri (bibliography): the lat-ter suggests that the "armed trading" of Europe's merchant empires in Asia after 1500 emulated Venetian precedents.

41. Craft guilds were found in many parts of the world; those in Europe seem to have had an unusual degree of autonomy.

42. Quality was of interest to the city because products like silverware and bolts of woolen cloth had town trademarks.

43. Merchants importing leather did not sell the shoes made by cobblers, but it was often the wool-importers who sold the finished woolens, giving them an interest in keeping artisan wages low.

44. Magnates claimed the right to avenge any and all injuries to any member of their extended family; their constant feuding dotted the cites with family fortresses, marked by tall towers from which boiling oil could be poured on besieging enemies. When the *popolo* took over the commune, these towers were torn down.

45. "Popolo" meant "the people," but not in an inclusive sense: workers not permitted to form guilds (like the wool-carders of Florence—see below) were not members of the *popolo*.

46. Like the Visconti of Milan: Chapter 8, p. 125.

47. When the Medici first took over.

48. One of the contested issues was the rate of interest for Florence's public debt, held by wealthy families, but financed from sales taxes that fell more heavily on the less wealthy.

49. In Florence, ruling boards chosen by lot necessarily included some ordinary guildsmen, but the boards made no important decisions without consulting an ad-hoc assembly of the city's political elite: see the splendid study by Gene Brucker (bibliography).

50. Fullers trod on the cloth passing through water-troughs to give the fabric an even finish by closing gaps between the warp and the woof. The water-powered fulling mills coming into use elsewhere did not provide the quality Ghent's fine woolens required.

51. Partly because travel was imperiled by the breakup of the Mongol empire founded by Genghis Khan (Chapter 15).

52. Fustian is a combination of linen and cotton.

53. Previously, the main qualification for becoming a master was to produce a "master work" of the craft that met the exacting standards of guild members. Only a master had his own shop.

54. In the late Middle Ages journeymen organized strikes, and masters blacklisted activist journeymen. Associations of journeymen, not the guilds, are the forerunners of modern unions.

55. Portugal's African adventures began with the conquest of Ceuta (Morocco) in 1415, a reawakening of the Reconquest, a centuries-old Iberian Christian tradition of warfare against peninsular Muslims originally from Morocco (Chapter 15).

56. In India's ports the bankers were often Hindu, the merchant-shippers Muslim.

57. Pumps drained water from deep-tunnel mines previously closed because of seepage, and new refining methods produced a higher-grade copper.

58. The price ratio of copper to silver was higher in India.

59. In this area the ruler had the right (never exercised by the Habsburgs themselves) to purchase ore coming out of the mine at slightly less than market value.

60. Mariners found better winds by sailing southwest from Lisbon rather than by sailing directly south along the African coast.

61. Chapter 8, p. 134.

62. Citizens (burghers) had well-defined privileges, not necessarily including the right to vote in local elections.

63. According to canon law, a cleric was a man who had been ordained as a sub-deacon or a deacon (the two highest of the so-called minor orders of the priest-hood) or as a priest. Monks and friars were not clerics unless ordained (many were not).

64. Chapter 3, note 23.

65. Above, note 10.

66. As developed in canon law since the thirteenth century, a corporation was a body (*corpus*) whose members were bound by the decisions of its head; heads came and went, the body never died.

67. The bishop was the celebrated philosopher, theologian, and would-be church reformer, Nicholas Cusanus (1401–1464). Archduke Sigismund (d. 1489) was the uncle of Emperor Maximilian. I.

68. Things like burial fees mattered to an ill-paid parish vicar.

69. There is evidence, at least for the sixteenth century, that men in some areas saw a priest with a "second-class wife" as one who would leave their own wives alone.

70. For original sin, Chapter 3, note 12. The doctrine of the Immaculate Concep-tion, that Mary was conceived without original sin, was opposed by St. Thomas Aquinas (d. 1274), a Dominican; favored by St. Bonaventure, a Franciscan (d. 1274); and proclaimed as a doctrine of the Catholic Church by Pope Pius IX (1854).

71. After the conversion of Constantine, the tax exemptions of temple priest-hoods were granted to Christian clergy.

72. The church claimed authority in cases relating to the sacraments (including matrimony) and oaths to God (used also in wills).

73. Many religious communities grew their own wine or brewed their own beer; taverns were an outlet for surplus production.

74. Creditors haled their debtors before church courts because of the oaths in-volved in loan contracts. Because moneylending was one of the activities from which Jews were not prohibited in engaging, moneylenders in some areas were of-ten Jewish.

75. Monasteries that had enserfed their peasants were centers for the Peasants' War, partly inspired by Protestant ideas; in a rural part of the canton of Bern, how-ever, peasants took up arms against their Protestant government (1528) for its sup-pression of a monastery known for its aid to the local poor.

76. Chapter 7, note 36. Prosecutions by the Inquisition for speaking against the clergy were infrequent.

77. Through coitus interruptus and through long periods of lactation, during which nursing mothers were less fertile.

78. Crucial documentation, such as town census records and parish birth and marriage registers, is available only sporadically from the late medieval centuries, hardly at all from earlier periods.

79. Cosimo de Medici (ruled 1434–1464) capitalized on this social need by cre-ating a hugely successful "bank of dowries." Parents of infant daughters invested

a sum that was returned with interest if she married at fifteen or later; if the girl died or did not marry, the investment was forfeit to the city treasury.

80. E.g., to feed a "family" enlarged by the presence of journeymen who could not afford to live independently and to exploit more intensely the family's small plot of ground.

81. Compare Burckhardt (chapter 1, note 23) with Alan Macfarlane and Aron Gurevich (bibliography).

82. See below, note 84.

83. Wealthy churchmen and other donors and confraternities had small chapels built against the interior of the outer wall.

84. The nave was the main body of the church, the space for lay people. The raised chancel, in front where the altar stood, was for the clergy. Nave and chancel were often divided by altar screens.

85. "Pax" is the Latin word for peace.

86. The domestication of grains.

87. High curtain walls of this era were in fact vulnerable to new-style siege artillery.

88. For the longbow, the crossbow, or the arquebus, a primitive rifle; these guilds were common in Germany and the Low Countries.

89. Chapter 3, note 25.

90. Regulating what people of different classes could spend on clothing or for family occasions, e.g., only men of patrician families were allowed to wear fur hats.

91. Receipts were often used not just for the city's needs, but also to pay the town's quota in subsidies demanded by the ruler.

92. This is the process to which historians of Germany in particular now refer to as "confessionalization." See Chapter 12.

CHAPTER 13

1. The historian who first made this point was Bernd Moeller (see bibliography).

2. Especially Luther's Augustinian Friars.

3. Famous mendicant preachers found an audience even if they spoke in Latin or Italian rather than in German. Near the north portal of St. Stephen's Cathedral in Vienna is a later monument to popular sermons preached here in the fifteenth century by the Italian Franciscan, St. Giovanni Capistrano.

4. Peter Blickle (see bibliography).

5. Chapter 5, pp. 66–67.

6. In German, Karsthans.

7. There is some danger in lumping townsfolk and peasants together, but scholars are now inclined to think we have erred by overstressing the differences between town and countryside. Urban-rural alliances formed during the Peasants' War show that less fortunate burghers and peasants had many of the same grievances.

8. Chapter 5, note 5.

9. Miriam Chrisman (see bibliography).

10. Erasmus sometimes referred to religious orders as "sects" (*sectae* in Latin), a term originally used by ancient writers to refer to rival schools of philosophers.

11. Thomas Brady's work on Strasbourg (see bibliography) illustrates this contrast.

12. Constance's Reformation preacher, Ambrosius Blarer (d. 1564), was the son of a town councillor. His brother Thomas (d. 1567), who had studied under Luther at Wittenberg, was a town councillor and later a burgomaster.

13. Chapter 5, pp. 57, 68.

14. This was the nephew and successor of Elector Frederick the Wise, Elector John, who ruled a part of the territory (including Zwickau) before succeeding his uncle in 1525.

15. Chapter 10, p 169.

16. Another reason was the French pensions for Swiss magistrates. The victory of Switzerland's forest cantons at Morgarten (1315) had effectively ended Habsburg control of the region.

17. Two important free cities were "mediatized" (subjected to princely rule), Mainz by its prince-archbishop in 1460, Reutlingen by the duke of Württemberg in 1519.

18. Following the First Schmalkaldic War (1547), Charles did force several Protestant imperial cities to reopen some churches to Catholic worship. See the discussion of Augsburg, Chapter 15.

19. Catholic Cologne is also an exception that proves the rule for conflict between cities and princes. Two prince-archbishops tried to introduce the Reformation: Hermann von Wied, who was deposed by Charles V and his army at the same time that he dealt with the duke of Cleves (Chapter 8, p. 139–140), and Gebhard Truchsess von Waldburg, who was forced to resign in favor of Ernest of Bavaria (Chapter 9, p. 160). Both times the city opposed the prince-archbishop's efforts to change its religious identity.

20. Both were men of exalted families. Prince-archbishop Christopher of Bremen was the younger brother of the duke of Braunschweig-Wolfenbüttel; Prince-archbishop Albert of Magdeburg (also cardinal-prince-archbishop of Mainz and prince-bishop of Halberstadt) was the younger brother of the elector of Brandenburg.

21. Chapter 8, p. 139.

22. E.g., by his confiscation of church properties, where some of the important salt-works were located.

23. Chapter 12, p. 221.

24. That is, followers of Martin Luther.

25. Chapter 10, p. 171. The money the city lent to Gustavus Vasa was in part borrowed from its own burghers.

26. See Chapter 14.

27. See Chapter 6, p. 83.

28. High German was based on the language of Luther's German Bible. Low German (in German, Plattdeusch) was a family of languages closer to the Netherlandish dialects than to High German.

29. For these Jesuit-inspired lay groups, see Chapter 14.

30. A broadside (e.g., Figure 13.4) was a one-page sheet with an illustration (often very elaborate) and a few lines of explanatory text.

31. Note that in Protestant rites the laity as well as the minister received the blessed wine.

32. Chapter 3, note 11.

33. For example, Luther saw Zwinglian zeal for "cleansing" the churches of religious images as a new form of works-righteousness (Chapter 5, pp. 59–60).

34. Chapter 5, note 5.

35. The sign of the cross is an ancient Christian prayer, used often in worship: "In the name of the Father, the Son, and the Holy Spirit."

36. Palm Sunday is the Sunday before Easter, commemorating the gospel story of people strewing palm fronds before Jesus as He entered Jerusalem.

37. See below for medieval Catholic marriage law.

38. For the formal rite of exorcism, reserved for cases when it is thought someone may be "possessed" by the devil, see Chapter 14.

39. Chapter 5, p. 57.

40. To the point at which priest and people prayed, echoing passages from the Gospels, "Holy, holy, holy! Lord, God of Hosts! Heaven and earth are full of your glory. Blessed is He that comes in the name of the Lord."

41. Apparently dating from the thirteenth century.

42. The main altar, as distinct from the altars used by chantry priests; in many parishes it would be richly decorated and set atop a platform of steps in the chancel.

43. This is another example of the difference alluded to above—for Zwingli, not for Luther, scripture was a form of law.

44. One name may suffice: Johann Sebastian Bach (1685–1750).

45. Zwingli made this analogy between the Jewish and Christian covenants as one of his arguments (against the Anabaptists) for keeping infant baptism.

46. This practice stemmed from medieval Catholic belief in limbo, a forlorn place in the afterlife for infants who had committed no sin of their own but had not been cleansed by baptism from the stain of original sin.

47. English Puritan wishes to relegate the altar table to a lesser place (Chapter 11, note 15) echoed the practice of Zurich, where it was normally set against the side wall.

48. Chapter 6, p. 74.

49. Children learned by rote, and teachers did not spare the rod or the paddle. In late medieval Germany, the schoolmaster is sometimes referred to in town records as "the ass-drummer."

50. Such as the *ABC des Simples Gens* (*ABC for Simple Folk*) of the Paris theologian Jean Gerson (1365–1429), and the *Christenspiegel* (*Mirror for Christians*) of the Franciscan circuit-preacher Dietrich von Kolde (1435–1515). Topics for these works, as for Luther's *Catechisms*, included the Ten Commandments, the Apostles Creed, and the Our Father.

51. The administrators were often appointed by the council, rather than by the parish or the heirs of the founders.

52. The friars were originally part of a spiritual movement that idealized the poverty of Christ and the apostles: Chapter 1, p. 4.

53. Lorenzo Valla: see Chapter 2, p. 15.
54. *De Subventione Pauperum* (*On the Subvention of the Poor*), 1526.
55. See chapter 14.
56. Reflecting traditional views, Vives in his treatise praised the voluntary poverty of the religious orders as a holy state.
57. The vows taken by members of religious orders—poverty, chastity, and obedience—were also referred to as "evangelical counsels," that is, things Jesus had recommended for those who wished to be perfect, but not commanded for all. The Reformers denied any such distinction among Christians.
58. A small city plus the eleven villages included within the bounds of its parish church.
59. The religious houses stormed by angry crowds during the 1520s were often, as in Strasbourg, Franciscan.
60. In Luther's view, the Christian does good works not as needful for salvation, but out of gratitude for God's mercy.
61. In Calvin's Geneva church order of 1541, the deacons of each parish were responsible for upkeep of the poor, just as in New Testament times ("deacon" comes from a Greek word meaning "servant").
62. Amsterdam's was the first (1596).
63. See Chapter 12, pp. 234–235.
64. See above, note 57. Chastity too was one of the "evangelical counsels."
65. Some canon lawyers argued that a valid marriage required sexual consummation as well as a promise of marriage freely exchanged by the parties, but a twelfth-century pope ruled against this opinion.
66. Announcement of the impending marriage from the pulpit of the bride's church on three successive Sundays, inviting anyone who knows of any impediment to the marriage (e.g., kinship between the couple within the degrees forbidden by canon law) to come forward.
67. Katherine von Bora.
68. *Hexe* is the German word for "witch."
69. Diana is the Roman goddess of the moon.
70. In Latin, *maleficia; maleficus* and *malefica* were the words for male and female witches.
71. *Malleus Maleficarum,* (*The Hammer of [Female] Witches*).
72. Brian Levack (see bibliography) gives an aggregate estimate of 75 percent.
73. *Maleficium* (note 70) was a capital crime in civil law, based on ancient Roman law; church courts did not have power of life and death.
74. Alan Macfarlane and Mary Douglas: see bibliography.
75. The person most likely to be accused of witchcraft was a poor older woman living alone—as in "Little Red Riding Hood."
76. The usual punishment.
77. Exod. 22:18.
78. Wittenberg (Electoral Saxony), Tübingen (Württemberg), and Heidelberg (the Palatinate) fall in the former category, Marburg in Hesse (1527), Königsberg in East Prussia (1544), and Jena in John Frederick's Ducal Saxony (1558) in the latter.
79. These seminaries, however, were not created in many places until the seventeenth century; Trent ordered bishops to create these new faculties of theol-

ogy but did not give them the resources to do so. Here, too, as in Protestant lands, reform of the clergy depended on active collaboration from the civil government.

80. Strasbourg had about 20,000 people in the 1520s, as compared with 5,000 for Zurich (the city), and a larger population of dissidents, including Anabaptists. For Bucer's complaints against the magistrates of Strasbourg, Chapter 6, pp. 87–88.

81. Individual confession of sins to the pastor (albeit not so detailed as in Catholic practice) was characteristic of the Lutheran as distinct from the Reformed Reformation.

82. This order was drafted by Johannes Brenz (1499–1570) and copied in a number of other Lutheran territories.

83. I have a letter from the priest of the parish of Carralacky in Kilmovee (Ireland) attesting to the good character of my mother's mother, Katherine Horkan, who came to the United States in 1882.

84. This paragraph simplifies a very complex discussion: see the bibliography for studies by Gerald Strauss and James Kittelson.

85. The Schmalkaldic League, open only to governments accepting the Augsburg Confession (chapter 6, p. 80), seemed to afford more protection against a Catholic emperor than a much smaller alliance of cities based on Zurich.

86. Chapter 6, p. 93.

87. The Catholic practice of praying for the dead—implying the existence of purgatory—was excised from Reformation liturgies. Prof. Willem Frijhoff (Free University of Amsterdam) stressed the idea of "appropriation" in a recent conference paper at the University of Minnesota.

88. Ibn Khaldun (1332–1406), *The* Muqaddimah: *An Introduction to History*, translated by Franz Rosenthal, abridged by N. J. Dawoud (Princeton: Princeton Univerisity Press, 1967), 127.

CHAPTER 14

1. Chapter 12, pp. 224–225.

2. E.g., the Cevennes region of southern France (north of Nîmes) and around Aalst in eastern Flanders.

3. Chapter 6, p. 94.

4. Under Heinrich Bullinger (d. 1575), Zurich too was a command post for the international Reformed movement. For struggling churches in Catholic lands (such as the Low Countries before 1572), differences between Zurich and Geneva were not of great importance.

5. Continental Protestants, especially from the Low Countries, had important refugee churches in London (under Edward VI, and again under Elizabeth I) as well as in Emden (East Friesland).

6. Chapter 7, pp. 117–118.

7. For Jeanne d'Albret, Chapter 7, p. 109. Catholicism was tolerated in Béarn after Henry IV's conversion (1593), and became the official religion when Béarn was conquered and annexed to the French crown (1620).

8. Among the more important nobles families it was common to arrange marriages across political boundaries.

9. Estimated for 1550 at 19,000,000.

10. Chapter 7, p. 112. In Holland, where the rebellion against Spain gained its key foothold, noble families were relatively few.

11. Chapter 8, note 59. The Habsburgs recovered central Hungary after the failure of the second and last Ottoman siege of Vienna (1683).

12. Chapter 9, p. 146.

13. Chapter 7, p. 116; Chapter 9, p. 158.

14. For examples in the Netherlands, Sherrin Marshall (bibliography).

15. Note that lending money to Charles V (see Chapter 8) was an important business for bankers in all of these cities except Lyon. The Fuggers were leaders of Augsburg's Catholic minority.

16. Chapter 7, pp. 112–113.

17. I.e., under persecution—a term used by Calvinists.

18. A term used by Johan Decavele (bibliography).

19. Not at this time; the radical Calvinist movement of the 1570s (chapter 9, p. 155) won support among guildsmen by restoring guild participation in city government, abolished by Charles V in 1540.

20. As distinct from the followers of a popular pastor, backed by the magistrates, who rejected some Calvinist teachings.

21. Chapter 13, p. 241.

22. This explanation was first put forward by Natalie Zemon Davis (see bibliography).

23. Such descriptions have to be taken with a grain of salt because writers of respectable background routinely attributed acts of violence to the poor. Also, some iconoclasm was carefully organized. In the Low Countries in 1566 (Chapter 7), image breakers were sometimes paid by the hour by radical Calvinist preachers.

24. Denis Crouzet (see bibliography) notes that this area was repeatedly crisscrossed by a popular apocalyptic preacher in the previous generation (1518–1528).

25. Including the agitator-preachers who sparked the iconoclastic riots of 1566 (above, note 23).

26. Chapter 7, note 26.

27. Associated with the Catholic doctrine that the mass is a representation of Christ's sacrifice on the cross: see Chapter 11, note 15.

28. Extreme unction (the last anointing) was one of the seven Catholic sacraments.

29. These laymen were known as "consolers of the sick" (*ziekentroosters*) in the Dutch Reformed Church.

30. See Chapter 6 for this key difference between Geneva and Zurich.

31. Chapter 6, p. 94.

32. See Chapter 7 for the Dutch distinction between members and sympathizers.

33. In France, Scotland, and the Dutch Republic—not in Germany, where, as in the Palatinate (Chapter 7), disciplinary powers were vested in councils appointed by the ruler.

34. Usually held four times a year.

35. Even today, declaring bankruptcy carries much more of a social stigma in Europe (not just in formerly Calvinist countries) than it does in the United States.

36. Jan Łaski (1499—1560); for Emden's defiance of its Lutheran ruler in the 1590s, Chapter 13, p. 259.

37. They worshiped in the bishop's cathedral, protected by successive truces in France's Religious Wars.

38. Meaning an ability to foretell the future, as in the case of a well-known preacher who predicted the manner of his dying.

39. One of Calvin's closest collaborators.

40. Chapter 7, pp. 114–115.

41. E.g., Dordrecht and Gouda, both in Holland. Where magistrates were divided on religion, as in most Holland cities, the church achieved an intermediate position, neither so strong as in Dordrecht nor so weak as in Gouda. This point is made in a fine dissertation by John Paul Elliott (Columbia University, 1990).

42. Out of respect for Calvinist norms, civil authorities banned drinking on Sundays, except for travelers; but Dutch townsfolk became "travelers" by strolling out to the nearest village tavern.

43. Said to be a desideratum of a good sermon, according to Dutch Calvinists.

44. Perhaps especially so in an age of sensory overstimulation and shortened attention spans.

45. The script has been "cracked" by Robert M. Kingdon and his students.

46. E.g., censure of church members for dancing, card-playing, or wearing clothing thought to be suggestive.

47. Heinz Schilling (see Bibliography) notes that the standard for sexual behavior was decidedly a double standard.

48. Known as kirk sessions in Scotland, church councils (*kerkeraaden*) in the Netherlands.

49. A backless four-legged stool, sometimes so constructed than the sinner who failed to sit bolt upright would topple over.

50. Reputation was a person's most precious asset; among other things, one's financial credit ("believability") depended on it.

51. See Norbert Elias (Bibliography) for a discussion of the growing social and cultural pressures to live according to proper "civilized" or "bourgeois" norms.

52. Chapter 12, pp. 220, 224.

53. Max Weber (see Bibliography) could not have imagined a day when the gross national product for historically Catholic Italy would rank ahead of that for England, a historically Protestant country of roughly the same population.

54. E.g., English Puritan diaries and spiritual handbooks, of which the most famous is John Bunyan's *Pilgrim's Progress* (1678).

55. Dillingen (1551), Würzburg (by 1582), and Graz (1588).

56. This point is made by Prof. Jaimé Contreras (Madrid) in a paper for a recent conference at the University of Minnesota.

57. The dean, usually a pastor himself, was designated by the bishop as presiding officer, with some judicial responsibilities, for a district encompassing a number of parishes. In some areas deans "visited" each of the parishes in their district annually.

58. Mostly for morals offenses: Chapter 7, note 35.

59. The language of Galicia resembles Portuguese, not Spanish.

60. E.g., in civic and religious processions, discussed below.

61. In 1584: see Chapter 9, p. 6.

62. In 1566: see Chapter 7, note 27.

63. See Marc Foster on the prince-bishopric of Speyer (bibliography).

64. "Ascetic" comes from a Greek word for athletic training. Christian asceticism, a disciplining of the body for spiritual aims, derives from the monastic movement, which began when St. Anthony (d. 255) chose to live as a hermit in the Egyptian desert.

65. For Spain's "New Christians," see Chapter 15.

66. Known as the Discalced Carmelites—those not allowed to wear shoes, only sandals.

67. Pierre Favre and Claude Jay.

68. Chapter 9, p. 150.

69. Author of *Introduction to the Devout Life.*

70. Cf. Angela Merici's Company of St. Ursula: Chapter 7, p. 100.

71. The canonical age limit for an abbess was seventeen.

72. Demanding to know why they could not see her except at newly appointed visiting hours, they were told: "Mother Angelica [her religious name] was not consulted by her family when they made her a nun; why should she consult them if she decides to be one?"

73. In the United States, the Charities are known as the Vincent de Paul Society, and the order of priests as the Vincentians.

74. Michel de Marillac (d. 1632) was the leader of those dismissed from the council in 1630: chapter 9, p. 163.

75. Of those mentioned in the previous two paragraphs, the church canonized Sts. Teresa of Avila, Ignatius Loyola, Francis Xavier, Francis de Sales, Jeanne Françoise de Chantal, Vincent de Paul, and Louise de Marillac.

76. For the earlier oratories, Chapter 7, pp. 99–100. Shown a genealogy claiming to prove his noble descent, Neri tore it up.

77. Chapter 7, pp. 97–98.

78. Even before pews were installed in Dutch Calvinist churches, there were hired "chair-keepers" who jealously guarded the front-row chairs picked by their employers.

79. But not the poor: Italian confraternity regulations banned the frequenting of taverns—the normal way of drinking for those who could not afford to lay in their own stocks of wine.

80. It is estimated that the population of the valley of Mexico declined from around 20,000,000 before the conquest to around 1,000,000 a century later, mainly due to the deadly smallpox virus.

81. Astronomers knew the solar year was minutes shorter than the $365\frac{1}{4}$-day Julian or Roman calendar. Some Protestant lands did not accept this papal "theft" of time until the eighteenth century.

82. Galileo supported the heliocentric theory of Nicholas Copernicus (d. 1543) with mathematical arguments and by observations of the heavens with a telescope. He drew the unfavorable notice of church authorities by saying that biblical passages referring to the sun as "rising" must be metaphorical. He was placed under

house arrest after disobeying an order not to write about Copernicus's theory as fact.

83. The Council of Trent authorized bishops to "visit" all confraternities (1562), even those run by laymen, and Pope Clement VIII decreed that any new confraternity must be approved by the clergy (1604). These pronouncements effectively ended an era of lay initiative in founding and controlling confraternities.

84. Gabriele Paleotti, bishop from 1566 to 1597.

85. Chapter 2, note 8.

86. For overseas missions, see Chapter 15. One French priest described a forlorn island off the Breton coast as part of Canada.

87. Such as St. Bernardino of Siena (Chapter 3, p. 35).

88. See chapter 3, p. 37 and Chapter 4, p. 49.

89. Chapter 7, p. 101.

90. Saint-Cyran and Jansen were classmates at Louvain. The most famous document of the anti-Jesuit campaign is the *Provincial Letters* of Blaise Pascal (d. 1662), a great mathematician (he invented probability theory) and devout Jansenist.

91. Chapter 9, p. 166.

92. Mirroring urban society also in frequent lawsuits and outbreaks of fisticuffs over which group marched ahead of which.

93. In a work unfortunately not available in English, Willem Frijhoff (Bibliography) touches on Calvinist miracle belief.

94. Chapter 13, pp. 254–256.

95. Jewish belief involved possession not by the devil but by wandering spirits of the dead: see J. H. Chayes (bibliography).

96. Chapter 10, p. 180. Canisius, later canonized, was the son of a man often chosen as mayor in the Netherlands city of Nijmegen.

97. William Christian (bibliography) first proposed this idea.

98. This suggestion is made by Wolfgang Reinhard (bibliography).

99. *Doopsgezind,* the term still used in the Netherlands.

100. Chapter 6, p. 84.

101. When Haarlem's Reformed split in two congregations just prior to the Calvinist victory at Dordrecht (1618), the magistrates backed the Remonstrants.

CHAPTER 15

1. World production of spices like cloves and nutmeg was based on parts of the Indonesian archipelago, controlled after about 1520 by Portugal, later by Philip II of Spain, who in 1580 became king of Portugal as well. The Dutch East India Company, chartered by the States General in 1602, soon wrested control of key fortified outposts in the region from the Dutch Republic's Iberian foes.

2. Islanders not yet reached by the spread of Islam in this region were converted to Catholicism by Portuguese Jesuits. Converted to Calvinism, they became key auxiliaries of the Dutch commercial empire, as they had been for the Portuguese.

3. On reaching Calicut on India's Malabar coast (1498), Vasco da Gama said, "We come seeking spices and Christians."

4. It was hard for Europeans to grasp that a people never spoken of by any of the ancient writers could have a capital larger and more orderly than any they had seen; Tenochtitlán, now Mexico City, had about 1,000,000 people at the time of the conquest.

5. Thomas More's *Utopia* (1516) purported to describe a far-off land whose people had learned to despise riches and live at peace. *Utopia* means "nowhere" in Greek, but the English humanist's satiric intent was not grasped by readers who made "utopia" a byword for the perfect society to be built somehow, somewhere. Ventures of this kind in the New World include the Franciscan mission at Santa Fe (New Mexico) and the Jesuit "resurrections" in Paraguay.

6. See below, page 290 of this chapter.

7. The long "Chinese Rites" controversy ended with a papal decision (1742) that Chinese Christians were henceforth to be forbidden to participate in the ceremonies Jesuits had approved.

8. Seventeenth-century Jesuit missionaries to China (see above) translated "Heaven" as "God," but modern scholars believe that in so doing they confused the impersonal force of Chinese tradition with the personal deity of biblical faith.

9. According to William Theodore De Bary (see bibliography), an alternate translation of the Chinese term in question is "the moral mind."

10. Chapter 2, pp. 14–15.

11. "Established" is not the right term, since the emperors also patronized Buddhist and T'aoist monasteries.

12. These five "commandments" are the so-called five pillars of Islam.

13. The earliest texts of Aristotle available in Europe (twelfth century) were translations not from the Greek, but from Arabic translations used in the then Muslim-ruled areas of Spain.

14. Chapter 4, pp. 52–53.

15. The word "Sufi" apparently comes from an Arabic term for the woolen cowl worn by Christian monks.

16. Erasmus was of the same opinion, at least in regard to the cult of certain saints; see his *Praise of Folly*.

17. The Talmud is a vast compilation of commentary on scripture and application of its teaching to daily life, put together by scholars living in southern Iraq in the first and second centuries of the Common Era.

18. Muslim invaders from North Africa conquered much of the peninsula in 711. In what is known as the *reconquista* (reconquest), Christian principalities in the far north slowly extended their rule to the south. By 1215, most of Iberia was controlled by the realms of Portugal, Castile, and Aragon. The latter two were united in the marriage (1476) between Isabella of Castile and Ferdinand of Aragon, but retained their separate identities. The last Muslim principality, Granada, was conquered by Castile in 1492.

19. Fantastic charges that Jews had poisoned the wells were a common feature of such attacks.

20. A heretic was a baptized person who rejected the teachings of the Church. Thus New Christians practicing Jewish rites were subject to prosecution as

heretics, but Jews were not. For the Inquisition's persecution of New Christians practicing Jewish rites, see Chapter 7, note 35.

21. Chapter 12, pp. 224–225.

22. Poland-Lithuania disappeared as its lands were divided up among more powerful neighbors—Prussia, Russia, and the Austrian Empire—in a series of three partitions between 1774 and 1795.

23. The True Cross is believed to have been discovered by St. Helena, the mother of Emperor Constantine I.

Bibliography

Abel, Wilhelm, *Agrarian Fluctuations in Europe: From the Thirteenth to the Twentieth Centuries*, trans. Olive Ordish (New York: St. Martin's Press, 1980).

Abray, Lorna Jane, *The People's Reformation: Magistrates, Clergy and Commons in Strasbourg, 1500–1598* (Ithaca, N.Y.: Cornell University Press, 1985).

Ady, C. M., *A History of Milan under the Sforza* (London: Methuen & Co., 1907).

Al-Yassini, Ayman, *Religion and State in the Kingdom of Saudi Arabia* (Boulder, Colo.: Westview Press, 1985).

Bainton, Roland H., "Katherine Zell," in *Women of the Reformation in Germany and Italy* (Boston: Beacon Press, 1974).

Bangs, Carl, *Arminius: A Study in the Dutch Reformation*, 2nd ed. (Grand Rapids, Mich.: F. Asbury Press, 1985).

Barbour, Hugh, *The Quakers in Puritan England* (Richmond, Ind.: Friends United Press, 1985).

Barnard, L. W., *The Graeco-Roman and Oriental Background of the Iconoclastic Controversy* (Leiden: Brill, 1974).

Baron, Salo Wittmayer, *Poland-Lithuania, 1500–1650*, vol. 16 of *A Social and Religions History of the Jews* (New York: Columbia University Press, 1952–1983).

Benecke, Gerhard, *Maximilian I, 1459–1519: An Analytical Biography* (London, Routledge & Kegan Paul, 1982).

Benedict, Philip, *Rouen during the Wars of Religion* (Cambridge: Cambridge University Press, 1981).

Bennett, Martyn, *The Civil Wars in Britain and Ireland, 1638–1651* (Oxford: Blackwell, 1997).

Bergendoff, Conrad, *The Church of the Lutheran Reformation: A Historical Survey of Lutheranism* (St. Louis: Concordia Publishing House, 1967).

Biel, Pamela, *Doorkeepers at the House of Righteousness: Heinrich Bullinger and the Zurich Clergy* (Bern: P. Lang 1991).

Bilinkoff, Jodi, *The Avila of St. Teresa: Religious Reform in Sixteenth-Century Spanish City* (Ithaca, N.Y.: Cornell University Press, 1989).

Bireley, Robert, S.J., *Religion and Politics in the Age of the Counter-Reformation: Emperor Ferdinand II, William Lamormaini, S.J., and the Formation of Imperial Policy* (Chapel Hill: University of North Carolina Press, 1981).

Black, Antony, *Council and Commune: The Conciliar Movement and the Fifteenth-Century Heritage* (London: Burns & Oats, 1979).

Black, Christopher F., *Italian Confraternities in the Sixteenth Century* (Cambridge: Cambridge University Press, 1989).

Blaschke, Karlheinz, *Sachsen im Zeitalter der Reformation* (Gütersloh: Gütersloher Verlaghaus, 1970).

Blickle, Peter, *Communal Reformation: The Quest for Salvation in Sixteenth-Century Germany*, trans. Thomas Dunlap (Atlantic Highlands, N.J.: Humanities Press, 1992). Published in German 1985.

———, *The Revolution of 1525*, trans. Thomas A. Brady, H. C. Erik Midelfort (Baltimore: Johns Hopkins University Press, 1977).

———, ed., *Landgemeinde und Stadtgemeinde im Mitteleuropa: ein Struktureller Vergleich* (Munich: Oldenbourg, 1991).

Bloch, Marc, *French Rural History: An Essay on Its Basic Characteristics*, trans. Janet Sondheimer (Berkeley: University of California Press, 1966).

Blumenthal, Uta-Renate, *The Investiture Controversy: Church and Monarchy, Ninth-Tenth Centuries* (Philadelphia: University of Pennsylvania Press, 1988).

Bonjour, E., H. S. Offler, and G. R. Potter, *A Short History of Switzerland* (reprint, Westport, Conn.: Greenwood Press, 1985).

Bonney, Richard, *The European Dynastic States, 1494–1660* (Oxford: Oxford University Press, 1991).

Bornert, René, *La Réforme Protestante du Culte à Strasbourg (1523–1598)* (Leiden: E. J. Brill, 1981).

Bossy, John, *Christianity in the West* (Oxford: Oxford University Press, 1985).

Bouwsma, William, *John Calvin: A Sixteenth-Century Portrait* (New York: Oxford University Press, 1988).

Bowker, Margaret, *The Secular Clergy in the Diocese of Lincoln, 1495–1520* (Cambridge: Cambridge University Press, 1968).

Boyle, Marjorie O'Rourke, *Erasmus' Civil Dispute with Luther* (Toronto: University of Toronto Press, 1985).

Brady, Thomas A. Jr., *Protestant Politics: Jacob Sturm and the German Reformation* (Atlantic Highlands, N.J.: Humanities Press, 1995).

———, *Ruling Class, Regime, and Reformation at Strasbourg, 1520–1555* (Leiden: E. J. Brill, 1978).

———, "Settlements: The Holy Roman Empire," in *Handbook of European History 1400–1600*, by Thomas A. Brady, Heiko A. Oberman, and James D. Tracy (Leiden): E. J. Parill, 1994; paperback, Grand Rapids, Mich.: W. B. (Eerdmans, 1995), 349–384.

———, *Turning Swiss: Cities and Empire, 1450–1550* (Cambridge: Cambridge University Press, 1985).

Brandi, Karl, *The Emperor Charles V*, trans. C. V. Wedgwood (1939; reprint, London, 1980).

Brecht, Martin, *Martin Luther*, trans. James Schaaf, 3 vols. (Philadelphia: Fortress Press, 1985–1993).

Brigden, Susan, *London and the Reformation* (Oxford: Oxford University Press, 1989).

Brucker, Gene, *The Civic World of Renaissance Florence* (Princeton, N.J.: Princeton University Press, 1977).

————, *Renaissance Florence* (New York: Wiley, 1969).

Brundage, James, *Sex, Law, and Marriage in the Middle Ages* (Aldershot: Variorum, 1993).

Brunner, Otto, *Land and Lordship: Structures of Governance in Medieval Austria* (Philadelphia: University of Pennsylvania Press, 1992).

Burkhardt, Jakob, *The Civilization of the Renaissance in Italy*, trans. S. G. C. Middlemore, 2 vol. (New York, 1958). Published in German, 1860.

Cahnman, Werner J., *Ferdinand Tönnies: A New Evaluation* (Leiden: Brill, 1973).

Cantor, Norman, *The Sacred Chain: The History of the Jews* (New York: Harper-Collins, 1994).

Carlton, Charles, *Archbishop William Laud* (London: Routledge & Kegan Paul, 1987).

Chajes, J. H., "Judgments Sweetened: Possession and Exorcism in Early Modern Jewish Culture," *Journal of Early Modern History* I (1997): 124–169.

Chatellier, Louis, *The Europe of the Devout* (Cambridge: Cambridge University Press, 1989).

————, *The Religion of the Poor: Rural Missions in Europe* (Cambridge: Cambridge University Press, 1997).

Chaudhuri, K. N., *Trade and Civilisation in the Indian Ocean* (Cambridge: Cambridge University Press, 1985).

Chevalier, Bernard, "France from Charles VII to Henry IV," *Handbook*, vol. I, 369–401.

————, *Les bonnes villes de France du XIIVe au XVIe siècle* (Paris: Aubier Montaigne, 1982).

Chiffoleau, Jacques, "La Religion Flamboyante," in *Du Christianisme flamboyant à l'aube des Lumières*, ed. Jacques Le Goff et al. (Paris, 1988), 11–183.

Chrisman, Miriam Usher, *Conflicting Visions of Reform: German Lay Propaganda Pamphlets, 1519–1530* (Atlantic Highlands, N.J.: Humanities Press, 1996).

————, *Lay Culture, Learned Culture in Strasbourg* (New Haven, Conn.: Yale University Press, 1982).

Christian, William, *Local Religion in Sixteenth-Century Spain* (Princeton: Princeton University Press, 1982).

Clasen, Claus-Peter, *The Palatinate in European History, 1559–1618* (Oxford: Blackwell, 1966).

Cliffe, J. T., *Puritans in Conflict: The Puritan Gentry during and after the Civil Wars* (London: Routledge, 1988).

Cohn, Henry J., "Territorial Princes in Germany's Second Reformation," in *International Calvinism, 1541–1715*, ed. Menna Prestwich (Oxford: Clarendon Press, 1985), 135–166.

Cohn, Samuel K., *Death and Property in Siena, 1200–1800: Strategies for the Afterlife* (Baltimore: Johns Hopkins University Press, 1988).

Collins, James B., *The State in Early Modern France* (Cambridge: Cambridge University Press, 1995).

Collins, Ross William, *Calvin and the Libertines of Geneva* (Toronto: Clarke, Irwin, 1968).

Collinson, Patrick, *The Elizabethan Puritan Movement* (Oxford: Oxford University Press, 1990).

————, *English Puritanism* (London: Historical Association, 1983).

Conrad, Franziska, *Reformation in der baüerlichen Gesellschaft* (Wiesbaden: F. Steiner, 1984).

Coward, Barry, *Oliver Cromwell* (London: Longman, 1991).

Croce, Benedetto, *History of the Kingdom of Naples* (Chicago: University of Chicago Press, 1970).

Crouzet, Denis, *Les Guerriers de Dieu: La violence au temps des troubles de religion*, 2 vols. (Seyssel: Champ Vallon, 1990).

Davis, Natalie Zemon, *Society and Culture in Early Modern France* (Stanford, Calif.: Stanford University Press, 1975).

Day, John, *The Medieval Market Economy* (Oxford: Blackwell, 1987).

De Bary, William Theodore, *The Liberal Tradition in China* (Hong Kong: Chinese University Press, 1983).

————, *Neo-Confucian Orthodoxy and the Learning of Mind-and-Heart* (New York: Columbia University Press, 1981).

Decavele, Johan, *De Dagraad van de Reformatie in Vlaanderen (1520–1565)* (Brussels: Paleis der Academien, 1975).

Delumeau, Jean, *Catholicism between Luther and Voltaire* (Philadelphia: Westminster Press, 1977).

————, *Sin and Fear: The Emergence of a Western Guilt Culture, Thirteenth–Eighteenth Century*, trans. Eric Nicholson (New York: St. Martin's, 1990). Published in French 1983.

De Roover, Raymond, *Money, Banking and Credit in Medieval Bruges* (Cambridge: Mass.: Medieval Academy of America, 1948).

Deursen, A. Th. van, *Plain Lives in a Golden Age: Popular Culture, Religion, and Society in Seventeenth-Century Holland*, trans. Maarten Ultee (Cambridge: Cambridge University Press, 1991).

Dickens, A. G., *The English Reformation*, 2d ed. (University Park: University of Pennsylvania Press, 1989).

Diefendorf, Barbara, *Beneath the Cross: Catholics and Huguenots in Sixteenth-Century Paris* (New York: Oxford University Press, 1991).

Diffelen, Roelof Willem van, *De Leer der Wahhabieten* (Leiden: E. J. Brill, 1927).

Dinur, Benzion, "The Origins of Hasidism and Its Social and Messianic Foundations," in David Hundert, ed., *Essential Papers on Hasidism* (New York: New York University Press, 1991), 95–168.

Dipple, Geoffrey, *Antifraternalism and Anticlericalism in the German Reformation* (London: Ashgate Publishing, 1996).

Dixon, C. Scott, *The Reformation and Rural Society* (Cambridge: Cambridge University Press, 1996).

Dollinger, Philippe, *The German Hansa* (Stanford: Stanford University Press, 1970).

Donaldson, Gordon, *The Scottish Reformation* (reprint, Cambridge, Cambridge University Press, 1979).

Douglas, Mary, *Natural Symbols* (New York: Routledge, 1996)

Duffy, Eamon, "The Parish of Salle," in *Official Religion and Lived Religion in the Early Modern World*, ed. James D. Tracy (forthcoming).

————, *The Stripping of the Altars: Traditional Religion in England, ca. 1400–ca. 1580* (New Haven, Conn.: Yale University Press, 1992).

Duke, A. C., *Reformation and Revolt in the Low Countries* (London: Hambledon Press, 1990).

Duplessis, Robert, *Lille in the Dutch Revolt* (Cambridge: Cambridge University Press, 1991).

Dykema, Peter A., and Heiko A. Oberman, eds., *Anticlericalism in Late Medieval and Early Modern Europe* (Leiden: E. J. Brill, 1993).

Ebeling, Gerhard, *Luther : An Introduction to His Thought* (London: Collins, 1970). Published in German 1964.

Edwards, Mark U., *Printing, Propaganda, and Martin Luther* (Berkeley: University of California Press, 1994).

Eire, Carlos M., *From Madrid to Purgatory. The Art and Craft of Dying in Sixteenth-Century Spain* (Cambridge: Cambridge University Press, 1995).

Elias, Norbert, *The Civilizing Process* (New York: Blackwells, 1994).

Elliott, John H., *Imperial Spain, 1516–1714* (New York: Penguin, 1990).

Elliott, John P., "Protestantization in the Northern Netherlands—A Case Study: The Classic Dordrecht, 1572–1640," Ph. D. diss., Columbia University, 1990.

Elton, Geoffrey R., *Reform and Reformation: England 1509–1558* (Cambridge, Mass.: Harvard University Press, 1977).

———, *The Tudor Revolution in Government* (Cambridge: Cambridge University Press, 1953).

Engels, Friedrich, *The Peasant War in Germany* (Moscow: Progress Publishers, 1977).

Epstein, Steven R., *Wage Labor and Guilds in Medieval Europe* (Chapel Hill: University of North Carolina Press, 1991).

Esser, Kajetan, *Origins of the Franciscan Order* (Chicago: 1970).

Estes, James M., ed., *Whether Secular Government Has the Right to Wield the Sword in Matters of Faith: A Controversy in Nurnberg in 1530* (Toronto: Centre for Reformation and Renaissance Studies, 1994).

———, *Christian Magistrate and State Church: The Reforming Career of Johannes Brenz* (Toronto: University of Toronto Press, 1982).

Evans, R. J. W., *The Making of the Habsburg Monarchy, 1550–1700* (Oxford: Oxford University Press, 1979).

Evans, R. J. W., and Trevor V. Thomas, eds., *Crown, Church and Estates: Central European Politics in the Sixteenth and Seventeenth Centuries* (New York: St. Martin's Press, 1991).

Farner, Oskar, *Zwingli the Reformer: His Life and Work,* trans. D. G. Sear (Hamden, Conn.: Archon Books, 1968).

Fernandez-Alvarez, Manuel, *Charles V* (London: Thames and Hudson, 1975).

Fernandez-Armesto, Felipe, *Ferdinand and Isabella* (London: Weidenfeld and Nicolson, 1975).

Fichtner, Paula Sutter, *Ferdinand I* (Boulder, Colo.: Eastern European Monographs, 1982).

Fischer-Galati, Stephen A., *Ottoman Imperialism and German Protestantism, 1521–1555* (reprint, New York: Octagon Books, 1972).

Fix, Andrew, *Prophecy and Reason: The Collegiants in the Early Enlightenment* (Princeton, N.J.: Princeton University Press, 1991).

Ford, Alan, *The Protestant Reformation in Ireland, 1590–1641* (Portland, Ore.: Four Courts Press, 1997).

Forell, Wolfgang, James McCue, and Wenzel Lohff, *Confessing One Faith: A Joint Commentary on the Augsburg Confession by Lutheran and Catholic Theologians* (Minneapolis, Minn.: Augsburg Publishing, 1982).

Forster, Marc, *The Counter-Reformation in the Villages* (Ithaca, N.Y.: Cornell University Press, 1992).

Fraser, Antonia, *The Gunpowder Plot* (London: Weidenfeld and Nicolson, 1996).

Friedman, Jerome, *Blasphemy, Immorality and Anarchy: The Ranters and the English Revolution* (Athens, Ohio: Ohio University Press, 1987).

———, *Michael Servetus: A Case Study in Total Heresy* (Geneva: Droz, 1978).

Friedrichs, Christopher R., *Urban Society in an Age of War: Nördlingen, 1580–1720* (Princeton, N.J.: Princeton University Press, 1979).

Frijhoff, Willem, *Wegen Van Evert Willemsz: Een Hollandse Weeskind op Zoek Naar Zichzelf, 1607–1647* (Nijmegen, 1995).

Ganoczy, Alexandre, *The Young Calvin*, trans. David Foxgrover and Wayne Provo (Virginia: Books International, 1994).

Genicot, L., *Rural Communes in the Low Countries in the Twelfth Century* (Baltimore: Johns Hopkins University Press, 1990).

Geremek, Bronislaw, *The Margins of Society in Late Medieval Paris* (Cambridge: Cambridge University Press, 1987).

Gerhard, Dietrich, *Old Europe: A Study in Continuity, 1000–1800* (New York: Academic Press, 1981).

Gernet, Jacques, *China and the Christian Impact* (Cambridge: Cambridge University Press, 1985).

Gero, Stephen, *Byzantine Iconoclasm during the Reign of Leo III, with Particular Reference to the Oriental Sources* (Louvain: Secretariat du Corpus SCO, 1973).

Gerrish, Brian, *Grace and Reason: A Study in the Theology of Luther* (Oxford: Clarendon Press, 1962).

Geyl, Pieter, *The Revolt of the Netherlands* (reprint, New York: Barnes and Noble, 1980).

Gilbert, Felix, *Machiavelli and Guicciardini* (New York: Norton, 1984).

Gordon, Bruce, *Clerical Discipline and the Rural Reformation. The Synod in Zurich, 1532–1580* (New York: P. Lang, 1992)

Greengrass, Mark, *The French Reformation* (Oxford: Blackwell, 1987).

Grell, Ole Peter, ed., "The Emergence of Two Cities: The Reformation in Malmö and Copenhagen," in *Die dänische Reformation vor ihrem internationalen Hintergrund*, ed. Leif Grane and K. Hoerby (Göttingen: Vandenhoeck & Ruprecht, 1990), 129–145.

———, *The Scandinavian Reformation*, eds. Leif Grane and K. Hoerby, (Cambridge: Cambridge University Press, 1995).

Grell, Ole Peter, and Bob Scribner, eds., *Tolerance and Intolerance in the European Reformation* (Cambridge: Cambridge University Press, 1996).

Greschat, Martin, *Martin Bucer: Ein Reformator und seine Zeit* (Munich: Beck, 1990).

Guggisberg, Hans R., *Basel in the Sixteenth Century* (St. Louis: Center for Reformation Research, 1982).

Gurevich, Aron, *The Origins of European Individualism* (Oxford: Blackwell, 1995).

Gutton, Jean-Pierre, *La société et les pauvres en l'Europe* (Paris: Presses universitaires de France, 1974).

Haigh, Christopher, *English Reformations: Religion, Politics and Society under the Tudors* (New York: Oxford University Press, 1993).

Hale, John R., *War and Society in Renaissance Europe* (Leicester: Leicester University Press, 1985).

Handbook of European History, 1400–1600: Late Middle Ages, Renaissance, and Reformation, Thomas A. Brady, Heiko A. Oberman, and James D. Tracy, 2 vols. (Leiden: E. J. Brill, 1994; paperback, Grand Rapids, Mich.: W. B. Eerdmans, 1995).

Hanlon, Gregory, *Confession and Community in Seventeenth-Century France: Catholic and Protestant Coexistence in Aquitaine* (Philadelphia: University of Pennsylvania Press, 1993).

Hay, Denys, *The Church in Italy in the Fifteenth Century* (Cambridge: Cambridge University Press, 1977).

Hendrix, Scott H., *Luther and the Papacy* (Philadelphia: Fortress Press, 1981).

Herlihy, David, and Christiane Klapisch-Zuber, *Tuscans and Their Families: A Study of the Florentine Catasto of 1427* (New Haven, Conn.: Yale University Press, 1985).

Hermann, Christian, "Settlements: Spain's National Catholicism," in *Handbook,* vol. II, 491–522.

Hess, Andrew C., *The Forgotten Frontier. The Sixteenth-Century Hispano-African Frontier* (Chicago: University of Chicago Press, 1978).

Hibben, C. C., *Gouda in Revolt* (Utrecht: HES, 1983).

Hoak, Dale, *The King's Council in the Reign of Edward VI* (Cambridge: Cambridge University Press, 1976).

Hoffman, Philip, *Church and Community in the Diocese of Lyon, 1500–1789* (New Haven, Conn.: Yale University Press, 1984).

Hoffman, Philip, and Kathryn Norberg, eds., *Fiscal Crises, Liberty, and Representative Government, 1450–1789* (Stanford, Calif.: Stanford University Press, 1994).

Holt, Mack P., *The French Wars of Religion, 1562–1629* (Cambridge: Cambridge University Press, 1995).

Höpfl, Harro, *The Christian Polity of John Calvin* (Cambridge: Cambridge University Press, 1985).

Hsia, R. Po-Chia, *Society and Religion in Münster, 1535–1618* (New Haven, Conn.: Yale University Press, 1984).

Hughes, Philip Edgecumbe, *Lefèvre: Pioneer of Ecclesiastical Renewal in France* (Grand Rapids, Mich.: W. B. Eerdmans, 1984).

Hussey, J. M., *The Orthodox Church in the Byzantine Empire* (Oxford: Clarendon Press, 1986).

Inalcik, Halil, *The Ottoman Empire: The Classical Age, 1300–1600* (reprint, New Rochelle, N.Y.: Aristide D. Caratzas, 1989).

Ingrao, Charles W., ed., *State and Society in Early Modern Austria* (Lafayette, Ind.: Purdue University Press, 1994).

Israel, Jonathan, *The Dutch Republic: Its Rise, Greatness, and Fall 1477–1789* (Oxford: Oxford University Press, 1995).

Jannasch, Wilhelm, *Reformationsgeschichte Lübecks* (Lübeck, 1958).

Janz, Denis R., *Luther and Late Medieval Thomism* (Waterloo, Ontario: Wilfrid Laurier University Press, 1983).

Jedin, Hubert, *History of the Council of Trent*, 3 vols. (New York: Nelson, 1957–1961).

———, ed., *History of the Catholic Church*, vols. IV and V (New York, 1980).

Jones, Norman, *The Birth of the Elizabethan Age: England in the 1560s* (Oxford: Blackwell, 1993).

———, *Faith by Statute: Parliament and the Settlement of Religion, 1559* (London: Royal Historical Society, 1982).

Kamen, Henry, *Crisis and Change in Early Modern Spain* (London: Ashgate Publishing, 1993).

———, *Inquisition and Society in Spain in the Sixteenth and Seventeenth Centuries* (Bloomington: Indiana University Press, 1985).

Kaminsky, Howard, *History of the Hussite Revolution* (Berkeley: University of California Press, 1967).

Kann, Robert A., *A History of the Habsbug Monarchy, 1550–1700* (Oxford, 1979).

Kaplan, Benjamin, *Calvinists and Libertines. Confessions and Community in Utrecht, 1578–1620* (Oxford: Clarendon Press, 1995).

Karant-Nunn, Susan, "Luther's Pastors: The Reformation in the Ernestine Countryside," *Transactions of the American Philosophical Society*, 68/69 (Philadelphia, 1979).

———, *Reformation of Ritual* (London and New York: Routledge, 1997).

———, *Zwickau in Transition, 1500–1547* (Columbus: Ohio State University Press, 1987).

Kelly, Henry Ansgar, *The Matrimonial Trials of Henry VIII* (Stanford: Stanford University Press, 1976).

Kieckhefer, Richard, *European Witch Trials: Their Foundations in Popular and Learned Culture, 1300–1500* (London: Routledge & Kegan Paul, 1976).

Kingdon, Robert M., *Geneva and the Coming of the Wars of Religion in France* (Geneva: Droz, 1956).

———, "International Calvinism," *Handbook*, II, 229–248.

Kirk, James, *Patterns of Reform: Continuity and Change in the Reformation Kirk* (Edinburgh, 1989).

Kittelson, James, *Luther the Reformer* (Minneapolis, Minn.: Augsburg Fortress Publishers, 1986).

———, "Successes and Failures in the German Reformation," *ARG: Archiv für Reformationsgeschichte* 73 (1982): 153–175.

Knecht, Robert Jean, *Renaissance Warrior and Patron: The Reign of Francis I* (Cambridge: Cambridge University Press, 1994).

Krahn, Cornelius, *Dutch Anabaptism: Origin, Spread, Life and Thought*, 2d ed., (Scottsdale, Pa.: Herald Press, 1981).

Kreider, Alan, *English Chantries: The Road to Dissolution* (Cambridge, Mass.: Harvard University Press, 1979).

Kristeller, P. O., "The Humanist Movement," in *Renaissance Essays* by P. O. Kristeller (Rochester, N.Y.: University of Rochester Press, 1993).

Ladurie, Emmanuel Leroy, *The Peasants of Languedoc*, trans. John Day (Urbana: University of Illinois Press, 1974).

Lane, Frederic, *Venice: A Maritime Republic* (Baltimore: Johns Hopkins University Press, 1973).

Lapidus, Ira, *A History of Islamic Societies* (Cambridge: Cambridge University Press, 1988).

Laslett, Peter, and Richard Wall, eds., *Household and Family in Past Time* (Cambridge: Cambridge University Press, 1972).

Lee, Maurice Jr., *The Road to Revolution: Scotland under Charles I, 1625–1637* (Urbana: University of Illinois Press, 1982).

Leff, Gordon, *Medieval Thought: From St. Augustine to Ockham* (Chicago: Quadrangle Books, 1960).

Le Goff, Jacques, *The Birth of Purgatory,* trans. Arthur Goldhammer (Chicago: University of Chicago Press, 1984), published in French 1981.

Lehmberg, Stanford E., *The Reformation Parliament* (Cambridge: Cambridge University Press, 1970).

Levack, Brian P, "The Great Witch-Hunt," *Handbook,* II, 607–640. See p. 356.

Lewis, P. S., *Late Medieval France: The Polity* (London: Macmillan, 1968).

Lindberg, Carter, *Beyond Charity: Reformation Initiatives for the Poor* (Minneapolis, Minn.: Augsburg Fortress Publishers, 1993).

Lis, Catharina, and Hugo Soly, *Poverty and Capitalism in Pre-Industrial Europe* (Atlantic Highlands, N.J.: Humanities Press, 1979).

Loades, David, *The Reign of Mary Tudor,* 2d ed. (London: Longman, 1991).

Locher, Gottfried W., *Zwingli's Thought: New Perspectives* (Leiden: E. J. Brill, 1981).

Lockhart, James, *The Nahua [Aztecs] after the Conquest* (Stanford, Calif.: Stanford University Press, 1992).

Lockyer, Roger, *The Early Stuarts* (London: Longman, 1989).

Lopez, Robert, "The Trade of Medieval Europe: The South," in *Cambridge Economic History of Europe,* vol. 2, 2d ed., ed. M. M. Postan and Edward Miller (Cambridge: Cambridge University Press, 1987), 306–473.

Lottin, Alain, *Lille, Citadelle de la Contre-Réforme (1598–1668)?* (Dunkerque: Westhoek-Editions: Editions des Beffrois, 1984).

MacCaffrey, Wallace T., *Elizabeth I* (London: E. Arnold, 1993).

Macfarlane, Alan, *The Origins of English Individualism* (Oxford: Blackwell, 1978).

———, *Witchcraft in Tudor-Stuart England* (Prospect Heights, Ill.: Waveland Press, 1991).

Mackenney, Richard, *Tradesmen and Traders: The World of the Guilds in Venice and Europe, c. 1250–c. 1650* (Totowa, N.J.: Barnes and Noble, 1987).

Mackinnon, James, *Luther and the Reformation,* 4 vols. (New York: Longmans, Green and Co., 1925–1930).

Major, J. Russell, *The Monarchy, the Estates and the Aristocracy in Renaissance France* (London: Ashgate Publishing, 1988.)

Mallett, Michael E., *Mercenaries and Their Masters: Warfare in Renaissance Italy* (London: Bodley Head, 1974).

Mallett, Michael E., and John R. Hale, *The Military Organization of a Renaissance State: Venice, c. 1400–1617* (Cambridge: Cambridge University Press, 1984).

Mansfield, Bruce, *Erasmus: Phoenix of His Age: Interpretations of Erasmus, c. 1550–1750* (Toronto: University of Toronto Press, 1979).

Maritain, Jacques, *Three Reformers* (Westport, Conn.: Greenwood Publishing Group, 1970). First published in English, 1928.

Marnef, Guido, *Antwerp in the Age of the Refomation*, trans. J. C. Grayson (Baltimore: Johns Hopkins University Press, 1996).

———, "Protestanten in 'Noord' en 'Zuid': Kerkhistorische Beschouwingen na aanleiding van een recente Studie," *Bijdragen tot de Geschiedenis* 70 (1987): 139–145.

Marshall, Sherrin, *The Dutch Gentry, 1500–1650: Faith, Family, and Fortune* (Westport, Conn.: Greenwood Publishing Group, 1987).

Matheson, Peter, *Cardinal Contarini at Regensburg* (Oxford: Clarendon, 1972).

McDonnell, Kilian, O.S.B., *John Calvin, the Church, and the Eucharist* (Princeton, N.J.: Princeton University Press, 1967).

McFarlane, K. B., *The Nobility of Later Medieval England* (Oxford: Clarendon, 1973).

McGrath, Alister, *A Life of John Calvin* (Oxford: Blackwell, 1990).

———, *Luther's Theology of the Cross* (Oxford: Blackwell, 1990).

McLaughlin, R. Emmet, *Caspar Schwenkfeld: A Reluctant Radical* (New Haven, Conn.: Yale University Press, 1986).

McSorley, Harry, *Luther Right or Wrong?* (New York: Newman Press, 1968).

Meigs, Samantha A., *The Reformation in Ireland* (New York: St. Martin's Press, 1997).

Mentzer, Raymond A. Jr., *Heresy Proceedings in Languedoc, 1500–1560* (Philadelphia: American Philosophical Society, 1984).

———, ed., *Sin and the Calvinists* (Kirksville, Mo.: Thomas Jefferson University Press, 1994).

Midelfort, H. C. Erik, *Witch-Hunting in Southwestern Germany, 1562–1684* (Stanford, Calif.: Stanford University Press, 1972).

Minamiki, George M., *The Chinese Rites Controversy* (Chicago: Loyola University Press, 1985).

Misikimin, Harry A., David Herlihy, and A. L. Udovitch, eds., *The Medieval City* (New Haven, Conn.: Yale University Press, 1977).

Moeller, Bernd, *Imperial Cities and the Reformation*, trans. H. C. Erik Midelfort and Mark U. Edwards Jr. (Durham, N.C.: Labyrinth Press, 1982). Published in German 1962.

Monter, E. William, *Calvin's Geneva* (New York: Wiley, 1967).

———, "Heresy Executions in Reformation Europe," in *Tolerance and Intolerance in the European Reformation*, ed. Ole Grell and Bob Scribner (Cambridge: 1996), 49–64.

———, *Witchcraft in France and Switzerland* (Ithaca, N.Y.: Cornell University Press, 1976).

Mormando, Franco, *The Preacher's Demons: Bernardino of Siena and the Social Underworld of Early Renaissance Italy* (Chicago: University of Chicago Press, 1999).

Muchembled, Robert, *Popular Culture and Elite Culture in France, 1400–1700* (Baton Rouge: Louisiana State University Press, 1984).

Myers, W. David, *Poor Sinning Folk: Confession and Conscience in Counter-Reformation Germany* (Ithaca, N.Y.: Cornell University Press, 1996).

Nalle, Sara T., *God in La Mancha: Religious Reform and the People of Cuenca, 1500–1650* (Baltimore: John Hopkins University Press, 1992).

Nicholas, David, *Medieval Flanders* (New York: Longman, 1992).

Nischan, Bodo, *Prince, People and Confession: The Second Reformation in Brandenburg* (Philadelphia: University of Pennsylvania Press, 1994).

Oberman, Heiko A., *The Dawn of the Reformation* (Grand Rapids, Mich.: W. B. Eerdmans, 1992).

———, *The Harvest of Late Medieval Theology: Gabriel Biel* (Cambridge, Mass.: Harvard University Press, 1963).

———, *Luther: Man between Good and the Devil* (New Haven, Conn.: Yale University Press 1989). First published in German 1982.

O'Connell, Marvin, *The Counter-Reformation, 1559–1610* (New York: Harper & Row, 1974).

Olin, John C., *The Catholic Reformation* (New York: Fordham University Press, 1993).

O'Malley, John W., *The First Jesuits* (Cambridge, Mass.: Harvard University Press, 1993).

Origo, Iris, *The World of San Bernardino* (New York: Harcourt, Brace, 1962).

Ozment, Steven E., *The Reformation in the Cities* (New Haven, Conn.: Yale University Press, 1975).

Parker, Charles H., *The Reformation of the Community: The Diaconate and Municipal Poor Relief in Holland, 1572–1617* (Cambridge: Cambridge University Press, 1998).

Parker, Geoffrey, *The Dutch Revolt* (New York: Viking Penguin, 1989).

———, "Success and Failure during the First Century of the Reformation," *Past and Present* 136 (1992): 43–82.

———, *The Thirty Years' War* (New York: Routledge, 1997).

Pettegree, Andrew, *Emden and the Dutch Revolt* (Oxford: Oxford University Press, 1992).

———, ed., *The Reformation of the Parishes* (Manchester: Manchester University Press, 1993).

Pettegree, Andrew, Alastair Duke, and Gillian Lewis, eds., *Calvinism in Europe, 1540–1620* (Cambridge: Cambridge University Press, 1995).

Pocock, J. G. A., *The Machiavellian Moment: Florentine Political Thought and the Atlantic Republican Tradition* (Princeton: Princeton University Press, 1975).

Poska, Allyson M., *Regulating the People:: The Catholic Reformation in Seventeenth-Century Spain* (Leiden: Brill Academic Publishers, 1998).

Post, R. R., *The Brethren of the Common Life* (Leiden, 1968).

Potter, G. R., *Zwingli* (Cambridge: Cambridge University Press, 1976).

Press, Volker, "The Habsburg Lands: The Holy Roman Empire, 1400–1555," *Handbook*, I, 437–461.

———, *Calvinismus und Territorialstaat: Regierung und Zentralbehörden der Kurpfalz, 1559–1619* (Stuttgart: E. Klett, 1970).

———, *Krieg und Krisen. Deutschland 1600–1715* (Munich: C. H. Beck, 1991).

Prestwich, Menna, "Calvinism in France, 1559–1629," in *International Calvinism, 1541–1715* by Menna Prestwich (Oxford: Clarendon, 1985), 71–107.

———, ed., *International Calvinism, 1541–1715* (Oxford: Clarendon, 1985).

Prodi, Paolo, *The Papal Prince: Papal Monarchy in Early Modern Europe* (Cambridge: Cambridge University Press, 1987).

Reinburg, Virginia, *Practices of Prayer in Late Medieval and Reformation France.*

Reinhard, Wolfgang, and Heinz Schilling, eds., *Die Katholische Konfessionalisierung* (Münster: Aschendorff, 1995).

Reynolds, Susan, *An Introduction to the History of English Medieval Towns* (Oxford: Clarendon, 1977).

————, *Kingdoms and Communities in Western Europe, 900–1300*, 2d edition (Oxford: Oxford University Press, 1997).

Roberts, Michael, *The Early Vasas: A History of Sweden, 1523–1611* (Cambridge: Cambridge University Press, 1968).

Robbins, Kevin, *City on the Ocean Sea: La Rochelle, 1530–1650* (Leiden: E. J. Brill, 1997).

Robisheaux, Thomas W., *Rural Society and the Search for Order in Early Modern Germany* (Cambridge: Cambridge University Press, 1989).

————, "The World of the Village," *Handbook*, vol. I, 79–112.

Rodriguez-Salgado, M. J., *The Changing Face of Empire: Charles V, Philip II, and Habsburg Authority, 1551–1559* (Cambridge: Cambridge University Press, 1988).

Roelker, Nancy Lyman, *Queen of Navarre: Jeanne d'Albret, 1528–1572* (Cambridge, Mass.: Harvard University Press, 1968).

Roodenburg, Herman, *Onder Censuur: De kerkelijke tucht in de gereformeede gemeente van Amsterdam, 1578–1700* (Hilversum: Verloren, 1990).

Rubin, Miri, *Corpus Christi: The Eucharist in Late Medieval Culture* (Cambridge: Cambridge University Press, 1992).

Rublack, Hans-Christoph, *Die Einführung der Reformation in Konstanz* (Gütersloh: Gütersloher Verlaghaus G. Mohn, 1971).

————, *Gescheiterte Reformation* (Stuttgart: Klett-Cotta, 1978).

Rummel, Erika, *Erasmus and His Catholic Critics* (Nieuwkoop: De Graaf, 1989).

————, *The Humanist-Scholastic Debate in the Renaissance and Reformation* (Cambridge, Mass.: Harvard University Press, 1995).

Russell, Conrad, *Fall of the British Monarchies* (Oxford: Oxford University Press, 1991).

Russell, Paul, *Lay Theology in the Reformation: Popular Pamphleteers in Southwest Germany, 1521–1525* (Cambridge: Cambridge University Press, 1986).

Safley, Thomas Max, *Charity and Economy in the Orphanages of Early Modern Augsburg* (Atlantic Highlands, N.J.: Humanities Press, 1996).

————, *Let No Man Put Asunder: The Control of Marriage in the German Southwest: A Comparative Study, 1550–1600* (St. Louis, Mo.: Thomas Jefferson University Press, 1984).

Salmon, J. H. M., *A Society in Crisis: France in the Sixteenth Century* (London: Methuen, 1979).

Samuelsson, Kurt, *Religion and Economic Action: A Critique of Max Weber* (Buffalo, N.Y.: University of Toronto Press, 1963).

Sauzet, Robert, *Chroniques des frères enemis: Catholiques et Protestants à Nîmes* (Caen: Panadigme, 1992).

Scarisbrick, J. J., *Henry VIII* (Berkeley: University of California Press, 1968).

Schilling, Heinz, *Civic Calvinism in Northwestern Germany and the Netherlands* (Kirksville, Mo.: Thomas Jefferson University Press, 1992).

————, "Confessional Europe," *Handbook*, vol. II, 641–682). See p. 356

————, *Religion, Political Culture, and the Emergence of the Early Modern State* (Leiden: E. J. Brill, 1992).

Schmitt, Jean Claude, *Holy Greyhound: Guinefort, Healer of Children since the Thirteenth Century* (Cambridge: Cambridge University Press, 1983).

Scribner, R. W., *For the Sake of Simple Folk* (Oxford: Clarendon, 1994).

Sedgwick, Alexander, *Jansenism in Seventeenth-Century France* (Charlottesville: University Press of Virginia, 1977).

Sharpe, Kevin, *The Personal Rule of Charles I* (New Haven, Conn.: Yale University Press, 1982).

Simon, Walter, *Cities of Ladies: The Beguines in the Southern Low Countries* (forthcoming from Cambridge University Press).

Slicher van Bath, B. H., *The Agrarian History of Western Europe, 500–1850*, trans. Olive Ordish (New York: St. Martin's Press, 1963).

Smalley, Beryl, *The Study of the Bible in the Middle Ages* (Notre Dame, Ind.: University of Notre Dame Press, 1964).

Smith, Alan G. R., ed., *The Reign of James VI and I* (New York: Macmillan, 1973).

Soergel, Philip M., *Wondrous in His Saints: Counter-Reformation Propaganda in Bavaria* (Berkeley, Calif.: University of California Press, 1993).

Soman, Alfred, *Sorcellerie et justice criminelle: le Parlement de Paris, 16e–18e Siècles* (London: Ashgate Publishing, 1992).

Spaans, Joke, *Haarlem na de Reformatie* (The Hague: Stichting Hollands Historische Recks, 1989).

Stadtwald, Kurt W., *Roman Popes and German Patriots: Antipapalism in the Politics of the German Humanist Movement* (Geneva: Librarie Droz, 1996).

Starr, Chester, *The Influence of Sea Power on the Ancient World* (New York: Oxford University Press, 1989).

Stayer, James M., "The Radical Reformation," *Handbook*, II, 249–282.

————, *Anabaptists and the Sword* (Lawrence, Kans.: Coronado Press, 1972).

Steen, Charlie, *A Chronicle of Conflict: Tournai, 1559–1567* (Utrecht: HES Publishers, 1985).

Steinberg, S. H., *The Thirty Years' War and the Conflict for European Hegemony 1600–1660* (New York: Norton, 1967).

Steinmetz, David, *Luther in Context* (Bloomington, Ind.: Baker Books, 1986).

Steinmetz, Max, ed., *Die frübürgerliche Revolution in Deutschland* (Berlin: Akademie-Verlag, 1985).

Stephens, W. P., *The Theology of Huldrych Zwingli* (Oxford: Clarendon Press, 1986).

Stevenson, David, *The Scottish Revolution 1637–1644* (Newton Abbot: David & Charles, 1973).

Stoeffel, F. Ernest, *The Rise of Evangelical Pietism* (Leiden: E. J. Brill, 1965)

Strasser, Ulrike, "*Aut Murus aut Maritus?* Women's Lives in Counter-Reformation Munich" (Ph.D. diss., University of Minnesota, 1997).

Strauss, Gerald, *Nuremberg in the Sixteenth Century* (New York: Wiley, 1966).

Strauss, Gerald R., *Luther's House of Learning* (Baltimore: John Hopkins University Press, 1978).

Subrahmanyam, Sanjay, and Luis Filipe R. R. Thomaz, "Evolution of Empire: The Portuguese in the Indian Ocean during the Sixteenth Century," in *The Political*

Economy of Merchant Empires, ed. James D. Tracy (Cambridge: Cambridge University Press, 1991), 298–332

Taylor, F. L., *The Art of War in Italy, 1494–1521* (reprint, Westport, Conn.: Greenwood Press, 1973).

Taylor, Larissa, *Soldiers of Christ: Preaching in Late Medieval and Reformation France* (New York: Oxford University Press, 1992).

Tex, Jan Den, *Oldenbarnevelt,* 2 vols. (Cambridge: Cambridge University Press, 1973).

Tolley, Bruce, *Pastors and Parishioners in Württemberg during the Late Reformation* (Stanford, Calif.: Stanford University Press, 1995).

Tolmie, Murray, *The Triumph of the Saints: The Separatist Churches of London, 1616–1649* (Cambridge: Cambridge University Press, 1977).

Tracy, James D., *Erasmus of the Low Countries* (Berkeley: University of California Press, 1996).

———, "Heresy Law and Centralization under Mary of Hungary," *ARG: Archiv für Reformationsgeschichte* 73 (1982): 284–307.

———, *Holland under Habsburg Rule* (Berkeley: University of California Press, 1990).

Trinkaus, Charles, *In His Image and Likeness* (Chicago: University of Chicago Press, 1971).

Troeltsch, Ernst, *The Social Teachings of the Christian Churches,* trans. Olive Wyon (Louisville, Ky.: Westminster John Knox Press, 1992).

Trouncer, Margaret, *The Gentleman Saint: St. Francis de Sales and His Times* (London: Hutchinson, 1963).

Tyacke, Nicholas, *Anti-Calvinists. The Rise of English Arminianism c. 1590–1640* (Oxford: Clarendon, 1987).

Vaughan, Richard, *Valois Burgundy* (London: Allen Lane, 1975).

Verheyden, A. L. E., *Le martyrologe protestant des pays-bas du sud au xvième siècle* (Brussels, 1960).

Vries, Jan de, "Population," in *Handbook,* vol. I, 1–50.

Wakefield, Walter Legget, *Heresy, Crusade and Inquisition in Southern France, 1100–1250* (London: G. Allen & Unwin, 1974).

Waley, Daniel P., *The Italian City-Republics* (New York: Longman, 1988).

Walker, D. P., *Unclean Spirits: Possession and Exorcism in France and England in the Late Sixteenth and Early Seventeenth Centuries* (Philadelphia: University of Pennsylvania Press, 1981).

Walsh, James J., *The Thirteenth Greatest of Centuries* (New York: Catholic Summer School Press, 1929).

Walton, Robert C., "The Institutionalization of the Reformation at Zurich," *Zwingliana* 13 (1972): 497–515.

———, *Zwingli's Theocracy* (Toronto: University of Toronto Press, 1967).

Warmbrünn, Paul, *Zwei Konfessionen in einer Stadt* (Wiesbaden: F. Steiner, 1983).

Weaver, F. Ellen, *The Evolution of the Reform of Port Royal* (Paris: Beauchesne, 1978).

Weber, Max, *The Protestant Ethic and the Spirit of Capitalism* (Los Angeles: Roxbury, 1998).

Webster, Tom, *Godly Clergy in Early Stuart England* (Cambridge: Cambridge University Press, 1997).

Wedgwood, C. V., *The Thirty Years' War* (New York: Routledge, 1990).

———, *William the Silent* (reprint, London, 1989).

Wee, Herman van der, *The Growth of the Antwerp Market and the European Economy,* 3 vols. (The Hague: Nijhoff, 1963).

Wee, Herman van der, and E. van Cauwenberghe, eds., *Productivity of Land and Agricultural Innovation in the Low Countries* (Leuven: Leuven University Press, 1978).

Wendel, Francois, *Calvin: Origins and Development of His Religious Thought,* trans. Philip Mairet (reprint, Durham, N.C.: Labyrinth, 1987).

White, Peter, *Predestination, Policy and Polemic: Conflict and Consensus in the English Church from the Reformation to the Civil War* (Cambridge: Cambridge University Press, 1992).

Whiting, Robert, *The Blind Devotion of the People: Popular Religion and the English Reformation* (Cambridge: Cambridge University Press, 1989).

Wiesner, Merry E., "Family, Household and Community," in *Handbook,* vol. I, 51–78.

Williams, George H., *The Radical Reformation,* 3d ed. (Kirksville, Mo.: Thomas Jefferson University Press, 1992).

Wright, William J., *Capitalism, the State and the Lutheran Reformation: Sixteenth Century Hesse* (Athens: Ohio University Press, 1988).

Wunder, Heide, *He Is the Sun, She Is the Moon : Women in Early Modern Germany,* trans. Thomas Dunlap (Cambridge, Mass.: Harvard University Press, 1998).

Ye'or, Bat, *The Dhimmi: Jews and Christians under Islam* (London: Associated University Presses, 1985).

Young, Michael B., *Charles I* (New York: St. Martin's, 1997).

Zachman, Randall, *The Assurance of Faith: Conscience in the Theology of Luther and John Calvin* (Minneapolis, Minn.: Augsburg Fortress Publishers, 1992).

Index

Page numbers in *italics* refer to illustrations.

Waldensians, 4
Waldo, Peter, 4
Wallenstein, Count Albert of, 162,
 330n100
war:
 Erasmus' view, 45, 308n35; Grebel's
 view, 312n20; and honor, 122–23;
 and religion, 28–29; Zwingli's
 view, 58–59, 323n51.
 See also Dutch Revolt; Hundred
 Years' War; Peasants' War;
 Schmalkaldic Wars; Spain
Wars of Italy, 133–38
Wars of Religion, French, 146–53, *148*
Warwick, Earl of, 189–90
The Way, 290–91
Wentworth, Thomas, 204, 337n57
Wesley, John, 9
wheel of fortune, 33, *34*
White Horse Inn, 185
Whitgift, John, 195
Whore of Babylon, 53
William IV, of Bavaria, 243
William V, Duke, of Bavaria, 108
William of Ockham, 305n7
William of Orange, 111–12, 113–14,
 154, 155, 318n60
wills, 40–41, *42*, 227, 342n72.
 See also inheritance
Winstanley, Gerrard, 338n71
Wishart, George, 115
witchcraft, 8, 26, 237–38, 254–56, *255*,
 302n12
Wittenberg, University of, 48–49,
 248–49
Wittenberg Concord, 312n16
Wolsey, Thomas, 187, 334n8

women, 67, 100, 109, 218, 230, 262–63.
 See also Beguines; marriage; nuns;
 pregnancy
works:
 Catholic Reformation view, 100; of
 mercy, *39*, *69*, 100, *275*, 315n10;
 and poor relief, 251, 346n57; and
 repetition, 43–44; and salvation,
 18, 19, 37, 53, 59–60
Worms:
 Diet of, 89; Edict of, 55, 73, 77
worship, 21–24, 246–48, 336n33
Wycliffe, John, 185

Yiddish, 296
Ypres, 250

zaddik, 297
Zell, Katherine, 67
Zurich, *58*, 75, 258, 265, 327n49, 347n4.
 See also Zwingli, Huldrych
Zwickau, 241
Zwickau prophets, 57
Zwingli, Huldrych:
 on authority, 76–77, 118; on baptism,
 247, 345n45; on church government, 76–77, 118, 335n22; and craft
 guilds, 11; and divorce, 253; on
 God's law, 59, 310n5, 339n16; and
 humanists, 58–59; on iconoclasm,
 59; on Lord's Supper, 60–62,
 78–79, 81; and Peasants' War, 70;
 on popular rituals, 23; on saints,
 294; on salvation, 59, 67; on scripture, 59, 70, 76, 246; on war, *60*,
 323n51
Zwinglianism, 241, 247, 282–83

About the Author

James D. Tracy is professor of history at the University of Minnesota. His published works include *Erasmus: The Growth of a Mind* (1952), *A Financial Revolution in the Habsburg Netherlands* (1985), *Holland Under Habsburg Rule* (1990), and *Erasmus of the Low Countries*.